WAR

Also by Angelo Codevilla

Between the Alps and a Hard Place

Informing Statecraft: Intelligence for a New Century

Machiavelli's Prince

Modern France

No Victory No Peace

The Arms Control Delusion (with Malcolm Wallop)

The Character of Nations:
How Politics Makes and Breaks Prosperity, Family, and Civility

While Others Build:
The Commonsense Approach to the Strategic Defense Initiative

WAR

Ends and Means

Second Edition

Angelo Codevilla

and

Paul Seabury

Potomac Books, Inc.

Washington, D.C.

First edition published in 1989 by Basic Books.
Published in the United States by Potomac Books, Inc.

Library of Congress Cataloging-in-Publication Data
Codevilla, Angelo, 1943-
    War : ends and means / by Angelo Codevilla and Paul
Seabury.
      p. cm.
    Author statement reversed.
    Includes bibliographical references and index.
    ISBN 1-57488-610-X (alk : paper)
      1.   War. 2. Military art and science. I. Seabury, Paul. II.
    Title.

U21.2C63 2005
355.02—dc22
2005054957

Printed in Canada on acid-free paper that meets the American
National Standards Institute Z39-48 Standard.
Potomac Books, Inc.
22841 Quicksilver Drive
Dulles, Virginia 20166
First Edition
10 9 8 7 6 5 4 3 2 1

CONTENTS

PART III
How Wars End

PART IV
Wars of Our Time

PREFACE

PAUL SEABURY and I wrote this book's first edition in 1987–88 for Basic Books and the late Martin Kessler. "Through the gentle medium of the printed page," we presented war to a generation of Americans who had neither experienced nor studied it. In a 1990 preface to the paperback edition, we showed that, contrary to the reigning consensus, the revolutionary events of 1989 neither ended history nor began a new world order in which war would be passé. Rather, force would midwife future events no less than past ones. Paul Seabury died in 1991.

Since then, events have further illustrated the principles of warfare. Beginning with the Gulf War of 1991, the word "war" returned to polite company's lexicon after almost a half century's absence. But until 11 September 2001 most Americans regarded war as something that others would do and suffer—a spectator sport.

After 9/11, interest in the causes, ends, and means of war increased, and so did inquiries about this book, by then out of print. With the encouragement of Potomac's Don McKeon, I undertook this second, revised edition in the spirit with which Seabury and I had written it in the first place. But I alone am responsible for all differences between the first and second editions.

While the principles of warfare have not changed a bit, and the book's storehouse of classical illustrations remains, I believe, as valuable as ever, this edition reflects changes in the book's audience and in salient events. Just as readers in the 1980s were likeliest to understand—and needed to understand—principles of warfare with frequent references to the confrontation between the Soviet empire and the free world, so early twenty-first-century readers want and need to know about war in part through the contemporary world's experience with indirect warfare, now otherwise known as terrorism. References to ancient experiences serve today's readers, as they did yesterday's, by disabusing them of the temptation to re-gard their problems as unprecedented and hence as excuses for nonsense.

The major differences between the first and second edition are: The section of the introduction "For Whom We Write" is revised. In chapter 3 the discussion of victory is expanded. Chapter 8, "Political Warfare," is shorn of its brief section on indirect warfare, which is expanded into a wholly new chapter 9, "Indirect Warfare and Terror." Part IV is wholly new. Chapter 13 deals with the minor post–Cold War conflicts, while chapter 14 ("The Gulf War of 1990–91") and chapter 15 ("Terror and Iraq") illustrate the perennial "facts of life" of war.

Angelo Codevilla
Plymouth, California

INTRODUCTION

For Whom We Write

THIS BOOK was written to open contemporary minds to the essential truths of war, lest these truths intrude of their own accord.

Although most Americans and other civilized peoples experienced 11 September 2001 vicariously through television, the security measures that followed gave millions a firsthand hint of war's reality. Because President George W. Bush declared—and Congress approved—an undeclared "war on terrorism" and U.S. troops invaded Afghanistan and Iraq, news of battles, casualties, and shifting alliances became daily fare for the media. The involvement of reserve troops ensured that war would touch at least part of the U.S. civilian population. Interest in military history, especially on television, increased. Political candidates' ability to deal with military matters became important.

Still, 9/11 only dented the edges of upper-middle-class American and European life. For most of this magic kingdom's inhabitants, military matters are still not part of reality—especially since the absence of a military draft has confined military service in the enlisted ranks to the lower-middle class and made officers into something of a caste. For the rest, curricula and textbooks from elementary school through university treat wars, if they treat them at all, not by explaining who fought for what, who won, who lost, how, and why, but as opportunities to expatiate on the feats of favored groups and on the injustices of their societies. In sum, makers of policy, those who write and speak to the public about international affairs, and influential citizens have neither personal nor intellectual acquaintance with the realities of war.

On 9/11 some of these realities knocked violently on the magic kingdom's gates. The inhabitants knew enough to be frightened, but not enough to understand. This book means to break the spell of ignorance about war, to make it possible for readers to put themselves in the shoes of history's protagonists and of those caught in the middle. At best it will enable readers to make judgments about war with the responsibility of Swiss, Israelis, or pre-1960s Americans—if not of ancient Greeks, for whom citizenship and participation in war went hand in hand.

Education for citizenship includes military education because victory in war is the sine qua non of peace, and because the peace a people gets depends on what kind of war it is able to win. Liberal education is that which enables citizens to be free. When Thomas Jefferson founded the University of Virginia, he wrote that it would "enable every man to judge for himself what will secure or endanger his freedom." That judgment necessarily requires knowledge of war. Jefferson crafted the Declaration of Independence, of which he was as proud as he was of his university, precisely to define the war that Americans would fight. At the other pole of America's founding generation, John Adams agreed on the importance of studying war:

> I must study politics and war, that my sons may have liberty to study mathematics and philosophy, geography, natural history, and naval architecture, navigation, commerce and agriculture, in order to give their children a right to study music, architecture, statuary, tapestry, and porcelain.

Our generations confront the problems that the Founders' victory in war created: What knowledge of war must we fit into our comforts and gentler arts in order to preserve our freedom to engage in them? How long will this cruel world allow what David Brooks called "Bourgeois Bohemians" to enjoy themselves if they ignore or misunderstand the art of war that made possible their refined way of life?

The Commonwealth of Venice—tiny, rich, sophisticated, and independent for a thousand years—engraved on its armory the words, "Happy is the city that in time of peace thinks of war." That cribbed the motto of history's greatest success story, Rome: *Si vis pacem, para bellum,* "If you want peace, prepare for war." The most important part of that preparation is intellectual. Knowledge of disease is gathered most fruitfully while in good health. It provides the techniques of surgery and it softens surprise. So does study of war in time of peace yield the tools and the steadiness to survive adversity. Hence this book modifies the opening line of Virgil's *Aeneid: Arma virumque cano,* "Of arms and the man I sing." Of arms and the man I *study.*

Our Context

Enlightened folk know that the Great War of 1914–18 ended all wars, forever. Or at least it would have if only America had accepted Article X of the Versailles Treaty that established the League of Nations. But in 1928 America did join the Kellogg-Briand Pact that outlawed war. In World War II, the United Nations (Franklin Roosevelt first sprang the term on the world January 2, 1942) enforced both Versailles and Kellogg by crushing those who had broken the new world order. In 1945 the establishment of the UN organization, with U.S. participation, made war really impossible by correcting the errors of 1919. We all know that. So in 1950, when North Korean armies (on behalf of the Soviet Union, member of the UN) attacked South Korea, the United States opposed them with a "police action" under the UN flag. Though it felt like war to those who fought, there was no war. Gen. Douglas MacArthur said that in war there is no substitute for victory. But he was fired. Certainly there was no victory for the United States, and American troops police Korea two generations later.

The years 1948 to 1991, however, saw a "cold war" between the Soviet empire and the United States. To the Enlightened, it proved conclusively that real, major war was passé. The two antagonists would never come to blows because their nuclear armament had made real what Norman Angell's book *The Great Illusion* (1910) had predicted for his time: modern war is so destructive that it could never happen. Just as in 1910, victory was no longer an option. The only choices were peace for all or death for all. Neither advances in technology, nor disparities in effort or strategy, nor even political changes could turn back the clock to the age of war, ever. Polite company even banished the concept of enemy. By the 1950s the Soviet Union had become merely the "adversary." By the 1960s it was a "competitor." And by the '70s "containment" had become more about "cooperation" than "competition." The U.S. government declared war on disease, ignorance, poverty, and drugs, but not on any foreign enemy. Then, on Christmas Day 1991, the Soviet Union died. Soon, not-so-enlightened people pointed out that U.S.-Soviet war was about the only war that had *not* happened in the twentieth century.

It was a bloody century. While despots and barbarians ravaged the earth with their wars, enlightened Western elites opposed them and otherwise to put soldiers and sailors in harm's way, often determined to misunderstand what they were doing. Their will to believe that they were keeping the peace rather than fighting wars, their unwillingness to think of victory as the assurance of peace, made the century even bloodier and less peaceful. The "general peace" that followed 1945 has seen the cross-border takeovers of Tibet by China, of Hungary by the Soviet Union, of

West New Guinea by Indonesia, of Laos, Cambodia, South Vietnam by North Vietnam, Lebanon by Syria, Afghanistan by the Soviet Union, the Falklands by Argentina, and Kuwait by Iraq, as well as border wars between India and China, Israel and all its neighbors, East and West Pakistan, Iran and Iraq, Ethiopia and Eritrea, Serbia and Croatia and Bosnia—to mention but a few—as well as countless civil wars.

By the mid 1950s Great Britain and France, which had painted much of the world's map with red and blue, respectively, had given up trying to influence the world militarily. For them, the United Nations ceased to be a mandate to maintain a certain order in the world and became an excuse for retirement from responsibility. So, during the Cold War, as armies and irregulars made war, sometimes at the behest—direct or indirect—of the Soviet Union, the United States had to decide whether its interest in defending itself against the Soviet Union, its interest in world order, and sometimes its interest in human welfare required military intervention. But when American leaders have decided to intervene, they have done so with disregard for the realities of war. Typically, because they have ill understood that war is the clash of purposes, they have "sent troops" with the hope of brokering peace and calling it victory. That habit of putting the cart before the horse has carried over into the twenty-first century.

Enlightened Americans' revulsion at war also stemmed from the will to believe that human values are entirely subjective, and hence that none are worthier or less worthy than others. This led many Progressives to oppose opposing countries, like the Soviet Union or Communist China, that presented themselves as agents of human progress. For some American elites, taking sides with progress meant taking sides against America. Hence in the Vietnam War some American elites supported North Vietnam. Throughout the Cold War, they worked to minimize U.S. military power *vis-à-vis* the Soviet Union and to restrict its use. The interplay between American patriotism, progressivism, and the press of events is why, although American military action in the twentieth century was invariably successful, American blood bought stalemate in Korea; in Vietnam, defeat; in Lebanon, Somalia, etc. nothing but contempt; and in the Balkans, thin pretense.

By the turn of the twenty-first century, American troops were on guard over much of the globe. At most, their presence might be guided by an "exit strategy." This term begged the question of what accomplishment would justify that presence in the first place. The United States typically sought "stability," a thing inherently impossible, or "democracy," ill understood and unenforceable. Worse, the troops were to accomplish the unlikely and the impossible by not making too many waves.

Beginning in 1990, the U.S. government committed much blood and treasure to military action in the Middle East. Under President George H. W.

Bush, and less sonorously under his successor Bill Clinton, these actions aimed at affirming a liberal democratic life that had never existed in the region. But the U.S. government hardly noticed that neither it nor any other entity on earth had the power to endow any people with the capacity to transmogrify into liberal democrats. Because it had long since lost the habit of proportioning the things it actually did to the things it professed to desire, the U.S. government's demands ended up engendering hatred, while its incapacity to enforce them earned contempt.

On 11 September 2001 it became cruelly clear that inconsequential war making in the Middle East had brought an attack on America more deadly than that of 7 December 1941. President George W. Bush then declared that America was at "war" against "terrorism." Not surprisingly, American elites and the U.S. government combined foursqare commitment to war against an abstract noun with confusion about whether victory was possible, whether it was wise even to seek it, and what victory might mean. Hence arguments over what specific actions America should undertake in the war abstracted from the only significant question in any war: what do we have to do to earn the peace we want?

This then is the context of the second edition: Any number of people in the Middle East have shown the will and the skill to kill American civilians. Their news media and their regimes' religious leaders urge them to kill. The regimes' governments do not prevent them from doing it. In sum, war is not a nightmare. It is far more fearsomely real than that. Nor has the world outgrown it, as it has outgrown horses and buggies. Today's world is filled with more people animated by greater hatred and possessed of more means to make war than ever before.

Across the third world, from India to Cuba to Tanzania, well over a billion people live under governments that tend to be bellicose, some of which have accumulated, per capita, more guns, tanks, and airplanes than the United States and its allies.[1] Meticulous comparison confirms common sense: countries with Marxist, Islamic, or military governments devote more of their resources to war material than countries governed otherwise.[2] There are a lot of men in the world with guns pointing the wrong way.

This mass of humanity lives in squalor and brutality that is difficult for Americans to imagine. For most of mankind, life is cheap. For example, in 2000–2001 Russia "pacified" Chechnya by razing its capital and killing some one hundred thousand human beings. In 1987–88 India "pacified" northern Sri Lanka at the cost of perhaps ten thousand lives. Ethiopia killed at least half a million "rebels." Tiny Mozambique snuffed out about four hundred thousand lives—about the same number killed in the Iran-Iraq War. In 1994–96 Serbians killed some hundred thousand Bosnians, and in 1994 Rwandan Hutus killed perhaps a quarter million Rwandan Tutsis. By

2004 Sudanese Arabs had killed perhaps two million Sudanese blacks. All told, the toll of human beings killed *since 1945* was close to thirty million.[3]

Furthermore, over the past generation this overarmed, underscrupled mass of humanity has been saturated with print media, radios, and televisions that have sharpened and focused hate. The "information revolution" has done everything *but* pacify the hearts of men. Also, it is most important to note that when third-world media have whipped up hatred against this or that nearby target, they have often indicted the United States as the arch villain, the party ultimately responsible for the evil that must be rooted out here and now. America's image as the best-fed nation in the history of mankind has proved to be a successful stimulant for rousing hateful envy, as has the fact that Americans make up about 5 percent of the world's population but consume about one-third of what the world produces. But of course since the propaganda does not mention that America produces more of value than it consumes, surely shortcomings in one's life must be due to America's superabundance, and vice versa! As a result, there is no shortage in the world of people who lack only the opportunity to wage war against the United States. What they make of these opportunities is a matter of reasonable concern.

The Soviet empire's disintegration eliminated history's greatest concentration of military power, the greatest engine of anti-American animus and enabler of anti-American action. Indeed, when the empire died—roughly between 1989 and 1993—anti-American terrorism well nigh ceased. But communism's collapse did not eradicate the hatred of America that three generations of communists had sown into progressive regimes around the world and into the very language of so many political activists. Nor did it change America's status as the focus of envy, or the third world's penchant for violence. On the other hand, the Soviet empire's disappearance prompted Americans to dally with the hope that violence belonged to the past, and that, as the *New York Times'* Thomas Friedman put it, the cooperative, universalist culture of "the Lexus" would overcome the nasty, particularist one of "the olive tree." This dalliance fed contempt. No one should have been surprised when in 1993 a new wave of terrorism burst upon America from the Middle East.

It would indeed be ostrich-like for Americans to fail to consider what *kind* of peace we could expect in our world, or what kind of war such a peace might force on us, or how we might arrest or reverse a hostile trend, and what role violence might play in our doing so. Surely we will live the kind of life that we are willing and able to fight for. This raises a host of specific questions: Who among us will fight (not just serve in peacetime armed forces, but actually bleed), and what will we as a society have to do to earn that service? What concrete threats or opportunities will we consider sufficient causes for which to put ourselves through the hell of war? We know it will not do to wait to bestir ourselves until enemies have struck. But what *will* do? And if we do fight, whom do we kill, and why? It would be silly to follow the models of the 1940s and 1960s and blindly strike out against the enemy's cities. But if not, then how do we bring the war to a close? What kind of knowledge of the enemy must we have? Good intelligence would help, but it cannot dictate what we want to accomplish or provide the means for accomplishing it. This requires material preparation, strategic planning, and moral reasoning lest we do more harm than good. Of course, the American people have available a variety of economic and political instruments of conflict. But how do we employ them so that they will have their intended effect and not simply convey impotence and heighten contempt? Above all, what kind of peace are we after, and what are we willing to do to get it?

To conduct international politics without having a realistic, practical image of the ultimate sanction of such politics is a bit like conducting flirtations while innocent of sex and all its consequences.

Americans have to decide what offensive and defensive measures to take. But senior U.S. government officials are no more acquainted with the principles of warfare than are those who write for the news media or most of the experts whom they interview, any more than is their audience. Hence they have only the haziest notions of the relationship between war and peace; of why wars start; of what "strategy" means; of the role of public support, allies, and intelligence; of how to win battles; of the distinction between battles and wars; of indirect warfare; of what makes for justice and injustice in war; and of the various kinds of peace that result from war. That is because, for the most part, they are strangers to the likes of Thucydides, Tacitus, Sun Tsu, Machiavelli, Clausewitz, Washington, Lincoln, and Churchill. This book distills their teachings.

Our Argument

This book is inspired by the fact that the modern age has obviated neither the lessons of past wars, their political origins and outcomes, the general relationships between war and peace, nor the particular relationship among war, strategy, and politics. Clausewitz, in his *On War,* made much of the idea of the "fog of war," which beclouds those who wage it. We write about war's "unthinkable" but all too real nature so that the fog of ignorance shall not blind citizens who must make decisions about war and peace—and who must live with the consequences. What, then, do we believe our generation—especially its young men—must know about war? What are the basic realities we cannot afford to befog?

First, it is altogether normal for human intercourse to produce circumstances in which reasonable people choose between killing and being killed. Those on the offensive are often animated by hating the enemy—whom they see as standing in the way of what they want and on whom they want vengeance for past hurts or slights—by contempt for the enemy and hence by confidence in victory, and by fear of what the enemy might do in case the enemy should prevail. Those on the defensive are usually limited to fear, hate, and hope that they won't have to fight—otherwise they might well have attacked preemptively.

Second, the natural purpose of each combatant is to produce a set of results that he can enjoy in peace. Some sweep away opposition to what they want, others get swept away. We call the first winners, and the others losers. One may judge that the cost of achieving the result one seeks is more than the result is worth, cut one's losses and accept the enemy's victory. But anyone who thinks as did America's leaders in the Vietnam war, that victory is not worth it for both sides, and that the other side just *must* know that, is likely to end up as did the Americans—surprised when the enemy answered subtlety with directness and sealed victory by crashing tanks into one's headquarters.

Third, war is hell. War means death, destruction of families, cold, hunger, and subjection to harsh authority. So why is so much of mankind at war? One answer is that peace is no picnic. The very evils we associate with war have fallen upon mankind more fully in times and places well removed from battlefields and in conditions conventionally called peace. Especially in the twentieth century, the victims of peace outnumbered the victims of war.[4]

In that century perhaps thirty five million people, of whom twenty five million were civilians, died as a direct consequence of military operations. These people were killed by armies, navies, and air forces using the latest equipment and techniques. The soldiers who died this way suffered in the days and weeks before their demise, as well as during the final minutes. Nonetheless, they not only had a fighting chance, but their governments were also making at least some efforts to keep them comfortable. As part of war, governments afforded some measure of protection even to civilians.

During the same period, however, at least one hundred million human beings have been killed by police forces or their equivalent, which almost never used heavy weapons but relied on hunger, exposure, barbed wire, and forced labor to kill the bulk, executing the rest by shooting them with small arms, by rolling over them with trucks (a favorite technique in China around 1950), by gassing them, or, as in the Cambodian holocaust of 1975–79, by smashing their skulls with wooden clubs. These one hundred million usually suffered for months or years before the end and perhaps suffered most of all by their helplessness in the face of monstrous acts committed against them and their families. Those who killed these one hundred million men, women, and children did not have to overcome resistance, much less armed resistance. Because the victims could not (while others would not) make war on their own behalf, the killers did their killing in peace. Regardless of whether the victims were Armenians, Jews, Tutsis, Ukrainians, Chinese, or Cambodians, the stories of these historic horrors of peace are very similar.

One of the primordial causes of war is fear of this kind of peace. One does not have to stand on the threshold of a gas chamber, watch one's family starve on a train to Siberia, or choose between jumping from a burning skyscraper and being burned in it to prefer combat to the absence thereof. From time immemorial people have learned that if they did not take up arms and risk their lives in battle, quick death or mild slavery was the best fate they could expect. On the other hand, another major motive for war has been the desire of some men to gain the opportunity to slaughter other men peacefully. The tendency to think of combat strictly as a means of killing or subjugating your neighbor before he does it to you has been the rule rather that the exception in history.

Fourth, the popular American playground slogan "fighting never solves anything" is a historical howler. In fact, for better or for worse, the great issues regarding how men ought to live have been settled by war. Had Persians rather than Athenians won the battle of Marathon (490 BC) Greece would have become part of the Persian empire. No Plato and Aristotle. No philosophy. Had the Battle of Poitiers (AD 732) gone the other way, Europe would have become part of the Islamic world. Arabic rather than Latin would have been the language of courts and universities in Europe, and all subsequent history and literature would have been about struggles very different from the ones that actually occurred. Because European Christians defeated North African Muslims at Poitiers they earned the chance to defeat the tribes of the new world. Because of Poitiers, English, French, and Spanish became the languages of business and culture from Manila to Bombay, from Mombasa to Dakar and Buenos Aires. Later, the fate of aristocracy in Europe was sealed by the Napoleonic Wars, just as surely as Negro slavery was terminated by the American Civil War and Nazism by World War II. Indeed, military force is one expression of a myriad of moral, intellectual, political, and economic arrangements. But history teaches that if any given set of these factors cannot produce military victory, that set of factors, that complex of civilization, has a high chance of disappearing.

This leads us to refute a fifth misunderstanding; namely, that a nation's survival depends on the "ultimate" military capacity inherent in such measurable quantities as the size, health, wealth, and technical skill of its population. No doubt "potential" is always important. But potential never wins wars any more than it wins athletic contests. As an astute sports commentator points out, "that's why they play the game!" Wars are won or lost, nations live or die, primarily by the people's willingness to fight, their ability to impose discipline on themselves, and their readiness to subordinate themselves to chiefs who know what they are doing, thereby turning potential into actual force at the right place at the right time.

The early Roman Republic was inferior to its enemies, especially to the Etruscans, in size, economic strength, and sophistication. Culturally, it did not exist. Yet it was rich beyond measure in the public spiritedness of its citizens and in the military skill of its leaders. For this reason, it was able to conquer many nations that were superior to it in other ways. The late Roman Empire, by contrast, was incomparably superior to its enemies by every measurable factor. Culturally, the barbarians were just that. But when Alaric's Goths broke through the maldeployed border legions, the rabble and leading citizens of the Imperial capital did not have in them the feats of arms that their republican ancestors had performed when the barbarian chief, Brenner, and Hannibal the Carthaginian had presented even greater military challenges. So Rome died. Its wealth, which could not buy military salvation, was carted away.

Accordingly, we correct the popular view that military power is something a nation can buy—like health care or transportation. In fact, military service is less like a commodity and more like filial love. People—especially in peacetime—may be paid to go through the motions of military service. But there is not enough money in the world to cause a man to push himself purposely through the hell of war. History shows that Machiavelli was correct: mercenary armies will usually ruin a nation both when they lose and when they win. In the end, people fight for themselves.

This leads us to our sixth point: The widely held view that wars arise out of certain sets of circumstances—arms races, economic competition, crises, and so forth—resembles more the medieval view that maggots originate from filth than it does truth. In fact, when people do not fight for self-preservation they fight for causes—causes that are espoused so strongly that they overcome the natural instinct against sacrificing one's children as well as one's self. These causes of war range from the extreme of trying to establish the Kingdom of God on earth to the extreme of, in Shakespeare's words, quarreling over the length of a straw. The final refutation of those theories that describe causes of war as subrational is the fact that whenever men want others to fight they speak to persuade them that what they are doing is necessary and worthy. Only when this persuasion is successful will their audience espouse their cause.

Seventh, because wars are started and fought by complex human beings for complex human motives, we argue against the view of modern social science, which holds that either the onset or the outcome of wars can somehow be predetermined if enough facts are fed into computers. In fact, history's clearest teaching about war is its utter unpredictability. A war that proceeds from beginning to end as its initiators planned is perhaps the rarest of phenomena. War's unpredictability results from a set of complex, interactive factors. Soldiers and equipment on both sides always perform either better or worse than planned. The ever-present stratagems, deception, and surprise sometimes backfire. Above all, as each side reacts to threats and opportunities, it creates new ones. Sometimes things go as foreseen in the military realm, but the unfolding of events changes the purposes, the personnel, and even the political character of the parties. Nothing is done until it's done. Though Goliath usually wins, overconfidence, mistakes, an inspired opponent, or the hand of God can defeat him. In this "fog" of war, the winners are those who combine flexible minds with inflexible will—and who get the breaks.

Eighth, we show that, among all the uncertainties of war—including new weapons and/or tactics—the principles of military operations have not changed through the centuries. Once one has identified the people whose undoing will give one victory, and figured out which military operations will undo them, the rule for operations can be summed up in Gen. Nathan Forrest's dictum "get there the fustest with the mostest." We show that there are no recipes for successful military operations and that to seek them is to invite disaster. Any and every conventional stratagem, from "taking the high ground" to "exploiting a break in the enemy lines" can make for success or for failure, depending on one's capacity to make something of it. The only rule is that there is no rule—only the pressing need to size up a constantly changing situation, while making the most imaginative use of the forces at one's command. There is, however, one exception to the rule: surprise. It can turn the weak into the strong, and conversely, can make the strong into the unchallengeable.

Ninth, the destructiveness of war depends on the intentions of the warriors rather than on the tools at their disposal. It is sobering for us in the nuclear age to remember that genocide was routine in the ancient world and that the great slaughters of our time have been carried out with decidedly low-tech means. Moreover, whereas the first target of nuclear weapons, Hiroshima, returned to being a thriving city, Roman fire, sword, and plows followed by men spreading salt erased Carthage forever. We argue that nuclear weapons have become useful only as advances in miniaturization and delivery vehicles have made them smaller and more accurate—less indiscriminately destructive and much more lethal to their intended military targets and useful to the commonsense purpose of war: victory. Only peculiarly unmilitary minds confuse destruction with victory. It also takes a peculiarly unmilitary mind to confuse high-technology weapons with military effectiveness.

Tenth, we maintain that low-technology or low-intensity conflicts are not inherently more or less effective than their high-tech counterparts in producing victory. While it is commonplace in post-Vietnam America to think of special operations—guerrilla warfare and the like—as the invincible tool of our time, we argue that, like every other kind of operation, their usefulness depends on coordination with other measures and, above all, on circumstances. Light, mobile, chaos-causing forces in the enemy's rear are as useful riding helicopters as they were when they rode horses. Troops specially trained for sabotage, coups de main, or rescue missions can affect the outcome of wars. The raising of native forces in enemy country is an art essentially unchanged since ancient times. These arts weaken the enemy militarily a bit. But their main worth lies in their ability to demoralize and confuse the enemy—to help subvert him. Nevertheless we show that, contrary to popular opinion, the success of such forces nearly always depends on what happens at the front. In other words, we insist that special operations, like nuclear weapons, infantry divisions, and the orders and arguments that form armies and direct them, are parts of war that should not be mistaken for the whole.

Eleventh, indirect warfare is subject to the same principles as any other kind of warfare. Indirect warfare consists of concealing as much as possible one's own responsibility for forces that harass the enemy, and subverting his attachment to his purposes. To the extent that concealment makes it difficult for the people attacked to identify their enemy, the attacker enjoys the privilege of posing as the political expression of the purposes of forces doing the damage, of enjoying the fruits of attacks without bearing the costs of retaliation. However, the "cover" cannot be perfect. Hence indirect warfare succeeds to the extent that the peoples attacked are already seeking excuses for inaction.

Hence whoever would wage indirect war must know his enemy well enough to be confident that he will not simply disregard the "cover." Conversely, to resist indirect warfare, the target peoples must be able to do simply that. The principle applies to all types of subversion: just as no one has ever been seduced without his or her cooperation, no one has ever been subverted without cooperating with the subversion to some extent.

Twelfth, because knowledge itself is only a part of war, we demystify the role of intelligence. Intelligence is the discovery of facts that may be useful in conflict. Of course, any party to any conflict that knows a great deal about the other's weaknesses and plans while hiding its own has the chance to create the most decisive event of war: surprise. But in war superior knowledge does not necessarily imply sound judgment, any more than knowledge implies virtue in Greek philosophy. In war, as in other human activities, the more competent an individual the less information he will require in order to act as he should. That is often because excellent people impose their agenda on others by taking the initiative. Weak decision makers, for their part, never seem to have enough information—perhaps because they want the situation to dictate their decisions. They often get their wish!

We also point out that nations and armed forces on the defensive, wondering where and how the enemy's blows will fall, need far more intelligence than those that have the luxury of choosing where to concentrate their initiatives. In war as in other activities, knowledge is but one constituent part of judgment. The analysis of intelligence—the process of judging the significance of facts—must be part of the larger process of strategic judgment. It is the intellectual process that ties together the ends sought, the means at hand, and the circumstances.

Thirteenth, we argue that perhaps the most important connection between ends and means is moral. Contrary to what many believe, not all combatants stand on the same moral plane, and the difference in moral status depends on far more than on who struck the first blow. It depends upon a combination of the relative justice of each side's quarrel and of the proportion between the goodness of the ends pursued and the harm done in their pursuit. Of course nothing ever sanctions the use of means that are unjust in themselves, such as deliberately harming innocents. Such a failure to discriminate between combatants and noncombatants is morally inexcusable. We show that while it is counterproductive to try to meld these guidelines into enforceable laws—especially ex post facto, as at the Nuremberg trials—the guidelines do help us to go beyond mere opinions about right and wrong, or at least about better and worse. We also affirm that these objective moral standards for judging wars and combatants are as valid in the age of nuclear weapons and indirect warfare as ever before. This is because, contrary to popular opinion, modern technology permits at least as much discrimination as ever in warfare, and because the differences in the moral stature of the combatants is as great as any that has ever existed.

Fourteenth, since war (insofar as it is not madness or mere tribal conflict) is the clash of different moral standards, we agree with Clausewitz that violent means are rightly the mere servants of political considerations. Nevertheless, we maintain that any attempt to resolve definitively the natural tension between the demands of military operations and those of political authority is fraught with danger. Both sets of demands are legitimate in their own right. When, as in World War I, a General Ludendorff dictates to the Ministry of the Interior, the results are as bad as when, during the Vietnam War, a President Johnson picks bombing targets. On one hand, the art of politics in wartime consists of guiding military operations without in any way fouling up military logic. It is difficult to find historical examples of military failures leading to political successes. On the other hand, part of the general's art consists of keeping his military choices within the perspective of the war's purposes and of the nation's good.

By a similar token, we argue that the essence of war consists of the political decision that a given cause is worth killing and sacrificing for. The means chosen to further that cause may be unbloody. Planting information in the right places in an enemy country and fanning the subsequent flames, using agents of influence to tear down some and build up others in the enemy camp, using one's power in international markets to affect an enemy's economy—none of these measures will necessarily spill blood. Nevertheless, they can be real measures of warfare if they are pursued as such. We insist on a caveat, however: there is a misconception in contemporary America that the unbloody arts of political influence can substitute for a lack of willingness to push military operations to victory. Nothing could be further from the truth. The effect of political warfare depends almost exclusively on the assumption by everyone involved that it is part of an open-ended commitment to victory.

Fifteenth, because war involves the commitment of so much, and applies so much stress to society, it is often the midwife of social change. Nevertheless, we challenge the widespread view that war necessarily brings about revolutions, or that it tends to produce more authoritarian governments. In fact, wars usually accentuate or bring to the fore features or possibilities already present in a given society. The most characteristic thing about any society is how it manages to squeeze blood and treasure out of itself. No one can tell how this will affect any given society. De Gaulle pointed out that war is the "gravedigger of decadence." Thus, war acts like a windstorm against trees whose roots no longer grip the earth. On the other hand, as blood and treasure flow, they can form wholly new roots so that new trees grow to replace the old ones. One of the primary threads of our civilization resulted from European kings progressively enfranchising their societies out of a practical need to gain support for war.

Sixteenth, the effect of any war depends to a large extent on whether a nation wins or loses. The trauma of defeat may or may not linger, but it surely comes all at once. Streets are filled with the country's own defeated soldiers who are hungry, bitter, and dispirited, and also with the winner's men, all of whom are outside the law. At best they will search out and kill or deport or restrict only a few of those associated with the losing regime.

But they are free to do whatever they please, and the normal behavior of conquerors is for the worse. Then there are refugees and economic dislocations. Hunger and disease are usually there too. In this atmosphere, the never-ending struggle for primacy takes on a truly Hobbesian cast. The spectacular rebirths of West Germany and Japan under kind conquerors are the exceptions to history's rule: don't *ever* lose a war!

Finally, we point out that the end of war is not necessarily the kind of peace in which everyone lives happily ever after. For example, looking at the Versailles Treaty of 1919, Marshal Foch declared, "This is not peace. This is an armistice for twenty years." And so it turned out to be. When a war does not pronounce final judgment on its causes, the result is a *bellum interruptum* rather than peace. Furthermore, when the winner thinks that he can secure his wishes only by killing or imprisoning the losers, as in the case of the Soviet Union and communist movements such as Cambodia's Khmer Rouge, the result is the peace of the penitentiary or the peace of the dead. But as Machiavelli pointed out five hundred years ago, unless the enemy people are thoroughly destroyed, their children will remember their parents' fate and will wait for the winner to stumble. This is not what people usually mean by peace either. Rather, peace is a kind of satisfaction or tranquility in the order of things. What the losers will and won't be satisfied with depends in part on the winners' readiness to resume the war. But as long-term winners have always known, peace also means an order under which a given people can live in a way that more or less satisfies their essential needs. Yet no peace is permanent, and nothing so surely guarantees war as dissatisfaction with contingency and the attempt to establish perpetual peace.

Peace, War, and the Unity of Mankind

Peace and war flow from contrasting desires in the hearts of men. What visions of peace in the bush can lead one to give up the peace at hand? What are the moral and political consequences of any given choice to fight or not to fight? Such questions have arisen only within Western civilization—and then only since about the year 500 BC. Prior to the Socratics in Greece and the prophets of Israel—and even in our day in other civilizations—human beings have lived by the tribal mentality, according to which people belonging to other tribes may be as useful as fish or cattle, but are much more dangerous. In tribal languages, the name of one's own tribe is typically the same as the word for "people." The tribe's relation to others is typically the same as to wild animals, which may be captured and domesticated, perhaps eaten, and certainly defended against. For example, even though Arabs have been sophisticated by Islam for over a thousand years, their language still reflects tribal practices: the word for "black person," *iswid,* is the very word for "slave." We call this state of things war. Most of the world's peoples typically do not call it anything. That's just the way things are.

The distinction between peace and war exists fully in the West because only the West fully draws the consequences of the distinction between animals, humans, and God: namely, human equality. Tribal culture does not inculcate thoughts, habits, or scruples that might restrain behavior toward foreigners. On the contrary, war against other tribes is something of a duty owed to the gods of one's own hearth.[5]

In addition, war against other tribes serves practical purposes. It provides land, goods, and slaves. The essence of tribal war is to conquer a territory and to kill or sell all those inhabitants one does not wish to use as slaves. The Spartans, for example, conquered their spot on earth from the Helots, whom they kept as slaves. Each new king of Sparta began his reign by redeclaring war on the Helots.

Only when what came to be known as Western or Judeo-Christian civilization gradually accepted that, as one formulation put it, all men are created equal, did this civilization come to deem armed hostility a departure from the normal state of peace, a departure that only good reasons could render legitimate. For St. Augustine and for the entire Christian tradition that has followed, the primary purpose of government is the maintenance of peace.[6] The classic Christian title for the ruler is *Defensor Pacis,* "the defender of the peace." The Christian tradition approves of war under a variety of circumstances. It leaves no doubt that war is an aberration to be justified in detail, contrary to a standing presumption in favor of peace. Hence Western literature has always been full of people agonizing over the moral claims of waging war or making peace. Surely no traditional Chinese or Indian manual of statecraft ever agonized over the legitimacy—as opposed to the prudence—of attacking a neighboring principality or of oppressing foreigners. Thus, peace, the kind characterized by people treating each other more or less as they would like to be treated, is the peculiar and hard-won creature of Western minds.

Although that creation is chock full of ancient Jewish and Greek elements, its synthesis is very peculiarly Christian. The Christian tradition values peace so highly because peace is conducive to spiritual life. Spiritual life, in turn, is of overriding importance because of the Christian imperative of saving one's immortal soul. God's saving grace judges individuals only for themselves, not as parts of groups. Hence temporal quarrels between groups become inherently less important, and peace becomes the primordial goal of Christian statecraft.

This line of reasoning is shared by no other tradition. Our nearest intel-

lectual neighbor, the Muslim tradition, though it recognizes the brotherhood of all men under God, defines peace as the state proper only among
the *Umma*, "the believers in Islam." Nonbelievers, by definition, live in *Dar
al Harb*—literally, "the place of war."[7] It is proper for Muslims to cut back
this realm by the sword.

The bulk of mankind, though, lives under neither the Christian nor the
Islamic tradition. China's billion-plus were never westernized. India's billion, along with the bulk of the world's former Western colonies from Borneo
to Zanzibar, acquired only a patina of Western elements. As Western influence recedes around the world, it is increasingly undeniable that in most
of Africa, much of the Middle East, and in some of Asia, the Western slogans spoken by political leaders reflect Western culture much less than
they do a barely scratched tribal ethic: the boundaries of humanity do not
extend much beyond the tribes.[8] The one Western modification to this ethic
widely accepted in the third world is itself a corruption of the Western
tradition: The boundaries of humanity do not extend beyond one's own
party.

In the twentieth century we became accustomed to thinking of total
war (mass violence aimed at eliminating, enslaving, or driving out alien
populations) as a modern phenomenon. It actually is a return to a practice
that was routine before Greeks and Jews separately discovered that there
was such a thing as mankind. Today it is all too easy to realize that, even in
the West, the distinction between peace and war is fragile. But few have
stopped to examine the ideas that gnaw away at the Western notion of
mankind and hence at the war/peace distinction. Five centuries ago,
Machiavelli began to impress on generations of rulers, would-be rulers,
and shapers of minds the image of the successful modern man, emanci-
pated from Christian civilization. This man's mind, if not his body, is always engaged in what fashion nowadays calls a violent zero-sum game,
that is, a contest for primacy in which the need to kill in order to live is ever
present. When Machiavelli's paragon of modern virtue is riding in the countryside, he asks himself and his friends what one might do if this or that
enemy appeared on a hill. When this modern man looks at any other man,
he considers him his potential assassin, his potential victim, or the potential executioner of his enemies. Thomas Hobbes followed. Dispensing with
Italian subtleties, he taught that what Machiavelli had counseled to the
few was nothing but the "state of nature" in which all of us necessarily
live, the state of war by all against all: *homo homini lupus*—"man the natural predator of other men."

The illustrious modern thinkers who have purveyed similar views are
legion. Indeed, much of the modern intellectual tradition intends to liberate man from the "Christian fairy tale" that all men are equally God's chil-

dren, that human compatibility is the natural law, and that peace is the mandate of God. Thus, the primary challenge to the Western understanding of peace comes from within the Western tradition itself. Many modern westerners have shed all spiritual concerns and have adopted mentalities—if not yet lifestyles—according to which absolutely all human intercourse is, by rigid definition, a form of war.

The most popular of these modern mentalities is Marxism, folded into most subjects—implicitly after the Soviet collapse—at every university in the Western world. Karl Marx teaches that the history of human relations must be necessarily that of exploitation. Friedrich Engels's *The Origins of the Family, Private Property, and the State* argues that the relationship of parents and children in all societies that have ever existed—never mind the relationship between husband and wife—is necessarily one of mutual exploitation unto death. The only question that Marxists can consider about any human relationship whatever is who can manage to live off whom. Of course Marxism is far from an anomaly on the modern Western intellectual scene.[9] Various species of social Darwinists, including some conservatives, believe that fitness is the only right to survival and that they are among the fittest. Life is a struggle in which one's gain is another's loss. They therefore commit what Abraham Lincoln called the primordial political sin, one form or another of the maxim: "You work, I'll eat." Diverse groups easily adapt this nasty logic to justify their rapacity.

The modern world is also filled with social movements that, although they do not have the power to unleash holocausts, nevertheless spread the "bad news" of the incompatibility of interests, the natural unsociability of man. Whether the "cause" is supposed to be sex or vanishing natural resources, the question posited by such movements is the same: how to make certain that the "right" people ride in the lifeboat and the "wrong" people are in the water. For people who think like this, the imperatives of race, party, or even sex wholly obscure the bonds even of kinship—never mind those of mere humanity. For many of these modernists, no less than for Marxists, Wahhabis, or primitive tribesmen, the only question is how best to wage the war that is life.

Furthermore, even people who sincerely adhere to the tenets of Western civilization tend to cast them aside when they are overcome by hate and when the issue at hand seems to be more important than anything else. This also happens when long periods of war cause loss of perspective. The dynastic struggles of the Hundred Years' War, the constant strife between the Italian cities during the Renaissance, the devastation of Germany after the Reformation, and the continental war during the generation following the French Revolution are poignant reminders that even people well schooled in the distinction between war and peace, and who sincerely avow a preference for peace, can let constant war become a way of life and thus become inured to atrocity. Habit and trend are as influential on the ways of war and peace as they are in all other human affairs.

One of the passages of history that has drawn the most nods over the centuries is Thucydides' account of how the Peloponnesian War gradually changed the habits and expectations of all Greece so that violence toward both foreigners and countrymen became frequent and normal.[10] People's willingness to blur the distinction between war and peace, their willingness to wage war, and the vehemence with which they fight stem from their habits, from desires or fears, and from their intellectual landscape.

We are conscious that the Western distinction between peace and war is a minority opinion in the world, that it is accepted but misunderstood in much of the West, and that the philosophic bases of that tradition are anything but popular in Western universities. Nevertheless, we use this distinction as the basis of our discussion not just because it is a bastion of our civilization, but also because it can explain both itself and much of the political and historical landscape. For a variety of reasons, nothing else on the intellectual landscape can do that.

PART I

How Wars Start

1

THE MEANING OF WAR AND PEACE

It is not that they love peace less, but that
they love their kind of peace more.
—Saint Augustine
City of God

P EOPLES DEFINE themselves by the kinds of peace they live and the kinds of war they fight. The Civil War, so goes an old saw, is the most typical event in American history—not because Americans fight civil wars frequently, but because the war showed most clearly the issues that make America what it is. One of these is the conflict between liberty and equality. Another is the battle between those who try to exclude others from equal protection under the law—and those who rally under the banner, "all men are created equal." What is the relationship of this country's parts to its whole? To what extent should race, age, or lack of power affect how people are treated? What can be bought and sold, and what cannot? In the 1860s, just like at the time of the constitutional convention, and just like today, these issues were fought out in the context of commercial interest and religious fervor.

The American people have fought nine major wars lasting a total of twenty-five years and have lived through more than two centuries of so-cial change. Yet never were the inner seams of this national structure so clearly on display as when they were strained to the breaking point be-tween 1861 and 1865, forcing people out of comfortable ambiguity to bet their lives on which of their country's aspects they wanted to predominate.

Two contrasting sets of views about these matters had grown up within the northern and southern parts of this country since well before the War of Independence. Each part of the country was at peace with itself about the choice it had made. Indeed, had either side lacked this internal peace and coherence, it could not have organized itself to fight. In the years leading up to 1860, the contrast sharpened as each side tried to prejudice the other's future to the point where Lincoln noted, "a house divided against itself cannot stand." Thus, the war was fought as if two different nations were involved. The American people can be grateful for this. Had the adversaries been interspersed, the seriousness of the issues might have produced an even more frightful slaughter.

War as the Ultimate Election

Both the practical and the moral consequences of any war depend in substantial part on the purposes for which it is fought. So, incidentally, does the war's ferocity. Why were wars in eighteenth-century Europe such courtly affairs while at the same time battles between tribes along the west coast of Africa were depopulating vast areas? While the Europeans were fighting to decide whose flag would fly over a particular province, the African tribes of that time were fighting over which would sell the others to Arab slave wholesalers. Why, during World War II, did Germans (never mind Italians) easily surrender to American units but fight the Soviets much more strenuously? Undeniably, it was because the character of the United States and hence the nature of the war with the United States were such that any reasonable German could expect better treatment from the Americans than from the Russians. The Germans knew that regardless of Hitler's global rhetoric, their war with the Soviet Union meant something substantially different from their war with the United States. By the same token, why did the fighting of the Christian crusades so resemble the jihad that spread Islam across ten time zones? Could it be that the purposes of both these sets of wars were so similar? It stands to reason that wars fought for annihilation or survival, to impose or maintain religion, to impose or avoid slavery, to conquer or lose a province, or to gain or lose markets will differ vastly from one another.

Yet we must note that purpose and habit by themselves do not *determine* the meaning of war. A war's character is the result of decisions actually taken. For example, during World War II the Soviet regime never bombed German cities even though it had murdered millions of its own citizens prior to the war. Thereafter it did not hesitate to destroy whole classes of innocents in occupied territories (for example, the massacre of much of the Polish officer corps in the Katyn Forest) to remove obstacles to creating communist societies. By contrast, the American and British regimes, habituated to nonlethal politics and built on a moral base that stresses protection of innocents, exterminated hundreds of thousands of innocents by deliberately bombing German and Japanese cities. Why the reversal of roles? The reason seems to be that the Soviet leadership was able to exercise retail self-discipline to pursue wholesale barbarism. Soviet leaders put aside their hatred of the Germans and their plans for socialism because defeating Germany most efficiently was more important. After victory, they indulged their hatred to the full. In contrast, the great democracies during the war indulged themselves in talk about wiping away the absolute evil embodied in Germany and acted accordingly. Similarly, Germany's Nazi regime overrode the advice of its professional military and indulged its race hatred on occupied populations on the eastern front—with disastrous consequences. None of these countries had to behave the way they did. But by behaving as they did they made the war mean what it came to mean.

War is always both the violent negation of the enemy and the violent affirmation of what one's own side is all about. War and the prospect of war demand that people bet their lives and the future of their families on one side or another of allegiances, quarrels, propositions, faiths. Often, war is the logical end of those allegiances or quarrels. Thus, it confronts people with the consequences of their commitments. It asks: Do you *really* want to bet your life on *this?* So, from society's humblest soldier to its biggest pillar, war forces men to choose the causes to which they will or will not lend themselves.

True, the bonds of group discipline are tightest in wartime. Still, wartime affords more opportunities and incentives to defeat, overthrow, or change one's own regime than does peace. The enemy usually welcomes defectors. But one does not have to resort to treason if one does not fully espouse the aims of one's own side or dislikes its leaders. Apathy is usually quite enough to ensure that the other side will prevail. Domestic factions are usually ready to exploit the discontent that always accompanies wars. Furthermore, regimes are seldom as open to change, for better or for worse, as they are during life-and-death struggles. In sum, because wars require the active, enthusiastic participation of large numbers of people to resolve the most important issues with which men deal, they are the ultimate form of election. And wars offer unusually effective ways of registering one's vote.

The most consequential of all choices is whether or not to fight. "What if they gave a war and nobody came?" This saying, popular among Americans who opposed this country during its war against North Vietnam between 1965 and 1975, reflects an essential fact: wars cannot be the private quarrels of rulers. Those who fight have to "buy into" the rulers' agenda or they will not fight. Any ruler who—like Presidents Lyndon Johnson and Richard Nixon—presents an ambiguous, cold, or otherwise unappealing agenda, while his opponent argues that the agenda is unworthy, is sure to lose both the war and his influence over his population. Even during the European Middle Ages—an anomalous time in history when rulers tried to fight their own battles personally—rulers had to convince people who would otherwise have no interest in the quarrel to fight for their cause. They also had to convince an even wider group of people to pay for the war. Of course, recruiting, equipping, and paying for an army that must fight far away requires more explanation than recruiting an army to fight at home against invaders. But even the job of getting people to show up for a war of home defense is not a trivial one. True, once people are put in a situation in which they must fight for their lives, they often fight regardless of the reasons they were put there. Yet, sometimes being in the face of the enemy will only heighten the sense of meaninglessness and hasten the collapse. In short, war is the most public of business.

The act of raising and paying for armies may well be the most typical act that any regime performs. It is the act for the performance of which any regime must call upon the deepest allegiances it has. When a regime calls upon people to leave their daily lives for certain discomfort and possible death, it must, as the contemporary saying goes, cash in its chips. Only then does it find out just how deep and sincere those allegiances are. Perhaps the most distinguishing features of any regime are the bases on which it claims military service—the chips that it cashes in, whether they be feudal oaths, habits, hatreds old or new, hopes, fears, appealing visions, and so on. The problem is only superficially absent in societies that put into the field armies composed largely of slaves or people who are there strictly because they are compelled to be there. In such cases, the political problem merely resides among those who drive the slaves. They are the ones "who count." What if the ruler "gave a war" and the cadre, or slave drivers, didn't show up—or showed up half-heartedly? Herodotus tells us that Xerxes, emperor of Persia, was sure that his armies were superior to the Greeks' because the Persians feared their masters. He could not understand that Greek citizens revered their laws more than his armies feared their masters. Surely the most important feature of any society is how and how well it ensures that when it does give a war, the right people show up and perform in a way that will allow the society to survive and stay independent.

Perhaps these are the most important questions one can ask of any society: Who will fight for it? How well will they fight? What will it take to call forth this allegiance? In what form will it come forth? In the Greek *poleis* and during the Roman republic, military service was one of the privileges of citizenship. Those most responsible for making their city what it was were also most responsible for fighting its battles. They eagerly paid for their own weapons. Centuries later, vast wealth and high culture could not save the seat of the Western empire when those who counted in the city of Rome did not even think of taking sword in hand against the barbarians. Their ambitions were not the empire's.

A country's war making always reflects "who counts" in society. For example, in medieval France those who counted, the mounted noblemen who were the only real "constituents" of the realm, were as eager to fight for their country as any republican Roman ever was. Indeed, they were so jealous of the right to a preferred place in combat that they relegated infantry and archery to a place on the battlefield comparable in significance to their lowly place in society. Hence, the French suffered defeat after defeat by English kings, whose zeal for combat and pride in rank did not blind them to the usefulness of peasants wielding longbows and pikes. The "scientific" mercenary armies of eighteenth-century Europe were trained to dispassionate, robot-like performance by that small portion of the elite who retained a taste for battle. That was enough for kings and nobles to play in the international arena for limited stakes. But kings, nobles, their societies, and their armies were swept away by the French Revolution's call to all men to fight for a new way of life. The armies of the French Revolution engaged the entire nation in passionate efforts perhaps even more demanding than those of republican Rome. The entire population now "counted." By 1914 the whole Western world, plus Japan, had imitated them.

But by 1914 the peoples of Europe were no longer fighting to free themselves from elites who had become parasites, nor for political independence, nor for any purpose that a detached observer would find reasonable. The stakes in their conflicts were not high by historic standards. Yet the societies of Europe were enthusiastic and organized to feed military organizations for "total efforts, regardless of cost." Families and communities deprived young men of any choice and pushed them into the meat grinder of trench warfare. They all counted, but their decisions doubly decimated Europe's young manhood for causes that obviously could not justify the carnage. Thus the proposition that war itself is senseless and that states that make war are senseless as well gained currency. Because of this World War I, and its enormous aftershock, World War II, dealt blows to the raison d'être of European states from which they never recovered.

Today, as one looks at the wealthy societies of Europe and of European descent—societies that seemingly have everything—there are no obvious answers to the questions: What might move "those who count" in these societies to fight or even to make the preparations without which an eventual decision to fight would be meaningless? Do they find in their own society any meaning, noble or base, for which they would kill or be killed? To say that these societies now find their meaning in peace begs the question: Whose peace?

Kinds of Peace

Peace is as much an election as war is. Whereas war is a kind of movement that proceeds from dissatisfaction, peace is rest that proceeds from satisfaction. But satisfaction with what? The condemned man, the slave, the stymied, the man who got half a loaf, the pillar of the community, and the conqueror each may be satisfied enough not to struggle. But what are they satisfied with? There is the satisfaction of communion with God, the satisfaction of the pig at the trough, of purposelessness or of purpose, of building up or of tearing down, of a fulfilled vision, of acquiescence in monstrosities, or of ceasing to care. In other words, to say that peace is the absence of fighting is to try to escape the inescapable question: What is one satisfied with? And why?

St. Augustine noted that everyone wants peace, and that everyone, however dimly, understands it as a kind of order that is generally accepted. Even the members of a gang who live by killing and robbing others expect to receive orderly forbearance from one another in order to enjoy the fruits of their crimes. Augustine's point is that if anyone follows the logic of this natural desire all the way, he will end up treating others as he himself would want to be treated. But Augustine is the first to admit that people will do whatever they can to shortcut the logic of peace—to cause others to acquiesce in the order that they want. Still, Augustine and every other perceptive thinker and statesman has realized that force alone may only bring about the peace of the dead by exterminating another people or the peace of the prison by constantly guarding unbowed enemies. To bring about anything beyond solitude or momentary acquiescence, one must also to some extent engage the affections or habits of the people with whom one wishes to live in peace.

Different people will accept peace on different terms. For example, given the Afghan people's indomitable resistance to the Soviet Union's occupation of their country, it became commonplace to say that the Afghans would die to the last man rather than let any foreigner rule them in any way. But this is not so. The British ruled the Afghans in the nineteenth century, never totally but with much less trouble than the Soviets. The explanation is simple. The Afghans never saw the British as a threat to what they hold dearest: Islam. Whereas the Afghans saw the British occupation as a bother that most of the time was not worth resisting, they saw the Soviet occupation as a mortal threat to their immortal souls. The British for a time got most of what they wanted in Afghanistan because all they wanted in Afghanistan was outposts to guard the Indian subcontinent from Russian influence. Thus, the Afghans did not so much mind giving up. Beginning in 2001 the U.S. armed forces occupied parts of Afghanistan. Like the British, the Americans were after mostly non-Afghan enemies. But like the Soviets, they sought to reform Afghan society. Hence the American's stay, though less peaceful than the Soviets', was not as peaceful as Britain's.

The Romans made clear to those on whom they would impose peace that they did not mean to change their internal customs. This helped to establish the Pax Romana, but not without violence. After all, the customs of the various Mediterranean peoples had not included paying tribute of money and men to Rome and the indignity of hosting foreign rulers on sacred soil. Hence the Pax Romana was punctuated by revolts, such as that of the Jews in AD 70, which resulted in the Diaspora. The Jews were the only nation who suffered dispersion without the death of its culture.

It is easier to impose any and all conditions on peoples who lack the intense cultural identity and religious faith of the Jews and Afghans and who lack the discipline that is necessary to face hardship. Consider the primary model of peace in the modern world drawn by Thomas Hobbes. According to Hobbes, each human being is inescapably interested above all in self-preservation. All other loves, hates, hopes, and fears fade away before the fear of violent death. Such people bestow to one among themselves the absolute power of life and death over each and all strictly because they fear death at each other's hands. For such people, peace means cringing surrender to the most powerful force around, regardless of its demands, as long as it promises safety from others.

Machiavelli long ago noted how easy it is to impose one's own peace on people who are accustomed to being subjects. One need only defeat the master in one battle and he will be abandoned. Then, with the former master out of the way, the people will be satisfied with a new master, almost regardless of what he does. If the people have some reservations, Machiavelli gives us Cesare Borgia as a guide to successful pacification. First, Borgia hired a henchman named Orco to sow terror in the land. Then, to draw resentment away from himself without losing the capacity to overawe, he had Orco cut in half. The bloody mess left in a public square along with the knife, he tells us, made the people both satisfied and stupefied. This is the peace, because this is the satisfaction, of people whose primary preoccupation is attachment to their own skins.

Note, however, where this sort of peace can lead. The managers of both the Soviet and Nazi extermination camps kept peace among the condemned by conspicuous cruelty *and* by giving the impression that those who were not killed at any given time might be allowed to live. Alas, these murderous managers had little trouble in turning tomorrow's victims into today's collaborators. Thus attachment to life, untempered by anything that might lead them to risk their lives, led millions to the slaughterhouse—the peace of the dead.

But as we have seen, some peoples are not satisfied with mere life. They will not rest in peace as long as a wrong, real or imagined, remains unrighted. This can have a variety of effects, depending on the nature of the outstanding grievances. Some peoples are in the grip of causes that cannot possibly be appeased. The Anabaptists of Renaissance times could never rest in peace because the New Jerusalem of perfection would simply not come about, regardless of how many priests and burghers they slaughtered. Real peace came to Bohemia, Munster, and other places only after the Anabaptists themselves had been killed. Nor could real Marxists ever rest in peace while alive, because no matter how many "enemies of the people" they killed, the "new communist man" was never a biological or moral possibility. Nor, similarly, can adherents to Islam's Wahhabi heresy live in peace because no one can set bounds to the purity they claim to seek. Hence no more than other heretics and Marxists can Wahhabis ever have peace among themselves or with others. Is it possible to pacify the ideologically unpacifiable by means other than killing them? Historical experience shows that if one tries to put down such ideologies solely by killing, one will fail. Ideas can be conquered only by other ideas. Thus St. Dominic, in his thirteenth-century campaign against the Albigensian heresy in southern France combined the sword and the sermon, as well as practical demonstrations of rightly ordered clerical and civil authority. His campaign restored peace to the region because he distinguished correctly who could and could not be convinced—and killed the latter.

Those whose dissatisfaction comes chiefly from their desire to possess more in order to enjoy themselves more are in another category. Indeed, it happens that passion's grip can be loosened easily enough by raising up obstacles to its satisfaction that would be unpleasant and dangerous to overcome. This is known as deterrence. For example, readers of Shakespeare are familiar with the process by which Henry V decided to invade France. First he wanted more domain and glory. Then he checked and found that the enterprise was feasible without undue strain. Only then did he listen to a legal-moral argument. It is clear that this argument would have had a much different impact on him had he previously judged that the enterprise would be difficult. Deterrence is like a cold shower on passion. However, a note of caution is in order. Some passions are unquenchable, and there is no guarantee that any given deterrent will quench the quenchable ones. Still, deterrence is usually an aid to reason because if any person's passion could be pursued cheaply, it would be very difficult for that person to listen to reason.

But the desire to possess more, particularly to have more glory, is sometimes so powerful that deterrence is not enough, especially when able men are involved. Neither Napoleon nor Caesar, for example, was an ideologue. They simply combined so much self-confidence with insatiable appetite for glory that no difficulty loomed large enough to deter them. This is not to say that deterrence is always the friend of reason. There are, after all, the pacifist passions: self-indulgence and fear. Because deterrence cuts both ways, much depends on a comparison of the character of both sides' leaders.

This does not mean that those who are coolheaded will hence be pacifists. In fact, dispassionate judgment sometimes argues against fear, against being deterred from war. Also, lack of passion is no guarantee against wrong or perverse judgment. For Machiavelli, Hobbes, and the tradition that follows them, reason is a mere scout for the passions, and hence predisposes people to war. But in the classical tradition from Plato to Hooker reason goes along with a preference for the right order of things, namely justice, the state of things in which everyone gets what he deserves. Thus oriented, a man is at peace with himself and potentially with others as well.

Anyone, whether a private citizen or a ruler, who has his passions under control and his priorities in order seeks only what is rightly due to each. But of course most people seek not right but their own safety, honor, and interest. Moreover, the right order of things is not to be made on earth, and the attempt to make it so makes not for peace but rather for permanent dissatisfaction and unending war. How far it is possible to approach either the right order of things or one's own true interest at any given time in any given place is a prudential judgment. By making such judgments, men and nations make the kinds of peace of which they are worthy.

War, the Gateway to Peace

Regardless of rightness, reasonable combatants must fight for peace. Napoleon was a master of battles. But he failed utterly as a warrior because he did not design his campaigns to produce a state of things in which France could be content. At any rate, he was never content, and neither was the rest of Europe as long as he lived. In the end, he bled France physically and morally to the point that it was no longer capable of winning battles against the opposition that he had stirred up. More than two thousand years earlier, though Sparta forced Athens' surrender in the great Peloponnesian War, Spartans enjoyed the aftermath almost as little as Athenians. Had the military result been the opposite, the Peloponnesian War would still not have given rest to anyone, because neither Athens after Pericles' death nor Sparta after King Archidamus' political eclipse was fighting for a vision of peace. In the deepest sense, military operations that do not reasonably aim at some kind of peace are unnatural. The safety and pleasures of peace are the natural ends of war, the reason people accept unpleasantness and risk death, just as wheat and wine are the reasons farmers plow fields and prune grapes. The reasonableness of any plowing or bombing depends on how well calculated each is to produce its natural fruits.

When—as so often happens—human beings' notions of right, their visions of peace, not to speak of their pride and perceived interests, are irreconcilable, force becomes their natural arbiter. Hence force is essential not just to establishing one vision of peace over another, but also to maintaining it against enemies foreign and domestic.

Sometimes, force is essential to maintaining a certain state of peace against even nonviolent assaults. After 1945 European states, whose borders, predominant languages, institutions, and character resulted from five centuries of wars, psychologically disabled themselves from fighting wars. For them, the second half of the twentieth century was a time of unprecedented albeit precarious peace and stability. By the turn of the twenty-first century, however, the accelerating flow of third-world immigrants was destabilizing European life in ways difficult for Americans to understand. The causes and justice of this flow are beside the point that force is the only way that it could be stopped and that European states had become incapable of using force. Hence, there seemed to be no way in which European states, unable to defend their borders, could maintain the institutions and character that they had made for themselves by war.

2

THE CAUSES OF WAR

Why do the nations so furiously rage together?
—Psalm 2

THE ELEMENTARY question has echoed down the ages. Countless wounded and bereaved and others simply contemplating the destruction of war have cried out, "Why?" Men have speculated about the causes of war in general and of particular wars. But *what is a cause?*

The dictionary offers two strikingly different meanings of "cause." Both answer the "why" of war. A cause, says the dictionary, is that which "produces an effect, result, or consequence." But then, it says, a cause also is "a goal or principle served with dedication and zeal." Thus, causes may be those forces, factors, and events that are supposed to drive nations into conflict. But causes also are the purposes that animate nations, that their leaders choose, and that men deem worth fighting and dying for. The fifth line of the final stanza of the "Star-Spangled Banner" exemplifies the latter meaning: "Then conquer we must when our cause is just."

In our times, social scientists typically explore the *first* meaning of cause and neglect the second. This approach is deterministic. Wars happen because of a confluence of generic factors, however defined. The fact that individuals decide to get involved seems beside the point to these social scientists, who claim to understand protagonists better than they understand themselves. War is supposed to happen without anyone really wanting it. After all, how could anyone want hell? So to the extent that "factors" don't explain any given war, it must have been an accident.

Others, however, including practitioners of statecraft, philosophers, poets, and many historians dwell on the voluntaristic meaning of "causes." This second view focuses on what actual people want out of any given war. To them wars are contests between causes, contests which, as the Greek storyteller Homer says, destroy "the glorious deeds of men," but which nevertheless men desire not only because of base motives—envy, greed, lust, revenge—but also because they offer the chance to display noble qualities—bravery, courage, prowess, judgment, and honor. Thus, the classical scholar, F. E. Adcock, tells us of Homer's *Iliad:*

> The greatest moment of Achilles is the moment when, as the Greeks are being driven back after the death of Patroclus, he stands unarmed at the Trench, and the sound of his sole voice strikes fear into the ranks of Troy.[1]

Throughout his history of the Peloponnesian War, the great Thucydides gives examples of how fear and perceived interest, in addition to honor, lead men to make war.

There is a third alternative: Until recent times, most westerners, like the Psalmist, have thought war to be a natural, if odious, aspect of human existence, akin to other calamities and challenges such as storms, earthquakes, famines, physical afflictions, and ultimately, mortality. The Jews of the Old Testament often described the ravages of war as Yahweh's chastisement for the transgressions of the chosen people. By contrast, Christians see war as merely another manifestation of free will exercised by imperfect human beings. War arises from the same inexhaustible fountain as every other man-made ill, from robbery to adultery to fraud. The Christian concept differs from the Jewish in that although Christians, like Jews, believe that war ultimately arises from human imperfection, they also believe that people actually *choose* the wars they fight.

A fourth theory became popular in the twentieth century. Shortly before World War I, the American steel magnate-philanthropist Andrew Carnegie in his will funded what was to become the first major American center for the study of the subject, the Carnegie Endowment for International Peace. So confident was he that war might someday disappear from the face of the earth that he specified that after perpetual peace was achieved, the trustees of his legacy then would shift remaining trust funds to other worthy causes. A century later, the endowment's peace work is still very active, and such "peace research" is lavishly supported by governments, foundations, and other benefactors.

Thus influential thinkers came to regard war as a gruesome clinical abnormality—a pathological practice to be cured rather than something with which we must live as best we can. This attitude has given rise to attempts to search for war's causes even as medical scientists search for causes and cures for diseases. But note that such researchers see the root of the disease neither in imperfect, imperfectible individuals, nor in the God of Abraham. Rather, the root cause is imperfect—but perfectible—social organizations. Hence, they believe peace is to be sought not through personal spiritual growth, nor in instruction about why some kinds of peace are preferable to others or about the most prudent ways of achieving one's ends, *but rather through the social surgery that they believe must be done.* Thus, this kind of peace research is a form of war—a way of increasing the likelihood that one's favorite social surgeons will put the knife to the least favorite causes and people. For many peace theorists, those offering explanations contrary to their own are themselves warmongers upon whom war must be waged for the sake of peace.

Thus, these sets of explanations—based on generic circumstances, human will, human imperfection, and social organization—really fall into two categories: the generic and the volitional. Let us examine them in turn.

Generic Causes of War

The prototypical example of generic causality theory is Quincy Wright's monumental *Study of War.* At the heart of Wright's method for deciding whether any given war will break out is a mathematical formula that expresses what Wright contends is the relationship between the many factors involved in any nation's decision to go to war with another.[2] Wright finds the many factors that determine the decision on all levels of human existence: the biological and cultural level, the social and political level, the level of legal institutions, and the level of technology. Each factor, like each human desire, can lead to war if it is not counterbalanced by another. War comes when the balancing act fails. The formula expresses the balance and purports to explain and perhaps predict breakdowns. It purports to be more than a simple mechanism for assigning numerical values to such factors as hostility and expectations of economic gain and loss. It attempts to use mathematical expressions, such as integrals and derivatives, to treat these phenomena in what appears to be a sophisticated method. But in the end, the formula requires the arbitrary substitution of numbers for qualities and even for imponderables and is an obvious example of the principle, garbage in, garbage out.

All other theories proposing generic causes are in a way partial versions of the Wright formula.[3] Instead of attempting to explain definitively the onset of war by drawing together and "objectifying" all factors affecting the onset of war, they take just one or just a few of these "objective factors," whether race, religion, or arms competition, as the sole explanation. In fact, however, the factor they mention may not even be an explanation, or not a terribly important one in the minds of those who start any given war. For example, standard Marxist explanations for World War II stress the importance of German industrial cartels such as I. G. Farben.[4] But how important is such an abstract factor compared with the actual presence in the Nazi Party of the master rabble-rouser, Joseph Goebbels? Given that Goebbels attributes his becoming a Nazi to his mother-in-law, is she to be ranked as a cause, or are mothers-in-law in general?

But while those who follow Quincy Wright may have difficulty convincing the man on the street that their "objective factors" and formulae mean anything, the U.S. military services and the CIA pay tens of millions of dollars each year for their wares. While other social scientists can only claim to provide the wisdom by which government officials may judge for themselves who is likely to fight whom over what, "objective" social scientists sell the ready-made results of complex, presumably authoritative processes.

Those social scientists who have sought the roots of war in causal theory have investigated many levels of human behavior and experience (psychology); particular human cultures (anthropology); particular political strategic orders (political science); particular economic systems; and particular arrangements and dispositions among nations and nation-states (international relations). None of this research and speculation has succeeded in predicting any war or any peace. Even when modern social science finds objective correlations between any one event or condition and the onset of war, for instance, an increase in armament levels, it cannot make the intellectual leap that separates correlation from cause. To say that the relationship between two generic events or conditions (for example, industrial expansion and social mobility) is the cause of a third event or condition is to abstract from what actually happens in particular places at particular times, and from what particular individuals are trying to accomplish.

Empirical studies have indeed confirmed what common sense teaches. Some cultures are indeed inherently more peaceable than others, and particular types of polities are more peaceable than others. It is not irrelevant that the ratio of the military budget to the gross domestic product of communist and Islamic countries is four times that for all other kinds of countries.[5] Particular economic systems may even be inherently more peaceable than others. Karl Marx himself pointed out that capitalism shuns war because of its depressing effects on stock markets, while "Oriental despotism" thrives on war. And perhaps certain particular arrangements between states, for example, fluid balances of power rather than blocs of alliances, are more conducive to peace than others.

Nevertheless, knowing all this, one is still far from understanding why any given war actually occurs in the real world. Ironically, peaceable kingdoms, being nice, may tempt aggressors to devour them, while nations armed to the teeth, whether they are nice like Switzerland or nasty like Afghanistan, may live undisturbed for generations. Thus an inclination to peace is no guarantee of maintaining it. However, peaceful nations, having taken up the sword, may fight with greater vigor and perhaps with less reasonable restraint than ones known for their martial spirit. All of this uncertainty exists because the disposition to fight arises from truly important contests of purpose and will between nations in concrete circumstances. It is impossible to predict what such contests may bring about.

The final proof that cultural characteristics do not bring about war is that while a nation's culture changes only slowly, its propensity to war changes quickly. The supposedly war-prone Japanese, who carried their savage military conquest deep into China, Southeast Asia, and the Pacific Islands in the 1930s and 1940s, seem today nearly bereft of martial spirit. Yet, Japanese culture, with its emphasis on discipline and clannishness, has changed little, while Japanese genes have not changed at all. The Jews of Israel, who now command one of the world's most effective armies, contrast vividly with their immediate forebears, the many Jews of Europe who allowed themselves to be herded into boxcars en route to Auschwitz and other Nazi extermination camps. Surely Jewish genes have not changed. Rather, Jews, Japanese, and all other peoples behave as they do at any given time because they are animated by particular regimes that call forth certain human qualities and suppress others. People also behave as they do because, at any given time, they either have or do not have particular leaders who succeed in making a cause out of the situation in which they find themselves. For example, Moses molded the Jews into a fearsome nation through the process of delivering them from Egyptian captivity. What some see as disasters, others see as opportunities.

Does this mean that man is infinitely malleable, and that while some particular cultures, states, and other conditions corrupt him, making him into a bellicose beast, other regimes could make man good and incapable of war? After all, the credo of the United Nations Educational, Scientific, and Cultural Organization (UNESCO) is because "wars begin in the minds of men," and because the mind is malleable, peace can be firmly and permanently planted there. This is the credo of social engineers of all kinds. By examining it, we shall see why it is mistaken.[6]

One theory on the generic causes of war stands outside of this deterministic framework, but rather is anchored to the rock of common sense about human affairs, namely that that human beings choose to make war or not to make it, just as they choose to do or not to do anything else.

The Christian realism that St. Augustine teaches in the *City of God* locates the source of war in the will of sinful men. Augustine thus assumes the ever-present possibility of war. Christian realists of our times, such as the American theologian Reinhold Niebuhr, however, have questioned the logical causal relationship between war and human imperfections, whether individual or collective.[7] As they see things, by no means does it follow that all imperfect men are aggressive; nor does it follow that the aggressive behavior of nations is caused by the aggressive compulsions of individuals. A *nation* of submissive robots may more easily be led to battle than one of aggressive individualists. The key to these possibilities lies in Plato's well-known point that a country reflects its leaders to the point that, for practical purposes, it is those leaders "writ large"—with all their virtues, passions, and shortcomings. If the leaders are aggressive, and circumstances allow them to follow their bent, others will either go along or revolt to change the regime.

Still, there is a non sequitur in any theory that grounds collective warlike behavior of nations in the aggressive attributes of individuals. Collective aggression and personal aggression are two different things. Determinists simply could not imagine that warlike leaders might impress their character on nations of sheep, and vice versa. But they do. When the young Bolshevik Stalin clandestinely visited Germany to meet with German communists, he concluded that, inured as they were to authority, they were utterly contemptible as revolutionaries. Stalin imagined that if his German counterparts were ordered to seize a railroad station they would first meekly line up at the ticket window to buy admission passes. He could not imagine these peaceable Germans whipped up to the sort of violence that suited his tastes. But in 1941 Stalin saw orderly hordes of these obedient Germans nearly topple his regime. Had the Germans been less prone to be obedient subordinates, they might not have lent themselves so easily to Hitler's aggression.

Each generation in the liberal West has been exposed to a particular intellectual fad that has named a particular culprit for war. In eighteenth-century Europe and in the American colonies, the main malefactors were widely deemed to be monarchs and dynasts.[8] There seemed to be a superficial plausibility to their logic. The main wars of the previous centuries had been waged among the courts of England, France, Austria, Prussia, and Spain. The will of European aristocrats, so went the accusation, was unchecked by public opinion. These aristocrats' objectives were said to be irrelevant or contrary to the real needs and aspirations of the people. This being so, truly peace-loving polities would be republics, in which decisions about war and peace would be made by men who would represent the people's desire to avoid becoming cannon fodder. The authorities would have no right to make war arbitrarily. Secret diplomacy and secret alliances and commitments would be anathema. To paraphrase George Orwell, "Monarchies bad, Republics good." The United States of America, born in this period, adopted a constitution incorporating these sentiments.

The view that war is spawned by the absence of democracy heavily influenced the worldviews of English liberals and the American Founding Fathers. Jefferson and Tom Paine, author of *Common Sense,* the most influential piece of writing in American history, saw the causes of wars as ceaseless struggles by dynastic courts in Europe waged over the whole globe. Thus, progressive Americans came to see the principle of the "balance of power," which evidently regulated the affairs of European cabinets in war and peace, as a cause of war made worse by its cruel disregard for the wishes of ordinary people. (By contrast George Washington, Alexander Hamilton, John Quincy Adams, and the tradition that flowed from them believed that republics and popular passions were as likely to breed war as monarchies.[9] Paine himself followed his equation of republicanism with peace with advocacy of a U.S. Navy capable of controlling the balance of power in the western Atlantic.) A simple-minded, supercharged version of the Jeffersonian creed was the rhetorical chariot on which Woodrow Wilson carried America into World War I. It was part of the basis for U.S. hostility to European colonial power after World War II, and remains a factor in U.S. foreign policy today.

Karl Marx, for his part, taught that the true progressive engine of modern history was the class conflict between the exploiting oppressors and the exploited oppressed—in our time, the bourgeoisie and the proletariat. The old ruling classes would vainly use any means to postpone their inevitable overthrow. Marx depicted this conflict as basically a *vertical* conflict between upper and lower classes. Lenin carried Marx's doctrine to include the clash of capitalist powers for the right to subjugate overseas markets, and sources of raw materials. This was the "highest" form of bourgeois exploitation and the chief cause of modern war. The only real peace, the peace of socialism, would come when all vestiges of capitalism, including vast categories of human beings, were "liquidated." In fact, perhaps as many human beings were "liquidated" in the name of Marxism-Leninism as were killed in the two "conventional" world wars.[10]

In our time, Samuel Huntington built the fact that the Islamic world has "bloody borders" into a thesis that the "clash of civilizations" is the nursery of war. But whether the war is between regimes, nations, or civilizations the fact is that war happens only when some individuals choose to fight. But why do they choose to fight? What is the cause?

Accidental War

The epitome of the view that war is caused by something other than the will of those who start it is that it has no cause at all, that it is an accident. The misconceptions, misunderstandings, miscalculations, and technical malfunctionings of international affairs may combine to produce unwanted conflagrations in much the same way a traffic accident occurs. A visual impairment, a flaw in the road, or bad weather may cause two cars to collide. The hapless drivers who swerve into each others' paths do not intend to hit each other. Each later might be held for negligence, but no more.

Now, it is almost always true that those who deliberately take up arms are uncertain what will ensue. One might indeed argue that any war might not take place if both sides knew the consequences. But all human decisions are taken in ignorance of the future, and nations have regretted decisions not to fight as much as they have regretted decisions to go to war. Moreover, the argument for accidental war is based on the assumption that no one really wants war, but that many let themselves be put into situations where somehow they are "forced to choose" war. But "forced to chose" is self-contradictory. Perhaps analogous is the familiar claim that college students don't really choose drunken sex in the basement of fraternity houses—it just "happens"—much the same way, some say, paraphrasing Emerson, that World War I "happened"—"Things were in the saddle." Today, those who oppose the spread of advanced weaponry regardless of the character of the regimes that might come to possess it argue that "things," the weapons themselves, are dangerous because they might displace their masters in the saddle of decision making. But if that were so, why are we afraid that some people might get these weapons and not at all afraid that others have them? Evidently, who happens to be in the saddle makes a difference.[11]

Hence the skeptic must ask, is it really true that there can be accidental wars? If so, when have they happened in history? As the Australian historian Geoffrey Blainey observes in *The Causes of War*, while "political scientists have tended to accept the idea that some wars are accidental, historians have been wary."[12] It is difficult, he says, to find a war which on investigation fits this description. This is not to say that an accidental war has never happened; perhaps one has. We do not know of one, though, and the likelihood of such a war being discovered in history is exceedingly remote.

Miscalculations and misperceptions are not accidents. Are misperceptions of the "other side's" actions or intentions fortuitous at all? Blainey cites events at the onset of the Russo–Japanese War of 1904 as an example. He asks:

Why did Japan so seriously misconstrue Russia's intentions? . . . [The answer] may lie in an observation made . . . by a Cambridge philosopher and literary critic, I. A. Richards. . . . [A]ll we have to do is substitute "diplomatic dispatch" for "poem": fundamentally, . . . when any person misreads a poem it is because, *as he is at that moment,* he wants to. The interpretation he puts upon the words is the most agile and the most active among several interpretations that are within the possibilities of his mind. Every interpretation is motivated by some interest, and the idea that appears is the sign of these interests that are its unseen masters.

Blainey concludes:

It seems that an "accidental war" becomes more likely in proportion to the presence of other conditions making for war. Ironically, an "accidental war" is more likely if the non-accidental factors are strong. Translated from war to law, the concept means that a murder is more likely to be unintentional if the prisoner had strong intentions of committing murder.[13]

One can carry Blainey's thoughts further. Those different intentions are the causes. Though cars clash in highway mishaps, intentions do not. The motorists seldom know each other and, in any event, have had no previous personal dislike of one another. Any previous acquaintance would not have contributed to the disaster. Not so among nations. "Accidental wars" rarely, if ever, occur between nations that do not fear or hate each other or see their interests as fundamentally antagonistic and unresolvable by peaceful means. Canadians today do not spend nights of terror in fear of an American strike, accidental or intentional. Conversely, should a crazed Canadian pilot bomb a U.S. border post, the United States would most surely not make war on Canada. When suspicions arise or accidents take place, friendly nations deal with them by means other than violent reprisals, "second strikes."[14] By the same token, common sense rather than hypocrisy explains why Americans were energized to war by the slightest suspicions that Iraq's Saddam Hussein possessed chemical and biological weapons. They simply had plenty of other reasons to want to undo him and his likes. When war follows from accidents or suspicions regarding an enemy, there is nothing accidental about it.

Nor does war follow inevitably from longtime enmity. Enemies may regard each other warily but not want to fight. Note that the centuries of hostility between Russia and China have never produced a major war. Every "cause" for war (in both senses of the word) has been present, but no one has caused a war. In our time, we must note that the now almost-forgotten shootdown by Soviet aircraft of an innocent Korean airliner carrying 287 people (including a U.S. congressman) in 1983 was a classic casus belli, cause for war. The United States had entered World War I after 128 Americans had died when Germany torpedoed the British liner *Lusitania*. Journalist Seymour Hersh contends that in 1983 the Soviets mistook the airliner for an intelligence aircraft. In fact the Soviets had both the airliner and the intelligence plane on radar at the same time. But whether the slaughter was accidental or intentional is beside the point. Even if the United States had declared the killing of the congressman an "act of war" it is highly unlikely that it would have deemed this as a casus belli. That is quite simply because war between the United States and the Soviet Union would have been a very big deal indeed, and would have to have been caused by a complex of causes important enough to justify something that size. All of this is to say that decisions about who is and is not an enemy are intensely political—they are the very opposite of accidents. Getting into war is not like catching a cold. It is more like catching a sexually transmitted disease. It's not easy. Adults who get it have chosen the things that make it possible.

We come here upon a profound philosophical matter: the nature of enmity. As the German legal philosopher Carl Schmitt pointed out years ago in his *The Concept of the Political,* most modern Western languages, in contrast to Greek and Latin, do not distinguish between public and private enemies.[15] In Latin, however, the public enemy is *hostis*, not *inimicus.* The distinction corresponds to that among evils: *malum prohibitum*—"bad because a decision has been made to prohibit it"—and *malum in se*—"evil in itself". In *Republic,* Plato also sharply distinguishes the political enemy from the private one.[16] This distinction is supremely important. As Schmitt points out, Western languages fail to distinguish between the enemy who embodies evil and the political enemy who is simply on the other side.

> The enemy in the political sense need not be hated personally, and in the private sphere only does it make sense to love one's enemy, i.e., one's adversary. . . . [The] state as an organized political entity decides for itself the friend-enemy distinction. The political [enmity] is the most extreme antagonism. For to the enemy concept belongs the ever present possibility of combat. . . . War follows from enmity. War is the existential negation of the enemy.[17]

Political enmity is anything but accidental. Nor does the fact of political enmity dictate war. What, if anything, one does to an enemy is a matter for prudence to decide.

When all is said and done it remains true, despite Blainey, that hostile powers have a great stake in the rational control of force to achieve strategic ends. Of course, inadvertence and miscalculation are inherent both in the actual conduct of war and in tactical crisis situations in which there are known enemies. But whether or not deep predisposition to enmity translates into actual warfare is for prudent statecraft to decide.

Voluntaristic Theories of War

When we inquire into the voluntary causes of war—into the motives of those who decide to fight—we not only examine the motives of those who fire or threaten to fire the first shot, but also of those who choose to respond. Any war is at the least a *duellum*. In August 1914, for instance, Serbia's refusal to submit to an Austrian ultimatum signified Serbia's choice to go to war rather than to remain peacefully within the Hapsburg sphere of influence. War thus entails a mutual agreement to fight. (The agreement may also be rejected by capitulation. In October 1938 democratic Czechoslovakia peacefully accepted Hitler's demands and was widely, if briefly, praised for its reasonableness by the leaders of "peace-loving" democracies.)

When we investigate the variety of purposes that war has served in history, and the variety of purposes for which men have chosen to fight, we enter the realm of the *political*. If we believe Clausewitz was correct in saying that war is "a continuation of politics by an admixture of other means," then purpose is the very essence of war. Purpose is manifest in benign and malevolent guises far too numerous to catalogue: despoliation, enrichment, and conquest; revenge and retribution; establishing or unifying nations and empires; instituting a just order of things for one nation or among all nations; subjugating and punishing evil; carrying civilization and secular or religious faiths to other peoples and places; and, of course, the defense of the realm against foreign and domestic enemies.

It is true that leaders often feel driven by forces beyond their control and despairingly succumb to "necessity." Yet even in the direst of circumstances, and regardless of how awful the alternatives, leaders are still responsible for choosing one course over another. In October 1938, when Czechoslovakia's civilian leaders peacefully capitulated to Hitler, they did so knowing that the option of a lonely defensive war advocated by high military advisers would likely have led to defeat and violent occupation. The Czech generals knew as well as the civilians that Czechoslovakia's Western friends had abandoned her. But they believed that if they fought, they would force the West to intervene. The civilian leaders did not want to take that chance and believed that their only choice was between a war followed by Nazi occupation or Nazi occupation without a war. They chose the latter in the hope that it would be milder. In retrospect, they made the wrong choice.

The choice of surrender is as deliberate as the choice of war. In September 1918, as the fortunes of war turned against Imperial Germany, the high command controlled by General Ludendorff convinced the kaiser to surrender while Allied armies were still far from German soil. But in 1945, with most of Germany already occupied and all her cities in shambles, Hitler continued to execute as traitors people suspected of harboring thoughts of peace. Obviously, circumstances in and of themselves dictate neither war nor peace.

Nor do circumstances dictate the degree of commitment to a particular war. For example, from 1915 to 1918 the Italian army conducted a successful offensive war on terrain that strongly favored the Austrian defenders. This mountainous front moved by miles while the French, British, and German armies, fighting on terrain that favored offensive operations, moved their front by yards. By contrast, between 1940 and 1943 the Italian army proved generally unfit for even easy operations, despite the far greater regimentation of Italian society introduced by fascism. Clearly, the regimentation and military orientation of fascism were not enough to overcome the Italian people's lack of enthusiasm for sharing Germany's cause in World War II.

The same point may be seen from a different angle if we look at how the behavior of Soviet troops changed during the year following the German invasion in 1941. At first Soviet troops surrendered by the hundreds of thousands, as millions of Ukrainians, Baltic peoples, other minorities, and even Russians, welcomed the Germans as liberators from communism. Clearly, neither the Russian army nor the populace would fight for the communist cause against Germany. But both the Soviet army and the Soviet people learned rather quickly and brutally that the invader was not so much Germany as it was Nazism, from which they could expect only death and slavery. Suddenly the cause was no longer a regime, but life itself. At the same time, Stalin realized that although the Russian people would not defend communism, they would fight for Holy Mother Russia. Given causes they cared about, the Russian people fought heroically.

Thus, also, one does not wonder that in 1861 an American public accustomed to biblical injunctions to fight for right, and led by Abraham Lincoln, should have fought even its own brothers for the abstract ideals of the Union and against slavery while singing "The Battle Hymn of the Republic." Nor is it surprising that in the 1970s another American polity, accustomed to the *Playboy* philosophy and led by presidents of somewhat ambiguous moral standing who repeatedly and emphatically refused to identify the enemy, label him evil, and call for his defeat, should have stood by and watched the peoples of Southeast Asia—on behalf of whose freedom it had made a half-hearted commitment—sink wholly into slavery.

War is a test of, among other things, how much and how wisely peoples love the things for which their regimes stand. For example, World War II quickly told the leaders of Italian fascism how little the people's attendance at their rallies meant. By contrast, during the Falklands-Malvinas War of 1982, the Argentine people showed perhaps even greater adherence to the objective of securing those worthless islands than the military government had expected—all out of genuine patriotism. It turned out that the people loved the islands more than they loved their government. But popular dedication could not make up for the Argentine military government's diplomatic miscalculation that Britain would not fight and for the Argentine military's incompetence in the fight. In both of these cases, though for different reasons, the regimes flunked the test of war. Because the people did not love the principles on which the regimes stood enough to suffer and lose with those regimes, they withdrew their allegiance and the regimes died. Indeed the people took just revenge on them for their miscalculations. The Argentine generals wound up in jail, and Mussolini ended up hanging from a meat hook outside a Milan gas station.

Anyone who counsels his fellow citizens to make war—or to stop fighting or to try to avoid a war—bears heavy responsibility both for judging what will be gained or lost by the decision and for divining what the outcome of the conflict will be. The first task requires the highest test of prudence; the second seems to be beyond human power. Thucydides named fear as the most frequent reason why people decide to fight: fear of growing enemy power, fear for one's fate in a situation that seems to be worsening, or even fear lest a long-sought prize should escape from one's hand. But surely fear is as likely a reason for staying out of war: fear that one's own nation is not up to the task, that the rewards will not be worth the effort, or that the war will foster alliances, unleash energies, or justify attitudes that could prove ruinous. Thus it seems that Thucydides' point is that regardless of where it leads, any calculation made under the shadow of war is necessarily fearful and less likely to yield the fruits of dispassionate reflections than it might.

Rare indeed is a testimony like that of Winston Churchill about that night in May 1940 when World War II ceased to be a "phony war." Having watched his country riven and weakened by the desire not to look the looming Nazi danger in the face, he slept peacefully because he was relieved that the issue was now unmistakably clear and so was the bloody task ahead.[18] Such calm can come only from profound confidence, if not in one's own nation (in 1939–40 Churchill was surely *not* confident of a good outcome), then in one's own judgment that the course chosen is the best under the circumstances.

This sort of firmness in judgment rarely comes from accurately, almost geometrically, calculating the results of the many vectors affecting the situation. Neither the direction nor the force of each vector is precisely knowable. But the most important and the most variable of variables is the moral evaluation that the combatants make of one another. So firmness in judgment can only come from an evaluation of the moral stakes. For example, in June 1940 the dominant faction of French politics represented by General Weygand and Marshal Pétain calculated the correlation of military forces competently and thus reasonably surrendered to what they wrongly thought was the equivalent of Wilhelmine Germany. Churchill could count German superiority as well as the French generals. Hence his peace of mind in his determination to fight to the death was not based on a different calculation of the correlation of forces. Rather, it was based on a moral evaluation of Nazi Germany entirely different from Pétain's. These differing moral evaluations made a decision that was unreasonable for Pétain inescapable for Churchill. Thus did the balance of Churchill's fears calmly weigh on the side of an outcome he could not plan in 1939–40.

Thus, the *volitional* approach, emphasizing purpose, shows that the causes of war are far more easily understood by concrete occurrences of history rather than by general, theoretical explanations of war. The future is unknowable precisely because it depends on decisions that free human beings have not yet made.

Past Causes

We conclude from all this that the only intellectually respectable investigation of the causes of war is that of the unique origins and causes and nature of past wars. The lessons of past wars, if used with caution, can help illuminate contemporary crises. The ordinary human mind understands the past better than it understands the present, which is filled with uncertainty. The future, with all its surprises, is unknowable. The obvious danger in applying the lessons of past wars to present or future wars is that we tend to deceive ourselves with our favorite images from the past. As some generals busily prepare to fight the last war, civilians succumb to the all too human temptation to *prevent* the last war: "No more Vietnams!"; "No more Sarajevos!"; "No more Munichs!" In 2006 many Americans said "no more Iraqs!"

The philosopher Santayana once said that those who "fail to learn from the past are condemned to repeat it." Unfortunately, Santayana did not specify *which* past or whose version of the past. In the 1930s particular "lessons" learned from the way in which America was allegedly drawn into World War I provided ammunition for persons who did not wish a repetition of the same scenario. The result was a series of so-called Neutrality Acts prohibiting measures to aid the Western democracies' resistance to Nazi Germany: Never again! Immediately after World War II, many American minds were powerfully influenced by remembrances of how U.S. passivity to Axis aggression in the 1930s—from Manchuria to Czechoslovakia—contributed to the national catastrophe of 1941. So in 1950, when communist armies invaded South Korea, President Truman's mind automatically turned to the tragic sequence in the 1930s of unresisted totalitarian aggression in Asia and Europe. He swiftly posted American military forces to Korea with full, if tacit, support from his cabinet, Congress, and the American public, which also "remembered": Never again! The U.S. commitment to Vietnam flowed from this lesson. But the United States lost that war. So, ever since Vietnam, vivid recollections of the particular ways in which the United States "allowed itself" to become incrementally involved in it have played a powerful role in debates about whether the United States ought to be involved in Africa and even in Central America: Never again! Since the late 1980s the opposing sides in Americans' debate over Middle East policy have called upon different lessons from the past. Should one think of involvement in that region in terms of America's experience in Vietnam or do other experiences apply?

So, which "lessons of the past" illuminate the future?

Many scholars in the interwar decades of the 1920s and 1930s agreed that the Great War had been caused by two great and ominous processes. The first was the polarization of Europe into two opposing alliance systems. Before the 1880s the great powers had lived in a fluid balance of power alignments within a concert of Europe more or less unchanged since Napoleon had been vanquished in 1815. Ideological conflict such as we now know had no significant place in the European diplomacy. Yet by 1914, on the eve of World War I, the great powers squared off in opposing armed camps, the Triple Alliance (Germany, Austria-Hungary, Italy) and the Triple Entente (Great Britain, France, Russia). They accused each other of being the harbingers of the end of culture and civilization, and their alliances were on hair triggers. Small flare-ups thus gained the potential for starting a huge conflagration, which is exactly what happened at Sarajevo in July 1914.

The second reason most commonly postulated for bringing on World War I was a supposedly dizzying arms race between the two European alliances. The two armed camps allegedly kept stockpiling armaments and expanding their armies. They prepared for war for no specific reason. Most destabilizing, beginning in 1899, was the German-initiated race for superiority in dreadnought battleships, that era's version of world strategic weaponry. The Germans were determined to match the British, and the British were equally determined to stay ahead. This ended up terrifying Britain into closer ties with the Franco-Russian alliance, which ensured that the next war between Germany and Russia or Germany and France would be a world war. Thus Europe devoted more and more of its resources to building military power. It was expensive, and in 1914 it turned out to be destructive.

The specter of bloc polarization, arms races, mutual misunderstandings, and of a "war nobody wanted" shaped liberal interwar (1919–39) thinking. Hence, alliances and attempts to balance power were seen as dangerous in and of themselves. Instead, the dream of universal collective security through the League of Nations disguised the unwillingness of the Western democracies to provide for their own security, never mind anybody else's.

Yet there is good reason to challenge the basic view that "nobody" wanted World War I. Major historians today again point the finger at Imperial Germany for deliberately aiming to dominate Europe and to challenge British sea power decisively; for deliberately egging Austria on to war with Serbia; and for using Russian troop mobilization as a pretext for armed aggression against France. The "myth of Sarajevo," that war broke out accidentally, that an action-reaction chain of events caught statesmen up in a maelstrom beyond their control, does not correspond to the true sequence of historical causation, in which deliberate choices for war were made *in Berlin*.[19] The kaiser wanted war, and the other nations of Europe consented to it. Moreover, no one can read the newspapers or letters written in the first year of that war without being impressed by the alacrity, dedication, and even the joy with which every nation of Europe threw itself into that meat grinder. If any proof be needed, note that the socialist parties of Europe, for whom pacifism was holy writ, wholeheartedly threw it away and became their respective countries' biggest war boosters. The two significant exceptions in 1915 were named Benito Mussolini and V. I. Lenin.

But the supposed impersonal causes of World War II do not resemble those of World War I. How, then, can we generalize about the causes of modern wars? Whether one believes in the significance of culture, or of arms races, or of economics, one cannot deny that the origins of World War II lay in an international situation utterly different from the one that preceded World War I. Not only were arms races and competing alliance systems absent in the 1930s. But the very same things that supposedly caused World War I might well have made World War II unnecessary or impossible had they again been present in the 1930s. It seems, then, that the two wars happened in wholly different circumstances and for different reasons. Yet in both cases some people thought they could gain by war, and they persuaded nations to follow.

As in the years before World War I, in the years before World War II, Germany engaged in a massive arms buildup. But the 1930s arms race was a one-sided, unreciprocated affair. Unlike the period from 1904 to 1914, German rearmament in the 1930s drew no response from the Western democracies—mired in the Great Depression and political instability—until the end of the decade when it was already too late. Western liberals tried to placate Adolf Hitler by showing him that he would not need all the weapons he was acquiring because they themselves would not arm. But while reciprocal military buildup might have sobered Hitler, the democracies' restraint made Hitler's buildup much more cost-effective at the margin. Restraint thus fostered madness and gave the madman disproportionate force.

In the immediate years before World War II, no alliance system opposed the growing German threat. Even though an early anti-Hitler consensus might well have deterred him, the Western democracies—England, France, and the United States—failed to link up among themselves and present a common front out of a general revulsion to what was supposed to have happened in 1914. When France attempted to act in the 1920s, Britain and America held it back. Had either Britain or America tried in the '30s, France would not have joined them. Stalin, who held no illusions about 1914, made frantic overtures to the West from 1936 until 1938, trying to form an anti-Hitler alliance. Stalin's accommodation with Hitler in 1939 came only after he decided the West would never come around. The United States was aloof from European balance-of-power politics in the 1930s, thus confirming the fact of Western weakness that encouraged Hitler. When Hitler started the war in 1939, he had sound reasons to believe that the British and French would not come to the aid of Poland and that America would not come to the aid of Britain and France. He was right, until he pushed his luck too far.

After World War II, the liberal-democratic West extracted one important moral lesson from the 1930s: appeasement is no way to treat an aggressor bent on world dominion. Appeasement, it was widely believed after 1945, only whets the appetite of the aggressor while revealing the weakness and irresolution of the appeaser. The League of Nations had failed to take appropriate action when Japan invaded Manchuria in 1931, when Italy invaded Ethiopia in 1935, and when Germany reoccupied the Rhineland in 1936. To Western liberals, the lesson to be drawn from this failure was the importance of deterrence for protecting peace.

But since the late 1960s, the "lessons of Vietnam" have cut directly against that conclusion and thus have revived the "lessons of World War I."

The specter of "the war nobody wanted" in 1914 parallels the agenda of many of today's American peace researchers: to wit, that America's "War on Terror" risks igniting a world "war that nobody wants." This supports two policy options that only seem different: that America withdraw from world affairs or that it take part only as part of a system of collective security—led by the United Nations or the European Union. At the same time, the lessons of World War II guide American statesmen in the opposite direction: strike at dangers before they strike you. President George W. Bush might well have quoted Franklin Roosevelt's radio address of 11 September 1941: "But when you see a rattlesnake poised to strike, you do not wait until it has struck before you crush him."[20]

Aggression as a Cause of War

Whatever the ultimate causes of war, the willful setting in motion of violence, actually loosing the dogs of war, striking the first blow—in a word, *aggression*—is what Aristotle might have called a proximate and efficient cause of war. Its image is formidable. Armies smash across borders. Ships, planes, or missiles sweep down to strike vital targets with premeditated fury. The party that suffers aggression has his cause handed to him—if he can stand it, given that the first fruit of aggression is often that most precious strategic good: surprise.

The nature of surprise is best appreciated when we see that the aggressor holds the key advantage of the *initiative,* with the added advantages of the "Three Ds"—duplicity, deception, and disinformation. In this respect, the Japanese attack on Pearl Harbor did not wholly surprise. The tradition of Japanese surprise tactics was well-known in naval and military circles. The "sneak attack" on Russian-held Port Arthur had given Japan a strategic running start in the Russo-Japanese War of 1904–5. Japan's general intention to attack was a well-known political fact, and this fact had been sharpened by the decoding of Japanese messages. Although it was not a strategic surprise, Pearl Harbor was a tactical surprise because the United States did not know when, where, and how Japan would attack. The information the United States possessed in the first week of December 1941 was sufficient for American leaders to decide that the war had started and that the United States should go on the offensive, although they did not consider this course of action. Yet the information was not detailed enough to be useful for defensive purposes. On 8 December 1941, Roosevelt made the best of a bad situation by turning the U.S. losses at Pearl Harbor into a battle cry, a date that would "live in infamy."

Such is the normal peacetime popular attitude to "sneak attack" (sometimes called "unprovoked aggression") that many people instinctively sympathize with the victim and condemn the aggressor out of hand. In 1914, when Imperial Germany launched its Schlieffen attack into hapless, neutral Belgium, "world opinion" rallied impotently around "poor little Belgium." In 1939, when the Red Army launched its "winter war" against Finland, "world opinion" rallied impotently around "brave little Finland," as it did around Afghanistan after the Red Army invaded it. In any event, sympathy is of little value if it is not backed by positive support, or if the victim quickly succumbs to the shock of surprise.

Even when faced with imminent aggression, wise statesmen sometimes have *allowed* an aggressor to strike first while realizing the risks of such strategic passivity. They have done this to demonstrate their yearning for peace and their unwarlike demeanor to their own public, to allies, and to onlookers. They have thought it worthwhile to pay a price to show unambiguously who fired the first shot—*who began it!* This was the case during the last days of peace before the German attack on Belgium and France in 1914. France commanded its forces to withdraw thirty kilometers from the German border to brand the attacking Imperial German troops as aggressors and invaders. In 1941, fully aware of the likelihood of Japanese aggression, the Roosevelt administration took no measures and drafted no plans to preemptively beat off imminent attack. In 1973 Israeli authorities, seeing the shadow of imminent Syrian–Egyptian attack, chose for political reasons to await it and to accept the risks of receiving the blow. To act preemptively would have cost Israel its precious image as a beleaguered, imperiled nation among its friends abroad, particularly in America. Thus, when Hitler finally struck in August 1939 (as Churchill had often warned would happen), Churchill complimented the peaceful instincts and aims of the Chamberlain government whose appeasement policies he had previously opposed as harbingers of war: "In this solemn hour it is a consolation to recall and to dwell upon our repeated efforts for peace." These efforts for peace, he said, had been "ill-starred," but they also had been faithful and sincere. "That," he said, "is of the highest moral value."[21]

Yet a decision to face the first blow of aggression in order to prove one's peaceful intentions risks destruction. If the first blow is bad enough, one's own people may not be aroused at all, but cowed into submission instead. It is especially fateful and perilous if by passivity and by signaling his own dedication to peace the potential victim expects clemency or forbearance from his enemy. In most cases, the moral comfort that comes from being the victim of aggression is purchased at an exorbitant price.

Moreover, while "firing the first shot" seems to mean quite a bit, its true moral significance is much less. "Firing the first shot" is not conclusive proof of the aggressor's culpability. What if a potential victim of attack comes to know what is in store for him and preempts his attacker? Is he then the aggressor and the cause of the war or merely someone who does the best he can with a situation he did not choose? Why should he not have attacked first? Is it right to condemn to death untold numbers of one's fellow citizens by deciding to take the blow lying down? What an immoral price to pay for the privilege of feeling morally blameless!

In 1967 the Israeli air force began the Six Days' War by destroying Egypt's air force on the ground. Six days later, after after Gen. Moshe Dayan had led his country to military victory, a TV newsman asked him, "General, who started this war?" He answered, "Who do you think started it?" Egypt had closed the Suez Canal, blockaded the Gulf of 'Aqaba to Israeli traffic— acts of war.

Still, as in the case of France in 1914, America in 1941, Israel in 1973, and so on, modern democracies have made calculated decisions, based not upon morality but rather upon raison d'état, to take the first blow. Modern democracies rarely have been aggressors in the strict sense that they have planned and carried out armed attacks on other countries with which they have been at peace. Even if, as Benjamin Franklin aphorized, "distrust and caution are the parents of security," democratic peoples tend to suspect leaders who are the first to strike even against foes whose aggressive intentions and plans are well-known. Democratic leaders know this all too well. For example, had Roosevelt and his advisers secretly planned, and carried out, the preemptive surprise blow, the ensuing public uproar might have been politically fatal to his administration and, possibly, to the nation's destiny. No doubt, Roosevelt's decision was also influenced by the cold calculation that anything that Japan could dish out would not cripple America. Roosevelt balanced these two concrete facts in a reasonable way. But Japan did more harm than expected!

It is one thing to await attack, confident that the blows can be repelled or that they will not inflict strategically fatal consequences. It is quite another to risk everything. This was why on the evening of Pearl Harbor a profound sense of relief pervaded the White House because the blow had been taken, the long months of uncertainty were over, the aggressor had struck![22] In fact, the attack proved that nobody was about to defeat mighty America. Roosevelt in 1941 might well have echoed the sentiments Lincoln expressed in 1838.

> All the armies of the world with a Bonaparte at their head and disposing of all the treasure of the earth, our own excepted, could not by force make a track on the Blue Ridge or take a drink from the Ohio in a trial of a thousand years.[23]

As things turned out, after Pearl Harbor the somber premonitions of Admiral Yamamoto—"we have awakened a sleeping giant and filled him with a terrible resolve"—came true to a degree, perhaps even beyond his imagination, for the giant rose indeed. America, savagely divided only days before between interventionists and isolationists, became one. (Scarcely weeks before, the U.S. Congress *nearly* had voted to abolish military conscription!) Only one member of Congress voted on 8 December against the declaration of war that followed the attack.

Other nations, however, are not so geographically well endowed as America. Britain's margin of safety in 1939 was much smaller than America's. Nevertheless, after Hitler's attack, Churchill was satisfied that being the victim of aggression was not so bad overall. Over the radio he told his people, "The storm of war may blow and the lands may be lashed with the fury of its gales, but in our hearts this Sunday morning there is peace. Our hands may be active, but our consciences are at rest."[24] But whereas Britain's margin of safety, largely consisting of the English Channel and the Royal Air Force, gave its people the luxury of such feelings, the people of Poland had no such luxury. As Churchill spoke, they were being bombed, shot, and herded into concentration camps. Their consciences were clean. They were united and very, very brave. They had a cause. But it was a lost cause.

So we must conclude that whether or not aggression provides the victim with a cause and the political benefits that flow therefrom depends entirely on circumstances. A sudden display of unexpected enemy power, to the degree that it is successful, can do more than break material resistance. It also tends to deprive political leaders of legitimacy, especially if they are perceived as having either provoked the attack or as having failed to prepare for it, or both. For example, the military blow that fell on France in 1940 discredited a whole political system and set its chief exponents against one another.[25] The world's sympathy did not help much. Neither did the world's sympathy for their causes mean much to the peoples of Hungary, Czechoslovakia, and Poland when in 1956, and again in 1968 and 1981, the Soviet Union overwhelmed them with its own army and proxy forces. Causes must be embodied by leaders—and so the Soviets killed or jailed them. And although, as Poland shows, the mere survival of a cause is not entirely dependent on the expectation of military victory, that hope really helps.

Thus it was that on 11 September 2001 much of the world seemed eager to give Americans condolences for having suffered some three thousand killed by terrorists who had crashed airliners into New York's World Trade Center and the Pentagon, and to offer support for whatever war America might choose to wage against terrorists. Yet this seeming solidarity vanished quickly when it became apparent that the U.S. government had no idea how to end terrorist activities. Most of the governments, news media, and peoples who had expressed support not only resumed their courtship of the Arab countries that embodied the terrorists' causes but actually increased their hostility to America. Aggression altered the balance of fear in the world, and the world reacted predictably by altering its appreciation of America's causes and of others' causes as well.

What about nuclear aggression? As we shall see in chapter 7, modern technology has increased the importance of the opening phase of war. Today, by means of accurate nuclear-tipped ballistic missiles one side may begin by destroying the other side's capacity for rational military operations. Unless and until a nation can either hide its own stock of accurate nuclear-tipped ballistic missiles and other key military assets (ships, armored divisions, and so on), or until it can "shoot down" the missiles that might be sent against them, that nation will be forced to decide whether to be the aggressor or the sure loser. Hence, because aggression now seems to be more militarily advantageous than ever before, it may be more of a "cause" of war than it ever has been in the past.

Of course, in our time, as always, aggression does not have to consist of spectacular acts. From time immemorial there have existed ways of prejudicing the outcome of a war without ever unfurling a banner and marching across a frontier. Political subversion, which includes acts ranging from planting rumors, cultivating secret allies, and sabotaging key installations, to assassinating key leaders, can prejudice the outcome of a war just as much as strikes by ballistic missiles. For example, when Soviet troops invaded Afghanistan in 1979 their way had been cleared by—among other events—Soviet advisers to the Afghan army who had taken the rotors out of the engines of the military vehicles, and sympathizers in the Afghan Communist Party who staged a coup against the country's president. The Afghan government never offered any resistance. The Soviets managed to cause the Afghan War in a manner that made it impossible for the Afghan government to have a cause. The Afghan people's cause against the Soviets had to arise from two nongovernmental sources: xenophobia and Islam.

As a surrogate for open military aggression, covert or indirect aggression may more economically attain the political ends of war. It resembles direct aggression in that it aims to cripple the will and the political integrity of an adversary. Sometimes the connection between means and ends is open and avowed. Such was the case on 11 March 2004, when Arab terrorists killed some two hundred people in Spain to punish the Spanish government for having supported the United States against Iraq. The attack took place just before national elections and had its intended effect. The government was voted out of office.

Sometimes aggression is surrounded with fogs of ambiguity and disinformation. Was the unsuccessful 1981 assassination attempt against

Pope John Paul II a Soviet contrivance (via Bulgarian and Turkish proxies) to kill the spiritual inspiration (dare one say a cause?) of the Polish people's resistance to Soviet rule? Strong evidence to this effect was presented by Italian prosecutors in the 1982 trial of Bulgarian agents in Rome. Judicial confirmation of such a plot was not forthcoming—perhaps because publicly to have established Soviet-Bulgarian responsibility for the planned murder of Christianity's best-known leader might have endangered the delicate state of East-West relations.[26]

Causes and People

What are causes of war for some people in some circumstances are not causes of war for others, or even for the same people in different circumstances. This shows that causes are perceptions in the minds of men rather than external things. Nevertheless, like fire, perceptions are fueled by palpable things. That is to say that prominent people, institutions secular and religious, and regimes are the visible symbols of causes—the things that lend substance to the images that rally men to fight. In this sense, they are like flags. If one's banner makes enemies "tremble" (as goes one of America's patriotic hymns), the cause it symbolizes will thrive. If a flag is captured and dragged through the dust, its cause may die. But the human embodiments of causes do more than symbolize. They organize, lead, and provide material support for the cause. Causes, in short, need physical roots.

In the twentieth century, Nazism and communism threatened the world militarily from Germany and the Soviet Union, respectively. Perhaps worse, multitudes of native Nazis and communists plagued the rest of the world. Wise men of the time were sure that because these ideologies tapped into deep sources of human discontent, they posed challenges that transcended the Nazi regime in Berlin and the Soviet one in Moscow. Besides, they argued, since these regimes did not control Nazis and communists in the world's four corners, doing away with the regimes would not eliminate the causes they represented. But when World War II killed Germany's regime, Nazism became a dirty word and the world's Nazis dwindled to nasty curiosities. A half century later, when Mikhail Gorbachev's incompetence killed the Soviet regime, communism became the butt of jokes and ceased being a cause for any but third-rate Western professors. What happened to all those Nazis and communists who willingly suffered for their causes, who caused so much trouble even without direct orders from Berlin or Moscow? When the sun of their causes set in Berlin and Moscow, many of these noxious sunflowers just withered.

The hardiest, however, sought other causes. Thus some of those who, for a variety of reasons, wanted to fight Western regimes and prior to 1991 had found intellectual, moral, and material support by identifying their causes with Marxism, thereafter found those very things in Islamism. Indeed, the intellectual categories of Marx, Heidegger, Nietzche, and Islamism had merged well before the 1990s in the works of such as Tariq Ramadan.[27] Similarly, the anti-Russian Chechen leader, Shamil Basayev, who had grown up as an aficionado of the Argentine communist Che Guevara, morphed into an ostentatiously ultra-pious Muslim. Only in novels do people fight for lost causes—in reality, warriors rally to causes that provide hope of victory. Hence fighting wars is really a matter of stripping hope from the enemy's causes—of killing causes rather than people.

Conclusion

We are no closer to finding the philosopher's stone about war's causes than was the Psalmist. Nevertheless, some concluding thoughts are in order.

First, generic-determinist theories of war's causes, while interesting philosophically, have no practical, predictive value in providing indicators of present dangers and future wars. Some highly generalized ones that proffer stereotypes of particular cultures and political orders may have some value but are susceptible to exploitation by propagandists with hidden agendas.

Second, voluntarist theories, stressing that most if not all wars are deliberately caused and waged over important causes, are more instructive if only because they focus inquiry on real people and their agendas. They show that wars are intentional and serious undertakings, not accidents or frivolous ventures. Further, historical examples of "chosen wars" help us to understand how future ones may be deterred, fought, or won. By the same token, however, selective lessons from the past may be dangerously misapplied to contemporary situations of choice. "Honest history" in all its breadth and comprehensiveness offers many and often contradictory lessons.

This is not all bad. Knowing these contradictions should compel us to inquire into the strategic characteristics of present conflicts. Historical analogies, as warnings, as solace, and as practical advice can be powerful stimuli to policies; like prescription drugs they may help to cure, but they also can be deadly when taken in excess or as a remedy for the wrong affliction. Above all, causal analogies may be useless in the contexts of truly surprising events that admit of no known or apparent precedent. In circumstances of novelty and uncertainty, in which no guideposts exist, strategic thought about purposive action must take over. The very notion that the world is run by the contrasting wills of men leaves us on our own, but sober.

PART II

How Wars Are Fought

3

THE FOG OF WARS

The movement of events is often as wayward and incomprehensible as the course
of human thought.
—Pericles of Athens

War is carried on in the dark.
—Archidamus of Sparta

NOT THE LEAST of war's daunting aspects is its unpredictability. No one knows how any given battle will come out. Even less can one foresee what shape the war will take, who will win it, or what its consequences will be for winners and losers.

Anyone who has ever been in battle has experienced its confusion. The battle is not always to the strong, because individuals under stress at any given moment prove either better or worse at seeing through the mess, at rallying efforts at key points, and at changing expectations about what will happen next. King Charles VII of Sweden and Napoleon are famous among military professionals both for winning battles against superior forces by their "eye"—which saw the correct time and place to apply maximum efforts—and for their talent in leading enemies to divide their forces. But at Waterloo, Blucher, the Prussian general, did not fall for Napoleon's divisive ploy, and Napoleon's "eye"—under which the Imperial Guard charged the Scottish infantry—was foiled by an unseen, low-lying road across the guard's path that tripped hundreds of horses.

The uncontrollable chaos of battle is but one example of a larger truth: life (and death) is what happens to you while you are making other plans. This confusion was never better described than in Tolstoy's *War and Peace*. Tolstoy borrowed his description from the French reactionary philosopher-diplomat, Joseph de Maistre. De Maistre was no pacifist, yet he shared with many pacifists a contempt for those war "commanders" who pretend to be in charge of the direction of combat in battles and wars, a view reflected in Tolstoy's contemptuous portrayal of Napoleon. *No one* in the heat of battle can ever fully know what is happening; much less fine-tune events. Thus, strictly speaking, military science is impossible. Tolstoy was inspired by this paragraph from de Maistre's *St. Petersburg Nights:*

> Many speak of battles without knowing what they are like; above all, one is prone to consider them as points on the map, whereas they cover two or three leagues of countryside; people say gravely: How come you do not know what happened in that fight, since you were there? But one could often say precisely the contrary. He who is on the right, does he know what is happening on the left? Does he even know what is going on two steps away from him? I easily conjure up one of those horrid scenes: in a vast terrain covered by the where-withal of carnage, and which the feet of men and horses are tearing apart; in the middle of fire and of billows of smoke; dumbstruck, carried away by the shock of firearms and of military instruments, by voices that command, scream, or flicker out; surrounded by the dead, by the dying, and by mutilated corpses; posessed in turn by fear, by hope, by rage, by five or six different crazy passions, what does man become? What does he see? What does he know after a few hours? What power has he over himself and over others? Among this crowd of warriors who have fought all day, afterward there is not even one, not even the general, who knows the winner. You do not need me to tell you of modern battles, of famous battles whose memory will never perish; battles which have changed the face of Europe, and which were lost only because this or that man believed they were; so that supposing all circumstances to be equal, and not one more drop of blood shed on one side than on the other, another general would have had the *Te Deum* sung on his side, and would have forced history to say everything to the contrary of what it will say.[1]

Tolstoy wrote from experience—the Russian defeat of Napoleon had not sprung from superior military or political genius. Neither Napoleon nor his Russian opponent, Kutussov, had won at Borodino, the principal battle of the Franco-Russian War of 1812. The Russian victory came from Russia's unwillingness to accept defeat, and from a primordial determination to continue fighting. This determination might not have paid off. But pay off it did, because Napoleon made the unforeseeable mistake of staying in Moscow too late into the autumn. Thus, Tolstoy concludes, victory and defeat are not to be understood as consequences of rationally managed physical and political engagements; rather, they are the consequences of profoundly moral-psychological conditions.

Tolstoy's conclusion is valid, yet the "fog of war" does not negate the value of capable commanders. As Clausewitz recognized, the fog of war is a profoundly important aspect of reality which, though it cannot be wholly eliminated, the commander must anticipate and struggle with rather than submit to.

It is true that many battles, once begun, "run themselves" while the commanders are passive witnesses to the carnage, as the historian Bruce Catton has written of the Civil War battle at Antietam (1862), which the Union army narrowly won at immense cost.

> Masterpiece of art it assuredly was not: rather, a dreary succession of missed opportunities. Not once had the commanding general put out his hand to pull his battle plan together to undo the mistakes of his subordinates. The battle had been left to fight itself, and the general was a spectator.[2]

But Antietam is not simply proof that Clausewitz was in error when he said that military leaders must try to control the chaos of battle, nor is it a simple confirmation of Tolstoy's and de Maistre's contention that such chaos is uncontrollable. Rather, the events at Antietam were an instance of *deformation* and collapse of strategic principles in the heat of war. The general in charge, McClellan, was soon to be replaced by Grant, who though not up to the standards of Stonewall Jackson, never mind Napoleon, controlled events better and produced more decisive victories.

Because societies and regimes react more unpredictably to war than armies react to battle, wars are even "foggier" than battles. A regime like the Turkish Empire in the seventeenth century may look wealthy and invincible, but may have filled positions of authority with losers, fit only for impressing one another. Another regime, like the American Confederacy of 1861–65, may be led by the ablest of men and yet prove to be totally handicapped by its lack of central command for marshalling resources. Moreover, a weapon that initially appears to be decisive may not be so if the enemy develops countermeasures under the lash of war. This is what happened to the German submarine fleet in World War II after the British developed sonar and the Americans covered the North Atlantic with anti-submarine patrol planes. By a similar token, in that war the United States and Britain to all appearances wasted enormous resources in strategic bombing because of a belief in its effectiveness that was based on nothing but a priori conjecture. But in a wholly unexpected sense, strategic bombing did not turn out to be a waste at all. It channeled so much technical, manage-rial, and financial help to the U.S. aircraft industry that it has dominated the world's civil aviation market ever since the war.[3]

The fog that surrounds the outcomes of war has always tempted people to spin theories about what lies on the other side. Yet reality is always a surprise. For example, the twentieth century's wars played havoc with the predictions of its most notable ideology, Marxism. Contrary to Marxist ex-pectations, none of the century's wars consummated a revolution in the advanced capitalist nations. As for under-developed colonies, Britain made the key commitment to Indian independence between 1919 and 1936 for reasons wholly moral-psychological while France gave its colonies the bum's rush beginning in 1958, long after it had surpassed prewar economic lev-els. Moreover, while Marxist doctrine had predicted that decolonization would be followed by the collapse of capitalist economies, the very oppo-site happened: instead of becoming impoverished, decolonized Europe enjoyed the biggest and fastest rise in prosperity it had ever known.

The fog of war is thickest for those least willing or able to impose their will on events, and it is most transparent for those most able to affect the conditions in which they operate. For example, many American military planners responsible for the central front in Europe in the 1980s, conscious of the Warsaw Pact's 3 to 1 superiority in materiel and 1.5 to 1 superiority in manpower,[4] found solace in the hope that non-Soviet troops in the Warsaw Pact armies might not fight well because they hated everything Russian or communist. But the Soviets, facing that same uncertainty, engineered cir-cumstances to force people who hated them to fight on their side. Special East European units whose members had personal ties to the Soviet Union had special responsibility for policing the others. East Europeans were de-ployed so that they would come under the West's fire—and under Soviet fire too—if they were to retreat. The Soviets' actions were like building dikes to channel a possible flood, while American military planners hoped for fair weather. Still, in 1989 the political weather so wrecked the Soviet empire that all military calculations turned out to be irrelevant.

By a similar token, in the days that followed the 11 September 2001 terrorist attacks on America, no one who measured America's military ad-vantages over all the possible sources of terrorism combined could imagine that anything could stand in the way of America eliminating those sources. Nor was there significant objection to America doing "whatever it takes" to do that. The problem was that America's leaders did not agree on the proper response to terrorism. Even those who agreed that defeating terror-ism must involve undoing the regime of Iraqi dictator Saddam Hussein dis-agreed as to why it should be done, how to do it, and what to do afterward.

Hence, four years after the war had begun, the fog in which American policy-makers worked had only become thicker and less endurable.

What Makes the Fog?

The fog of war is the result of the unpredictable interaction of incalculable human factors. "No one," Clausewitz wrote, "starts a war—or rather, no one in his senses ought to do so—without first being clear in his mind what he intends to achieve by that war and how he intends to conduct it."[5] This is because one's own intentions and plans are all one can be sure of. If one is not sure of those, any and all knowledge of the enemy is irrelevant.

Yet no one can fully know the other side's intentions. Those who choose to start a given war usually take great pains to conceal their intentions from their enemies or to misrepresent their plans, capabilities, and deployments. As warfare unfolds, it tends to becloud its own ebb and flow. Years later, military historians may learn things about great battles that never dawned on astute and observant commanders at the time. By then the information is useless, except for didactic purposes in war colleges.[6] For good reasons, military establishments set great store in maintaining a precious system of "C³"—command, control, and communication—but when this fails or fails to perform effectively, battle tends to become blind and anarchic.[7] That is when subordinate commanders, on their own in some corner of the battlefield, make the difference by performing better or worse than expected, by seizing opportunities, or by panicking. All this is doubly true for wars than for battles. Either side's capabilities are a matter of opinion. What will actually happen, that is, how long the war will last and what will become of it, no one should pretend to know. One reason for this is that, in wartime, as Clausewitz put it, "the will is directed at an animate object that reacts." To put the matter differently, wars are contests between active wills. Moreover, unpredictable contrasts exist within as well as among the contenders. The expression "the dice of Mars" suggests the uncertainties of fortune even when, at the onset, the dice seem to be loaded one way or another. This "uncertainty principle" applies particularly to wars among great powers.[8]

No one can foretell which side will more quickly change its own ways to minimize the other side's strengths. For example, in the first battle of the Anglo-Zulu War of 1879 some fifteen hundred rifle-armed British soldiers were killed by perhaps twice their number of spear-carrying Zulus. But on 4 July, in the final battle at Ulundi, although the Zulus had some rifles, their twenty-thousand-man army was destroyed while killing only twelve British soldiers.[9] Machine guns broke the formidable, disciplined Zulu lines. British cavalry then ran down the scattered warriors. The British had learned simply that hand-to-hand fighting with disciplined lines of Zulus was not a good idea and found the weapons to deal with them, while the Zulus failed to abandon the style of warfare that had given them so much success against opponents both black and white in favor of the only style that might have defeated the British in the long run—guerrilla war.

But the principal reason major wars are unpredictable is that their scope, duration, intensity, and purposes depend to some extent on how hard each side tries and on the degree to which the war engages the nation's energies and ingenuity. For example, observers of the Napoleonic Wars were startled by the unexpected military and political consequences of a revolutionary principle—the "nation in arms." Since then, societies have poured more of their bodies and souls into war than Clausewitz ever imagined. Not surprisingly, those who have managed to marshal more of their strength have had an advantage, not the least of which has been surprising their enemies with unexpected power.

The relationship between the latent power of nations and their forces-in-being is inherently unclear. With the advantage of hindsight, we know that great errors can be made by over- or underestimating both the military potential of adversaries and the belligerence of peaceful peoples once aroused.

Consider, for instance, the state of American war preparedness and morale before and after Pearl Harbor. Before the Japanese attack, American army conscripts were being trained with broomsticks in lieu of rifles and America's gross national product was about $100 billion. Three years later, the United States was producing more war materiel than all other belligerents combined, and the United States military budget alone was near $100 billion. A peaceful people had become the "arsenal of democracy." Static analyses of human phenomena are bad analyses.

Similarly, in the 1850s few could have imagined either the vast human and material resources that the American North and South would soon mobilize for war or the continental scope of the military operations that would ensue. Anyone who tried to predict this war's intensity by keeping track of military buildups would have gotten it all wrong. Neither side had prepared materially either to wage or deter the Civil War. But the thirty-year political buildup to that war sufficed to make it the nineteenth century's bloodiest. So unexpected was the war's fury that Washington's fashionable ladies drove out under parasols to view the first encounter between Union and Confederate forces at Manassas (or Bull Run). They came back screaming, some covered with the blood of the wounded in their carriages. North and South were soon mobilizing in ways they had never imagined. The point here is that moral buildups—and their counterparts, moral corruption and decay—contribute to the fog of war by being so important and so easy to mistake.

Perversely, reasonableness itself contributes to fog. That is because reasonableness, which should count in war as in all other human affairs, often does not. In August 1914 European military experts' plans were based on expectations that, although reasonable, turned out to be wrong. Most thought the European war would be brief. And why not? The experience of a whole century's continental European wars had been that the decision would come in a few weeks or months. The Schleswig-Holstein campaign of 1864, the Austro-Prussian War of 1866, the Franco-Prussian War of 1870, and the Balkan Wars of the late nineteenth and early twentieth centuries were all short. In each the strategic decision came quickly. In 1914 many believed all of the factors that made for the bold and swift movements of armies had increased in importance. Besides, everyone knew that the sheer cost of modern war would exhaust the belligerents' treasuries and drive everyone to the peace table. The experts' facts were correct. The disproportion between costs and stakes should have driven all sides to the peace table—and fast. Instead, aroused peoples backed mindless military leaders while the wonders of modern transport merely fed blood and treasure into fixed fronts that consumed them.

Size, Commitment, and Competence

Why are some wars bigger and others smaller, some more and others less violent than expected? Our contemporary jargon would suggest that we are considering "escalation"—as if there were a ladder of size and intensity that nations can dispassionately choose to mount or to dismount. We, however, argue that each of the factors contributing to a greater or lesser "totality" of war—for instance, political commitment, popular enthusiasm and hatred, economic mobilization, military strategy, weapons employed, competence of commanders, and the number of nations involved—is subject to change in unpredictable ways. The individuals involved are not dispassionate technicians in white coats, nor are they blind representatives of impersonal forces. The nature and outcome of wars are unpredictable precisely because they are determined by a complex of emotional, high-pressure decisions. In the real world, nature and outcome can paralyze the will to deter or limit war. On the other hand, what seems a timely application of force may fuel war by *aggravating* passions and purposes.

Consider the natural propensity of those facing superior forces to call in allies. Whether or not this turns out to be unwise (for example, the Greeks invited Roman dominion this way), it always widens the war. During the American Civil War, for example, the South ardently sought help from Britain and France, and almost got it. In fact, during the war France seized control of Mexico. If the European powers had acted more boldly, the size of the war and its repercussions throughout the world would have grown significantly. That is why Lincoln, knowing that nations almost never embrace losing causes, sought big victories quickly.

Indeed, as Britain and France were on the brink of recognizing the Confederacy, news came that the Battle of Antietam had stalled and the Battle of Gettysburg had dashed the South's chances of success. Britain and France stayed out. Eighty years later, however, Adolf Hitler bet mistakenly that "lightning war" against Poland would present Britain and France with a moot cause. He was right that the two democracies would not lift a finger for Poland. But instead, they concluded that Hitler was an unappeasable danger to them and went to war on their own behalf.

The competence of commanders can only be guessed at before it is tested. This applies as much to the leaders of major powers as it does to Latin American dictators. Nicaragua's Anastasio Somoza or Cuba's Fulgencio Batista, who were committed above all to pleasant living, fled before fighting while two others, Guatemala's Lucas Garcia and Rios Montt, a primitive and a preacher respectively, defeated communist guerrillas and apparently never considered doing otherwise.[10] At first glance, disarray was Josef Stalin's reaction to Germany's 1941 attack on the Soviet Union. But after three weeks' silent seclusion, Stalin emerged as World War II's most coherent and successful leader. By contrast, partisan charges of passivity in the hours following terrorist attacks on 11 September 2001 notwithstanding, U.S. President George W. Bush almost immediately rallied his country for war. In the years that followed, however, he failed to identify the enemy, much less to defeat him. Performance, not posturing, makes the difference.

Obviously, people's commitment to a war changes during the war. Despite almost daily declarations about how the Vietnam War was a test of America's credibility, Presidents Johnson and Nixon never took the war seriously enough to declare it formally, and thus effectively diminished their own and their country's political commitment even while pouring in more money and troops. Watching their enemy's political weakness strengthened North Vietnam and its allies far more than American bombs and bullets could weaken them. We will never know how North Vietnam's commitment would have fared if the United States had not engaged so many troops but had declared war instead.

Although it is generally true that success breeds commitment, and defeat the opposite, success can also bring on insouciance. For example, the awe-inspiring early successes of Hitler's blitzkrieg partly explain the Third Reich's failure to mobilize the German economy. German confidence in swift total victory meant that German troops on the eastern front in 1941 were logistically ill equipped for Russia's none-too-secret weapon, winter. Even in the darkest months of Russia's agonies in 1942, Soviet factories' tank production vastly exceeded Germany's lethargic output. As Albert Speer later admitted in his memoirs, German total mobilization was not seriously attempted until 1943.[11] By then, the American, British, and Soviet war economies had been fully mobilized for years. Although German women worked in domestic service and agriculture, they were not conscripted for factory work until well after the siege of Stalingrad in 1942–43. While American women were becoming "Rosie the Riveter," the German wartime hausfrau typically kept the home fires burning.

The mobilization of technology also depends on the level of the belligerents' commitment. Albert Speer, for example, recounts how the famed German physicist Werner Heisenberg was asked by Hitler's government to investigate the technical feasibility of the atom bomb. But Heisenberg did not want the Nazis to win the war.[12] So his truthful report intentionally emphasized the enormity of what would have to be done instead of laying out an appealing plan for what was admittedly a large job. Meanwhile in America, scientists—many of them Jews or refugees from Hitler's Europe—had every incentive to be positively ingenious and to get the atom bomb built as quickly as possible. By a similar token, in the 1980s the American technical community was split on the question of whether antiballistic missile defenses were feasible. Naturally, those who, like Edward Teller, had a history of opposition to the Soviet Union tended to describe the task of building antimissile defenses in ways that invited effort. Others, like Val Fitch and Sidney Drell, both presidents of the American Physical Society who had a history of leftist activism, described the task in ways that discouraged effort.[13]

The principal reason for the fog of war is that so much depends on human purpose, and human purpose is so variable.

Piercing the Fog

The Greeks consulted oracles. The Romans tried to read the entrails of sacrificed chickens. The tradition of staging "war games" for both training and prediction has no known beginning. Soothsayers, magicians, and charlatans of every kind have long purported to tell rulers how the next war would come out—for a price. In our time this hoary habit wears the "uniform of the day": the computer scientist's white coat. Today's soothsayers are at least as expensive as Roman chickenologists—and about as accurate. In 1988 the Pentagon announced a one-billion-dollar project for a computer facility whose sole job would be to run various simulations of battles between hypothetical Soviet ballistic missiles and hypothetical American antimissile defenses.[14] This would have been only the showiest of the dozen major simulation centers within the U.S. military establishment that mathematically model the performance of everything from components of individual weapons to tactics and procedures and entire wars. Since the early 1960s computer simulation, which is part of a larger intellectual and bureaucratic process called "systems analysis," has largely replaced "command judgment" as the basis for most major decisions in the U.S. military.

Advocates of this approach to decision making claim that it removes uncertainty from choice by objectifying and testing the consequences. But the best it can do is to discover the consequences of the assumptions inherent in the test scheme. Systems analysis can come up with entirely different judgments depending on the assumptions with which it starts. At best its results are tautologies recognized as such. Its appeal, however, lies in its bureaucratic effects. By buttressing their choices, or their deferral of choices, with studies that seem objectively to pierce the fog of the future, military bureaucrats exercise power while keeping the option of claiming that they are not responsible for eventual failures because they acted "by the numbers." Another example of this is the practice of the U.S. Joint Chiefs of Staff to hold high-level war games in which they themselves are both the "blue team" *and* the judges of the outcome. Not surprisingly, whenever the games are held like this the chiefs give themselves As. Real wars don't grade so generously.

The results of systems analysis can be shocking examples of what the ancient Greeks called hubris. For example, in 1964 Secretary of Defense Robert McNamara claimed that his newly established Program Analysis and Evaluation Department had figured out the precise numbers of 105-mm towed howitzers and 4.2-inch mortars that the Pentagon would need for the next war, that the United States had 270 percent of the former and 290 percent of the latter, and that it was going to sell the remainder![15] While it makes sense to judge that the number of cannon (or anything else) may be too high or too low or about right, it is utter nonsense to live by precise predictions of wartime needs. Although it is sensible to try to thin the fog of war by formulating as good an idea as one can of what may lie beyond, the worst thing one can do is to hypostatize assumptions about how this or that weapon or tactic will work and then treat these assumptions as if they were reality. As Stalin used to remind his generals and intelligence officers, to live by one's own assumptions is to fall into self-made traps.[16]

One reason why systems analysis has become so popular in our time is that one important aspect of war in the period circa 1965–90 was rather easily predictable. Given the assumption that no defenses existed against long-range ballistic missiles, and given a certain number of missiles of known reliability, warheads with known explosive yields, and targets of known location and vulnerability, predicting the results of missile strikes is a matter of mere arithmetic. But note: Long before 1990 it became clear that antimissile defense was a growing reality and that the increasing mobility of strategic targets had deprived the simple yield-on-target calculus of much of its utility. Furthermore, even the limited applicability of systems analysis to predicting missile battles does not extend to predicting war in which missiles are involved, much less other types of warfare.

Yet it is true that, here and there, the fog can fleetingly be pierced to some extent. Having knowledge of the enemy's strength and plans, and given time, it is possible to rehearse attacks. The Japanese pilots who attacked Pearl Harbor in 1941 practiced by looking at a scale model of the area from the angles at which they would be approaching it. The Israeli soldiers who attacked the Ugandan soldiers and terrorists at Entebbe Airport in 1976 practiced in a mock-up of the airport hastily thrown together according to its original Israeli designs. Almost everything went as planned. In 1971, however, a group of American special forces built a mock-up of a North Vietnamese prisoner of war camp so accurately that even the hinges on the cages opened the right way. They rehearsed a rescue mission to perfection, only to find that by the time they struck, the American prisoners had been moved.[17]

Rehearsal is wonderful, but it is terribly dependent on good intelligence and flawless security. To the extent that the intelligence is flawed, rehearsals prepare the troops for the wrong fight. The longer rehearsal takes, the likelier it is that circumstances will have changed. And if the enemy learns the details of one's rehearsal, he can prepare a surprise that will be all the more devastating because the attacking forces will be going through a rigid drill. That is why there is never any excuse for rehearsed operations not having a "plan B." Alas, rehearsal is far more useful for attack than for defense because it is easier to plan one's own attack than to predict the enemy's.

All attempts to pierce the fog must be based on knowledge of the enemy. Knowledge of the enemy before the war starts is difficult enough to gain because of the enemy's concealment and deception. But such knowledge is not to be confused with knowledge of the enemy's actual performance. That can only be gained the hard way. One major battle may confirm or nullify previous impressions and give rise to wholly new impressions. One strategic victory or defeat can change the reputations of victors and vanquished alike. Military historians now recount how Western analysts at the time of Hitler's attack on Russia in June 1941 mistakenly predicted the defeat of the Red Army in a matter of weeks.[18] By the same token, General

Howe, commanding British troops in Boston in 1775, believed that a whiff of grapeshot would tame the colonials' rabble-in-arms at Bunker Hill. A catalog of such underestimates in history would be as long as a catalog of adversary overestimates. The outcome of battle confirms or refutes estimates, just as the proof of a pudding is in its eating. Such uncertainties are no monopoly of the military; they are present in other contests—in sports, in democratic electoral politics, and in the stock market.

Nations have been built on one great victory that gave heart for others. Similarly, the loss of one battle can begin to unravel the psychological and military fiber of empires. For example, the British surrender to the Japanese of their great Asian naval fortress, Singapore, in early 1942 echoed throughout Asia. Here was the mightiest European empire bested in battle by Asians! This startling event inspired in non-Western nationalist leaders a hitherto chimerical vision of independence, even though Japanese victory made them all far less independent than they had been before. Although three years after the British surrender at Singapore another Western power, America, broke the Japanese empire, the British, French, and Dutch empires in Asia had already all but collapsed psychologically.

How then is the fog of war to be pierced? Since the fog results from turbulent human emotions, it can only be pierced (to the extent to which piercing it is possible) by the assertion of human qualities that master those emotions.

Machiavelli's portrait of Cesare Borgia is a paradigmatic account of competent hedging against uncertainty. Borgia stuck to the basics. Build the best and most reliable armed forces you can, and place your allies into positions from which it would be arguably suicidal for them to desert. Win battles that encourage your side and raise the enemy's incentive to negotiate. Strike the decisive blow when it is least expected. Never assume that anyone will forbear doing all the harm of which he is capable or that the next step into the fog will not be your most difficult. Never rely on the gratuitous help of others. Make sure that in every move your reach is equal to your grasp, and think several moves ahead. Above all, keep your eye on the objective.[19]

Victory

Anyone entering the fog is best advised to fix his eye on the only reliable compass, victory—the portal to the goal for which he is fighting—and to view everything through that perspective. Victory is not the most important thing in war. It is the *only* thing that gives any meaning to any war. It is the natural end of war, in the sense that harvest is the natural end of farming. Imposing one's will upon the other is a necessary condition of victory—but not a sufficient one. Winning requires having chosen correctly *what* to force upon the enemy. Only when one's military objective is chosen correctly do military successes eliminate the problems that led to war in the first place, and free one to go on to other things. Only through real victory do the operations of war lead to peace. Indeed, peace is both the acid test of victory and the lodestone that draws the needle of victory's compass.

Victory means putting the enemy's military forces in a position from which they are unable to resist further pressure. This does not necessarily mean annihilating enemy forces, or that further prosecution of the war would be without cost to the victor. But victory comes when the vanquished recognize that the military situation would become increasingly worse, without hope of reversal. Also, for the vanquished to so consider themselves, they must believe that the enemy is willing, even eager, to continue the war, that the war will become more and more "total" unless its demands are met. Otherwise, the situation is not hopeless at all.

Again and again over a half century, events have belied American statesmen, who believe that victory is an archaic concept, and that military pressure must be carefully graduated to "send signals" for securing specific objectives (the "Pol. Mil." doctrine taught as gospel in the U.S. State Department, the Pentagon, and the CIA). In Vietnam, the more U.S. presidents said they were not interested in victory and proved it by not trying to undo the enemy regime—or even calling it the enemy—the more Ho Chi Minh and Le Duc Tho learned that they could safely disregard everything else that the Americans said and did. In December 1972 President Nixon mined North Vietnam's harbors and bombed the country in a way that might have portended the North Vietnamese communist regime's destruction. But this change in action did not cancel the overriding fact that Nixon was no more interested in victory than he or his predecessors had ever been.

By 1972 American leaders had finally realized that North Vietnam's politburo, rather than socioeconomic conditions, were the obstacle to peace in Vietnam. But they had not decided to do away with that obstacle. A fortiori they had not designed military operations for that purpose. Throughout the course of the war, they hoped to get peace in South Vietnam without undoing the regime of North Vietnam. They wanted peace without victory. It was impossible. Ho Chi Minh forced the Americans to choose. When Nixon's Christmas bombing showed that the Americans once again were raising the specter of real war rather than actually waging it, Ho knew *he* did not have to choose between abandoning his war aims and seeing his regime destroyed. The Americans were less interested in the reality of the promises of peace that North Vietnam made in exchange for U.S. withdrawal than in what Henry Kissinger called a "decent interval" between U.S. withdrawal and North Vietnam's victory. The margin of military superiority is less important to victory than the expectation that the "winner" is willing to go "all the way" to get his peace.

Shakespeare's *Henry V* gives us another example. Having tried twice unsuccessfully to take the French city of Harfleur, Henry warned its citizens that unless they surrendered, he would not be responsible for the rapes, the dashing of infants' skulls, the dishonoring of the aged that English troops would commit were the next assault to succeed. Harfleur surrendered. Shakespeare was following an older tradition: Virgil's *Aeneid* tells us that the hero's merciful efforts to spare civilians by drawing the enemy champion, Turnus, into single combat were counterproductive, and that Turnus succeeded in convincing his people to fight for his cause—until Aeneas started attacking to raze the city.

What must the winner force upon the loser in order to have won? The U.S. performance in the Persian Gulf War of 1991 provides perhaps the clearest negative example. Saddam Hussein, Iraq's dictator, had occupied Kuwait with the bulk of his army. By so doing he had made himself the world's second biggest source of oil exports, and put himself in position strongly to influence the biggest, Saudi Arabia. U.S. President George H. W. Bush deployed some half million Americans to Saudi Arabia and demanded that Saddam vacate Kuwait. When Saddam didn't do that, U.S. forces pounded Iraq, cut off its army in Kuwait, and expelled it. Bush declared victory. Since Bush demanded the wrong thing, no one should have been surprised that though America won the battle, it lost the war.

Saddam's invasion of Kuwait in 1990–91 was not the problem, but only one manifestation of what a ruthless regime atop a regional great power could do to American interests. Merely reversing the invasion not only left the problem untouched, but also contributed to its manifesting itself in an even more noxious fashion. Saddam had survived America's onslaught, and America had shown remarkable lack of ruthlessness. Thus Saddam was able to inspire hate and contempt for America throughout the Arab world and to put himself at the head of it. When, in 2003, another President Bush took American forces back to Iraq, this time to overthrow Saddam and a few of his cronies, it fixed the problem that had existed a dozen years before. But it did not fix the problem that had grown up since, namely the (correct) impression that America was afraid to kill entire regimes, that it would target only individuals. And so the U.S. occupation of Iraq that began in 2003 produced not peace but only more hatred and contempt. A proper understanding of victory would have made this outcome, too, visible through the fog of war.

The ultimate weapon for sealing victory is the foot soldier, whose bayonet against the enemy's belly can compel obedience and thus perform what some American political scientists believe to be the quintessential political act—determining who gets what, when, and how. Not even the bayonet, however, is omnipotent in this regard. History is full of examples of peoples whose armies were defeated and who nevertheless rebelled, resisting bayonets and police truncheons through paramilitary means. Nevertheless, history teaches that resistance movements, no matter how inspired, lead only to executions and deportations unless they somehow combine their activities with a war waged against their oppressor by a third power. One need only recall what would have happened to Americans after 1776 had France not made war on Britain. Movements of resistance or insurgency succeed by themselves only when the enemy lacks ruthlessness because of moral incapacity or political divisions at home—or when the enemy is grossly incompetent.

Just as there is an art to winning wars and maximizing gains, there is also an art to losing wars and minimizing the consequences of defeat. The trick, for the defeated, is somehow to avoid occupation. "In defeat, defiance," counseled Winston Churchill; that can be done very well—if one avoids occupation. The defeated party must retain enough military power and fighting spirit to limit the winner's demands, or perhaps even to limit the winner's gains to the ones he was able to seize on the battlefield. This, of course, is what Britain managed to accomplish in the early days of World War II. It suffered a huge loss in France and was also compelled to withdraw from Norway. The Soviet Union similarly suffered enormous defeats and retreats. But because Churchill and, to a lesser extent, Stalin were prudent enough to cut their losses in losing battles, they were able to save sufficient forces to defy the winner. There should be no illusion. By June 1940 Hitler had won the war. In 1940 Britain spurned German peace offers that could only be described as generous, and was able to build on what remained, ultimately to seal its victory by occupying Germany.

It is interesting to note that as German troops were put on the defensive beginning in 1943, traditional German commanders drew conclusions similar to those Churchill had drawn three years before: conserve troops, retreat, and fortify so as to be able to defy the enemy to obtain either a not-too-onerous peace or time in which to prepare new offensives. But the Nazi regime would have nothing to do with such prudence. It could not deal with the unknown by continuously adjusting the balance between its millenialist political objectives and military strategy. Students and practitioners of the military craft must bear in mind that such irrationality and incompetence can and do exist. But the basis of the craft must be balancing the length of one's reach with the strength of one's grasp.

The war councils must constantly consider the questions that every fighting man as well as every father, mother, wife, and sweetheart of such a man constantly asks: When do we win? How will this attack or this defense help end the war and get us the things for which we are fighting? However thick the fog of war may be, those vital questions are always crystal clear.

4

THE POLITICAL CONDITIONS OF BATTLE

Stiffen the sinews, summon up the blood,
Disguise fair nature with hard-favor'd rage;
Then lend the eye a terrible aspect. . . .
Now set the teeth and stretch the nostrils wide,
Hold hard the breath, and bend up every spirit
To his full height.

—SHAKESPEARE
King Henry V 3.3

SINCE NAVIGATING through the fog of war is the most politically willful of activities, we begin our discussion of military operations with some observations on the practical political questions that every belligerent nation must resolve: Who will fight? Who will lead? How? What will the basic plan be? Nations tend to change their answers to these basic questions as they move through wars.

Who Will Fight?

Who will pay the blood tax? Will the armed forces be composed of men for whom arms are a family tradition—a self-perpetuating military caste—or of men for whom the armed forces are merely a reasonably well-paid career? Or will the armed forces be drawn principally from society at large so that men serve only for a short time and without much pay? If so, will all able-bodied men serve, or only some? If some are exempted from the blood tax, how will they be chosen? Will men be enticed into the armed forces with pay and benefits, or will they be drafted?

In Western civilization, where the Oriental tradition of slave armies never took root, military service has always been regarded either as something that goes with citizenship or as something that the ruler manages to purchase on behalf of the polity (in which case the citizen as taxpayer is merely obliged to help pay the bill). Arguments in favor of these two contrasting approaches shed light on primordial questions about the nature of citizenship.

Purchasing military service is an old practice. Thucydides tells of commanders in the Peloponnesian War augmenting their forces by going to towns near their lines of march to engage bowmen or stone-slingers. Athens used its treasure to lure foreign and domestic rowers to its *triremes,* the battleships of the day. During the Renaissance, Switzerland was known throughout Europe as the exporter of its prime commodity: fine pikemen. A vestige of this tradition remains today in the Swiss Guards, who police the Vatican and serve as bodyguards of the Pope. Today also, Pakistanis serve for pay in the armed forces of Saudi Arabia. France permits foreigners to serve in its foreign legion, which, however, is not so much a means of purchasing foreigners' services as it is a vestige of the time when foreigners chose to fight for the supranational ideals of the French Revolution. Britain still today allows persons from northern India to enlist in its Gurkha regiments; they fought ferociously in the Falklands War. But that is a vestige of the time when Britain fielded the vast army of an empire that included the Indian subcontinent, Arabia, black and white Africa, Canada, and Australia.

The Turkish Empire once employed yet another kind of soldier—the janissary. These young men had been taken from their homes as children and raised to be elite troops. Well fed, trained, and equipped, loyal to the sultan alone, the janissaries stiffened armies throughout various parts of the empire, guarded the sultan, and served as shock troops. Similarly forcible abductions of native children for long-term service were carried out by Cubans in Angola and the Soviets in Afghanistan. Forcible abduction of boy soldiers is common in modern Africa's tribal wars.

The art of recruiting and managing armies from subject countries was fully developed by Rome and described by Livy. The imperial power usually places its own imperial officers in key positions in the subject countries' armies. It must ensure that the subject countries' leading officers, and certain special units enjoying special privileges and equipment, are more loyal to the empire than to their own people. Above all, the imperial power must see to it that when subject armies are mobilized, their soldiers know that if they revolt, the empire will kill them and devastate their homes and families. Subject armies may hate the empire with all their hearts. But if their lines of command and communication are controlled by the empire, and if they are far from home—sandwiched perhaps between the empire's troops to their rear and facing in front enemy forces that regard them as part and parcel of the empire—they are most likely to do the empire's work.

Thus it was with Rome. France and Britain used vast contingents from their colonies in the twentieth century's two world wars. After about 1950 the chief practitioner of this art was the Soviet Union, which appointed its own Marshal Rokossovski as Poland's minister of defense. He was a Russian general in a Polish uniform.

Alliances

Armies may also be purchased wholesale by forming alliances. Nowadays, as in the past, this is the primary means of purchasing armies abroad. Perhaps the best example of a modern mercenary alliance was Mussolini's participation in Hitler's war against Britain and France in 1940. This case illustrates one of the two possible outcomes of such a purchase. Because the purchased armies of Italy had no interest in the fight, they performed miserably. This forced Hitler to take troops he could not spare from the Russian front to reinforce fronts in Greece, North Africa, and Italy that would not have existed in the first place had he not brought Italy into the war. Thus, much of the time, "bought" armies are dangerous because they tend to lose.

But if foreign-bought armies win, they may be even more dangerous to the purchaser than when they lose. In 1494 the pope brought the king of France into Italy to help him in a quarrel with Milan and Venice. France's King Charles won, but France was not finally expelled from Italy until 1870! During World War II, many Americans and some Englishmen argued that it was clever to spare Western lives and efforts and to allow the Soviet armies to bleed in order to defeat the Wehrmacht in Eastern Europe. In a sense, the West bought Soviet services on the eastern front by leaving that front to Stalin. The Soviets did indeed pay a heavy price for Eastern Europe, but having paid it, they were not about to give up their prize simply because the Atlantic Charter's democratic principles would have obliged them to permit Poles, Hungarians, Czechs, Rumanians, Germans, and Bulgarians to choose their own governments and to align themselves with the West.

Purchasing allies in hope of avoiding war is perhaps the riskiest and most self-deceptive means of increasing one's forces. As Machiavelli has pointed out, one's own countrymen (never mind foreigners) are all too ready to promise fidelity in battles that seem improbable or are in the indefinite future. But as prospects of death and privation take shape, allies tend to remember that the purpose of their adherence in the first place was to *avoid* fighting. Hence, they tend to urge accommodation with the enemy—at the price of real military power—as a condition for maintaining the alliance.

In the 1930s both Britain and France found that their alliance weak-

ened rather than improved their ability to deal with Hitler's growing men-
ace. Neither country would act without the other, and each found in the
other's reticence an excuse for its own. Each also saw in the other's armed
forces a reason not to increase its own. France desperately wanted British
troops on its soil, not so much for what they could do against Germany but
as an assurance of a political commitment, which by itself, it hoped, would
keep war from starting, or from becoming serious. Britain agreed to send
troops for precisely the reasons the French wanted them, but with insufficient thought about what would actually happen if the Germans attacked
seriously. The British Expeditionary Force was thus hostage to a certain
political design that served to lull both Britain and France into compla-
cency.

When Germany attacked in May 1940, it quickly became clear that both
countries would have been better off had each committed itself to its own
defense fully though separately, rather than trusting in its own and in its
ally's half commitments. During the Cold War many Europeans wanted U.S.
troops stationed in Germany not so much for what they could do to stop a
Soviet invasion, but rather as a token of an American political commitment.
The United States kept troops in Europe for that very reason. Along with its
allies, it hoped for deterrence and gave little thought to what it would have
actually done if the Soviets had launched a large-scale attack.

Expectations of help from allies, even well-founded ones, always reduce intellectual vigor. Thus as World War II approached, Switzerland continued to rely on what seemed to be a law of nature: If French armies
threatened to cross Swiss territory to attack Germany, the Germans would
help secure Swiss borders. If German armies threatened, the French would
help. And if neither helped, surely Italy would. So Switzerland could simply move its old-fashioned heavy infantry to whichever border needed it.
But in 1940 Germany occupied France and made Italy its vassal. Surrounded,
the Swiss scrambled to do what they should have done calmly years before—modernize their forces and move them to the Alps.

Alliances purchased at the cost of nefarious limitations of war aims or
military operations are most dangerous. Since the most important step in
any war is settling on the right reason for fighting in the first place, no
good that any ally can bring could possibly outweigh the harm that surely
comes from acceding to a demand to fight for the wrong objective as the
price for alliance. At best, one will end up fighting the ally's war rather
than one's own. Usually, one ends up fighting a senseless war. No problem
can be solved if it is defined badly. That is what happened in 1990–91
when, in order to obtain the nominal concurrence of the dying Soviet Union
and of several Arab states, U.S. President George H. W. Bush limited U.S.
war aims to expelling the Iraqi army from Kuwait.

"Collective security" is the pons asinorum, the asses' bridge, of alliances. The idea is that nations can "league" (1919) or "unite" (1945) against international evildoers. Each is allied with all, but against no one in particular and for no particular purpose, only with good and against evil. The trouble is that different nations come to different conclusions at different times about what is good or not, and about whether or not to care about anything. Some Europeans and Americans have argued that military action is legitimate only when part of, or sanctioned by, a collective security arrangement, and that ad hoc "coalitions of the willing" are illegitimate. But history does not record any instance of any government making war despite being unwilling to do it. In fact, all wars and all alliances result from choices made at particular times in particular circumstances.

In sum, allies are available in inverse proportion to the need for them, and any alliance that reinforces its members' tendency not to think seriously about fighting does more harm than good.

Mercenaries

The practice of purchasing the military services of one's own citizens developed in the West during the Renaissance, when kings could no longer count on noblemen to bring along to battle a sufficient number of infantry and bowmen who would serve out of feudal loyalty. The rise of cities free from feudal obligations provided pools of manpower. Since no one in the premodern, Christian West believed that secular authorities had the right to compel military service, money became the mother's milk of armies. Money had been important in Thucydides' time. But now it became nearly everything. The armies of King Louis XIV and of the Duke of Marlborough that fought for control over the valleys of the Rhine and upper Danube at the beginning of the eighteenth century were made up of an aristocratic core of officers; professional, long-service noncommissioned officers; and fighting men hired for long terms or "for the duration." The only change in this pattern up to the French Revolution was that the European officer corps became somewhat less aristocratic as kings commissioned more commoners as officers, and these officers tended more and more to draw their livelihood and status from their royal commissions. The French Revolution gave impetus to this trend even in the countries that remained monarchies. The best example is Prussia, where titles of nobility came to be the result of rank earned by performance. The Napoleonic Wars ushered in the age of secular ideology, and hence spawned the drafting of simple soldiers.

After 1815, however, even France—which under both the revolution and Bonaparte was a "nation-in-arms"—returned to the previous practice of enlisting soldiers through financial incentives. This was widely decried by the political left as a bourgeois body blow to both patriotism and national power. In the 1830s France introduced a novel combination of compulsion and incentive: selective service. Theoretically, every young Frenchman was obliged to lend his person to his country's glory. Theoretically, everyone, regardless of class, would share the same soup and barracks. This pleased the French imperialist left. But France did not have any use for, and could not afford, the huge army that would have resulted from universal service. France's wars for the foreseeable future would not be in Europe but in Africa and Asia. Short-term draftees would not do for those campaigns. So men were drafted for as long as eight years, and were paid reasonably well. This produced a small, professional army. Since bourgeois families would not tolerate having their sons randomly taken for such big slices of life, the law permitted anyone to satisfy his military obligation by hiring someone to fill his place in the military, a practice also followed by the U.S. federal government during the Civil War. Of course, this system produced reservists both few and old. Consequently, the system worked only until France had to fight a European power, Prussia, in 1871. Prussia had also used selective service, but the Prussian system's enlistments were shorter, its base was wider, and it produced a bigger base of reservists for mobilization. After its defeat by Prussia, and with the return of the left under the reestablished Republic, France returned to universal military service, which produced the huge army of World War I. In the modern world, all major armed forces use universal service all the time, or plan to do so in time of major war.

The practical question of how to arrange peacetime forces depends both on how the society regards itself and on how it thinks of the wars it might have to fight. Nowadays, for instance, Britain maintains a small armed force made up of long-term enlistees enticed by pay, many of whom make a career of the military. Despite its tiny reserve forces and a population that stopped thinking of such things long ago, Britain is committed by the North Atlantic Treaty Organization, and by virtue of its ties to its former colonies, potentially to fighting a world war—but only nominally. The rest of western Europe has the same nominal commitment, and most of it retains peacetime universal military obligation, but only theoretically, and only because of the judgment that the draft fosters integration among the various social classes and some sense of civic responsibility. Europe keeps about one million men and women in the military at the cost of some $200 billion annually. Europeans own four thousand tanks, eight thousand armored infantry vehicles, three thousand aircraft, and even aircraft carriers. Thus Europe would be the world's second-ranking military power—if its people were at all willing to fight for anything, which they are not.

Until World War II, the United States followed the British tradition of a small, relatively well-paid, long-service, standing armed force that could be augmented by wartime conscription. But the United States faced the problem of reserves very differently from the rest of the world. America's frontier origins, reflected in its federal system, had provided it with state militias—the National Guard. The United States, unlike the rest of the world (save Switzerland and, to some extent, the other English-speaking pioneer societies of Canada, Australia, and South Africa), had no lack of civic responsibility. After World War II selective service relied on local draft boards to select young men who were both qualified and representative of the general population. Between 1954 and 1964 a cross-section of rich and poor, black and white, unschooled and educated alike were either drafted or, with their draft boards breathing down their necks, enlisted as privates or "volunteered" for officer training. True, young men who continued their education or were obliged to take care of families could defer their responsibilities. But few who pursued Ph.D. studies until they were too old for the military, or who started families, did so to escape the draft.

The Vietnam War changed all that. Then, draft avoidance through deferment became so widespread it largely exempted the upper-middle class from military service. When this happened, the draft became a cause of national disunity rather than unity. So, after a brief (1969–72) experiment with selective service by lottery—with sharply curtailed deferments—the Nixon administration abandoned the military draft altogether.

The chief argument for doing away with the draft was a combination of classical liberalism ("no innocent person should be deprived of liberty unless the nation's requirements are so dire as to demand that everyone be so deprived for a short period"), pragmatism ("by offering the right pay we can recruit the forces we need quite efficiently"), and finally, whistling in the dark ("military service should be performed out of patriotism, not coercion, and the United States is full of patriots"). The fact that many of those who urged the "volunteer army" most strongly were the ones least likely to volunteer pointed to the main reason politicians felt pressure to end the draft. Perhaps the most influential portion of the U.S. public, the upper-middle class, wanted to "drop out" of the obligation to support the U.S. armed forces with their bodies and the bodies of their loved ones. Significantly, most people in this group did not object to America's playing an active role in the world. Indeed, except for a few extreme leftists, most thought that an active foreign policy and powerful armed forces were necessary. But they no longer wanted these things badly enough to commit themselves or people they cared about. They may not have thought of international affairs as a spectator sport, but they wanted no part for themselves in any of the rough stuff.

Republican and Democratic presidents since Richard Nixon have turned the political question—who shall pay the blood tax?—into one of market economics: Have the armed forces been attracting enough qualified people so that they can accomplish their mission?

Yet the political implications of the American "all-volunteer force" are obvious. More than one-fourth of its numbers are black (some two-and-a-half times the percentage of blacks in the population). Ten percent are women. Most important, practically none are from this country's upper and upper-middle socioeconomic groups. The families of those who make national policy have effectively "dropped out" of the institution that enforces such policy, and the families of those who pay the blood tax have only a theoretical connection with the policymakers—people with vastly different tastes and habits. So until the 2003 U.S. invasion of Iraq there was debate about how properly and effectively national policy can be made by leaders who do not feel its consequences personally and about how long those who pay the blood tax are likely to accept directions from those who lead but do not bleed.

The Iraq War of 2003 reignited the debate because almost half of the U.S. dead (some two thousand at this writing) were reservists, civilians from around the country who had not signed up intending to go to war. After Vietnam, the armed forces had transformed the reserves into auxiliaries of regular forces, ensuring that ordinary citizens would be involved in all but the smallest wars. This was to ensure that after the end of the draft the professionals would be sent to war only if the rest of the country went with them. The plan in fact helped fuel a national debate about the war, and ensured that no part of the American political spectrum would malign the troops regardless of its position on the war. Still, it is by no means clear that U.S. war policy in Iraq would have amounted to a seemingly endless commitment had a significant number of the dead been from the country's most influential families. Nor is it clear that these families would support using U.S. troops to police the world or to act as outmanned, outgunned "trip wires" in outposts such as Korea.

Contemporary America also offers perhaps the most extreme answer ever given in history to the question, should women fight? Throughout history the standard answer has been "No!" Mostly, this protective attitude toward women has not been a product of tenderness. Most men at most times have exploited the weaker sex rudely, more or less as slaves for precisely the same reason that masters exploit slaves—because they can get away with doing it (note Aristotle's definition of the "barbarian" as one who equates women with slaves). In all civilizations but our own the life expectancy of women has been lower than that of men. Why then have men kept the bloody business of battle to themselves? Is it possible that they have wanted to exclude women from something they considered glorious? This is unlikely because men have kept women out of combat even in times of direst necessity, when auxiliary corps of women fighters might have made the difference between victory and defeat. Yet in all but a few odd cases, more prominent in books than in reality, men who otherwise routinely used women for the roughest, meanest labor have chosen not to use them in battle.

The reasons are twofold. First, the natural attraction between men and women is so strong that if it is allowed to be present on the battlefield, commanders can be certain that it will distract fighters from a task to which they must give their undivided attention. Also, because that natural affection gives rise to special attention by some individuals to others, it is sure to detract from the loyalty that fighters must give to their unit.

Second, and even more powerfully, separation of women from combat is rooted in mankind's basic instincts for survival. A society's women are the living assurance that no matter what happens, the society will survive. An army of men may be destroyed one year, and twenty years later the sons born to the dead men's wives, sisters, and daughters could reverse the result. A war may decimate a society's men. But as long as the women are not touched, the demographic catastrophe will last only one or two generations. For example, if in World War I France had lost 1.5 million young *women* rather than young men, its loss would not have been made up in a generation, but would actually have become worse before improving.

But the question of the role of women in war has become pressing in our time because modern war involves all of society, and because equality of the sexes has become one of the principal tenets of modern conventional wisdom. All modern countries have encouraged women to work in war-equipment industries and to replace men mobilized for military service. In World War II, the Soviet Union and Britain drafted female labor. The Nazis, initially averse to women in workplaces, used female as well as male forced laborers. After 1943 when the war took a turn for the worse, they recruited free German women as well. The armed forces of all modern countries, especially in wartime, make use of women in staff functions far from combat and in medical functions immediately behind the lines. Israel trains women's units to protect their homes and farms while the men are at the front.

The United States, however, made a historically unique attempt to fully integrate women into the armed forces while still barring them from combat. It has done this out of a combination of the push of egalitarian ideology and of the pull of necessity—the shortage of qualified male "volunteers" in the armed forces. In the United States, women enter military service through the same avenues as men (enlistment followed by basic training, officer candidate schools, reserve officer training corps at colleges, and service academies). Like men, women trainees shoot rifles, crawl through the mud, fight hand to hand, and so on. However, they are not asked to do this as much or as vigorously as men. Furthermore, by law they are assigned to jobs that require none of those things. One often hears that the integration of women has gone very well, and that the U.S. armed forces function perhaps better with women than they have without them. This is true. But it is surely due to the fact that the U.S. armed forces in peacetime are almost indistinguishable from civilian society in their daily duties. The average working day of the average member of the U.S. armed forces when not deployed is not so different from that of his or her civilian friends. In wartime, however, all military forces are vastly different from *any* civilian society. They work around the clock in makeshift conditions; they kill and get killed. So today, because women make up such a substantial part of U.S. forces and above all because they hold so many kinds of jobs (ranging from piloting transport aircraft to processing battlefield intelligence), their involvement in battles is certain. The number of women being killed is far too small to make a demographic impact, but more than enough to cause both a disruption in U.S. forces and arouse bitter recrimination over having hired women to do duties that men would not compel one another to perform.

Who Will Lead?

War brings military considerations into the everyday business of government. By its nature, that business is nonmilitary, even if the man running it happens to be a general. However, the moment that any government, whether headed by a civilian or a military man, makes the decision to go to war, it must wrestle with the fact that the art of government in wartime has both a political and a military dimension. Its primary task is to balance both dimensions. General Ludendorff, Germany's dictator in World War I, and President Franklin D. Roosevelt, who led the United States through World War II, were equally wrong to say, in Ludendorff's words, "Overall, politics must serve the war." The art of wartime leadership is not to destroy the natural tension between political and military requirements, but to synthesize it.

The fluid connection between the actual conduct of battles and the political aims of war may be seen in the American Civil War. Clausewitz's maxim regarding the supremacy of the political aim in war in no way implies that war aims are unalterably fixed once war begins. Rather it implies that the politicians in command must be sensitive to the course of battle. Battlefield necessity may actually work to modify, lower, or dramatically elevate the political objectives of war. So, although Gettysburg, not Antietam, proved to be the true military turning point in the American Civil War, the news of Antietam led Lincoln to make a major change in political strategy. No longer was the war to have as its sole, overriding purpose the mere restoration of the Union.

American history's bloodiest day of battle, Antietam made Lincoln's Emancipation Proclamation a necessary and possible war measure. It declared that Negro slaves in secessionist states from then on would be free from bondage. Lincoln knew this would subvert enemy-held areas by stimulating slave defections, as well as win the loyalty of Negroes to the Union. Nearly 180,000 negroes quickly donned the Union blue uniform. But the proclamation also elevated Union war aims to a morally higher plateau than had the goal of recapturing wayward Southern states. Later, in 1863, Lincoln thus described the intimate connection between the moral and the material exigencies of combat: "The emancipation policy, and the use of colored troops, constitute the heaviest blow yet dealt to the rebellion."[1] In hindsight, the moral force of Lincoln's subsequent Gettysburg Address and its moving affirmation of human freedom can scarcely be imagined had it not been preceded by the Emancipation Proclamation. And that was possible only because Antietam's heavy casualties required elevating the goal.

Once such political thresholds, such Rubicons, have been crossed, there is no going back. As the Civil War drew to a close, Lincoln was reminded that he had issued the Proclamation solely on his authority as commander in chief of the armed forces during wartime. When the war ended, the argument went, so too would his authority to deprive slave owners of their property. Unless and until the Constitution could be modified, Lincoln would have to reimpose slavery. But Lincoln rejected this reasoning. The war and his peculiar war measure, the Proclamation, had already changed the Constitution. The text would have to catch up with reality somehow. At any rate, he himself would not reenslave anybody for any reason whatsoever. If Congress passed a law to the contrary, it would have to find someone else to enforce it. Here was political leadership conscious of the civil effects of military measures.

But political and military elements do not always combine so harmoniously. The quest for battlefield victory may overwhelm the political leadership, which then abdicates and stares impotently at the storms of war. Conversely, ignorant or imprudent civilians may saddle the generals with political-strategic objectives that they for professional reasons come to view as impossible.

For example, in the First World War, the German generals froze German statecraft into accepting a rigid prewar strategy dictating an automatic two-front war against both France and Russia. Moreover, the Schlieffen Plan's insistence that the French army be outflanked on the western front through Belgium ensured that yet another country, Britain, its channel coast then threatened, would enter the war against Germany. When the war broke out, the political leadership in Berlin further capitulated to the generals' definitions of the necessities of war. By 1917 Germany had come under the military dictatorship of Gen. Erich Ludendorff, and his extreme dictates for battle and victory were accepted even by the kaiser himself, subordinating all other political possibilities. A catastrophe ensued.

Twenty years later, Germany went to the other extreme, civilian super-supremacy, and suffered even worse catastrophe. From what we now know, from 1938 onward many if not most high-ranking Junker generals were genuinely alarmed by Hitler's war plans. In 1938 some of them engaged in desperate and treasonous actions during the Munich negotiations, planning to arrest Hitler while secretly urging the British government, then under Prime Minister Chamberlain, not to appease but to resist Hitler's political ultimata.[2]

When Hitler in 1941 ordered the German Wehrmacht into his war on the eastern front against the Soviet Union, the generals' professional military aim—defeating the Red Army—quickly came into fundamental conflict with Hitler's political aim, destroying Slavic culture in all of Eastern Europe and Russia. The generals cited the battlefield necessity of continuing to be welcomed by Ukrainians and Great Russians as liberators from Stalin's tyrannous rule. But the civilians would have none of this. So, behind the Wehrmacht came Hitler's political army, the SS, which soon rallied most (but not all) Russians behind Stalin, Hitler stubbornly clung to his absolute political aim of a new racial order even after he recognized that he was suffering defeat on the battlefield.

Excessive civilian control is as harmful in democracies as it is in dictatorships. During the War of 1812, when President James Madison as commander in chief took personal charge of army units defending the nation's capital, the White House was captured and burned. Even when political-military relations are going smoothly, political leaders' preoccupation with military matters may unconsciously subordinate the higher, political goals of war to immediate battlefield concerns. For example, the Roosevelt administration in World War II came to regard the political and military objectives as aimed directly and exclusively toward "winning of the war" and punishing the enemy. This pushed all other political considerations out of sight, and out of mind. FDR remarked that "Dr. Win-the-War" had replaced "Dr. New Deal." This single-mindedness had some good side effects. Roosevelt, somewhat like Stalin (but wholly unlike Hitler), suspended his controversial domestic social programs for the duration of the war. By 1945 it would have been impossible even for Roosevelt to reimpose the dead hand of New Deal economics upon a bullishly antisocialist America.

Alas, that was only half the story. In his direction of the war, Roosevelt also forbade military commanders to divert resources from the goal of de-feating the Axis powers to shape the postwar world. Thus his administra-tion resolutely opposed any battlefield actions that could have checked the relentless advance of Soviet political-military might in Europe. American troops were forbidden from liberating Prague and Berlin. They were even ordered to retreat from portions of Germany that they had already occu-pied. The legacy of that (successful) resolution was the Soviet subjugation of half of Europe to a totalitarian system as severe as the Nazi system that American armies were destroying on the battlefield. Thus, because Roosevelt took his eye off the ball that counted most, American men unwittingly died to help create a Soviet threat to America far bigger than the German threat they were in the process of destroying. The battles were being won, but the war was being lost politically.

Excessive involvement by political leaders in actual operations may also usurp the necessary functions of the field commander, introducing confusion and complications. The advent of sophisticated and reliable com-munications has increased civilian leaders' temptations to meddle. In the *Mayaguez* incident of 1975, in which Khmer Rouge Cambodians seized an American freighter, President Ford and Secretary of State Henry Kissinger micromanaged the recapture of the vessel from the White House situation room, using satellite photos and radio to monitor and command the assault to the point of conversing directly with the pilots. One Marine commander on the spot reportedly became so confused by conflicting orders that he finally "just turned the radio off."[3]

Perhaps the best example of diffusion, indeed confusion, of command was the U.S. operation to rescue diplomatic personnel being held hostage in Iran in 1980. The complex operation was planned by the Office of the Joint Chiefs of Staff. Service chiefs and senior generals settled questions about the composition of the force. Other generals settled questions of tim-ing. The plan was then assigned to an Army colonel to execute. The plan was not his. Indeed it was not anyone's. If he found fault with the training and equipment of the people assigned to him, he could not change them or ask a single responsible individual to change them. To change anything before the beginning of the operation would be a time-consuming political process far above his pay grade. Moreover, communications were so good that he could be in contact with all of his many superiors throughout the operation. All could offer suggestions or make criticisms. But none would be responsible. Of course, neither would he. So the hostage rescue force flew its prescribed path although a blinding dust storm was raging, going neither to its left nor its right, not above it, nor landing to let it blow over. It lost helicopters to dust and confusion, and argued across half the world about whether to go on. The commandos were so unused to working with one another that they crashed into each other.[4] But everyone got medals.

Who, then, should decide what? There is only one sound principle: authority must be proportionate to responsibility. The person in charge of planning any given operation must also be the one responsible for making it succeed. When this principle is violated and several people have something to say about what is done but nobody is in charge, only luck can avoid disaster.

Leadership: Making Things Happen

Anyone who thinks of command as the mere flow of orders from higher to lower ranks is likely to fail as a leader and to weaken even the authority that mere rank has given him. Any military unit that merely fulfills the letter of its orders will fail even more surely than a company whose unionized employees "work to rule."

Human organizations function if their members believe in what they are doing and don't just go through the motions. Anyone who has ever been in the military has noticed that ships or battalions, sometimes whole divisions or armies, reflect the personality and competence of their commanding officer. The troops are generally good judges of the character and competence of their commanding officers. They quickly answer such questions as, What's driving him? What's he after? Does he give a damn about us? Does he know what he's doing? Can he get us out of this scrape? Above all, troops know *what* their commander is serious about. Is it the mission? Is it medals? Is it show? The troops can spot a phony. Usually, the commander gets out of his troops what he shows the troops *he* is really after.

No operation is likely to succeed if the people who are supposed to make it work don't want it to, or if they are discouraged, disconsolate, morally defeated, sullen, uncooperative, inattentive, or lazy. In war more than in most human contests, success goes to those who want it, who keep their heads up and look for ways of winning, and who work hard and hopefully. But war is not inherently appetizing work. How, then, to keep up essential morale?

Gen. Douglas MacArthur once summed up the requirements for morale as follows:

> The unfailing formula for production of morale is patriotism, self-respect, discipline, and self-confidence within a military unit, joined with fair treatment and merited appreciation from without. . . . It will quickly wither and die if soldiers come to believe themselves the victims of indifference or injustice on the part of their government, or of ignorance, personal ambition or ineptitude on the part of their military leaders.[5]

In World War II, General Patton expressed one age-old recipe—convince one's soldiers that they ought to fear the enemy less than they fear their own commander. Hannibal, Livy tells us, kept his army on its toes by exemplary displays of "inhuman cruelty" toward his troops. Hannibal's armies stayed together also because he had taken them deep into enemy country. Thus, his soldiers knew that desertion would surely have meant death or slavery. Their only hope of survival lay in following orders, and Hannibal gave daily proof that he knew what he was doing. This is the basic insight that led Hernán Cortés to burn his ships upon landing on the shores of Mexico so that his troops would know that they had only two choices— conquer the Aztec empire or die—and that he was the only one who had a plan. Still, no one has ever been able to dispense with at least some fearsome examples of what happens to slackers.

Morale also involves being nice to troops who do their jobs. No human being will be generous with his work or his life if he feels unappreciated. It is remarkable how much of themselves people will give in return for being made to feel appreciated by the great. It is worth noting that in December 1981 before ordering its ZOMO special troops to crush the Solidarity trade union, the Polish government issued those troops that rare treat: chocolate bars. Perhaps Poland's General Jaruzelsky was trying to imitate Napoleon, who used to issue brandy, eau-de-vie (the water of life), on the eve of battle.

Wise commanders always tell their troops the importance of what they are doing, and how the folks at home are counting on them. Alas, they usually overdo it, engendering cynicism. A few words frequently have a greater effect than a long speech. Thus de Gaulle's message, written in classical French, to the first Free French division (the first major French unit to beat the Germans since the debacle of 1940) upon its successful delaying action at Bir-Hakeim on 10 July 1942: "General Koenig! Know and tell your troops that all France is looking at you and that you are her pride."[6] When apparently sincere discussions of the importance of the current campaign are accompanied by material signs of appreciation, the invigorating effect is visible. The opposite is unmistakable. In 1916–17 soldiers on the western front not only lived miserably but saw that their likely deaths would surely be meaningless. Hence morale dropped, and armies were kept together in part by exemplary executions.

Of course, morale also depends on habits of loyalty. British and German units in World War II each had been accustomed to being together for a long time. Thus, their members kept up high standards of performance even during demoralizing times in order not to let one another down. The Japanese, for their part, maintained fighting morale apparently because it was inconceivable for them to do anything else.

Morale also depends on faith in leaders and on hope of victory. If the two disappear, soldiers tend to believe they have been sold out and throw away their weapons. Surprise is so devastating to armies in part because it destroys the men's confidence in their leaders. This is what happened to much of the French army in 1940. The German advance was so unlike what their leaders had led them to expect that the army drew the (correct) conclusion that their leaders had no idea what they were doing and no convincing answers to the question, what's next? Surprise can wreck the morale of nations as well as of armies. When a whole political establishment weds itself to the proposition of "peace in our time" and then war comes, that establishment loses credibility. It is impossible for people identified with a discredited policy to lead a nation in the opposite direction. In practice, hope must be personified by credible people.

Another case in point is the morale of U.S. forces in Vietnam. Contrary to the movies on the subject, U.S. forces had no morale problems until well into 1969, when it became unmistakable that the United States was not going to try to win the war and was going to turn it over to the South Vietnamese as quickly as possible. That is when the drugs, the insubordination, and the practice of just going through the motions took over. Indeed, the decision to stop building up and start building down turned domestic opposition to the war from a fringe position that had lost out within the Democratic Party, which then had lost the election of 1968, into something with obvious legitimacy. It is true that Americans in Vietnam lived very comfortably. But the answers to their natural questions—"What am I doing here? Am I on the right side? Do my leaders know where they are taking me? What will people say and do if I slack off?"—were so historically unsatisfactory that it is a wonder morale was as high as it was.

American leaders in the war that began on 11 September 2001 have equivocated on whether eliminating terrorism is at all possible or whether terrorism is a part of life in the twenty-first century to which Americans must adapt. When political necessity has forced them to say that they intend to defeat it, they either promise to hunt down terrorists "one at a time" or to transform Middle Eastern politics and culture. They do not say how they propose to do any of these things, especially since they do not point to enemy individuals or regimes which, if eliminated, would give Americans what they want. One reason for that is that American leaders have not defined what they do want out of a war being waged against an abstract noun. Hence as time passes, casualties mount, and acts of terror against Americans increase, the confidence that civilians and soldiers place in their respective leaders cannot help but fall.

Leadership consists of providing and of personifying (as Churchill did) good answers to the questions that move people. The leader must prove by deeds that he knows where he is going, that the goal, once reached, will be worthwhile, and that those who stick with him will be taken care of. Regardless of how good he is at charming or cajoling, events must prove him right. Christopher Columbus calmed his men by lying about the distance they had traveled each day, lest the magnitude of their separation from home overwhelm them. And Columbus was a charmer. Nevertheless, he was on the verge of falling victim to mutiny when land came into view on 12 October 1492. In World War I, Germany's spring 1918 offensive ground to a halt because the troops had been told too many times that the next assault would be the last. In contrast, troops follow all too blindly those leaders with a reputation for success, or who can evoke wonderful vistas of what lies beyond the horizon. Shakespeare gives us an example in Henry V's speech before the Battle of Agincourt of one kind of leadership—the promise that participation in this enterprise is ennobling. But Dante, in the eighth *bolgia* of the eighth ring of hell (reserved for deceivers) shows us Ulysses' punishment for using the gift of leadership to take men where they should not go. As every soldier knows, there are some leaders who men will eagerly follow to hell itself, and others who have not earned the trust to show the way to the latrine.

Strategy: Where to Go, and How

"Strategy" is a fancy word for a road map for getting from here to there, from the situation at hand to the situation one wishes to attain. Strategy is the very opposite of abstract thinking. It is the intellectual connection between the things one wants to achieve, the means at hand, and the circumstances. It is a mistake to give the name "strategy" to a set of particular attitudes, prejudices, or wishes. Thus, anticommunism was not a strategy, nor is a penchant for, say, controlling the sea, or for courting allies, much less for being "strong." For that matter, John Kennedy's "strategy" of building a "wall of freedom" around Cuba, and the U.S. government's "strategy" between 1947 and about 1969 of "containment" of the Soviet Union were wishes, not strategies, because they did not envisage chains of specific acts that would produce specific results leading to the desired outcome. All such inclinations beg the vital questions, what are you after, and what reason do you have to believe that what you want to do will get us to where we want to go?

To be a strategy a plan does not have to succeed. It just has to consist of components that have been thought through reasonably well, and that have a reasonable chance of success. The Schlieffen Plan for the invasion of France in World War I, for example, failed because of flawed execution and because of General Joffre's especially spirited counterattack. It also brought Britain and eventually America into the war. But it was arguably a reasonable plan for employing Germany's resources to defeat France. The finest contemporary examples of successful strategy are General MacArthur's island-hopping campaign in the Pacific in 1942–45 and North Vietnam's political-military rout of the United States in 1965–73.

To make war strategy, on any level of command, is to answer five sets of questions. First, what do I really want out of this situation? What will rid me of my fears or satisfy my needs so that I will be able to rest in peace or go on to something else? Have I thought things through well enough to be satisfied that the thing I'm after is neither a mirage nor the lid to Pandora's box? Second, whom or what do I have to kill, destroy, besiege, intimidate, or constrain to get what I want? Once I have done these things will I have achieved what I want? In other words, at what point do I win? Third, what can my enemy do to keep me from killing, destroying, or constraining as I must? What forces does he have and how best could he use them to his own advantage? Fourth, what forces are available to me to defeat the best opposition that my enemy can throw at me, and how can I use them? Can I entice more forces to my side? Can I entice any away from his? Can I deal with an expansion of the war? What military options are available to me and to my enemy at any given time? Fifth, am I willing to do what is necessary in good time to win? Do I have a realistic estimate of the costs? Is the whole thing worth the trouble?

To clarify one's ends is not easy—mostly because of the common human tendency to want to have one's cake while eating it too. Thus, for example, the United States in the 1980s joined in a war against Nicaragua's communist regime with the obviously contradictory goals of overthrowing it and reaching a modus vivendi with it. In addition, and, as happened to the United States in World War II, the hatred that war engendered can narrow the goals of the war to simple destruction of the enemy regime and crowd out consideration of what is to happen after the fighting is over.

The acme of mindlessness, however, is to enter a war as the United States did in Lebanon between 1982 and 1984 for the purpose of stopping the fighting. This begs all the questions. What kind of peace do we want to see? Who stands in the way of peace? What actions of ours will remove the obstacles to peace? Mindlessly inserted into Lebanon, U.S. Marines were used for target practice by various factions in the war. Since the United States had not designated a political enemy and the Marines lacked the power to search out their tormentors, as a police force in control of a country would, they continued to die without fighting back until they were withdrawn.

Sometimes the problem is indecision about the scope of the conflict. In 1950 General MacArthur and his superiors in Washington agreed that the

North Korean army was the enemy, and that the objective was to defeat it militarily. Thus, Washington agreed with MacArthur's plan to outflank the enemy troops via the amphibious landing at Inchon. Both Washington and MacArthur realized that there was a chance that victory over North Korea would bring China or the Soviet Union into the war. But while MacArthur did not mind this possibility, and was willing to use the full power of the United States to defeat what he believed was the real enemy, Washington abhorred it and was unwilling to treat either China or the Soviet Union as the enemy. Hence, in 1950 the United States pursued the defeat of North Korea without having thought through whether it would be willing to deal with the consequences of victory. Events in 1951 forced choices.

In the operations of war, intentions don't count as much as calculations. Thus, the United States killed thousands of people in South Vietnam whose deaths made absolutely no difference to the outcome of the war, while sparing the few dozen in North Vietnam whose deaths would have ended the war. In 1991 U.S. forces killed countless Iraqis whose deaths made no difference while consciously sparing Saddam Hussein's regime, whose demise would have fixed the problem of the day. During and after the invasion of Iraq of 2003, U.S. forces targeted some fifty five leaders of Saddam's regime, but made no sustained attempt at uprooting the thousands who made up the regime—and prevented their internal enemies from doing it. Whatever goals U.S. leaders had, shooting the people they shot did not achieve them.

By a similar token, Israel went to war three times in one generation without any idea of what it would have to do to win what Israel really wants—its enemies' recognition of its right to exist. Thus, although it thrashed its enemies each time, it is no surprise that Israel failed to win its objective.

In contrast, Bismarck was aware that Austria was the chief obstacle to the unification of Germany under Prussia, and that if Austria were defeated in the field, its links with Bavaria and the Rhenish protectorates would snap. In fact, after Prussia beat Austria in 1866, it found no further obstacles to gaining its objective.

Churchill once cautioned British military strategists that sometimes it is necessary to take the enemy into account. The enemy will have his own strategy and his own means of carrying it out. During the American Civil War, for example, it was all very well for the Union Army to take the thousand-mile route along the Mississippi to cut the Confederacy in two during 1863. But in the meantime Robert E. Lee had taken his Army of Northern Virginia deep into Pennsylvania. Had Lee won at Gettysburg, which he almost did, a march of 150 miles would have allowed him to cut the Union in two. The Union would have regretted the overconfidence that led to dispersing its forces. By the same token, as the United States was landing in the Philippines in 1944, it realized that the Japanese navy would make a major effort to wreck the landings, and prepared to meet it. But the United States did not realize that the Japanese would make *two* powerful thrusts at the landings.[7]

The strategist would always like to know what the enemy plans to do. But he seldom does. So he has no choice but to put himself in the enemy's shoes and to figure out what the enemy's best shot would be. This exercise tests the strategist's intellectual honesty, his willingness to see the challenge as neither more nor less daunting than it is. Overestimating the enemy is often as fatal as underestimating him. Thus, for example, in 1948 and again in 1961 when East German and Soviet soldiers blocked roads to Berlin and in the city as well, the United States respected the barriers because it feared that these moves were backed by Soviet resolve to start World War III. They were not.

What do I have to do to avoid or defeat the best shot that the enemy is realistically going to throw at me and to destroy his ability to resist me? Realism is necessary not only in estimating forces available to either side, but also in making calculations about time. Britain and France, for example, grossly neglected this element in September 1939. Both had just declared war on Germany in retaliation for its attack on Poland. Both knew that Germany had left only skeletal defenses in the West, but that after Poland was crushed, no later than mid-November, those defenses would be back up to strength. The British and French knew that they had clear superiority, but that it would last for only a short time. Thereafter, it would take years for Britain and France to match the power Germany had built up. So, the allies could choose to pay a small bill immediately, or a huge one later. Their choice to wait in the hope that the war that had just begun would somehow continue to be a "phony war" was irresponsible. It was phony only for them, not for Hitler.

The effect of the forces one has available also depends on the tempo of operations. The German advance into France in 1940 was so devastating because its speed left no time for recovery. But the tempo of the American bombing in North Vietnam was so slow that it allowed the enemy to recover from each operation. There is no case in history of a war won through the piecemeal commitment of resources. Victory comes when the enemy's will to fight is broken by a specific defeat. The whole point of strategy is to figure out what that defeat would be and to inflict it.

Finally, strategy consists of a commitment to do whatever is necessary to make the plan work. This does not imply that once a plan is made it should be followed inflexibly. But it does imply the realization that to fight "on the cheap" either materially or politically is to court disaster.

5

THE MATERIAL CONDITIONS
OF BATTLE

He maketh the rain to fall on the just and the unjust.
—MATTHEW 5:45

WHOEVER FIGHTS, whoever leads, and whatever his strategy, any combatant must slug it out within the variable limitations imposed by nature and materiel. There is no magic in war. Assuming one is meeting the political conditions necessary for success in battle, the only trick one can muster is to match one's objectives and capabilities to the environment in which one must operate: to avoid destruction by the weather, to match one's tactics to one's weapons, and not to let men and equipment be consumed without good results.

Weather and Terrain

Weather is perhaps the most obvious illustration of the proposition that nature is but the neutral backdrop for military operations, and that its various features may be considered helpful or harmful, even decisively so, according to the wisdom, technology, and energy with which commanders adjust their plans to those features. Many have noted, for example, that both Napoleon's and Hitler's soldiers were defeated in part by Russia's cold weather. But surely cold itself did not defeat them, because Russian flesh freezes at the same temperature as European flesh. Rather, the Europeans were simply not prepared to live and fight in the cold. In December 1941, for example, as the German authorities were requisitioning civilians' fur coats to send to the Moscow front, Russian troops were arriving from Siberia in what the German generals enviously described as "superb winter clothing." In fact, given Russia's predominantly flat, wet topography and lack of good roads, cold weather actually facilitates the movement of armies overland *if* they are suitably equipped. The Germans did not enter Russia intending to winter there.[1] In 1941 winter came a few weeks early. Had it waited a bit, the Germans might well have taken Moscow. No one could have known when it would come. But all should have known to prepare for it. The Germans, however, were prepared neither for winter nor for cutting their losses; hence, their scramble for fur coats.

Extremes of weather may intervene in battles. But they seldom change the fundamental balance of forces. At a certain point, however, preparations become so elaborate and troops consume so much attention keeping the cold from freezing them and incapacitating equipment that fighting ability ceases to exist. Thus, places that are too far north or south simply are the scene of military operations only when they are as strategically located, such as the North Cape, Russia's gateway to the North Atlantic. During World War II the waters off the cape were the scene of battles in which German forces tried to stop American convoys from delivering arms to the eastern front.

Conventional wisdom holds that the German counteroffensive in the Ardennes in December 1944 was wrecked by the onset of clear skies on 23 December, allowing the American air force to enter as a factor in the Battle of the Bulge. The skies in fact had been cloudy since before the start of the battle on the 16th, during which the Germans had been able to act as if the American monopoly of the aerial "high ground" did not exist.[2] During that period it was almost as if the airplane had not been invented or Germany had not frittered away its air force during the previous four years. But it was unreasonable for the German high command to expect this variable environmental factor to long obscure what had become a decisive deficiency in their forces. General Von Rundstedt could not command permanent cloud cover.

Still, weather can be usefully taken into account for tactical purposes. A major ground offensive, meant to advance over long distances and to hold territory, would not be launched when the earth is expected to be soaked. Such offensives require much in the way of supplies, and mud slows or altogether halts the movement of heavy transport. In Angola in the 1980s, for example, the Soviet Union's heavily armed Cuban and Angolan proxies timed their annual offensives against Jonas Savimbi's bush headquarters to coincide with the onset of the Southern Hemisphere's dry season. By contrast, lightly armed forces fighting against heavily armed ones prefer wet weather because mud hampers small groups of men and mules far less than it hampers heavy transport. Moreover, small groups of lightly armed troops can use bad weather as a screen behind which to sneak up on the enemy. George Washington did this when he led his men across the Delaware River in December 1776 for a surprise attack on a stronger British garrison in Trenton, New Jersey. So the rainy season favors the guerrilla, while good weather favors the regulars. When both sides rely on heavy weapons and transport, both wait for good weather before fighting. Thus, in the early spring of 1943, both the German and Soviet high commands made no secret that the plains near Kursk would be the site of a major tank battle, but both waited for the ground to dry out first.

Semipermanent good weather (as in the desert) imposes certain requirements on those who operate in it. Because desert distances are long and supplies nonexistent, the desert makes unusual demands on logistics. Desert forces need plenty of water, food, and especially fuel. In 1941 and early 1942, when Rommel's Afrika Korps was well supplied, the superior tactical talent of German and Italian officers manifested itself in quick, daring moves, and the British came to call Rommel "the Desert Fox." But during 1942 the British navy won control of the Mediterranean and prevented adequate supplies from reaching the Afrika Korps. With his soldiers hungry, on foot, and without air cover, Rommel could not be nearly so foxy.

Another factor in desert warfare is that neither vegetation nor weather provide hiding places. Hence, an army's safety and its ability to surprise enemies can only result from seeing the enemy first and/or being able to move faster. In the old days sharp eyes and fast horses made the difference. Nowadays air and satellite reconnaissance, strike aircraft, and motorized land forces do the job. In 1987, for example, Libyan tank forces were defeated by Chadian machine guns and antitank rockets mounted on trucks. This modernday desert light cavalry was able to lay a good ambush thanks to information provided by U.S. satellite reconnaissance.

Because there is normally nowhere to hide in the desert, air superiority, as regards both reconnaissance and combat, has become very important. On the other hand, the same unobstructed view that makes airplanes so fearsome also makes them vulnerable to surface-to-air missiles. Indeed, in the Sinai Desert in 1973 Egypt made the best showing of any Arab country against Israel by keeping its ground forces under the umbrella of high-altitude and low-altitude surface-to-air missiles. As long as it did so the Israeli air force spent itself against these well-prepared defenses with little effect. But when the Egyptians foolishly departed from this plan, and moved out from their umbrella, the Israeli tank-plane combination chewed them up.

The fact that aircraft are so vulnerable to surface-to-air missiles in "big sky" country means that only the fastest and finest aircraft are suitable for desert fighting. Helicopters, because they are slow, cannot fly within line of sight of the enemy for long lest they be shot down.

The openness of the desert means that more shots of every kind will find their mark there than elsewhere. So, desert battles tend to be quick and violent and to consume huge amounts of material quickly. The desert is tough on soldiers, too. Human beings cannot function normally for more than an hour at a time in tanks under the desert sun. Once the enemy is in view, however, the pace of desert operations makes rest impossible. Thus, in the Arab-Israeli wars a large part of Israel's advantage lay in the ability of its troops to function with minimal rest.

The desert, however, is sometimes so hot and dusty as to impede military operations or just to stop them. Americans planning the 2003 invasion of Iraq knew that starting a campaign any later in the year than early March would subject the troops both to violent sandstorms and, later, to debilitating heat. And in fact, American forces in March 2003 were stopped dead in their tracks not by enemy fire but by a four-day sandstorm.

Jungle fighting is very different. Hiding is easy, and overland movement is painfully slow, even during relatively dry times. Lines of sight are short. All of this means that tanks are virtually useless and the speed of aircraft means little or is even a liability. By contrast, helicopters are wonderful for moving people from jungle clearing to jungle clearing. But it is also easy to sit under a canopy of trees with a machine gun or a crude antiaircraft missile, wait for a helicopter to come over, and shoot it down before its occupants know what is happening. While firing out of a jungle is easy, firing either bullets or bombs into a jungle is not terribly productive since the thick vegetation tends to absorb bullets and bomb fragments.

This means that whereas deserts are fit for quick offensive warfare, jungles are better suited for protracted defensive campaigns. While desert ambushes are unusual, especially in an age of air reconnaissance, jungle ambushes are the rule. To be sure, jungles are full of other discomforts, but none are as pressing as thirst in the desert or arctic cold. This means that jungle fighting is inherently slow, and that the battle must be carried by many small, lightly armed groups who slug it out almost hand to hand.

High Ground

Nature imposes a rule of thumb: Take the high ground. The rule proceeds from the immutable fact that it is more difficult to walk up a ridge or throw a spear or shoot an arrow upward than it is to stand on a ridge throwing things down. The invention of firearms, which shoot as well up as they do down, did not change this law except that the longer range of firearms made valuable the conquest of heights that had been useless before. Even the invention of nuclear weapons has not negated the value of mountains as natural fortresses, as anyone knows who is familiar with Switzerland's preparations to use tunnels in mountains as sheltered runways for its combat aircraft. Thus, until very recently, mountain peoples, however armed, could count on confronting invaders with the fact that as invading forces moved up, straining men and machines, retreating defenders could be "covered" by their fellows stationed higher. These defenders would be fresh and relatively well supplied. As the battle continued to move up, the attackers would weaken and the defenders would grow stronger. This is how Afghan tribes resisted both Genghis Khan's Mongols and the British army.

But changing technology has affected the military usefulness of high ground. Generally, high ground is still useful if one possesses the technology to exploit it, but it will not make up for a lack of technology or military skill. After 1979, for example, the Soviet army's helicopters significantly reduced the mountains' value to the Afghans. Helicopters simply climb faster than humans, and can deposit attacking troops above the highest layer of defenders, as well as astride the defenders' routes of supply and retreat. Of course, helicopters are not immune to the logic of mountain warfare: Mountains provide excellent vantage points from which to see helicopters and to shoot them down—*provided* one has the missiles with which to do the job. Thus in 1986, as the Afghans began to receive serious U.S. missiles with which to fight Soviet helicopters, they recovered some of the advantages that nature had given them but that the huge disparity between their technology and that of their Soviet enemies had taken away.

The Synthetic High Ground

Let us now briefly consider the question of the "high ground" as it regards the air and outer space.

Until the mid-nineteenth century, armies would battle for possession of high ground in part because it offered the only means of observing their enemies. Beginning in the American Civil War, however, armies began to use tethered hot-air balloons to lift observers in sight of enemy positions. No sooner did the first balloon come within the range of enemy guns than it was treated just like what it was: an enemy outpost on a nearby hill. The battle for control of the "synthetic high ground" had begun. How important has this contest been?

During World War I, the amount of machine-gun fire and explosive ordnance delivered by aircraft was negligible in comparison with the mountains of explosives fired from the ground. Aircraft did not determine the outcome of any major battle. The airplane was used primarily as an observation platform. Yet, for the privilege of observing, and also for the sheer desire to win mastery of the sky, flyers in airplanes of wood, canvas, and wire fought like the knights of old.

During the Spanish civil war, almost twenty years later, airplanes that could carry a ton of bombs became truly useful for purposes other than observation. Airplanes became a kind of very long-range, very flexible artillery. Dive-bombers became especially useful for clearing the way for fast-moving forces far faster and more accurately than artillery could. Airplanes could also disrupt enemy artillery before it ever came into the range of battle. This tank-plane combination proved to be the queen of World War II battles. The modern airplane potentially placed enemy forces in a predicament similar to the one they would have had to face had they been located just under a cliff, from the edge of which enemy forces are dropping bombs. Given the growing ability of airplanes to carry bombs, a force unable to control the "high ground" above itself stood little chance. This became especially obvious in naval warfare during the battle of Midway—the first naval battle in history in which none of the ships of the opposing sides ever saw one another. Aircraft did all the fighting. Since aircraft operate most efficiently from land bases, they extended to almost mid ocean the coastal areas that could be controlled from land.

Aircraft have also improved in their ability to carry out their original function: reconnaissance. Miniaturized, high-resolution cameras, infrared detection equipment, side-looking radar imagery equipment, electronic intercept recorders, and radiation detectors have made it possible for modern aircraft, respectively, to record tiny objects on the ground, to notice whether an airplane is fueled or a car has been driven lately (by the amount of heat it gives off), to see large objects through clouds, to listen to conversations, or to determine if there are nuclear weapons in the vicinity.

Does this mean that the airplane is the decisive weapon? Only sometimes. After all, the battle for control of the high ground can also be waged successfully from below. Ground-based radars that see aircraft against the sky and modern interceptor missiles directed by modern computers can impose frightful attrition upon intruders. If the defender also employs radars carried by high-flying aircraft that can distinguish low fliers against the ground and can direct its own missiles to intercept them, then even the finest modern aircraft can be made ineffective as offensive weapons—unless the way is cleared for them by bombs falling from an even higher ground: outer space.

Long-range ballistic missiles are essentially very long-range artillery, whose projectiles arch up through and then fall out of outer space. In order for such missiles to be useful at all, however, the location of their targets must be known precisely, as must the effect of their fire: Was the target destroyed, or not? Where else should we shoot? Between the 1960s and the 1980s these questions became vitally important as missiles became the queens of strategic warfare and as they, as well as other strategic assets, became mobile. Whoever makes the high ground of orbital space safe for his own sensors and unsafe for the enemy's can theoretically keep his enemy under constant surveillance, while preventing his enemy from knowing where to shoot. The fall of the Soviet Union only increased the appetite of aggressive governments for ballistic missiles that travel through space, and did not slow the development of space-based sensors.

As we will see below, the very techniques that have allowed mankind to place satellites in orbit, and that allow satellites to point cameras and antennae precisely at points on the ground and at each another, also allow them to destroy each other or to destroy ballistic missiles flying through space. In this function, too, altitude makes a difference. Geometry says that if a satellite is in orbit three hundred miles above the earth, its line of sight will be unobstructed by the earth's horizon for about sixteen hundred miles in any direction. But if that satellite is traveling eight hundred miles above the earth, its line of sight will be unobstructed for some twenty-five hundred miles.[3] Satellites at these altitudes can see ballistic missiles. But can they do anything about them?

At the outset of the space age the means for making use of satellites for antimissile purposes were lacking. In 1962 American scientists learned how to make one object in orbit rendezvous with another. Theoretically, this constituted the capability to destroy enemy satellites. Yet satellites did not have the means to do such maneuvers fast enough to destroy ballistic missiles. Even if such a satellite had carried an interceptor rocket able to add, say, 6 kilometers per second (13,600 miles per hour) to its orbital velocity, that interceptor rocket would not have been able to catch up to the missile before its telltale engines cut off, and it became very difficult to see. But to ensure that a defensive satellite would be close enough to any given missile path, it was clear that there would have to be many hundreds of defensive satellites. Since the speed of chemical reactions sets a limit to how fast any rocket can go, this kind of defense, despite twenty-first-century technology, must "trade off" the rockets' relatively low speed, and hence their short effective range, by basing them on a high number of orbital stations.

When it became possible to design laser and particle-beam weapons with beams that travel at or near the speed of light, it became obvious that the height of the orbits in which defensive stations could be placed would depend only on the maximum range at which these weapons could deliver a fatal dose of energy upon a missile. Whereas a rocket can destroy a missile from perhaps two hundred miles away, a contemporary laser can do it from two thousand miles. Hence, today's lasers could usefully be stationed in orbits perhaps eight hundred miles up. Instead of hundreds of satellites, dozens would do. The more powerful and accurate lasers become, the more suitable they will be for higher orbits, and therefore the fewer will be required to cover the areas from which missiles might be launched. But with lasers, as with rockets, there is a trade off between having fewer, more powerful models, and greater numbers of less powerful but more conveniently located ones.

Higher orbits also confer upon the satellites located there the relative safety of fortresses on high ground: rockets, just like infantrymen, take longer time and require more energy to get to higher elevations. Whereas the world's biggest rocket (Russia's *Energia*) can deliver up to 400,000 pounds to low-earth orbit in one shot, the biggest payloads delivered to geosynchronous orbits (22,300 miles high) weigh only some 10,000 pounds. Moreover, whereas the journey to low-earth orbit takes a few minutes, the trip to geosynchronous orbit takes hours. That means that the higher a satellite is, the more energy it takes to attack it and the longer the missile attacking the satellite will be exposed to being hit from above. Also, just like a defender on a mountain crag, the higher the "ground" that the satellite holds, the more difficult it will be for sensors on the ground to see it, and for ground-based beam weapons to shoot at it accurately.

None of this is to say that whoever holds the highest orbits will prevail in space any more than whoever holds the highest ridges will prevail on the ground. In space as on the ground, the numbers of combatants, the quality of their equipment, and the tactics with which they are employed have more to do with the outcome than the altitude at which they are deployed.

Transportation and Logistics

Even when armies moved by muscle power, their comparative abilities to transport themselves and their goods made a difference. The Roman legions were superior to their enemies for, among other reasons, the excellent discipline and organization that enabled them to carry what they needed to survive and fight in relatively good health. This discipline extended to such matters as preventing troops from rushing to drink from rivers. While other armies would drink muddy water, the Romans carried small wooden bridges to allow the drawing of clean drinking water from the main current of streams. Roman discipline also allowed the legion to make and break camps quickly. Hence, the Romans moved more high-quality human muscle power faster. No one would argue that this did not contribute to their success. Still, no one can argue that mere logistics were decisive. After all, the Roman legions of the fifth century AD enjoyed as much logistical superior-

ity over the barbarians as had their predecessors five hundred years earlier. But by the fifth century, the Romans had become inferior in other
respects. Logistics, then, is but one factor among many.

Beginning with the Austro-Prussian War of 1866, in which the mobilization and concentration of armies was done primarily by railroad, a period began during which many held logistics to be the essence of warfare.
The reason for this belief is easy to grasp. If boarded quickly, a single train
can move an army division two hundred miles in an afternoon. By arranging the efficient employment of rolling stock, as well as the loading and
unloading of units, an army can be mobilized and placed in a strategically
advantageous position before the enemy can react. But even in the Austro-
Prussian War the railroad stratagem did not work as intended. The armies
were moved with historically unprecedented speed, all right. But the result
was due more to disparity in the armies' performance in the "fog of war."
The generals' plans for bringing their forces to battle were based on elaborate networks of train watchers, who would instantly transmit their intelligence by telegraph. However, cavalry units from both sides took Luddite
joy in pulling down the telegraph poles along railroad lines. The Prussian
army, however, stuck to its plans, dismounted the trains, marched over
passes, and closed the ring on the Austrian staging area for the decisive
battle of Königgratz.

The mechanistic emphasis on railroad timetables resurfaced during
World War I, when the art of war seemed to have been reduced to the grim
calculus of how many pounds of artillery shells could be made to fall on
each square yard of the enemy's front lines, and the planning of battles
consisted almost exclusively of concentrating more and more men and explosives on sections of the front in murderous efforts to force a breakthrough "at all costs." Yet the decisive breakthrough at Amiens in August
1918 came not so much because of superior logistics but because a new
tool, the tank, allowed troops to cross the no-man's-land between opposing trenches and dislodge the machine guns that had held the western
front immobile for three bloody years.

In World War II the United States performed logistical wonders such as
the world had never imagined. It built 100 aircraft carriers, 285,000 aircraft, and millions of vehicles. It laid pipelines under the English Channel
to fuel the fighting in France. It sent bombers to the South Pacific to land on
runways that would be completed only as the planes were in the air. Medi-
cines and blood products stayed refrigerated all the way from the laborato-
ries in the United States to remote corners of jungle or desert. New roads
connected China with the Bay of Bengal and Alaska with the main body of
North America. Never had soldiers been so superbly equipped, so well fed,
and so healthy as Americans in World War II. Nevertheless, German soldiers

continued to exact about a three-to-one casualty ratio against Americans until the closing months of the war. Surely, without logistical superiority, it would have been worse.

Vietnam surely dispelled the illusion regarding the benefits of logistical superiority. There is no truth to the widespread supposition that the communists fought with field-made or captured weapons. Indeed their southern front was supplied by containerized trucks rolling on a four-lane highway from the Cambodian port of Sihanoukville (now Kompong Som) to the Parrot's Beak area of South Vietnam, while the northern front was supplied by a good network of truck roads called the Ho Chi Minh Trail. Nevertheless, not even the shadow of a comparison is possible between how well the communists and the United States and South Vietnamese troops were supplied. Until 1973. Americans in Vietnam lived and fought in physical comfort unimaginable even by their fathers in World War II. Any wounded American usually could count on being in a state-of-the-art hospital within minutes of being hit.

America's firepower in Vietnam was overwhelming. An American infantry lieutenant recalls once mentioning on the radio that a sniper had fired on his platoon from a tree line ahead, at which time he was offered assistance by three different kinds of American gunships in the area. Poor sniper! Suffice it to say that the United States dropped three times more tons of bombs on tiny Vietnam than it had in all of World War II.[4] Had those bombs and bullets been spread at random, they might have had a greater military effect. Instead, the bulk was expended on a computerized "target list" that was drawn up in Washington and that was well-known to the North Vietnamese army, which of course used these American bomb dumps as accurate guides where not to put men, trucks, etc., as well as for installing antiaircraft equipment. The United States simply wasted its logistical superiority. After the U.S. departure in 1973, the logistical balance—especially with regard to ammunition—shifted in favor of North Vietnam, which knew how to use it.

In the Gulf War of 1991 and in the Iraq War of 2003, America outdid all previous logistical feats. Troops could walk from the battlefield to hamburger stands and pizza parlors, and by computer order for themselves the good things available to their families at home. None of this however made up for their leaders' misidentification of objectives.

Terrain

Assuming that both sides know the terrain equally well, drawing particular advantage from it depends on the opposing commanders' imagination. Consider, for example, an armed force confronted by an enemy-held city on its line of advance. Buildings, basements, sewers, culverts, and terraced hills are ideal places for defenders to hide. Rooting an enemy army out of a city is perhaps the dirtiest and most time consuming of all military operations. It is also dangerous. If the enemy has reserves elsewhere, he can wait until his opponent is embroiled in house-to-house fighting, and then call them in with disastrous effect. The Germans lost World War II this way, when the Soviets cut off their retreat while they were bogged down in house-to-house fighting in Stalingrad in 1942–43. Twenty-two divisions, comprising 230,000 men, ceased to exist, and only 90,000 of the men survived to suffer the fate of prisoners of war in Russia.[5]

The traditional military recipe for cities calls for either bypassing them or for laying siege. Bypassing cities is preferable because it prevents tough fighting, preserves the city's wealth intact so that it can be plundered in the future, and allows an army to seek a quick decision elsewhere. But what if a decision can be reached only by attacking the city? This was the case with regard to Berlin at the end of World War II. Then there is no choice. What if the enemy uses the city to shelter forces so large that it would be imprudent to bypass them? Thus, in 1944 the Germans strongly garrisoned Warsaw and dared the Red Army to come in. The Red Army then used the best possible stratagem under the circumstances—the use of allies who were already within the city. It called on the strong Polish underground in Warsaw to revolt openly against the Germans so that the Germans, occupied with their rear, could not make efficient use of the urban terrain when the Red Army advanced.

But the Soviets went beyond this reasonable military measure. As the Polish underground rose, the Red Army stopped. For three weeks the Red Army watched as the German garrison and the Polish underground bled one another. Only after nearly all the Polish fighters—the natural leaders of Polish society—were dead, did the Red Army enter Warsaw. The house-to-house fighting was easier than it would have been had the Polish underground not fought, but harder than it would have been if the Red Army had joined the fight while the underground remained alive. But on the other hand, after taking Warsaw this way, the Soviets did not have to deal with a lot of independent-minded and armed Poles.

Wilderness poses problems different from the ones posed by cities, but just as great. Suppose for a moment that an army from the Northern Hemisphere were to try to invade South Africa. Unless that army tried to come ashore through an amphibious operation, it would have to come either from Namibian or Mozambican ports or from points even farther away. Imagine the sheer effort that would go into supplying the food, fuel, spare parts, medical supplies, bridging equipment, and other provisions that perhaps half a million fighting men would need, depending on which route they took, in order to cross the Namib Desert, Limpopo or Zambesi Rivers, or the Great Rift Valley, traveling over a thousand miles through desert and semi-desert country or perhaps coastal swamps, and surely some rugged mountains without good roads or with no roads at all! As road-building crews worked and as the supply lines lengthened, South African light forces could harass them. Who would want to bet on the condition of the attacking force when it reached Johannesburg? The awaiting defenders would be fresh, healthy, and covered by nearby airfields. Any equipment that broke down could be fixed close by. Any wounded defender would be minutes from a hospital. But for the attackers any wounded soldiers or disabled vehicles would most likely be lost. In short, any army that tried to attack South Africa overland would face problems worse than those that the British encountered in their war against the American colonies in 1776–81.

In the 1980s the classic attempt to attack through wilderness was that of Soviet- and Cuban-led Angolan forces based in northwest Angola against the forces of Jonas Savimbi, headquartered in the southwest corner of that semiarid country. Prior to 1985 the attacking forces, consisting almost exclusively of motorized infantry, had been stopped by guerrilla attacks against their supply lines. In 1985, however, the Soviets and Cubans included tanks in their attacking force, and covered their advance with aircraft and helicopters. Savimbi's forces were finally able to defeat the attackers only one hundred miles from their headquarters because the attackers lost many tanks in transit and could not provide decisive air cover operating from fields as much as five hundred miles away. In 1986 and 1987 the wilderness became an even better shield for Savimbi when his forces received American Stinger shoulder-fired missiles with which to defend themselves against the best wilderness-shrinking devices ever invented, namely airplanes.

So, in sum, wilderness is excellent cover for light troops, but it is terribly hard on regular forces. For that reason wilderness is excellent for guerrilla war, whether defensive or offensive. It is also good for defensive conventional conflict. The caveat of course is that wilderness also hampers the irregulars' efforts to supply themselves. Hence wilderness is most useful to irregulars if it lies between them and the enemy and especially if it "backs up" to friendly territory.

Rivers and canals are also generally good lines for defense. Before World War II, Winston Churchill hoped that "the broad, deep, swift-flowing Rhine" could easily be garrisoned as an effective barrier against the German army. The Rhine, even more than most rivers, is indeed difficult to cross against opposition. On any river, even if the attackers' artillery can keep the opposite bank clear of defenders, the defenders' artillery can sit far back from the bank and smash pontoon bridges as they are being built. On the Rhine, however, the fast current makes it even more difficult than normal to build pontoon bridges, even without opposition. Generally, river crossings succeed when the attacker moves quickly to places that are not heavily defended and bridges have not been destroyed. This is precisely how the Germans crossed the Rhine delta in May 1940—and how the Allies recrossed it upstream at Remagen in 1945.

Once a crossing is secured, the river is no longer much of an obstacle. It becomes significant again only if the attacker is forced to retreat quickly. Then, equipment gets abandoned because it can't be moved across the river fast enough, and troops must swim for their lives. If it happens to be cold, those lives will be shortened. This is what happened in January 1813 when the remainder of Napoleon's Grande Armée escaped from Russia to Prussia across the Berezina River. Over one-third of the fleeing mass did not make it across a hastily built bridge near Studienka. In 1973 the Egyptian army that had surprisingly dashed across the Suez Canal to attack Israel found itself unable to get back across as fast because Egypt lost control of the airspace over the canal to the Israeli air force. Thus Egyptian forces were trapped.

Because crossing even small rivers is never a trivial matter for an army, it is generally good military practice to plan the movement of troops so that they cross any river just once, rather than marching along the river's course. It is foolish to inhibit maneuvers by operating with a river alongside, and foolhardy to fight with it directly behind. Doing so threatens to turn any setback into a disaster. Nevertheless in the Second Punic War, Hannibal broke this rule of thumb and defeated Rome's best armies by marching down the Tiber River Valley. He risked much, but gained the prize of surprise.

Technology

When the Spanish Armada approached the English fleet in 1588 it was superior numerically but not technically: the English ships had deep keels. Whereas the Spanish ships could not sail in directions far from the axis of the wind, the English ships could maneuver much more freely. The English also had mounted their cannon on four-wheel carriages. This made for faster loading and more accurate shooting. That is why the English were able to pick off the Spanish at will, so weakening the armada that its survivors fled. Superior technology applied by a knowledgeable commander made a decisive difference.

But superior technology by itself is no guarantee of superior weapons. For example, gallows humor in the U.S. Navy at the time of the battle of Midway (1942) had it that its weapons were either experimental or obsolete. The American torpedo bombers were so outdated that casualties were near 100 percent! The Navy simply had not acted as if war in 1942 was a real possibility. So, although the United States had the finest aircraft technology in the world, Japan had the Zero, the best fighter in the air over the Pacific in 1942. Nevertheless, the United States, not Japan, won the battle of Midway because of superior intelligence and because American airplanes were lucky enough to find Japanese carriers while their planes were refueling on deck.

Sometimes inferior weapons can defeat superior ones if cleverly used. By the late 1930s and certainly after Pearl Harbor, "everyone" knew that battleships were sitting ducks for airplanes. But the United States simply filled up deck space on battleships with antiaircraft guns that could literally put a wall of shrapnel around the ship. The result? On a particularly good day, the USS *South Dakota* shot down *thirty-five* Japanese aircraft.

Weapons technology is pointless if it is not used to actually build weapons and if these weapons are not deployed. For example, in the 1960s the United States developed the technology for producing highly accurate ballistic missiles—and indeed curiously sold a key part of this technology to the Soviet Union in 1972. But not until December 1986 did the United States deploy its first ballistic missile, the MX, with the combination of accuracy and explosive power adequate to destroy other missiles on the ground. Meanwhile, the Soviet Union had begun deploying its version of the MX, known as the SS-18, in 1976. Of course, the MX is a more technically advanced weapon than the SS-18. But the two weapons performed essentially the same task, and the SS-18 was deployed not only earlier, but in 308 copies rather than the MX's 50! In sum, during the 1970s and 1980s, while the United States continued to develop militarily applicable technology at a vertiginous pace, the pace at which it embodied new technology in major deployed-missile systems slowed from an average of five to an average of fifteen years.[6] This hiatus gave the Soviet Union the chance to acquire American technology and introduce it into its own weapons before the United States did. Perhaps the starkest example of this imbalance is the Soviet Union's incorporation of optical-guidance technology stolen from the American Strategic Defense Initiative program into its operational SH-11 antimissile interceptor. While the United States was deliberating whether to deploy or even research antimissile defenses, the Soviet Union was building them, in part with stolen American technology.

Possession of superior weapons does not guarantee that they will be used wisely. For example, in 1987 the U.S. frigate *Stark*, on patrol in the Persian Gulf, was equipped with a self-defense Gatling gun (the Phalanx) able to literally and automatically put a wall of bullets between the ship and an attacking cruise missile. But when an Iraqi cruise missile approached the ship, the Phalanx system had not been turned on.

Perhaps the most striking example of wasted technical superiority was the U.S. Navy's announced plan, the Maritime Strategy, to send aircraft carrier battle groups into the Norwegian Sea at the outset of any war with the Soviet Union without first destroying the hundreds of Soviet airfields within range of the Norwegian Sea.[7] Now, U.S. aircraft carriers have the indubitable technical capacity to dominate the air over the ocean, *but only in places out of reach of massive land-based airpower.* The rule, "Thou shalt not bring sea-based airpower within range of superior land-based airpower," is more valid in the age of jet aircraft than ever before. American carriers are infinitely superior to their Soviet counterparts. In mid-ocean, or close to friendly coasts, they are invincible defensive weapons. But not in an offensive against the teeth of land-based airpower.

Finally, we must remember that the effect of superior technology—indeed of any innovation—is strictly limited in time. After 1588 no serious navy ordered warships without deep keels or wheeled guns. If Spain's Golden Century had not ended, a second armada fifty years later would likely have succeeded. In our century the major European powers did not understand the impact that the machine gun would have on ground combat until 1916. But once they did, they all started to use tanks. The effectiveness of tanks, of course, depends on who constructs better guns, sighting devices, armor, and antitank missiles. Much also depends on the tactics with which tanks are used. By the same token, the effectiveness of aircraft centers on the constant technological competition for better speed, maneuverability, and the ability of on-board radar systems to "see" and "lock-on" to faraway targets by overlooking clutter from ground reflections and from electronic countermeasures.

Today's decisive innovation becomes tomorrow's standard, and is sure to be obsolete sometime thereafter. No one can know how long novelty will last. Only one thing is sure: there is no such thing as an ultimate weapon. Thus, time is perhaps the most crucial element in technical innovation. *The longer an idea takes to reach the battlefield as hardware, the shorter will be its period of usefulness.* In military technology, seeking the best is the enemy of choosing the good.

But the race for technical supremacy should not be misconstrued. In the war between Israel and Syria over Lebanon in 1982, the box score was eighty-one Syrian fighters destroyed and zero for Israel. This does not mean that Israel's American equipment overwhelmed Syria's Soviet equipment, but that the Israelis used what they had incomparably better than did the Syrians.

Attrition

Contrary to boasts, hardly any army fights "to the last man." Nor do competent commanders point vaguely in the direction of the enemy and simply order: "Kill." Battles, much less wars, are seldom won by inflicting indiscriminate attrition. Nevertheless, attrition of trained people and key supplies (or even just fatigue) can deprive an armed force of substance.

For example, in the 1973 Yom Kippur War, Israel won the battle for the Golan Heights simply by imposing dreadful attrition on Syria's tanks. Israel's technique was simple. Its tank commanders had noted every boulder and depression that could provide cover for a tank, had plotted routes of withdrawal from shelter to shelter, and had assigned small groups of tanks to cover each other's retreats. When the numerically superior Syrian tanks rushed in, the Israelis made them pay for every rock and hollow. Before the battle had reached the precipice leading down into Israel proper, the Syrian tank force had been much reduced, and Israel, now enjoying numerical superiority, was free to move forward.

In 1940, during the Battle of Britain, trained pilots were the crucial element. Airplanes could be manufactured more easily than pilots could be trained. Hence it was of enormous significance that the battle was conducted over British soil or over the English Channel, where the Royal Navy ruled. Whereas every downed German pilot (regardless of his physical condition) was lost to Germany, German aviators actually had to kill British pilots before they would be lost to Britain. Because of the importance of trained pilots, Winston Churchill had implored the faltering French government in Tours to turn over to Britain the four hundred-odd German pilots that France had captured during its losing struggle of May–June 1940.[8] Britain would go so far as to excuse France's acceptance of an armistice if only it would turn over these pilots. The fate of one hundred thousand ordinary troops would not have meant so much to the outcome of the war as did the fate of those four hundred pilots.

Since equipment has become more important in war, so has the attrition of equipment. Since the primary mission of aircraft is to achieve mastery of the sky, the chief target of aircraft must be other aircraft. Using aircraft for any other purpose requires a good reason, for instance, killing soldiers or destroying tanks on a particular battlefield if it will achieve a goal more important than air superiority. One classic example of a misuse of airpower was Goering's mad commitment to use the Luftwaffe to supply the German Sixth Army encircled at Stalingrad. The Luftwaffe lost so many planes and pilots that it was never a major factor in the war again.

All operations of war entail losses on both sides. These are foreseeable, though rarely calculable. Hence, commanders must ask themselves whether the attrition they are imposing on the enemy will be worth the attrition that their own forces will suffer. But—and this is the crux—*the importance of the attrition on either side can be measured only in terms of the effect that it has on either side's ability to achieve its strategic goals.* It will not do to count bodies on either side, because each set of bodies can mean something entirely different to its side's plans.

In our century there has all too frequently existed an awesome contrast in the value that the respective belligerents place upon the lives of their troops in battle. The "human waves" of Chinese communist "volunteers" who poured against American firepower in Korea in 1950–53 suffered casualties four times as great as those of American, South Korean, and UN forces—1,600,000 to 437,000. (In all, only 37,000 American soldiers perished in the war—scarcely three times the number of Union soldiers who perished in the one-day Battle of Antietam!) Similar ghastly asymmetries were observed on the eastern front in World Wars I and II in engagements between German and Russian forces, in the Vietnam War, in the Iran-Iraq War of 1981–88, in the 1991 Gulf War, and in the 2003 Iraq War. In such instances a cynic might distinguish between "capital-intensive" and "labor-intensive" fighting forces. Thus, a belligerent with small regard for human life is far less sensitive to taking casualties than one accustomed to cherish life highly—a factor that surely must enter into strategic calculations. The American practice of "body-counting" enemy casualties in the Vietnam War was mindless in innocently assuming that these deaths had a bearing on North Vietnamese capabilities and willpower. Similarly, the Americans' attention to their material successes in the Middle East obscured their understanding of their political failures.

The weight of burdens, up to some unknowable point, is relative, as anyone knows who has ever gazed at the statue in front of Boys Town, Nebraska: one boy carrying another over the inscription, "He ain't heavy. He's my brother." What some consider burdens—for example, digging ditches—others consider good sense and the chance to build good morale. Nor will it do to try to calculate the economic costs of each side's losses or efforts. Not only do peoples put different values on things, but more important, *military goods are valuable not for the materials and labor that go into them, but for the strategic gains that can be got out of using them. No one in wartime has ever been struck by an amorphous piece of gross national product.*

6

WINNING THE BATTLE: LAND, SEA, AND AIR

Just win, baby.

—AL DAVIS
owner, Oakland Raiders

W HEN ARMIES march and navies sail, what makes the difference be tween victory and defeat? From time to time throughout history, usually after a major victory or defeat has occurred—especially if it was unexpected— military writers rush to explain that the "laws of war" ordain a certain formula for success. But the only answer consistent with history is that the success of military operations depends largely on how creatively command- ers impose their will on a particular set of circumstances. A prescription for success in one set of circumstances can lead to disaster in another.

The wisest commentators on the operations of war, from Livy and Machiavelli to Napoleon and Soviet writers such as V. D. Sokolovskii, have stressed the contingent nature of warfare: the supreme need to adapt what- ever human and material means are at hand to avoid or defeat the enemy's peculiar strengths while exploiting the enemy's vulnerabilities at any given time whether on the ground, at sea, or in the air.

Decision on the Ground

From time immemorial, most battles on the ground have been decided when one side succeeded, by force, maneuver, or both, in placing enough force to the side or the rear of the enemy to disorganize him. Again and again Thucydides tells of various battle alignments in the Peloponnesian War:

heavy infantry in the center or on the flanks, archers and stone-slingers on one side or the other, and cavalry on the line or in reserve. The battle would be decided when one part of the line routed those opposite it, made a breakthrough or a flanking movement, and then wheeled right or left, thus bringing overwhelming force to bear on a line that now had to fight in several directions at once. The decisive break could be caused by anything: the shock of cavalry, a hail of stones or arrows, or the patient chopping of swords and spears. At that point, either the defeated side would retreat and close ranks again, leaving the field in good order, or there would be a rout. That is when the major killing would occur.

The development of ever more powerful firearms has changed the means for causing breakthroughs. As late as 1914—almost six hundred years after the introduction of gunpowder in the West, two hundred years after the introduction of trench warfare, and despite the experience of the Franco-Prussian War in which only 10 percent of the casualties were caused by bayonets, swords, and lances—the so-called white arms—the field manual of the French army counted on the bayonet to break enemy lines. "There is no individual act of preliminary preparation of the attack by the artillery. Artillery and infantry operate together." But the wholesale slaughter of attacking infantry by dug-in defenders soon taught everyone that, in Marshal Henri Pétain's words, "fire kills." Since then, armies have relied on some kind of bombardment to break a path for both infantry and armor. Over the years this bombardment has drastically increased in intensity, has struck ever deeper behind the front, and has shortened considerably. Thus during France's Verdun offensive of August 1916, 3,360 artillery rounds were fired every hour, on every kilometer of front, ten hours a day for a week. In 1944, however, as the Soviet army prepared for the Vistula-Oder attack, its artillery fired for only twenty-five minutes—but at the rate of sixty thousand shells per kilometer of front, per hour![1] The shock opened the breach.

By the end of World War I, the amplitude of offensives had increased so much that in order to facilitate the movement of forces exploiting a breakthrough, the bombardment had to extend beyond artillery range. Airplanes became mobile artillery. Thus some fifteen hundred airplanes took part in the preparation for the "breakthrough" at Amiens in 1918. During World War II, fleets of bombers ranged far beyond fronts to strike both fortifications and enemy reserves. In our time "attack helicopters" are both mobile field artillery and mobile machine-gun nests. The lesson seems to be that "breakthrough bombardments" are increasingly violent and concentrated in time, and that they tend to extend ever farther and more accurately into the enemy's rear.

Today ballistic missiles armed with nuclear or chemical warheads are replacing airplanes and to some extent artillery as the battering rams, the great prejudgers of ground combat. This does not mean that in modern ground combat the defense stands no chance. Dug-in infantry and armor, backed by strong reserves, have an enormous advantage over attacking forces that expose themselves, but only to the extent that the defenders can protect themselves against the long-range battering rams.

Today, as always, the attacker has the enormous advantage of concentrating his fire on the point of attack and on the routes that his infantry and armor will follow to exploit the breakthrough. The idea is the same as it was in Thucydides' time: roll up the flanks, destroy the enemy's supplies, and cut off the dug-in defenders. But modern firepower has changed the role that infantry and armor play in ground offensives. Now more than ever they follow a line of action already traced, if not predetermined, by the high-power salvos that cleared the way, well or badly, for them. Modern ground troops legitimately expect to be covered constantly by their own planes and helicopters as they move through and beyond enemy lines.

Wise commanders of units both large and small have always kept perhaps one-third of their ready forces away from the front as battlefield reserves. This serves the needs of both offense and defense. The reserves can be rushed into a sector where the enemy is about to break through or into a sector where one's own forces are breaking through. The reserves can help prevent a rout on one's own side or cause one for the enemy. All great battlefield commanders (Napoleon at Austerlitz and Marlborough at Blenheim come to mind) have been masters at feeling the pulse of battle and deciding just when and where to engage the reserve forces for the supreme effort.

The absence of strong, highly mobile reserves—from the platoon level to that of an empire—must be counted as one of the most fatal errors in warfare. Rome was sacked in AD 410 because once the barbarians had broken through the border legions, the reserve forces under Romulus Augustulus were simply too weak. Rome would not have been taken if this last Roman emperor of the West had had under his direct command even a small fraction of the legions still intact on the far-flung borders of the empire. Reserves are especially important in modern combat. In May 1940, when German troops had broken through French lines on a narrow two-mile front at Sedan, Winston Churchill asked the French government, "Where is the maneuver mass?" French generals looked at the floor as their leader said, *"Aucune"*—there wasn't any.[2] Moreover, because the Germans who had broken through were riding tanks and trucks, it was out of the question for French forces on the front to pull back fast enough to constitute a mobile army to give battle to the intruder. The French were doomed.

The importance of mobile reserves does not diminish the importance of fortifications. The Maginot line, for example, has been unjustly maligned. Like all fortifications it was supposed to economize troops at the front precisely so that they could be used as mobile reserves. After all, if any enemy has to work to get through a fortified line, or to go around it, he presents an inviting target to "linebacking" reserves. Unfortunately, the French chose to look at the Maginot line not as a strategic tool but as an excuse to economize overall.

Some learned a lesson from this disaster, while others did not. In the late summer of 1940, Britain, while preparing for a possible German invasion, deployed a thin cordon of troops along the coast, but kept the bulk of its home forces as a mobile reserve "on which everything would depend." However, when the shoe was on the other foot and Hitler was preparing to meet the Allied invasion of the Continent, he repeated the mistakes that the French had made in 1940. He created brilliant spiderweb fortifications. But, as Churchill noted, *"he forgot the spider."*[3] There was no "maneuver mass" to smash the Allies as they broke out of the Normandy beachheads in August 1944.

The North Atlantic Treaty Organization (NATO) alliance, for its part, prepared a defense of West Germany that seemed to violate every rule of ground combat. American, British, and West German troops were spread out against the inter-German border, while Benelux and French contingents were layered behind. There was no mobile reserve, and indeed there were no nuclear minefields on the German border because of a twin contradictory commitment to "forward defense," that is, to limiting the fighting to the border and to making the fighting as nondisruptive as possible. In addition, of course, NATO forces were outnumbered in tanks by three to one, in artillery by five to one, and in infantry-fighting vehicles by five to one.[4] Under such conditions, the likelihood of a successful preclusive defense is zero. There were no plans for rapid withdrawal in the face of attack followed by sharp counterattacks when the force of the attack was spent. Instead of plans for the likely eventuality of a Soviet breakthrough there were vague words about the possible use of nuclear weapons.[5]

Yet since combat in Europe would have taken place in the context of the U.S.-Soviet military balance, it would have had to take into account that the Soviet Union had the capacity to inflict more damage on the United States than the United States could inflict on the Soviet Union. It was irrational to think of trying to avoid defeat on one level of warfare by inviting certain defeat on another, far more destructive, level. Modern conditions do not invalidate common sense about military matters. They strengthen it.

Amphibious Operations

Landing and fighting on a hostile shore multiplies the difficulties of naval and ground operations. First, one must defeat or evade the enemy's ships.

Then one must fight the waves, tides, sand, and Murphy's Law to get men and equipment on shore. If the beach is defended, ship-based aircraft and guns have the tough job of overwhelming land-based aircraft and guns. Then the invader must do it all over again and again to keep his troops supplied. On top of these difficulties are the pains of ground combat.

The advantage of amphibious operations is that they allow an attacker to move whole forces by sea at around fifteen miles per hour and land them wherever he chooses. They almost guarantee tactical surprise. Attacking forces can be concentrated at the point of attack very quickly to outflank or bypass or circle behind a defending force.

The first requirement of amphibious warfare is naval superiority. It is impossible to deal with nature and shore defenses while fighting a naval battle. So if the attacking navy has not yet eliminated its opponent, it must be prepared to screen the landing area. In World War II, Hitler did not invade Britain because he did not have a navy capable of challenging Britain's. He counted on being able to cripple the Royal Navy and control the channel with the Luftwaffe, but first it had to cripple the Royal Air Force. This is what the Battle of Britain was about. When the RAF beat the Luftwaffe, the Royal Navy was ensured control of the channel and Britain was safe from invasion. The Germans could have sneaked a few shiploads of men across the channel, but such operations would have been inconsequential. An amphibious invasion requires at least a naval screen, and Britain, not Germany, was in a position to provide it.

The U.S. Navy fought the battle of Leyte Gulf precisely to cover the invasion of the Philippines. The battle was fought in two separate parts. Had the Japanese commander of the essentially victorious northern fleet continued toward Leyte despite the damage to his fleet, he would have been able to cut through the invasion fleet and wreck the main U.S. landings. But he mistakenly supposed that he would be met by the other half of the U.S. fleet, and chose not to hazard Japan's few remaining capital ships. By contrast, with the exception of a few submarines, when the Allies invaded Normandy across the English Channel what was left of the German navy did not even attempt to break through an obviously overwhelming naval screen.

Naval protection of amphibiously landed forces is absolutely essential. History's greatest example of what happens when the fleet that was supporting a land force is defeated is the aftermath of the battle of Salamis, when King Xerxes's superior Persian forces were instantly transformed from potential conquerors of Greece to wretches trying to save themselves by walking around the northeast rim of the Mediterranean. By the same token, although World War II's desert campaigns in North Africa are not normally considered amphibious operations, in effect they were, because both sides' supplies came by sea. Allied victory in the sands of North Africa followed victory in the Mediterranean and Atlantic.

Unchallenged naval supremacy makes possible what appear to be strokes of genius. In 1950 Gen. Douglas MacArthur, commander of the U.S.-UN forces in Korea, landed an amphibious force behind the front, at a place called Inchon. The port was undefended because the North Koreans did not imagine that anyone would land there. Surprise was complete, and in a few weeks the now outflanked North Korean forces lost more than they had gained in the entire war.

MacArthur was adapting the oldest recipe in the book. Thucydides tells us that the Athenian Demosthenes cajoled a small naval force to land on Pylos, a small Peloponnesian peninsula (which looks like Korea on a small scale). He fortified the peninsula's narrow neck. The Spartans, unable to break through the wall, tried landing in overwhelming force on the peninsula's narrow beaches. Demosthenes persuaded his troops that the Spartans could land only a few at a time, encouraged them to prevent the landing, and called in the superior Athenian fleet. Frustrated, the Spartans laid siege by land and sea. When the Athenian fleet arrived, it defeated the Spartans at sea and trapped the flower of Spartan soldiery on an island. Thus did Athens win the first half of the Peloponnesian War.

Demosthenes and MacArthur were able to do their amphibious operations because their countries had already succeeded in the laborious task of sea control. Already twenty-five hundred years ago mastery of the sea required superiority in shipbuilding and ship handling, and these things, as King Archidamus reminded his Spartans, required years of commitment. In our day, sea control must involve the sky above the sea, the depths, as well as the surface. The greatest amphibious campaign in history, MacArthur's island-hopping campaign of World War II teaches hard lessons: Aircraft carriers can sometimes send their planes to fight against planes from enemy airfields (if they can manage to surprise them). But absent surprise, the carriers themselves must stay out of range of enemy land-based aircraft. The big amphibious landings in the Pacific, where major enemy air activity was expected, were covered by aircraft from American airfields hastily built on islands that had been lightly defended and were captured for this purpose. Then the naval screens were set out, and finally the aircraft and battleships hammered the hostile shore, with seldom a shot fired back. Only then would the Marines "hit the beach."

Naval Operations

While the purposes of naval operations have not changed since the dawn of time, their character is wholly determined by changing technology. In our time the purposes remain, first, securing the sea for friendly ships and denying it to the enemy's, and second, attacking enemy shores. These goals may be more important now than ever before. In simpler times land powers did not have to worry about the sea. China after 1433 is the classic example of a one-dimensional land power. But today no nation—even the Soviet Union, the quintessential land power—could expect to fight a major war successfully if its enemies are able to utilize the world's resources to supply themselves and can prevent it from receiving supplies and help from across the sea while landing on its coasts at will. Indeed, the Soviet Union could not have survived World War II if Germany had won the "Battle of the Atlantic" for control of the routes by which American trucks, airplanes, tanks, and food reached Soviet territory.

Coastal or island nations—Britain, Japan, and even the United States—are much more dependent on naval success. Quite simply, for such nations loss of sea control is defeat. Because occupying forces can come only by sea, as long as it is in friendly hands, worse cannot come to worst, and there should be time to repair losses. While the sea is in friendly hands the lifeblood of commerce will provide an unoccupied island the material means to repair losses and prepare for victory. But if an island or coastal nation loses control of the sea, it will run short of materials and time will become its enemy.

Thus, in World War I, the British were right in saying that their First Sea Lord, Earl Jellicoe, whose Grand Fleet did indeed "rule the waves," was the only man on either side who could "lose the war in an afternoon." He could not win it. Only lose it. Germany was largely the mistress of the Continent. Its inferiority at sea was a serious, though not a decisive, liability for its campaign on the western front. Germany could lose a major sea battle and not be much worse off than before. But if Britain had lost naval superiority, the position of its troops on the western front would have become untenable instantly.

Changes in technology have made controlling the seas today a vastly different enterprise than it has ever been before. Historically, naval warfare consisted of guessing where the enemy fleet would be, stumbling into it, and getting close enough to enemy ships to strike them with one's weapons—first ramming prows and arrows, and then guns. Gradually the range of guns lengthened until, by World War I, guns could shoot to the horizon and beyond. Since that time, war on the surface of the sea has relied on machines (airplanes, radar, and satellites) that can look beyond the horizon and on weapons (guns, but mostly airplanes and missiles) that can reach there. Also, whereas once all naval warfare took place on the surface of the sea, today's technology allows naval operations to take place under and over the sea as well. Let us look more closely at naval technology.

First, consider sensors. Until the twentieth century, ships could perceive one another only by human eyes and ears and could never detect each other if they were farther than the horizon. Today instruments make it possible (though never certain) to perceive ships, aircraft, and even submarines hundreds and even thousands of miles away. The bottom of the North Atlantic, for example, is sown with hydrophones. Similar strings of underwater ears are arrayed across the bottom of key straits in the Pacific as well. These devices transmit to stations on shore the noise made by passing ships and submarines. The ever-changing character of seawater does not allow these electronic underwater ears to tell precisely where submarines are, but they help antisubmarine forces know where to begin searching. Submarines and surface ships now carry large, sophisticated listening devices. Depending on ocean conditions, these can give a reasonably good "fix" on a submarine over a hundred miles away. Airplanes and helicopters, too, can drop into the water buoys carrying electronic ears. This is quite useful for following up imprecise leads provided by underwater arrays. Airplanes also fly low over the ocean carrying magnetic anomaly detection devices, essentially metal detectors, to pick up traces of nearby submarines.

Once a submarine is detected, weapons can be launched at it from far away. The most remarkable example of such a weapon is something the United States calls SUBROC. It is a rocket that a submerged submarine can launch at another submerged submarine. The rocket, carrying a homing torpedo, pushes itself out of the water and travels a ballistic trajectory toward a point above the enemy submarine. Then it dives back into the water and releases the torpedo, which listens for the nearby submarine and then homes in on it. Surface ships and airplanes can also fire rockets carrying homing torpedoes. Improved sensors for long-range detection, as well as the development of sensors that make weapons "smart," have put an end to the era when the only way to destroy a submarine was to drop depth bombs on it.

This is a good place to note that naval warfare was the nursery for "smart," or guided, weapons. That is because the sea, like the sky, is such a featureless background that streams of energy coming from ships, submarines, or aircraft stand out clearly against it, whether they be sound waves, radar waves, or radiated heat. To make any naval weapon "smart", it was only necessary to give it a sensor that could tell the difference between the sound, heat, radar coming from the target and those from the featureless background, and then to devise mechanisms for steering the weapon so that it kept heading for the source of the signal. When sensor technology became able to sort targeted objects out of the clutter of signals coming from the ground, "smart" weapons came to be applied to land warfare as well. But because of the peculiar characteristics of the sea, naval weapons are still the "smartest" of all.

But sensors, both offensive and defensive, can be defeated by false signals and by speed. Homing torpedoes can be lured away from their targets by underwater explosions that create false targets. In this regard, it seems that a Russian torpedo, the Skral, minimizes the effectiveness of countermeasures by traveling perhaps five times faster than anyone thought torpedoes could possibly go. It does this by creating an air bubble within which it travels and which eliminates the water friction that slows conventional torpedoes. The Skral's guidance cannot be very good. But its speed makes up for that. Speed is also the essence of the Russian antiship cruise missile known as "Sunburn." It cuts the time for defensive measures nearly to zero. China has bought Sunburn and perhaps Skral. The only obvious defense against such fast terminal weapons is to strike their carriers before they launch them.

High-flying airplanes carrying powerful radars can scan huge swaths of the ocean for surface ships. Satellites for detecting heat and the presence of metal on the surface of the ocean are feasible, as is satellite-borne radar—though of limited capacity. In addition, satellites, airplanes, ships, and land stations bristle with antennae that can detect and locate the radio signals that ships at sea normally send out. Of course, ships that want to hide (for instance, the Japanese carriers that struck Pearl Harbor) maintain strict radio silence. Nevertheless, as time goes by and various kinds of sensors proliferate, and better computers collate what they report, major naval powers increasingly gain an accurate and timely picture of where ships are located in the world's oceans. The problem of detection in naval warfare is smaller than it has ever been, and it is steadily diminishing.

Almost the same can be said of detecting aircraft in naval roles. Aircraft are normally visible to modern shipborne radar as soon as they come above the horizon. Just exactly when this happens depends on their altitude. That is why any aircraft that wishes to sneak up on a ship must fly low and pop over the horizon only a few seconds' flying time from the ship. Antiship cruise missiles (pilotless aircraft, otherwise known as flying torpedoes) are easy to stop if they fly high enough to give the ships time to aim their antiaircraft guns and launch their antiaircraft missiles. Absolute speed matters much less than speed relative to the horizon. Such speed is highest when altitude is lowest. In naval warfare, as in other kinds of warfare, designers of aircraft and cruise missiles also try to make it possible to avoid detection by shaping their products in ways that give low radar returns (stealth). Modern aircraft can also jam detection radars and carry out other electronic countermeasures.

In sum, modern naval warfare is characterized by generally easy detection and by weapons with increasingly high probability of hitting their targets. This is not to say that every antiship cruise missile launched from a ship or airplane will hit a ship, that every surface-to-air missile will bring down a plane, or that every homing torpedo will sink something. But it does mean that there is a big and growing premium in naval warfare in getting off the first shot. Since the success of a weapon is more and more taken for granted, the essence of modern naval tactics consists of taking whatever measures are necessary to get into position to shoot before the other side can get ready to shoot back or to protect itself. Submarines win by being quieter. Aircraft win by flying lower or with better electronic countermeasures. Surface ships try to be quiet in every way, to extend their eyes and ears as far as possible, and to be ready to repel attacks. Every naval unit tries for speed, uses electronic communications to find out from others where the enemy is, and attempts to stay out of range of his sensors, all the while trying to move its own sensors quickly into range so that it can strike.

Given these conditions, then, how do modern navies carry out traditional naval operations? Consider the blockade, and its counterpart, the protection of sea lines of communications. The airplane is the most common tool of modern large naval blockades because its speed and field of view allows it to cover wide areas. Satellites promise to be even more effective. During World War II, German planes based in western France could not locate and fight American convoys in the Atlantic because their speed, range, and staying power were not enough to maintain continuous coverage. Today, anyone trying to prevent American convoys from reaching Europe, could track them all the way with Radar Ocean Reconnaissance Satellites, keep them in view with long-range reconnaissance aircraft, and when the convoys got within perhaps five hundred miles of the Continent, hit them with swarms of naval bombers loaded with cruise missiles that would head directly for the ships. The cruise missiles would be launched on accurate headings well before the ships could see them and would pop over the horizon seconds before impact.

All of this is to say that the task of securing sea lines of communications today no longer means escorting ships directly, confident that it would be unlikely to meet an entire blockading force. Since evasion is unlikely, a convoy can be assured of getting through a blockade only if its "escorts" seek out and defeat the blockading forces themselves. Moreover, the speed and reconnaissance capacity of modern naval forces ensure that the battle to hold or break blockades would be on an oceanic scale.

Thus, given modern naval technology, an advantage for either side would depend on the overall rather than on the local balance of forces. Nevertheless, location remains important, because it seems that the character of modern naval weapons favors the side that is on the defensive, whose job is to stop the movement of ships, especially when it is trying to prevent enemy naval forces from getting near land that it controls. This is true for several reasons. First, submarines that are predeployed in defensive positions need not move much, if at all. Because the submarines that are moving in to dislodge them will be noisier ipso facto, the defense will have an important advantage. Second, even if the attacker is superior in aircraft carriers, it is difficult to imagine any realistic number of carriers that could put enough airplanes in the air at any given time to block a concentrated attack by a major air force operating from nearby land bases.

Conversely, if the defense were to send out a superior number of aircraft carriers, and these carriers were deployed under the cover of friendly land-based airpower, the carriers could project aircraft outward so as to be able to keep the offense from even reaching mid-ocean. Of course, control of the air above the sea also helps a country's own submarines fight underwater without having to worry about threats from enemy aircraft. Naval forces, subsurface, surface, and air, have always been mutually supportive.

Thus we conclude that naval bastions have always made sense, but that the recent extension in the range of sensors and weapons has increased their potential size and effectiveness. At any rate, the lethality of modern naval forces is such that no ship carrying troops or cargo would venture into the battle area, or possibly even out of port, before the battle for control of the sea was decided.

Modern technology has also radically expanded the geographic scope of another classic naval mission: attacking the enemy's shore. Before the invention of gunpowder, navies could batter enemy shores only by landing raiding parties or, occasionally, by shooting flaming arrows into coastal installations. The Byzantine Empire even used to squirt flaming oil at enemy ships and shore defenses: "Greek fire." Since the sixteenth century, naval guns have allowed ships to pound the enemy shore from ever farther away, with ever greater accuracy and effect. American battleships of the Iowa class, the Japanese *Yamato,* and the German *Bismarck* could hurl twenty-seven hundred-pound shells twenty miles with the accuracy of a dive-bomber. Thus, they could support friendly troops ashore or pulverize an enemy port. In World War II, the carrier-borne airplane extended the range of naval destructiveness beyond the horizon. In the years since, cruise missiles and ballistic missiles carried by ships and submarines have become capable of inflicting major damage from thousands of miles away. The only thing that such long-range weapons cannot do is change their targets rapidly enough to keep up with an evolving military situation. But rapid advances in communications may soon enable a commander looking at a hostile shore through the eyes of small pilotless aircraft or satellites to "call in" and direct fire from faraway ballistic missiles just as his predecessors in World War II used to "call in" fire from battleships, with words like, "Up 200 yards, right 50, fire for effect!"

Battering the shore from very far away has its advantages. One does not have to brave the hazards of a long voyage, which may include facing enemy submarines and aircraft, nor local defenses, which may include the threat of mines. But today one might ask, if the intention is to pound the enemy with very long-range weapons from a safe distance, why go to sea at all? Why not fire missiles from home soil instead? The answer is that probably the safest place for valuable weapons is under a patch of sea close to home, well protected by tons of water and by secrecy, as well as by both land-based aircraft and submarines. In other words, a naval bastion is the safest of places for long-range missiles.

But firing missiles accurately from the ocean requires knowing precisely the geographic coordinates from which they are being fired. Long ago, the United States developed inertial navigation instruments for submarines that recorded changes in location very precisely. Hence American submarines could fire accurately from anywhere. But such precision is unnecessary if one is firing from presurveyed points on the sea floor. The old Soviet Union focused much of its navy on one mission: to create a bastion on the edge of the Arctic icecap that contained a number of presurveyed points from which its ballistic-missile submarines could fire. This, and the fact that even noisy submarines are very quiet when sitting on the ocean floor, minimized the Soviet navy's technical weaknesses.

Why then should any navy try to take on the U.S. Navy in mid-ocean when it can bombard the U.S. shore from its own home waters and when its own fighting capacity in those waters is incomparably greater than in mid-ocean? And if the range of one's missiles requires that, to strike America, they be launched from hundreds rather than thousands of kilometers off shore, it is easier for a third-world country to carry its missile aboard a freighter, drop its canister into the water, and fire it from there. Being on the surface, the freighter can fix the missile's precise point of departure by using a global positioning system receiver available at any electronics store.

Thus, we see that modern technology, by expanding the geographic scope of naval operations, has blurred the traditional distinctions between them. The fate of blockades and shore bombardments may be decided in naval engagements thousands of miles away from the places concerned.

Technology has also heightened the importance of that least glamorous but perennially important naval operation: mining. The purpose of mining is not so much to sink ships as it is to close narrow waterways. That is why mining, although it is usually done secretly and often by submarine, is almost always announced. Often the announcement exaggerates the extent of the mining. For example, during the Civil War Adm. David Farragut entered Mobile Bay despite the well-advertised presence of mines, yelling "damn the torpedoes [mines], full speed ahead" because he suspected the minefield was thin enough to warrant the risk of going through it. Nowadays, minefields are more deadly. The oldest mines would explode only on contact. World War II's mines would detonate when they sensed the sound, pressure, or magnetic influence of a ship. Newer mines release homing torpedoes, hence they are deadly as far out as their sensors can hear and their torpedoes can travel—a range far greater than that of any explosive.

Clearing mines, usually by exploding them, is always dangerous, time consuming, and potentially incomplete. Nowadays, of course, there is always the further danger that the mines may be nuclear. These, whether real or bluff, can cause unprecedented problems. After all, if an enemy claims to have mined the entrance to a port with multimegaton bombs, one obviously cannot clear them by exploding them. What if the enemy claims that the mines are also programmed to go off if moved unless deactivated by a coded transmission? Even if divers found the mines, they could do nothing. Nuclear mines, then, raise the prospect of bottling up enemy nuclear submarines, and indeed whole navies, in port.

Aerospace Operations

Should air forces be considered in the same terms as armies and navies or should they be considered mere servants of ground and naval operations? This question is not about whether airpower can make a decisive difference in battle. Of course it can. Everyone also recognizes that some important battles, for example, the Battle of Britain in 1940, have taken place almost entirely in the air. No one doubts the usefulness of interceptor fighters, fighter-bombers, air transports, and long-range bombers. Rather, the question is whether or not, as airpower theorists of the 1920s (Giulio Douhet) and the 1950s (Curtis LeMay) believed, bombing the enemy's homeland can be the decisive tool of warfare.

The old Soviet Union had more military airplanes than the United States, but no air force. Instead, it organized its airplanes according to function, making sure that every kind of military operation would design, purchase, and operate the kinds of airplanes it needed. Hence its fighter-bombers and air-superiority fighters, helicopters, indeed all aircraft that served the army, belonged to "frontal aviation." The *Protivovozdushnoya Obrona* (PVO) contained air defense interceptors, associated radar complexes, surface-to-air missiles, antiballistic missiles, and space weapons—everything for defending the homeland. The "long-range aviation" and the "strategic rocket forces" were a kind of centrally directed, long-range artillery. Soviet military thought gave much importance to this latter function. But—and this is the point—Soviet military thought did not see strikes by long-range weapons as a principle around which to organize all air operations, much less all military operations

Because the "airpower theory" came into vogue in the United States during World War II, the United States has an air force that controls most of the nation's fixed-wing military aircraft that do not fly off ships or exist specifically to attack submarines. (The U.S. Army proclaims that it has more aircraft than the Air Force. But these are mostly helicopters.) Indeed, a bureaucratic fight between the Navy and the Air Force in 1947 resulted in the United States having no shore-based naval bombers. The centerpiece of the U.S. Air Force is the old Strategic Air Command, which controls both bombers and intercontinental missiles, and which is supposed to be America's principal sword. So, nominally, America's use of airplanes is very much as the airpower theorists thought. Reality has become increasingly closer to the old Soviet model.

Let us then begin by considering air defenses, which include various kinds of radars for detecting and tracking aircraft and cruise missiles, as well as the interceptor aircraft and various kinds of interceptor missiles used to shoot them down. Radar waves travel in straight lines. So, when airplanes fly high (say above twenty-five thousand feet), as they must in order to conserve fuel on long flights, they come into view of air-search radars two hundred or more miles away. Since such radars are usually set on the periphery of countries, on outlying islands, or, in battle, as far forward as possible, the planes will be evident to the defense many minutes (perhaps hours) before they reach the target. To kill the planes, the defense must keep track of them well enough to direct an interceptor to them. As long as the airplanes are flying high, regardless of how fast they are flying, their speed with regard to the horizon is low, and tracking them is easy.

During World War II, even primitive radars were able to give defenders excellent information about the high-flying airplanes of the day. But tracking bombers was useful only insofar as one's own interceptor aircraft were able to defeat the fighters that accompanied the bombers, since high-altitude bombers were invulnerable to fire from antiaircraft guns on the ground. After World War II, as surface-to-air missiles replaced antiaircraft guns, aircraft designers sought to diminish the vulnerability of bombers and reconnaissance planes by making them fly ever higher. But by 1960 the art of surface-to-air missile interceptors had advanced to the point of making impossible high-altitude penetration of defended areas—except by reconnaissance aircraft that fly so fast that they went beyond the interceptors' horizontal range. During the 1960s and 1970s attack aircraft of all kinds were designed to fly low in order to achieve very high speeds relative to the horizon and thus minimize both the time that radars would have to gather information and the distance at which they could do it. Airplanes also began to be equipped with short-range attack missiles (SRAMS), designed to fly ahead and destroy radars in the airplanes' path. Later, airplanes began to carry low-flying cruise missiles, small and specially shaped to be harder for radars to detect. In the 1980s long-range attack and bomber aircraft switched more and more from carrying bombs that are to be dropped to carrying cruise missiles that can be launched. Aircraft and cruise missiles were also equipped with electronic countermeasures to spoof defensive radars.

The response of air defenses to this trend was to equip radar with the ability to undermine spoofing by hopping from frequency to frequency, to increase the number of radars, and above all to interconnect them so that central computers can use many small glimpses to build a comprehensive picture of what is happening. In addition, radars were developed to be carried on patrol aircraft (AWACS) and to be set on high places that are able to look down and pick airplanes and cruise missiles out of the clutter of radar waves bouncing back from the ground. Interceptor aircraft have also been equipped with these "Look down, shoot down" radars. As a result, modern air defenses can cover the air from treetop level to the edges of the atmosphere. This is not to say that air operations are obsolete. But any and every airplane in combat has to be equipped to try to fool radars with countermeasures and counter-countermeasures. The simplest involve sending back radar waves in forms that cancel out the ones incoming. Devices that derive from this contest are available in electronics stores to ordinary citizens who seek to prevent police radars from gauging their cars' true speed.

Beginning in the 1980s, American aircraft designers sought to leapfrog this contest by applying a principle first discovered by German designers in 1944, namely that aircraft shaped in certain ways tend to scatter radar waves away from their source. Countless tests perfected shapes. Others perfected radar-absorbent materials and paints. The result was the "stealth" fighter, the F-117, and the "stealth" bomber, the B-2. Of course, nothing is perfect. It is impossible to scatter or absorb radar waves from any and all angles. Hence "stealth" aircraft are truly stealthy when mission planners know where enemy radars are and bring the aircraft past them over courses that maximize stealth. If enemy radars are mobile and mission planners don't know where they are, the radars can be switched on suddenly and catch the stealth plane from a nonstealthy angle. When that happens, the stealth plane's lack of speed makes it a sitting duck. This is how Serbians destroyed a U.S. F-117 during the Kosovo War of 1999. Our point is that while modern air defenses can be spoofed here and there for brief moments, they have ended the age when bombers could roam the enemy's country at will.

The job of frontal aviation is to keep the enemy under a man-made firestorm while one's own troops can look up at the sky unafraid. Frontal aviation must also operate the elaborate airborne reconnaissance and signal collection system that allows its artillery and aircraft to find their targets. The job of a fighter-bomber, also known as an attack aircraft, is to carry bombs or short-range cruise missiles over the battlefield "low and slow" enough so that the pilot can see where to fire them, yet fast enough so that it can come in and get out quickly enough to evade enemy antiaircraft defenses. The 1991 Gulf War produced a near perfect example of the proper use of U.S. tactical (the Russians said frontal) aviation. After cruise missiles and low-flying planes and helicopters had eliminated Iraqi air defenses and air superiority fighters had frightened Iraqi pilots out of the air, U.S. fighter-bombers freely struck enemy units toward which U.S. tanks were heading, while the tanks were yet out of range. They silenced enemy artillery. Then as the tanks came into range, cannon and machine guns on helicopters kept the enemy's heads down. As the helicopters left, enemy soldiers looked up to see the muzzles of U.S. tanks and infantry. That is how it is supposed to work, tactically.

How effective is frontal aviation strategically? One limit case is Vietnam. The United States enjoyed a monopoly of airpower over South Vietnam. Enemy soldiers could not concentrate for more than a few minutes without having an American airplane shooting at them. True, the United States lost some aircraft when it bombed. But the United States could choose to bomb any place in the country at any time. This was a potentially decisive advantage. Surely, had it been available in April 1975, North Vietnam would not have been able to drive three main columns totaling some quarter of a million men into the heart of South Vietnam. Nevertheless, the United States never even tried to use this superiority as part of a plan to defeat North Vietnam. There was no such plan. U.S. officials would not consider any such plan. They regarded such consideration as dangerous in and of itself.[6] Consequently, this monopoly of airpower over the front served only to hold off disaster.

Indeed, between 1962 and 1973 the United States lost 3,706 fixed-wing airplanes and 4,866 helicopters over Indochina.[7] The fundamental reason so little was purchased at such great cost is that this airpower was not part of a success-oriented military plan involving other kinds of forces. Take the air war against North Vietnam. Again and again, the fighter-bombers would clear away a set of surface-to-air missiles and bunkers, and lose a few planes doing so. But no American ground force would move through the breach. So, in a few weeks the enemy would rebuild the defenses, and the Americans would lose a few more planes knocking them out. Air strikes also avoided North Vietnam's leadership. They spared the country's vital infrastructure, including the dams on the Red River, without which much of Hanoi would have washed away. There also was no air and sea blockade of North Vietnam. This kind of air war did not shake the resolve of North Vietnam's leaders. It reassured them. The lesson here is that control of the air, unlike control of the ground, guarantees nothing and means next to nothing unless it is part of a plan to achieve something on the ground.

Another illustration of the function of frontal aviation was the U.S. plan for aerial follow-on-forces attack (FOFA) on the central front in Europe. The United States advertised that if superior Soviet ground forces attacked across the inter-German border, its arguably superior fighter-bombers would fly deep into East Germany and Poland and, using "smart" munitions, attack the Soviet tanks and supplies moving up to the front. But if the Soviet Union feared that a U.S. FOFA could put a serious crimp in its projected attack across the inter-German border, why would it not precede any invasion with a ballistic-missile attack on the undefended bases of U.S. fighter-bombers in Europe? All of this is to say that air superiority over a front does not make up for the deficiency of the rest of one's forces on that front, does not counterbalance the advantages that the enemy gains by seizing the initiative, and does not make up for deficiencies in overall strategy.

Now consider modern long-range or "heavy" bombers. The nature of their task differs from that of frontal aviation in that they must traverse considerable hostile territory to reach their targets. Heavy bombers, then, could have serious problems with air defenses—providing such defenses happen to be there.

For example, in the 1950s and early 1960s the United States built a formidable air-defense system against a possible Soviet attack. Eighty-one large radars made up the Distant Early Warning (DEW) line across the Arctic. Another 280 radars comprised the Pinetree Line across northern Canada and backed up the DEW line. Seaward approaches were covered by radars set on oil-drilling platforms and by 137 radar-picket ships. Behind these radars stood 2,612 interceptor fighters, 274 Nike surface-to-air missile batteries, and 439 long-range nuclear-tipped Bomarc interceptor cruise missiles. If the Soviet Union had launched its two-hundred-odd Bear and Bison bombers against this network, it is entirely possible that none would have gotten through. It is not surprising, then, that by 1959 the Soviet Union stopped building new heavy bombers. But in 1964 the United States began to dismantle its air-defense system. By 1974 it was gone. Not surprisingly, in 1976 the Soviet Union went back into the heavy-bomber business with its Backfire and later its Blackjack models.

If a long-range bomber does not have to face serious air defenses it can be an effective, flexible weapon, roaming enemy territory, destroying mobile military forces, nipping military preparations in the bud, and inflicting punishment at will. In addition, the long-range bomber can be very useful against enemy bases that may be in the process of being built in faraway places and that are not yet fully defended.

Against well-prepared defenses, however, a force of heavy bombers really has only one reasonable choice: to try to shoot its way to the target by progressively attacking the radars, surface-to-air missiles, and interceptor airfields in its path. Of course, this option entails losses for the bomber force. In a country with many targets covered by a network of air defenses it is not clear whether the bombers or the defenses would run out first. *But more important for our understanding, using heavy bombers in this way in fact reduces their role to that of frontal aviation.*

Finally, consider airlift operations. Nowadays it is possible to drive tanks and trucks directly into and out of wide-body aircraft. Since such aircraft are expensive, no nation has enough of them to land a division of fifteen thousand men, three hundred tanks, and one thousand trucks onto a given airfield in an hour. Nevertheless, modern airlift operations can be strategically significant. The Soviet Union, for example, began its invasion of Afghanistan in 1979 by sending a regiment of special troops via four heavy-lift cargo planes into Bagram Airfield outside of Kabul on 3 December 1979. After the troops had secured the airfield, the big aircraft shuttled in a division. Nearly all of the nearly eight million Americans who went in and out of the Vietnam theater of operations between 1965 and 1973 did so by air. In 1973 Israel was able to recover from the losses suffered from the Arabs' attack during Yom Kippur because the United States was willing and able to load tanks, trucks, antitank missiles, ammunition, and spare parts onto virtually every available heavy-lift aircraft and fly them to Israel.

This shuttle, like the Soviet shuttle of material to Egypt and Syria, did not have to take into account possible military opposition. But, of course, in full-scale war one of the objectives of any military force would be to thwart its opponent's attempts to outflank it by airlift. Hence, during full-scale war, airlifts would likely take place only under fighter escort and they would only go into areas that had been reasonably well secured. This would involve capturing airfields along the route for use by one's own fighters and denying them to enemy fighters. All of this is to say that, airpower theorists notwithstanding, air operations are the operations of war that should be most integrated with other kinds of operations.

7

MILITARY OPERATIONS IN THE NUCLEAR AGE

> The [American] planners seem to care less about
> what happens after the buttons are pressed than
> they do about looking presentable before the event.
> —HERMAN KAHN
> *On Thermonuclear War*

> Nuclear weapons have a decisive significance on the
> change in the methods of attack and on the employ-
> ment of other means of destruction: They caused a
> reduction in their density especially of artillery.
> —A. A. SIDORENKO
> *The Offensive*

WHEN THE FIRST atom bomb lit up the sky over Trinity, New Mexico, 16 July 1945, it raised a question that has troubled Americans ever since: what should we do with it? In 1945 the bomb was welcomed as a life saver (for Americans). During the Cold War it was accepted uneasily as a necessity, and as the repository of millennialist hopes and fears. Since the Soviet empire's demise, many have wished it could be disinvented. But it could not be. In the twenty-first century, Americans are beginning to come to grips with the real prospect of nuclear war.

In 1945 the United States faced the prospect of suffering a million more casualties to finish the war against Japan by conventional warfare. How could the bomb help? The United States planned to use the bomb to shock and overawe the Japanese out of their resolve to resist invasion. Could that be done best by dropping it on a military installation or on a Japanese city? If the United States dropped the bomb on ships in Tokyo Bay, the limitations on the bomb's power and the inaccuracy of the parachute drop from the B-29 might well have left every ship afloat. Army bases, for their part, had air-raid shelters, which would surely cut down casualties. On the other hand, if dropped anywhere on a warm-weather city made up of paper-walled houses, the bomb could not help but have an impressive effect. Alas, the policy of destroying cities was well established by September 1945. Certainly there was no moral difference between using the atom bomb or incendiary bombs to destroy cities. So Hiroshima and Nagasaki were hit.

Though other air raids had been more destructive, surely the atom bomb's novelty was impressive. But just as surely Japan was being starved by blockade, and had been asking to surrender since April 1945, if the United States would only spare the emperor. In July and August the United States hinted that it would. Then came the bombs. It is impossible to know whether they caused the surrender that quickly ensued.

Immediately, the debate over nuclear weapons erupted full grown into terms that have not changed much in the subsequent half century. Only in the 1990s was there substantial change.

The debate's starting point was a little book edited by Bernard Brodie within weeks of Hiroshima, *The Absolute Weapon*.[1] The book took both sides. It held that nuclear bombs could be used in the same way as other kinds of bombs. Although nukes would be more effective, and also more expensive, the logic of nuclear war would be the same as that of other wars: to strike the enemy's bombers and other armed forces on the ground and to shoot down as many as possible in flight, while protecting one's own airfields and other targets with concrete, sandbags, etc. The book made it clear that the power of nuclear weapons did not override the fact that their effect would depend on how they would be used and on the countermeasures the enemy would take.

But the book's other, intoxicating side has had a more profound effect. This side of the book assumed that the power of the bomb was infinite, indeed "absolute," and that cities would be the main targets. One bomb could destroy a city. Hence, it would make no difference whether one side had two thousand bombs or six thousand. Four years before the Soviet Union tested its atom bomb, before intercontinental aircraft existed, at a time when intercontinental missiles were thought impossible, the book postulated that the United States and the Soviet Union would have the power to destroy one another while lacking the ability to protect them-selves, and that this situation would never, ever change. Thus, nuclear weapons would be used by not being used. In this role they could estab-lish a perpetual peace that would overshadow ideology and indeed all other sources of human enmity. Why? Because fear of nuclear attack would "never be low." The silent postulate was that everyone in the world would fear nuclear weapons equally. Just as Thomas Hobbes had postulated that equal fear of death made all men equal, Brodie thought that fear of death by nuclear weapons would do that most surely.

Theory aside, nuclear weapons seemed to solve a pressing practical postwar problem: how the United States, eager to get back to the pleasures of peace, could defend much of the world against a Soviet military superior in numbers and surely far more willing to suffer casualties.[2] Presidents Truman and Eisenhower quickly concluded that if the United States were to attempt to play a global role using only conventional weapons, it would have to keep perhaps seven million men under arms, militarize society, and perhaps bankrupt itself. But nuclear weapons would allow a much smaller U.S. force to do the job because they provided "a bigger bang for the buck." So, although U.S. presidents from the beginning spoke loudly about putting the nuclear genie back into the bottle, they put the genie to work as fast as they could. But it wasn't easy.

In 1947, President Truman asked the Joint Chiefs of Staff how the United States could use atom bombs to stop a Soviet invasion of Europe. Answering that question had a sobering effect. To stop a three- or four-million-man army, spread out over hundreds of thousands of square miles would require hundreds, if not thousands, of Hiroshima-size bombs (each yielding the equivalent of twenty thousand tons of TNT, or twenty KT). Each would kill troops and destroy trucks and perhaps tanks in a four-square-mile area, but each would have to be delivered to just the right place at the right time in a rapidly changing military situation. The United States had only some twenty atom bombs at the time, each of which strained the capacity of a B-29.[3] Even if the United States multiplied that number, what would be the chances of getting a B-29 to the right places through undiminished Soviet fighter screens? So the conclusion was that if the United States were to rely on nuclear weapons to make up for its unwillingness to put millions of young American lives on the line around the world, it would have to make its nuclear weapons small enough to be delivered by fighter-bombers and even by artillery. It would have to increase the accuracy and reliability of delivery systems. It would also have to build these new warheads and delivery systems by the thousands.

But wasn't there a shortcut? Couldn't the United States just "nuke" Moscow in retaliation for a Soviet invasion of Europe? Doing that would not stop the invasion, but threatening it might deter the Soviet Union from the undertaking.[4] And besides, how better to fight the Russian hordes than through nuclear-strategic bombing? This was the idea behind Secretary of State John Foster Dulles's 1954 announcement that the United States would retaliate against Soviet aggression anywhere by striking "massively at times and places of our own choosing." But even this alternative required hundreds if not thousands of bombs. After all, one bomb would not affect the one hundred square miles of brick and concrete that was Moscow at the time the way it had affected ten square miles of papier-mâché Hiroshima. Also, penetrating thousands of miles of undefeated Soviet territory would be a different proposition than sending a lone B-29 to intrude a few miles from the sea over prostrate Japan. So the United States had to build a whole infrastructure for long-distance nuclear strategic bombing as well as for battlefield use of nuclear weapons.

Before looking at the preparations that the United States, the Soviet Union, and lesser powers have made for nuclear operations, it is necessary to make two points. First, the success of nuclear operations depends far more on the technology of delivery systems, on the defenses against the delivery systems, and on strategy than it does on the technology of nuclear weapons themselves. There is no factual basis for the widespread view that weapons research has aimed at producing weapons with ever bigger bangs. Almost the reverse is true, because for good or ill, the purpose of any and all military operations is not to destroy but to conquer. Hence, it can be argued that the development of the microprocessor, which is at the heart of delivery system technology, and not the nuclear bomb, is the great development of our time. The development of more reliable and more accurate means of delivering nuclear weapons has resulted in increasing the practical choices available to commanders who are equipped with them.

Second, these technical developments paralleled the growing nonsense of political rhetoric about nuclear weapons. According to that rhetoric, mankind's only choice was whether to "push the button" and perish, or to live happily ever after. At the same time, the military doctrines of states possessing nuclear weapons increasingly regarded nuclear weapons, their delivery systems, and the defenses against them as practical problems rather than as objects of millennialist fear or hope. The consequence of these conflicting tendencies is that states that are influenced by political rhetoric—chiefly the United States—pursued policies in preparation for nuclear operations that are both schizophrenic and fitful.

Let us now look at preparations for nuclear operations during the classical period, that is, before the collapse of the Soviet empire in 1989–91.

Ground Operations

Between the 1960s and the 1990s nuclear weapons were thoroughly integrated into the ground operations of the United States, the Soviet Union, Britain, and France. The basic weapon was the nuclear artillery round. The U.S. Army had some four thousand of these munitions in Europe alone, mostly for 105- and 155-mm guns and as munitions for fighter-bomber aircraft. The range of the guns is between ten and twenty miles, and the yield of the warhead is about one kiloton—enough to disable, though not necessarily destroy, unprotected ground forces within perhaps one thousand feet of where the warhead hits.[5] Then there are short-range, unguided rockets, like the Army's Lance or the Soviet Free Rocket Over Ground (FROG). They can hit targets thirty to seventy miles away with warheads from twenty to one hundred kilotons. There are also longer-range battlefield missiles like the Soviet SS-21 and 23, the French Pluton, and the American Pershing IA, which can carry warheads in the hundreds of kilotons up to five hundred miles away.[6] In addition, of course, modern fighter-bombers can carry nuclear bombs all over the battlefield.

The art of using such devices consists of finding worthwhile targets, hitting them quickly before they move, disperse, or hit back, and then exploiting the holes left in the enemy's order of battle. The scarcity and cost of nuclear munitions demand that they not be wasted. So, even after a commander has received authorization to use them, he must make sure that there are enough enemy troops, tanks, trucks, supplies, and so forth, close enough together to make expending a nuke worthwhile. The enemy, however, is not likely to bunch up and provide an inviting target unless he has the intention of using his own nukes to strike any place from where he thinks the same might be fired at him. By the same token, one is likely to regard an enemy unit thought to be armed with nukes as ipso facto a good target, no matter how small the unit. Hence, much depends on the intelligence, judgment, and speed of both sides.

On the other hand, any target at all is a good target for nukes if one's own plan calls for ensuring a breakthrough at a particular place. A barrage of nuclear explosives will clear a path, providing that one's own troops are ready with the anticontamination suits and the equipment necessary for traversing temporarily radioactive areas. All of this is to say that the nuclear battlefield is likely to be more chaotic than other kinds of battlefields, if only because of morale. But the character of nuclear weapons ensures that the range at which engagements take place is greater than in the past and that there will be a greater premium than ever on shooting first and on imposing one's own agenda onto the battle.

Nuclear weapons increased the importance of mines and of being dug in. Land mines, as always, are useful for channeling enemy movement, and most useful when mountains already do the channeling. Hence, the most secure part of the NATO front was the Soviet-Turkish border—mountain country full of passes and canyons where big nuclear mines were buried. Even after the Soviet Union's demise, Turkey kept them mined against Russia, Turkey's ancestral enemy. Switzerland's passes are also mined, but not with nuclear weapons. Perhaps their narrowness makes up for the mines' lack of yield.

Radiation, the peculiar characteristic of nuclear weapons, gives a definite advantage to those who are protected by yards of earth or concrete over those who are protected by inches of armor. Hence, in purely ground combat, the nuke tends to restore the kind of advantage to the defense that existed before the tank made it possible to cross fields of fire. In the 1970s, this fact led NATO to procure nukes optimized to emit more penetrating neutrons and fewer blast-producing X-rays. Since neutrons are stopped only by the atomic nuclei of the material they encounter, they travel far through the atmosphere and are stopped only by sheer mass. If the mass they connect with is human tissue, they kill. Hence, the occupants of a tank that had survived the blast of an enhanced-neutron weapon would be killed by its radiation, which penetrates the inches of the tank's armor. But that same radiation would not affect people nearby who happened to be in cellars or bunkers because the neutrons would likely be stopped by the nuclei of several feet of concrete or earth before reaching the dug-in defenders. Moreover, the reduced-blast feature of this "neutron bomb" tends to spare not just cellars and bunkers, but also buildings. So even more than other nuclear weapons, the enhanced-neutron bomb tends to favor those in ground combat who have taken refuge underground, meaning those who are not attacking. It is an effective defensive weapon. Conversely, the nuclear weapon of choice for ground attackers would emphasize blast and deemphasize radiation.

The lethality of any and all nuclear weapons places any but the most heavily bunkered of fixed military facilities at an enormous disadvantage. Airfields, command centers, supply dumps, nuclear weapons storage sites, and above all, fixed missile launchers are sitting ducks for any attacker armed with long-range, nuclear-tipped ballistic missiles—unless these installations are defended by antimissile devices or made mobile or both. The ability of nuclear-tipped ballistic missiles to destroy much of the defender's infrastructure and thus prejudice the outcome of a war in its opening minutes is an enormous incentive to shoot first.

Naval Operations

Nuclear weapons make a big difference in naval operations. Ships are inherently tough. The water they ride on is an excellent shock absorber. They really are hard to sink. During World War II, dozens of direct hits were necessary to sink aircraft carriers or battleships. Even with nuclear weapons, a blast must be fairly close to a ship in order to sink it. Thus, from the beginning of the nuclear age there has been incentive to put nuclear explosives on torpedoes and in depth bombs, as well as on aerial bombs and cruise missiles aimed at ships. The development of technology in recent years has increased this incentive. For example, despite the fact that sea-skimming cruise missiles give ships only a few seconds' warning, nowadays radar-controlled Gatling guns can put up a wall of bullets that will stop the cruise missile a few hundred yards from the ship. This can put conventionally armed antiship cruise missiles out of business. Only if the cruise missile is carrying a nuclear explosive will it stand a chance of having any effect at all.[7] Moreover, techniques for detecting naval targets at longer distances (say, eight hundred miles) are most useful only if there are means of striking those targets quickly. Ballistic missiles can indeed be programmed to hit close enough to moving fleets to damage them—providing they are armed with high-yield nuclear weapons. Similarly, a wave of naval bombers poses threats of different magnitudes to a fleet depending on whether their air-launched cruise missiles are armed with conventional or nuclear weapons. In addition, of course, navies can carry out their traditional mission of striking enemy shores much more effectively if their aircraft, guns, and missiles are armed with nuclear weapons.

The U.S. Navy, however, while it embraced nuclear weapons wholeheartedly for shore-strike missions, prepared to carry out sea-control missions almost as if nuclear weapons had never been invented. This may be because the existence of nuclear weapons made it more difficult for any navy to give equal weight to both missions and thus sharpened the conflict between the two.

During World War II, the Navy's carrier aircraft and heavy guns inflicted arguably as much military damage on the enemy in the Pacific theater as did Army Air Corps planes. As we have already seen, after World War II, the Navy and the Air Force vied for the prestige and the budget shares that went along with the job of delivering nuclear weapons on the Soviet Union. Of course, in the 1950s and 1960s it would have been difficult to argue that the United States needed modern attack aircraft carriers to protect the shores of the United States when the Soviet navy posed no threat to U.S. control of the world's oceans, much less to American shores. Nevertheless, geography alone should have been enough to convince the United States to maintain the finest possible capacity in this field. The Navy thus came to sell—and so to regard—the aircraft carrier primarily as something for the glamorous offensive job of striking the enemy shore. But even in the 1960s, carriers could expect to get close to a well-guarded Soviet shore only if Soviet shore defenses, both submarines and aircraft, were not armed with nuclear weapons—which of course they were.

Had the U.S. Navy sincerely asked itself, as apparently the Soviet navy had done, how nuclear weapons could be used in sea-control operations, it probably would have concluded (as did the Soviet navy) that it is far easier to use nuclear weapons at sea when defending the ocean approaches to a continent than when trying to force one's way into enemy waters.

This is not to deny that nuclear weapons can be used offensively at sea. The U.S. Navy had nuclear weapons for some of its antiship, antiaircraft, and antisubmarine missiles. Also, the Navy was well aware that the Russian land mass is vulnerable to having its navy shut in by nuclear mining, and the United States had the quiet submarines necessary for mining. Still, none of this was as glamorous as five-carrier battle groups shooting their way into the Norwegian Sea. This shore strike mission was where the Navy's heart—and budget—was during the Cold War. Yet the U.S. Navy never seriously considered how such a carrier armada would deal with literally hundreds of nuclear-tipped cruise missiles and ballistic missiles attacking it at roughly the same time. Nor, subsequently did it think this way about naval operations near a hostile Chinese shore.

In short, to think seriously about the role of nuclear weapons in sea control (against an otherwise undefeated enemy) is to think in terms of naval bastions and of expanding those bastions methodically by surface, air, and submarine units working together. It also means operating outside the bastions only with relatively cheap platforms designed to deliver nuclear weapons to enemy ships. But it has never been U.S. policy to think this way about sea control.

Air Operations

If during World War II Germany or Japan had had nuclear-armed cruise missiles capable of flying into the U.S. thousand-bomber raids, those raids would never have been mounted. After the war, American planners feared that the Soviet Union might mount such raids on America. So by the 1950s the United States had built some sixteen hundred U.S. nuclear-tipped "Genie" cruise missiles. But the problem they were designed to solve never materialized. The bombers of the fifties, carrying nuclear weapons, were fewer in number than a decade earlier, and would not travel in big formations. By the fifties, then, nuclear warheads on air-defense cruise missiles and rockets had an entirely different purpose, to hedge against inaccuracy. In some cases (such as the Nike), the hedge probably was not needed, but in other cases (such as the notoriously unreliable Terrier naval air-defense missile), it surely was. But by the 1970s, advances in guidance technology had shifted the debate from whether or not the interceptor should carry a nuclear or a conventional explosive to whether or not the interceptor should carry any explosive at all, given that it might be accurate enough to smash directly into the target. The swift advance of radar and data-processing technology made destroying large numbers of attacking aircraft a function of instruments that can track many of them simultaneously and direct interceptors to them.

The only surface-to-air mission in which nuclear explosives remained useful (though not for long) was the medium-to-low altitude interception of reentering ballistic-missile warheads. We will consider this in greater detail below.

The final thing to be said about the effect of nuclear weapons on air operations is that all modern military aircraft have been "hardened" to some extent to operate in a nuclear environment. That means chiefly that all-important electronic navigation, communications, and target-finding instruments have been shielded against the electromagnetic pulse and other effects of nuclear explosions. For some aircraft, such as bombers whose airfields are likely targets of ballistic missiles, this is essential. How effective the hardening turns out to be depends on a variety of factors, not least of which is how fast the airplane can escape the zone likely to be hit by a nuclear explosion.

"Strategic" Bombing

The most talked about aspect of nuclear operations is long-range bombing. Since about 1960, however, discussion of this subject has taken place almost exclusively in terms of the ballistic missiles that largely replaced airplanes (as airplanes had supplanted artillery) as the chief means of long-range bombardment. We will look at the discussion from this perspective as well as from the vantage point of the struggle over U.S. strategic policy, with occasional glances at the Soviet side of things.

By the mid-1950s the United States had transformed its nuclear poverty of 1947 into nuclear plenty. The United States had some five thousand hydrogen bombs for its fleet of B-47 and B-52 jet bombers. The United States had more bombs than it had intelligence about places to drop them. If "the balloon went up," so the saying went, the United States would disgorge its arsenal on everything of value in the Soviet Union, on what the jargon of the day called an "optimum mix" of both civilian and military targets. But beginning in 1957, photographs from U-2 intelligence aircraft showed the United States for the first time how big and spread out the Soviet strategic forces were and served to identify thousands of important military targets. By this time also, the Soviet Union was building ballistic missiles that could hit the United States, leapfrogging American air defenses. Literally no one questioned the need to hit Soviet missile-launching pads. The simultaneous increase in knowledge and in the threat caused a shift toward targeting more military and fewer civilian installations. "Optimum mix" targeting had been a compromise between the urge to eradicate communism physically while punishing the Soviet Union for aggression, and the need to destroy the Soviet Union's means of doing harm to the United States and its allies. The compromise had been easy to make because there had been lots of American bombs and little detailed information about the places in the Soviet Union where it might be good to drop them. But as the years brought more information, demand increased for "covering" this and that military target, and targeting became more thoughtfully oriented toward the Soviet military arsenal.

By 1959 Secretary of Defense Thomas Gates had done away with the ambiguity. The United States would bomb primarily with the intention of defeating the Soviet military—this was counterforce targeting. By the time President Kennedy and Secretary of Defense Robert McNamara came into office in 1961, the third generation of U.S. ballistic missiles, the land-based Minuteman and the submarine-launched Polaris, were in production. They had not been designed specifically for either counterforce or city bombings, but rather had been made as powerful and as accurate as the technology of the day allowed. Thus, at the time of the Cuban Missile Crisis of October 1962, the United States, using only a portion of its missile force, could have devastated the Soviet Union's few, highly vulnerable missile-launching pads, as well as much of its long-range aviation.

In 1963, however, the United States came up against a choice that did not fully resolve until after the Soviet empire had passed away and a new set of problems had developed. The Soviet Union had begun to put its late second-generation SS-8 ICBMs into underground silos. In order to strike them, the United States would have had to increase its own missiles' combination of nuclear yield and accuracy. In 1963 and 1964 it was clear that unless the United States did that or abandoned its strategy of 1959 through 1962, and its standard for judging forces, it would soon be underarmed. The Kennedy administration chose not to build counterforce missiles but rather to switch both the strategy and the standard. Henceforth, the United States would target the Soviet population and shape its weapons with the objective of killing people. The Kennedy administration did this for a variety of reasons. Among them was the millennialist hope that major war could be exorcised forever by the threat of mutual suicide. But there was also an immediate, concrete disinclination to keep pace with changing conditions by continually innovating weaponry. The Soviets could change both their missiles and their basing modes ad infinitum, so went the reasoning. But they could not remove their cities from under America's nuclear Damocles' sword. Thus, by focusing U.S. strategy on threatening the destruction of Soviet civil society, U.S. nuclear forces would remain adequate forever *regardless of what the Soviets did.* According to this new standard, the United States was seriously overarmed. Of course fiddling with definitions independent of the realities to which they refer is the very definition of solipsism.

What did it mean to destroy Soviet society? Robert McNamara defined it as destroying 25 percent of the Soviet Union's population and 50 percent of its industry.[8] He arrived at those figures by examining the demographics of the Soviet Union. According to McNamara, after expending four hundred "megaton equivalents" on perhaps as many targets, the United States would be running into the "flat of the curve." That is, any additional nuclear weapons and missiles expended would cost more to manufacture, keep, and launch than the people they would kill and the factories they would wreck were worth. Of course, this entire thought process rested on—indeed consisted exclusively of—his own arbitrary assumptions about the value of human life and on the assumption, first formulated by Brodie, that all mankind shared them.[9]

This targeting strategy raised practical questions. Just what would this "destroyed" Soviet Union be able to do? One thing it could surely do would be to launch its untouched missiles at the United States, whose denser demographic distribution would guarantee a higher percentage of fatalities. McNamara and the national security adviser, McGeorge Bundy, and a whole generation of the U.S. foreign defense policy establishment did not mind that. Indeed, they saw the obvious U.S. vulnerability under their strategy as the guarantee that the Soviet Union would recognize that the United States had no intention of ever carrying out any kind of strike. Hence, with mutual assurance of mutual assured destruction (MAD), both would live happily ever after.

The happy ending, however, required that both sides channel advances in missile technology away from the combination of yield and accuracy necessary to destroy hardened silos, and that both sides wholly refrain from developing the means to destroy missiles or warheads in flight. In 1972 many influential Americans believed that the SALT I and ABM treaties guaranteed that both sides would do just that. In 1977–80, when the Soviet Union deployed a fourth generation of ICBMs (the SS-18, 19, and 17) that indubitably possessed those very characteristics, any basis for those expectations collapsed. By the mid-1970s it was difficult to deny that the Soviet Union, using perhaps one-third of its new missiles, could have destroyed nearly all of U.S. land-based missiles, half of the U.S. missile- firing submarines in port at any given time, and most U.S. bombers on the ground. Thus, the Soviet Union could have gone a long way toward protecting itself and winning the war.[10]

Even before the intellectual edifice of MAD had collapsed strategically, it had failed an even more practical test. As U.S. nuclear targeters tried to follow McNamara's guidelines, they could not help noting that *which* quarter of the Soviet population lived or died and *which* half of Soviet industry stood or fell made a big difference in what the Soviet Union could do afterward. After all, although MAD sought to banish the thought that *anything* would ever happen after a nuclear exchange, it was obvious that 175 million surviving Soviets might think of *something*. So targeters argued about which industries were particularly crucial to Soviet recovery, and which workers would have been most difficult to replace. As they did so, they noticed that the Soviet Union had prepared deep, hardened shelters for precisely such industries and workers. Hence, the U.S. targeters had to conclude that the missile technologies required to do a thorough antirecovery job were not so different from those required to do the counterforce job.

Another thread of logic unraveled MAD. If the purpose of MAD is to deter war by threatening valuable things, MAD works best if we threatened the things and people the Soviet dictators valued most. But satellite photographs showed unmistakably that the things the Soviet leadership most valued and most sought to protect from nuclear attack—other than themselves—were military. Hence, even if one had not thought of fighting a war, but merely wanted to deter the Soviets, one would have had to have the ability to threaten the Soviet strategic rocket forces and long-range aviation. In other words, to deter a war, one would need the capacity to fight and win it.[11] This was news only to sophisticates.

The Soviets were never of two minds about targeting. Back in 1961, when primitive SS-7s still relied on inclined launch rails for their azimuth, U.S. satellites photographed the rails, and photo analysts drew lines from the rails over the globe to get an idea of what the Soviets were shooting at. To their surprise, the lines never crossed American cities—always air force bases. This was at a time when technology did not permit the kind of accuracy that would have ensured the success of a missile attack on an air force base. No matter. The Soviets did not want to waste precious nuclear missiles on killing useless people.

Thus, in the late 1970s all these threads of logic led the Carter administration formally to renounce MAD and to announce a new strategy. If the Soviet Union ever attacked, the United States would reply by putting at least one high-quality warhead on every Soviet missile silo. This would deprive the Soviet Union of the accurate reserve force that it would need for a coercive follow-up to its first strike. The prospect of being unable to follow up (and win) would presumably deter the Soviets.

This approach had at least three shortcomings. First, the United States did not yet possess any missiles and warheads of the type that would be required to do this—and that could survive a Soviet first strike. This changed only slowly after 1979. Second, by the mid-1980s the Soviet Union had put the SS-24 and SS-25 mobile missiles into full production, and thus was well on its way to putting all of the missile forces that would not be used up in a first strike out of the reach of American retaliation. Third, Americans faced the prospect of contending with growing Soviet antimissile defenses.

Briefly, Soviet preparations for missile defense consisted of nine huge (two hundred yards by three hundred yards) Pechora-class phased array radars, mostly on the country's periphery. Each of these would "see" incoming warheads from afar, create electronic files for each, predict each trajectory, and sort the files according to the destination of each warhead. The distinctive feature of these Soviet radars is that, unlike American ones of the same kind, they electronically transfer the bundles of files to hundreds of lesser radars around the country, telling each almost exactly where to look. These in turn would guide interceptor missiles to their marks. These lesser radars and interceptor missiles (named respectively Flat Twin and SH-4 to SH-8 later, and SH-11) were in mass production. In addition, the Soviet Union was producing the SA-12 surface-to-air missile system. Mounted on trucks and using data from peripheral radars, each unit of the SA-12 could intercept a small number of warheads coming into its area. Note that very few targets in the world even had more than two warheads assigned to them. Of course, there was also the modernized ABM system that covers the Moscow area with one hundred rapidly reloadable underground interceptor launchers. Because of their relative inaccuracy, Soviet interceptors carried nuclear warheads. What did this all mean?

It is clear that after an initial Soviet attack the United States could not have spread the perhaps twenty-five hundred (mostly submarine-launched) remaining warheads among hundreds of targets with confidence that chosen targets would be hit. No doubt the United States could concentrate its remaining bolts on a few cities, with reasonable hope that some would get through. But at what parts of the cities should it aim? And what good would destroying them do? The Soviet Union never ensured its safety from such an irrational American response. But it reduced any such response to irrationality.

The U.S. government's response to Soviet nuclear superiority and missile defense was a research program called the Strategic Defense Initiative (SDI). But while popular opinion had it that after 1983 SDI gradually rose like a shield to protect America, the reality is that SDI was a decision *not* to build antimissile defenses in the 1980s while researching the possibilities for defenses in the future. The same had been true in the 1970s and would remain be true in 2005. The only realistic question is what antimissile defenses are available at any given time, and what they could do against the threats of that time.

In sum, the United States could have produced mobile surface-to-air interceptor systems accurate enough not to require any warheads at all. High-altitude interception could protect broad swaths of the North American continent. Of course, the United States could have built large phased array radars and the rest of a conventional ABM system much like the

Soviet Union's—but superior because of the significantly better data-processing equipment available in the United States. But optical systems in space would have allowed U.S. antimissile systems to work even better without radars. After 1983, the United States had the option of producing optical systems (originally to have been mounted on high-flying Boeing 767s and subsequently on satellites) that could tell the difference between the thermal characteristics of warheads and decoys in space, track the warheads accurately, and transmit targeting data to antimissile interceptors. Also, finally, since the early 1980s the United States had the option of building space-based chemical lasers that could kill missiles in space from as far away as three thousand kilometers. The United States did not choose to build any antimissile systems at all.

What good would such devices have done? A half dozen space lasers and a few hundred mobile ground-based interceptor units would have so complicated any attack on U.S. strategic forces as to render it unattractive. Perhaps two dozen lasers and, say, a thousand ground-based units would have made such a strike unfeasible and protected the population from stray rounds as well as from the collateral effects of the attack, if ever it had been carried out. More would have done more; fewer, less.

Wars, like all other human contests, are won at particular instants in time with the tools available at the time. Robert McNamara and his followers recoiled at the thought of an open-ended contest for improving strategic weapons and thought that they could freeze for all time an instant in that development. They were wrong. In 1972 the most impressive of McNamara's defenders, Henry Kissinger, asked "What does one do with strategic superiority?"[12] The short answer is, "Whatever one wants to do with it." Preponderance of power in nuclear weapons, perhaps even more than any other kind of military imbalance, is something that casts a shadow even if it is unused. Nuclear superiority "covers" all of one's military-political moves, and smothers the enemy's. In the jargon of the 1960s, "escalation dominance" produces "extended deterrence." The Soviet Union's ability to drastically reduce U.S. strategic forces and to substantially protect itself against the rest could have inhibited the United States from doing anything about a defeat of NATO forces in Europe or from overthrowing a hypothetical Soviet satellite regime that had installed itself in Mexico. On the other hand, the shadow of a serious American missile force backed by U.S. ability to protect itself, its forces, and its allies against Soviet ballistic missiles would have covered U.S. military operations all over the world and perhaps even convinced the subjects of the Soviet empire that they could detach themselves from it with impunity.

But sometimes, rarely, historic international confrontations end, the world is transformed, without military confrontation. Thus it was that in 1989–90 the subjects of the Soviet empire detached themselves from it, the Soviet Union died, and strategic nuclear forces were quite uninvolved. Note, however, that these developments did occur in the context of the nuclear balance as it was. Had the balance tilted more to one side or the other, the weapons might have been involved. Happily, no one will ever know.

Nuclear Weapons Today

Confrontation between America and the Soviet empire obscured the fact that nuclear weapons, like all things that had ever been invented, were becoming commonplace. Whereas U.S. officials (who imagined that all men feared nukes equally) also indulged dreams that the possession of nukes had helped make Soviet dictators into responsible co-stewards of world order and would equally impress anyone else who possessed them with the awesome responsibility, the last quarter of the twentieth century made plain that diverse, ordinary governments would acquire whatever nukes they wanted and would use them as seemed most convenient. As the technologies of nuclear weapons and ballistic missiles improved and spread to smaller countries, preparations for nuclear operations changed somewhat from what they had been during the Cold War. We begin here by describing "third-world nuclear strategies" and end by considering the U.S. response.

The twin notions that "nuclear proliferation" is bad per se and that it can be stopped are apolitical and unhistorical, respectively. Just as the French people have every reason to consider U.S. nuclear weapons as contributions to their security, not threats, so Americans have reason to think similarly about French nukes. By the same token, Americans would have every reason to fear Fidel Castro's Cuba acquiring nuclear weapons. India had no reason to fear Israel's nukes, but every reason to fear Pakistan's. In short, because the significance of any and all weapons lies in who holds them and at whom they are pointed, it is common sense to try to keep nukes from spreading to the wrong people and nonsense to try to keep them from nations whose possession of them might do us good. Besides, nothing but war itself can prevent any government from developing nukes. Technology spreads naturally. A glance at any department of physics, chemistry, computer science, or engineering in any U.S. university shows that many undergraduates and most graduate students are foreign nationals. "Their" scientists are fully as good as "ours." The computers and other tools available on the open market are superior to the ones that Americans used to develop their nuclear arsenal in the first place. Nuclear reactors that produce electricity are natural "cover" for weapons programs, as well as sources of materials and expertise.

In fact governments have acquired nuclear weapons in part through indigenous effort, in part through help from friendly states, and in part through purchase of materials. Israel's acquisition of nuclear weapons in the 1960s was indigenous, but used French nuclear reactors. Israel has never acknowledged the well-known fact that it has nukes. South Africa's white regime developed an atom bomb in the late 1970s and tested it in the far reaches of the South Atlantic before dismantling it when the transition to black rule became inevitable. China built its first nuclear weapons in the 1950s with the formal help of the Soviet Union—which quickly regretted what it had done when China turned from a vassal into a competitor. France got its nukes at the same time, testing them in the pacific, despite America's and Britain's refusal to help. India and Pakistan got them in the 1990s mostly indigenously, except that Pakistan had help from China. North Korea seems to have followed the same path, except that some of its resources were coerced. Iraq and Iran have pursued nuclear weapons through a combination of openly purchased nuclear reactors, clandestinely purchased equipment for enrichment, and indigenous effort.

Because regimes such as those of Iraq, (pre-2003) Iran, and North Korea have used chemical and biological weapons in war, there is little doubt that they would use nukes if the occasion arose. India and Pakistan's likely behavior may be gauged by the fact that each country's announcement of nuclear tests led to crowds dancing in the streets chanting death to the other. Not least of the ways in which such states could use nukes to kill their enemies is to do so through irregulars—the indirect form of warfare typical of the vast regions from Morocco to the Philippines.

In the twenty-first century, the United States and Russia (and to a much lesser extent Britain, China, and France) are still the only states capable of the kind of nuclear operations described above. But for the most obvious of political reasons, these states are most unlikely to fight one another. Today's nuclear contenders are likely to use nukes differently from twentieth-century nuclear operations.

Deterrence is the exception. In 1991 India's minister of defense voiced openly the conclusion that many had drawn from the then-recent Gulf War: the United States would not have dared interfere with Iraq's conquest of Kuwait if Iraq had already tested a nuclear weapon. Hence, any government that wanted to make war on its neighbors without American interference could do so by acquiring nukes. Thus in 1996 China, which already possessed them, openly warned the United States that if it tried to save Taiwan it would "lose" Los Angeles to a Chinese nuclear-tipped missile. In other words, even a few nukes give a third-world government the power to raise the stakes for a major power that might otherwise be tempted to stand in its way. Nukes also confer status on those who have them. Thus in

2004 Iran publicly warned Israel that its newest version of the Shahab missile (prospectively armed with nukes) is targeted on Israel's nuclear complex at Dimona. This was meant to raise Iran's status in the Islamic world as much as to frighten Israel.

The new nuclear powers' quantitative nuclear poverty and relative technical backwardness, as well as their local conditions, dictate the kinds of nuclear operations they might carry out. Since these powers, including China, are relatively weak, the major result of their using nukes, or preparing to use them, might well be to involve major powers in unexpected ways.

Consider North Korea. As of 2006 it seems that it acquired nukes primarily to blackmail South Korea, Japan, and the United States into providing food, fuel, and other resources. Its most impressive acts have been the testing of missiles that overfly Japan and could reach Alaska and Hawaii. But the success of this venture depends on frightening its targets enough to get them to pay, yet not enough to cause them to use the overwhelming power at their command. North Korea's nukes in no way make up for its massive inferiority vis-à-vis South Korea, Japan, and the United States in every imaginable category. Though a North Korean nuke could cause havoc in downtown Seoul, or in Japan by striking a Japanese nuclear reactor, no one could design operations by which North Korea might win any war it started. By using nukes anywhere, North Korea's dictators would ensure their own deaths. But by merely brandishing nukes, North Korea has gone a long way toward convincing the Japanese public that because America can no longer be relied on for protection, Japan must take care of itself like a "normal" nation. Were Japan to continue in this direction, it would undo America's post–World War II primacy in the Pacific, and all Korea would be in Japan's natural sphere of influence.

By contrast, anyone can devise ways in which China's nukes might overturn America's primacy along the rim of the western Pacific. China's military strategy would be to deny the United States the capacity to use Taiwanese, Japanese, and Korean ports by destroying them, or merely by showing that it could easily rain nuclear-tipped missiles on them. In 1996 China gave more than a hint that it could do this by conducting ballistic-missile tests over the Taiwan straits. Any of those missiles could have carried nukes. In addition, China purchased Soviet/Russian Sunburn cruise missiles that could attack American ships from the coast or from small craft operating under coastal air cover. While this would not win command of the broad Pacific, it would push the U.S. Navy back to Guam and Hawaii. But while China's nukes would expel America, they would thereby stimulate Japan—which could build a world-class nuclear force that might make China wish America were back.

India and Pakistan have pointed nuclear-tipped missiles at one another, but have not integrated nukes into their land forces. That means that nukes are practically irrelevant to the wars that the subcontinent's two powers might fight with one another. Certainly they are irrelevant to the war over Kashmir, which the two have been fighting for a half century. Nor is there any likelihood that either country would make war on the other with the objective of conquering its capital: Hindus would not want to rule more Muslims, and Muslims would not want to rule Hindus. True, both sides hate one another enough to nuke each other's cities—which is the only thing of which their nuclear forces are capable. But since neither India nor Pakistan is able to defend itself against the other's nukes, the relationship between these two countries may well resemble what many (mistakenly) thought was the relationship between the United States and the Soviet Union during the Cold War.

Israel has nuclear weapons on fighter-bomber aircraft that can act as artillery on the battlefield and that can reach all the capitals of its enemies. Thus Israel would use nukes on the battlefield if Arab forces were breaking through its conventional units and heading into populated areas. Israel's tacit nuclear threat against Arab capitals is pure deterrence: if you set about slaughtering us, we will surely slaughter you. Of course, carrying out this threat once Arab forces really were in the process of genocide would not save any Jews. Nevertheless this threat is more credible than standard deterrent threats the execution of which is not in the threatener's interest, because the determination never again to allow Jews to be killed with impunity is modern Israel's cornerstone.

Iran's nuclear weapons program aims (as Iraq's aimed) to deter the United States. These programs also sought the capacity to achieve victory on the battlefield, and the capacity to destroy the enemy's capital. We can see this from the way that both countries used missiles and chemical weapons in the 1981–88 war against each other. Nuclear strikes are also the most efficient means by which either state could contribute to the defeat of Israel. On the battlefield, Iran and, especially, Iraq followed Soviet doctrine and preceded their attacks on major enemy concentrations with the most concentrated barrages of the deadliest weapons they could manage, including chemicals. Placing nukes on the missiles and bombs hitting such targets is simply logical. During the phase of that war known as the "war of the cities," both sides hit each other's capital as hard as they could. Fear of Iraq's missiles drove out one-half of Tehran's population. Again, putting nukes on the missiles makes it possible to do that job more efficiently. Using nukes, or just chemicals, in a first strike against Israel makes much military sense. Israel's armed forces consist largely of reserves. Such forces have two Achilles' heels: mobilization centers and equipment storage areas. Destroying or just contaminating these facilities in a surprise attack would prejudge the course of the war. Moreover, in a country so densely populated as Israel, where there is literally no place to which one can escape, the explosion of a few nukes at the outset of a war would start a panic difficult to contain.

8

POLITICAL WARFARE

Phyrrus used to say that Cineas had taken more
towns with his words than with his arms.

        —Plutarch

For to win one hundred victories in one hundred
battles is not the acme of skill. To subdue the enemy
without fighting is the acme of skill.

        —Sun Tzu

ARMS ARE TOOLS of war, but not the only ones. Words, ideas, and reputations may be even more powerful. We have said that the foot soldier's
bayonet against the enemy's belly is the ultimate weapon. But bayonets are
held by men who can be persuaded to thrust them home, drop them, or turn
them against others. Men are moved through their minds. One moves one's
own troops mainly by speaking words into their heads. One moves the
enemy to give up his cause by affecting his mind through a combination of
words and deeds. The art of heartening friends and disheartening enemies,
of gaining help for one's cause and causing the abandonment of the enemies' is called political warfare.

The term "political warfare" refers both to the *whole* of warfare directed at producing political results, and to that *part* of warfare that employs political means to attain the political goals of war in conjunction with
fighting troops—or even without the actual engagement of fighting troops.
Winning primacy for one set of ideas over others is sometimes the very
essence of war. But ideas are also weapons of war among many others.

The term "political warfare," often used synonymously with "psychological operations," is often misunderstood as the preposterous proposition
that words can substitute for deeds on the battlefield, or that diplomacy is
anything but the verbal representation of reality, or that the allegiances of

peoples in conflict can be manipulated by "public relation," "dirty tricks," or "big lies."[1] In fact words are powerful to the extent that they refer to powerful realities. Bluff is generally bad policy. Making people attend to one's words is a hard-earned conquest that is easily lost. Nothing is worse, said Theodore Roosevelt, than to combine "the loose tongue with the unready hand."

A second bit of nonsense is that the means usually associated with political warfare—propaganda, agents of influence, sabotage, coups de main, and support for insurgents—are not acts of war in the same sense that armies crashing across borders or airplanes dropping bombs are acts of war. They are in fact war, whether done in pursuit of victory during war or during unbloody conflicts as serious as war. If these political tools are not used seriously, they are not acts of war, but bloody foolishness. But then again, so are politically unserious bombings and glorious feats of arms. "It's magnificent, but it's not war," said France's military observer about the British Light Brigade's suicidal charge at Balaklava.

It is incorrect to think that political warfare includes only propaganda, subversion, and related efforts. Every battle undertaken must be calculated to have the effect of strengthening one's own supporters while weakening the enemy's. Planning battles, economic sanctions, and so on without having a reasonably good idea of how to stop what one has started is a sign of either incompetence or a death wish. So, an atomic bomb, a cavalry incursion into the enemy's rear, a lone saboteur, an agent whispering in the right ear, or a frightening set of battle cries is useful in warfare only insofar as it forms or breaks ideas in the enemy's mind.

The essence of war consists primarily of neither words nor deeds, but of *intentions.* The supreme decision in war—the one that makes a conflict a war—is designating an objective as important enough to kill and die for. Without such a decision, a country may, as the United States did in Vietnam, the Gulf War of 1991, or the War on Terror of 2001, mobilize millions of men, shoot off billions of dollars worth of ordnance, and yet not wage war, that is, neither bending an enemy's will nor eliminating him as an obstacle to peace. When the decision is made to kill and die for an objective, however, it may not be necessary to do very much because the skillful communication of that intention may be enough to so weaken the opponent that he either will not give battle or will fight it badly.

For example, Mongols developed such a reputation for torturing to death anyone who put up the slightest resistance to them that the appearance of a single Mongol horseman in a Russian village would provoke the inhabitants to line up, docilely offering their necks to be decapitated. Imagine then the psychological effect of Genghis Kahn's Golden Horde, riding out of clouds of yellow smoke generated by hundreds of pots burning sulfur, while the great war drums sounded out doom! The enemy might well have been focusing his mind on escape routes rather than on the impending battle. Herodotus tells us that Greeks had once been debilitated by the Persian soldiery's luxurious appearance. But at Marathon the Athenians discomfited the Persians by attacking at a run. The contest for human hearts and minds can be won in many ways.

The objective of this contest is to influence every individual who might become involved in the war. Each is a creature beset by private urges, hopes, and fears and endowed with the capacity to judge better and worse, good and evil. Each wants his own vision of the good life for himself and his loved ones and is therefore eager to relate what is happening in the world to his hopes and fears. He wants to know what the combatants intend to do that will affect him for better or for worse, what it's likely to cost him, and what the chances are that either side will win. Essentially, he wants to know which way the wind is blowing and what this means for him and those dear to him.

Those who win the contest produce hope for themselves and their cause, and desperation for the enemy and his. How much each side hates the other does less to encourage or dispirit than does each side's regard for the other's prospects. Contempt for the enemy is more encouraging than hate for the enemy. And contempt can be based as much on faith in the long-run outcome as on short-term events. Thus in 1943 Charles de Gaulle's radio broadcasts told Frenchmen to regard their German occupiers as future "cadavers or prisoners." But causes do not live on words alone. Had Allied victories not been forthcoming, or had the people who embodied the cause of Free France been eliminated, words such as de Gaulle's would not have inspired the French resistance.

Hence, the basic message that each combatant side must get across by deeds as well as words is as follows: "We are here to win. We have totally dedicated ourselves to winning. We have what it takes and we know what we are doing. You can count on our winning. You and everybody else will depend on us for your lives and for your futures. We have a well-deserved reputation for being kind to those who join us and for making those who stand in our way wish that they had never been born. Moreover, if you think about it, our side deserves your adherence because we are more in tune with the standards by which you live than are our opponents. These people will soon be either cadavers or prisoners. You have a rare and fleeting chance to show you belong on our side and not theirs. Don't miss it!"

The first element of the message is commitment. The audience must know that they are facing people who have made a basic choice, and hence will not waver. When Hernán Cortés burned his ships behind him, he not only forced his men to choose between victory and death, but also intimidated the Aztecs who faced him. What could make this man risk his life so completely? Perhaps he had powers they could not fathom. Such thinking may well have contributed to the Aztecs' defeat. Similarly, the American colonists who read the Declaration of Independence could only have been impressed by the boldness of the signers—prominent men who publicly bet their "lives, fortunes, and sacred honor." If *they* were willing to commit an act for which they surely would be hanged in case of defeat, then perhaps there was a good chance of victory; and the average man could take the lesser risk of joining Washington's Continentals.

Conversely, in 1988 anyone who asked himself whether to ally with Panama's military dictator, Gen. Manuel Noriega, after he was indicted by a U.S. court for dealing drugs, or with his opponents would have had to ask himself whether the United States would use force to put Noriega in a federal penitentiary or mock by inaction the justice system to whose seriousness they had committed. Few Panamanians would have supported Noriega's cause if it had been obviously foredoomed. But they heard American explanations that the indictment and talk of military action were only a "show of force." Hence, by showing force that was obviously not meant to be used, the United States earned contempt for itself and support for Noriega. But when two U.S. divisions invaded Panama in December 1989, Noriega's support evaporated swiftly.

By the very same token, between 1991 and 2003 U.S. leaders of both parties vied with one another in using "strong language" to denounce Iraq's Saddam Hussein. The U.S. Congress voted for resolutions that he be overthrown, and (oxymoronically) *publicly* approved money for *covert* actions to do it. President Clinton and his successor George W. Bush ordered numerous air strikes against Iraqi air defenses. Clinton even ordered cruise missiles to destroy the headquarters of Iraq's intelligence service—at night, so only cleaning ladies died. Two Bushes and one Clinton supported economic sanctions on Saddam. But sanctions increased rather than diminished Saddam's power over the Iraqi economy. No surprise, then, that these dozen years of ill-conceived "political war" bolstered Saddam's claim to be the Arab world's, and even the Muslim world's, leader against an impotent America. Nevertheless, when four U.S. divisions invaded Iraq in March 2003 Iraqis danced as they pulled down Saddam's statues. But as Americans occupied the country in an impotent manner, they were bedeviled by a resistance more powerful than any that Saddam had ever faced.

Commitment of resources does not necessarily convey commitment of will. The single Mongol horseman was a sufficient show of force because of the Mongols' reputation. Similarly, in Lebanon in 1984, the Soviet Union was able to wield power by a very small action that sufficed only because of its reputation. The various factions in the long-festering Lebanese civil war had become habituated to taking citizens of foreign powers as hostages in order to compel those powers to bring pressure against their client states in the area, who in turn would bring pressure on *their* clients in Lebanon on the kidnappers' behalf. Americans, Frenchmen, Egyptians, and Saudis all suffered this fate. In 1984 Soviet citizens were kidnapped for the first time. Soviet agents in league with Syria instantly kidnapped four members of a prominent Beirut family thought to be associated with the suspected kidnappers, killed one of them, and sent several of his body parts to his family. At the same time, Syria told prominent Lebanese thought to be close to the kidnappers that unless the hostages were released, the Syrian armed forces would wreak upon their neighborhoods and their inhabitants the slaughter they had previously done to Hama, Syria's third largest city. The Soviet hostages were released immediately. None were ever taken again.

Had the United States made a similar move on behalf of its hostages, a truckload of gore would have been a mere "dirty trick." That is because no one could imagine the United States wrecking a city to get at its enemies. Two decades later, Arab terrorists were kidnapping and beheading Americans in Iraq, Saudi Arabia, and Pakistan. The kidnappers' families, political connections, and causes were well-known. But neither the United States itself nor, of course, any of its nominal allies were willing to do what Syria had done on the Soviets' behalf. And so Americans continued to be taken and beheaded.

The reductio ad absurdum of the principle that commitment of resources can have a beneficial effect as a "show of force" was President Jimmy Carter's dispatch of a squadron of F-15 fighters to Saudi Arabia in 1979. This "show of force" was intended to reassure the Saudis against the threat posed by militant Shi'ite Iran. The United States had wanted to show forceful support for the Saudis. But it did not want to appear threatening to anyone. So it compromised by announcing that the F-15s would be *unarmed.* But the sight of airplanes deliberately stripped of their armaments conjured up the exact opposite of the intended image of a powerful ally ready, willing, and massively able to come to the rescue.

Even the commitment of resources to actual operations is politically ineffective unless these are part of a success-oriented plan. From 1981 to 1988 President Ronald Reagan spoke eloquently about the evils of Nicaragua's communist regime and of the dangers it posed to the United States. He also asked for money to support the armed resistance to that regime. But to do what? Reagan never said specifically. Reagan claimed that financing the war would bring pressure on the communists to negotiate and to change their ways. But since Reagan also claimed that the United States planned to get along with communist leaders in the long run, what sense did it make to bloody them? Because people cannot be made to forget past injuries by subsequent aid, it is common sense either to put one's enemies out of action or to get along with them.

The bottom line in war and hence in political warfare is who gets buried and who gets to walk in the sun. This was illustrated as well as it ever has been by the events that followed the assassination of Egyptian President Anwar Sadat in 1981. From his predecessor, Gamal Abdul Nasser, Sadat had inherited a country deeply enmeshed politically and financially with the Soviet Union. Egypt's principal daily preoccupation was war with Israel. Sadat wanted to turn his country to a worthier agenda. He fought a well-planned campaign against Israel in 1973 to gain leverage for a peace that would restore to Egypt land that it had lost in Nasser's war of 1967. Sadat also expelled the Soviets from Egypt, so that instead of paying for Soviet arms, Egypt became the annual recipient of some two billion dollars of American aid. For this he earned the status of public enemy number one of the Soviet Union and of its sympathizers around the world. In 1979 the shah of Iran, a longtime ally of the United States, was overthrown by Islamists allied with one of the Soviet Union's allies in the region, the Palestine Liberation Organization. "Progressive" propaganda blared that Sadat's end was near and began referring to him as "Shah-dat." As soon as Sadat died in a hail of bullets in October 1981, anyone in the world who turned the dial of a shortwave radio could not help hearing the following message in a variety of languages and formulations:

> Anwar Sadat is dead because he was on the wrong side. Who wants to be next? Let him do as Sadat did. Let him oppose the forces of progress in the world, and he will end up as just another corpse alongside the corpses of all others who have thought it possible to go over to the American side in the great worldwide struggle. On the side of progress there is success and life. Against us there is only dishonorable death. Who's next?[2]

In August 1988 the chief ally of the United States in South Asia, Mohammed Zia ul Haq, president of Pakistan, died in a fiery plane crash along with the U.S. ambassador and Pakistani officials in charge of supplying the anti-Soviet resistance in Afghanistan. Legal responsibility for his death was never established. But two facts are self-evident: anti-Soviet forces in South Asia lost their principal supporter, and once again America's allies died while their enemies lived.

These acts of war did not change the political alignment of Egypt or Pakistan. But they turned U.S. allies into passive partners.

Let us consider first the tools of political warfare and then the political element in several kinds of wars.

The Tools of Political Warfare

We have already noted that effective policy forcefully explained is the most powerful tool of political warfare, and that for any other tool to be useful it must be used consistently with an internally consistent, otherwise successful policy. This is not to deny the occasional usefulness of minor currents of policy that run secretly against the mainstream. Such undercurrents can prepare for eventual changes in course, or can even fool "some of the people all of the time or all of the people some of the time," but any covert undercurrent always carries the danger of disrupting the main current of policy. In short, political warfare is all about reality, not smoke and mirrors.

Gray Propaganda

Gray propaganda is the semiofficial amplification of a government's voice. Foreigners pay attention not only to what a nation's government says, but also to what nonofficial but authoritative voices in the country say. By enlisting the support of these voices, a government lets the audience know that it has domestic support. This strengthens its hand in political warfare. This is what the United States did in the late 1940s when it was trying to convince West Europeans to resist communism. Europeans who were wondering how deep was America's official commitment to fighting communism saw that commitment confirmed through a multiplicity of sources: U.S. newspapers, labor unions, chambers of commerce, and letter-writing campaigns by private citizens. These sources had been partly inspired and sometimes paid for by the U.S. government.

Gray propaganda can also serve to help foreigners deceive themselves. Thus the Nazi regime sent "Putzi" Haenfstaengl, Hitler's pianist, and others close to the führer, to mingle in high Western social circles to pass along the "good news" that the regime's ranting and raving, as well as its military preparations, should not be taken seriously. Hitler's antics were just show for the masses. Western socialites, eager to believe the best—and amazed that Nazis could eat with knife and fork—preferred what they were hearing to what they were seeing. As the comedian Groucho Marx used to say, "Who you gonna believe? Me or your own eyes?" During the Cold War, the Soviet Union's Georgi Arbatov, Vladimir Posner, and a corps of semiofficial Soviets who could pass for American yuppies served the same "gray" counter-reality function with the Western upper-middle classes.[3]

Beginning in the 1990s television station al Jazeera became arguably the biggest shaper of opinion in the Arab world. The station operates in Qtar. The Qtari emir owns it. The government is allied with the United States. But if al Jazeera represents only a minority faction in the government (it would not be allowed to operate if it represented no part of it), it certainly represents the country's regime—the people who count in the land. Because of its TV station, Qtar played an indispensable role in turning the Arab world against America while at the same time enjoying America's protection.

Finally, gray propaganda can provide a government with the dangerous pleasure of saying things that it doesn't really mean, or has not really thought through. For example, in the 1950s the U.S. semiofficial Radio Free Europe and Radio Liberty gave East Europeans the impression that it would be best for them to revolt against Soviet rule and that if they did the United States would come to their aid. The United States was not determined to do this. Nor was the United States determined not to aid an uprising. The U.S. government simply had not faced the question internally and had let its semiofficial voice run ahead of its official mind. When the Hungarian Revolution of 1956 forced the U.S. government actually to choose between the danger of aiding East European rebellions and the danger of permanent communist rule in East Europe, it had neither studied the consequences of either option nor made contingency plans. America stood by as Soviet tanks crushed the East German and Hungarian rebellions of 1953 and 1956. The lesson is that ideas have consequences, whether they are white, black, or gray.

Black Propaganda

Black propaganda is information (true or false) that appears to come from a source other than the one from which it actually originated. Information or suggestions that are black propaganda enjoy the appeal of appearing to come from a disinterested source when in fact they do not. For this reason black propaganda can be powerful. In 1979, in Islamabad, Pakistan, undercover Soviet agents spread the word that the United States had just committed a mass murder of Muslims. This ignited a crowd that burned down the U.S. embassy. In 2006 Islamists in Denmark, with the "black" help of the Syrian and Iranian governments, ignited deadly anti-Western riots across the Islamic world by flatting the publication of anti-Islamic cartoons in a Danish newspaper and exaggerating it into a civilizational casus belli.

In more complex and more important instances the effect of black propaganda is difficult to gauge. For example, it does not follow that because KGB money and personnel fed the 1980s campaign to turn public opinion in Europe against American nuclear weapons, because certain noncommunist media outlets followed the Soviet line, and because European public opinion *was* turned, that black propaganda made it happen. In fact, the Soviets worked on all levels to turn European opinion, and no one can distinguish the proverbial straw that broke the camel's back from the other straws in the bale.

Black propaganda must be consonant with other policy efforts in order to be effective at all. There is a constant temptation to run black propaganda, like other secret activities, not as an adjunct to policy but as a policy in itself. This often happens when an incompetent government refuses to choose between two appealing but contradictory courses of policy and tries one more or less openly and the other in the "black." Thus in the early 1960s the U.S. government used clandestine sources to spread facts about the copious sexual misdeeds of Indonesia's dictator, Sukarno. But at the same time the United States was openly refusing to its own ally, the Netherlands, the right to land aircraft in transit on U.S. territory when it was fighting Sukarno's attempt to grab the Dutch colony of West New Guinea.

Agents of influence are people whom the enemy mistakenly believes are on his side. Good ones cannot be bought. Their work is far more valuable, subtle, and dangerous than that of a mere spy. That is because by the very act of exercising influence an agent brings suspicion on himself. For example, the Soviet Union's agent in Norway, Arne Treholt, helped bring about his own downfall in 1985 by negotiating a too obviously one-sided treaty between Norway and the Soviet Union. Such agents can gain the help and protection of a domestic party by identifying their view of the "proper" relationship with the other country with that of the party. Thus in the final stages of World War II Alger Hiss, a Soviet agent and spy, helped shape U.S. foreign policy toward the Soviet Union. When he was exposed, he enjoyed the support of most of the Democratic Party's elites. He went to jail only because he had lied under oath about illegally passing documents to Soviet intelligence. By contrast Harry Hopkins, President Franklin Roosevelt's alter ego, fully identified his agenda with Stalin's but never went to jail. He exercised more power over U.S. foreign policy than anyone other than President Franklin Roosevelt. But he never did anything illegal, and his pro-Soviet attitude was widely shared within the Democratic Party.[4]

Sometimes when agents are particularly exposed there is no substitute for a great power's extending overt and even physical protection. Thus, in the 1930s, the German government openly encouraged ethnic Germans and their friends in Austria, Czechoslovakia, Switzerland, and Poland to agitate for unification with the Reich. The Reich government then threatened the governments of those coun-tries if they acted against Nazi agents. Only Switzerland resisted. In the 1970s and 1980s agents of influence in Lebanon were so open about their allegiances to Syria, Iran, Israel, Saudi Arabia, and the United States as to be outright proxies. Thus, they prospered or died according to the ability of their patrons to convince enemies that killing them would invite deadly retaliation.

Finding or making allies out of factions in the enemy camp or in neutral countries is an ancient art. The prospect of victory recruits allies. No one worth having joins a losing cause or merely enlists as a paid pawn. Recruiting allies requires at least pretending to be committed to victory. True, foreign factions are often used as pawns, and using them as such requires much deception. But doing this is as unwise as it is immoral, because it leads to the discrediting, isolation, and defeat of whoever does it. For example, in the 1960s the United States gave the H'mong tribes of Laos every reason to believe that the United States had come to Indochina to defeat the government of North Vietnam, which was also the enemy of the H'mong. These tribesmen then made up an army of thirty thousand men and, with American arms, held the northwest corner of Indochina until the United States abandoned them. Similarly, in 1975 and again in 1991 the United States encouraged Iraq's Kurds and Shi'ites to fight Saddam Hussein, only to abandon them to his tender mercies. Hence in 2003 as U.S. armed forces invaded Iraq there was no reason for Americans to wonder why Kurds and Shi'ites did not respond to America's invitation to rise. They waited to see what America's intervention would mean for them. Four years later they were still waiting.

Sometimes factions will accept—indeed seek out—foreign support even when they are highly uncertain about its purpose and reliability. They do this because they believe they have no alternative to accepting aid. Factions in this predicament have a variety of ways to guard against abandonment. One way is that pursued by the Nicaraguan resistance in 1981–88, which staked its entire future on shaky support from the United States and prepared for betrayal by arranging places of more or less comfortable exile. Another way is that of Jonas Savimbi, leader of Angola's UNITA party. Savimbi consistently assumed that all sources of aid are subject to cutoff; he diversified his resources to the best of his ability and had an endless number of plans for augmenting or cutting back his operations to match his supplies. In the end, being cut off from all foreign support forced the Nicaraguan Contras to come to terms with their enemies or to emigrate, and doomed the anti-regime Angolans to death.

In sum, a great power's ability to recruit foreign groups as allies for political and military operations depends on how desperate these groups are for allies, on how they gauge the reliability of the assisting great power, and what are the latter's plans for them. The usefulness of such allies to the great power depends less on their characteristics than on the ways in which it encourages, supplies, and above all supports them while preventing the enemy from concentrating its forces against them.

Political Warfare in Big Wars

The flash of big guns should not blind students to the importance of political warfare even in the biggest of wars.

Few remember that Hitler's conquests in Europe between 1933 and 1939 were almost bloodless. They were triumphs of will over victims wanting in conviction, resolve, and courage. Scarcely six years after he had seized power inside Germany from irresolute opponents, Hitler had torn apart the Versailles Treaty of 1919, massively rearmed Germany in violation of it, remilitarized the Rhineland, occupied Austria, and seized Czechoslovakia. In those six years Hitler's threats, invariably combined with protestations of peace, broke the will of those who might have combined to resist him. He knew the psychological dimensions of political warfare. As he told a Nazi comrade in the late thirties:

> The place of artillery preparation for frontal attack by the infantry . . . will in the future be taken by revolutionary propaganda, to break down the enemy psychologically before the armies begin to function at all. The enemy must be demoralized and ready to capitulate, driven into moral passivity, before military action can even be thought of.[5]

Hitler did not invent the idea of ideological precursor strikes. Classical historians such as Livy have commented on the "anti-imperialist" alliance of the Gauls with Carthage and on the Carthaginian "anti-ruling-class" propaganda directed at the Romans during the Second Punic War.

Breaking the will of a people by terrorizing it can be done in both war and peace. Bolshevik military leaders such as Leon Trotsky deliberately exploited latter-day comparisons of their assault on the West with that of the Mongols. A passage in Nikita Krushchev's famous twentieth party congress denunciation of Stalin in 1956 underscored the importance of terror in Soviet strategy. "The questioning of Stalin's terror," Khruschev said, " . . . may lead to the questioning of terror in general. But Bolshevism believes in the use of terror. Lenin held that no one was worthy of the name Communist who did not believe in terror."[6]

Even more than irrational fears, ideas have inspired as well as intimidated. The Roman emperor Constantine, embracing Christianity for himself and his subjects, led his armies to victory after victory, by filling them with hunger for Christian peace. Much later, under Bonaparte, French *soldats* plunged across Europe, carrying copies of the Declaration of the Rights of Man stowed in their knapsacks. Nazi SS units were outfitted with copies of *Mein Kampf*—presumably to strengthen the soldiers in their beliefs rather than to convince the *Untermenschen* that it would be best if they merged peacefully into the mud.

We should, of course, distinguish the thoughts that animate peoples and armies to fight from propaganda designed to affect the minds and wills of the enemy—civilians and soldiers alike. The first aims to generate and sustain morale. That which is aimed at the adversary in political warfare hopes to persuade or deceive and seeks to detach popular opinion from the wartime government ("we have no quarrel with you people, only with your leaders"). We should take particular note of the *different* forms and manifestations of ideology in warfare; particularistic ideologies—National Socialism, for one—differ greatly in their targets from universalistic ones—Jacobinism and Marxism-Leninism, for instance. And then there are the hybrids of our time—Khomeini's fundamentalism, for instance, is Shi'ite messianism merged with Iranian nationalism. The Wahhabi Islam emanating from Saudi Arabia combines hate of westerners with hate of the Shi'ites. Since the 1990s Islamism has contained ever less Islam and ever more every rationalization for anti-Americanism ever thought of.

Sometimes however ideas hinder military performance. Stalin had to store Marxism-Leninism in a Kremlin closet for the duration of what he was forced to call "the great patriotic war." The Russian people hated communism and would fight only for Holy Mother Russia—and to save their skins from the Nazis. Only after victory in 1945 did Stalin again proclaim the doctrines of communism and force the patriotic Russian people to repeat its slogans.

Sometimes, inspiration conflicts with military strategy. The flip side of the coin of Bonaparte's Rights of Man carried in triumph throughout Europe was its capacity to arouse homegrown, nationalist, anti-French sentiment in subjugated kingdoms and principalities. The decisive Battle of Leipzig, in 1813, in which Napoleon lost military superiority in central Europe, was called "The Battle of Nations" because the forces that fought Napoleon there truly felt themselves to be the upholders of their nations' identities against the French "nation-in-arms." Conversely, Hitler's ideology of German racial superiority feared and despised by most non-Germans, made nonsense of his political claim to be the defender of the European nations against the Bolshevik hordes.

Precisely because ideological warfare (or ideologically inspired war) involves human psychology with all its imponderables, it is not susceptible to fine-tuning. Political warfare, particularly when it expediently opts for a risky "radical" line to achieve battlefield victory, can backfire, have unforeseen effects, or spin out of control.

During World War I, "clever" Imperial German political-warfare strategists transported V. I. Lenin back from Switzerland to wartime St. Petersburg (in a sealed train so that he might not contaminate Germany with communism while passing through it) to aggravate an already grave revolutionary crisis and get Russia out of the war in 1917. The stratagem worked both better and worse than expected. The Bolsheviks, seizing power, sued for peace and granted Germany a settlement in Eastern Europe at Brest Litovsk in 1918 that was fabulously advantageous. But after the November armistice, German revolutionaries, Lenin's communist comrades, heartened by the Bolshevik Revolution, helped to bring the fall of Imperial Germany, and came close to seizing power in central Europe. The "clever" strategists didn't realize that Lenin's political shock troops also had pamphlets in their pockets! Worse for the Germans, Lenin's Soviet Union became so powerful that it ended up occupying Germany's eastern third for half a century.

Political warfare, no matter how appealing, works best in the service of realistic strategic aims. It works worst when objectives waver, are confused, or are contradictory. Woodrow Wilson's powerful though brief appeal to war-weary Europeans for peace without victory in 1917–18, the famous Fourteen Points, coincided with the growing popular consciousness that the war had become a tragedy for all sides. In November 1918, when the armistice took place, Wilson briefly towered above all other wartime leaders. But Wilson's vague principles, beguiling as they were for engagé intellectuals, were not the source of their mass popularity. On the contrary, they were universally popular because different peoples saw in them the promise that their very different—and conflicting—objectives would be realized. When Wilson tried to translate those principles into reality, he and America became the object of resentment.

In contrast, the flood of words from the Johnson and Nixon administrations about the Vietnam War did the very opposite of what propaganda should do. They sounded an uncertain trumpet. They held out no concrete promise of either political victory or justice, and they emitted confusing signals to friend and foe alike. Thus the words of American leaders contributed to public demoralization, and ultimately, to defeat. This was no product of political propagandists. Rather, it mirrored all too accurately the wavering confusions and contradictions of high policy. Because of this, the grim will and relentless political purpose of America's tenacious enemy, inferior in every other way, finally triumphed.[7]

Even outright propaganda can be directly counterproductive. Allied propaganda, in its proclaimed insistence on unconditional surrender and punishment of the German nation in World War II, was independent confirmation of everything the Nazi regime was itself generating about the Allies' plans for Germany's surrender. In 1944 Goebbels gleefully exploited Roosevelt's proposed punitive "Morgenthau Plan," with its threat of permanent "pastoralization" of a subjugated Germany. The increasingly punitive language of Western statesmen weakened the case of anti–Hitler opposition in the German public. This teaches that the propaganda of a clearly superior belligerent in wartime must not corner the enemy, giving him no choice but that of total and abject capitulation or resistance to a fatal end.

Political Warfare in Guerrillas, Insurgencies, and Civil Wars

When one looks at small wars (or *guerrillas,* the Spanish word meaning "little wars"), or even at the unbloody side of great conflicts, it becomes unmistakable that wars go on to the extent that people agree to fight, and that they stop when at least one side's fighters abandon the cause. This leads us to consider what it takes to recruit and keep fighters. A glance at any civil war or guerrilla is enough to remind us that recruitment is not always an automatic process as it was in World War I, when national leaders "pushed the button" and effortlessly turned out millions of soldiers. These leaders drew upon and depleted an unusually rich bank of allegiances built up over a thousand years. Moreover, the soldiers did not think they had much choice. Most of the time, however, the allegiances of potential draftees are more scarce, and their choices are more plentiful.

In civil wars or guerrillas, let alone insurgencies, the potential recruit is pulled in at least three directions: to join one side, to join the other side, or to stay aloof. Typically, such wars lead neighbors and even brothers to choose different sides. Also, because the opportunities for desertion are abundant in such conflicts, keeping the loyalty of one's own troops and weakening the other side's is a never-ending concern. Intimidation alone will not suffice.

This is not to say that individuals are not drafted into insurgencies or civil wars. Quite the contrary is true. Indeed, one of the more characteristic and despicable aspects of these wars is that some groups force young men publicly to commit murders and expropriations in order to preclude their return to normal life. Nevertheless, it is clear that since the opportunities to escape from an irregular force are greater than the opportunities to escape from a regular army, irregular forces know that to stand a chance of winning they must gain more and more adherents, and that they cannot do this through intimidation alone. Hence, irregular warfare is quintessentially political warfare aimed at winning over the hearts and minds of combatants.

"Guerrilla" is the term Spaniards gave to their ultimately successful struggle against the Napoleonic troops that occupied their country. Spain could not muster an army capable of challenging France's main force in battle. But it could and did muster dozens of small units that achieved local and temporary superiority over small fractions of the French army. By doing so, the Spanish, with the help of an English detachment under the Duke of Wellington, forced the French to move only in large groups, preventing them from becoming a widespread presence in Spain. Although the "little war" could not force French troops out of Spain, it prevented them from drawing a net profit out of their stay. Napoleon soon found he had more pressing needs for his troops elsewhere, the Duke of Wellington's British forces provided the nucleus for victory in a few medium-sized battles, and Spain returned to its native tyranny.

The "little war" has always been the natural recourse of those who know they cannot win a big one. As the Romans advanced deeper into North Africa, they came upon bands of archers mounted on fast horses and camels. The archers could not possibly have stood up to the legions' high-tech warfare, but their nomadic camps were always several days' march ahead, and the Romans soon pulled back, figuring that they did not want to be walking pin cushions in the desert.

Still, nothing is more erroneous than the modern view that a determined people fighting from their homes can always defeat an occupying army. The Romans, master conquerors, developed the standard for successful antiguerrilla operations: secure the most valuable parts of the conquered country through a massive troop presence and offer the inhabitants the choice between reasonably normal lives under Roman rule or certain death. They would then make impossible normal life outside the areas of their control. Over generations the pacified zones expanded gradually. Ivan the Terrible successfully pacified Chechnya this way in the sixteenth century. The Soviet Union did it against the Muslim Basmachi rebels of central Asia in the 1920s. In the 1930s it did so preemptively in its drive to collectivize the Ukraine, causing mass starvation among those who resisted or might have resisted. The Soviet Union repeated the pattern in the 1940s in the Baltic States and in the 1980s in Afghanistan. In the 1990s Russia repeated with modern weapons what Ivan had done to the Chechens four centuries previously. At the turn of the twenty-first century Sudan's Arab Muslim government defeated resistance from its black Christian citizens by enslaving the ones they could reach and starving the ones they could not.

The United States lost the military part of the war in Vietnam first because it chose to treat a foreign invasion—a big war that had a base of operations susceptible to attack—as if it were a little war that lacked such an enemy nerve center. Having chosen to fight a big war as if it had been a guerrilla, the United States also never considered the Roman-Russian approach. The United States found it easy to entice millions of Vietnamese into "secure" areas. But it tried not to upset normal life in areas it did not control, thus forfeiting such control to the North Vietnamese. In fact, the United States in Vietnam allowed its enemy to consolidate in rear areas subject to harassment but not subject to any strategic threat. This emphatically was not a classic guerrilla. Similarly, America fought the post-2003 war against the remnants of Iraq's former regime as a classic guerrilla although it was not. The Iraqis whom Americans called "insurgents" were in fact an established regime that represented a small minority of Iraqis and that had not been dismantled by invading American forces. The Americans never empowered their enemies' enemies. They hunted their enemies as individuals, refused to target the Sunni faction they represented, and indeed allowed that faction effectively to control parts of the country. Politically, the Americans pressed the Sunnis' demands on the majority Shi'ites and Kurds. The more the Sunnis killed, the more solicitous of them the Americans became. Thus Americans were prey as well as hunters.

Most guerrilla wars are actually civil wars in which guerrilla tactics are sometimes used, and in which foreign forces are usually the decisive factor. The Angolan war, which began in 1975, originally pitted the MPLA, a native political faction supported by the Soviet Union, Cuba, and East Germany, against Jonas Savimbi's UNITA, supported by France and South Africa. UNITA has its own remote capital from which it controlled a third of the country. However, the MPLA army on the communist side virtually ceased to exist. The Angolan war for the most part was the Cubans and Soviets versus UNITA, which fought with South African logistical and U.S. token support. After South Africa stopped its direct support and the U.S. Clinton administration switched sides and cut off UNITA's purchases abroad in the 1990s, UNITA was forced to fight a true guerrilla war. It lasted a decade longer on purely indigenous resources, but lost.

Rarely are civil wars fought autonomously, as was the American Civil War. Civil wars always represent a diminution of the power that a nation can exercise abroad, and they almost always produce at least one contender that is eager to accept help from abroad. Hence, almost invariably, civil wars lead to foreign interference and tend to make both winners and losers less happy than they would have been without the war. The Romans entered and conquered Greece as a result of being called into a civil war in the third century BC. The French entered Italy in 1494 when the Venetians as well as the pope summoned them in. Italy would not be free of them until 1870. In the 1930s the Spanish civil war squared Italy and Germany on one side against the Soviet Union on the other. But the Spanish were lucky that both sides' "helpers" soon found fighting each other more appealing, and that the civil war's winner, Gen. Francisco Franco, did not pay off any of the debts he had incurred. The Vietnamese were not so lucky. The leaders of North Vietnam could not have fought their war without the Soviet Union, and they paid their debts, in part by sending over a hundred thousand of their own people as forced lumbermen in Siberia. Since 1975 Israel, Iran, the PLO, the United States, and above all Syria have supported various contenders for power in Lebanon. But all Lebanese, except a few factional leaders, live lives that are far poorer, more brutish, and shorter than before the civil war began. All of the "helpers" except Syria lost more than they gained. Syria was the only winner in the Lebanese civil war.

The least destructive civil wars are the few, like the American Civil War, in which both sides are organized in regular armies and treat each other as international belligerents rather than as common criminals. Far more pernicious are those like the "dirty war" in Argentina in the 1970s between leftist elements in the population and rightist elements in the army and the police. Both sides hid among larger publics who shared their political views and social preferences to some extent. Each side was bent on annihilating the other because it loathed the other's ways. Hence, neither side particularly cared whether the people it killed were precisely the ones it meant to kill, as long as the intended people were among the victims. But the most murderous civil wars of all are the ones in which at least one side is organized into a regular army and fights to annihilate those who embody the enemy's ways. Thus the Red Armies of Russia and China, as well as the Cambodian Khmer Rouge, sought victory so that they might begin the serious killing, not end it. The small wars are sometimes the biggest killers of all.

Insurgencies are the smallest wars of all. But they are most obviously political because insurgents necessarily begin by representing no one but themselves. Their acts in violation of the law begin as private challenges and therefore as crimes. To the extent that the insurgents are legitimate, the government is not, and vice versa. The insurgent's hope is to wage a small war that will perhaps become a civil war. The insurgent's military task is no different from that of anyone fighting a small war: to survive long enough and attract enough supporters to win a war.

Special Operations

Special operations are often confused with guerrilla warfare because they employ similar tactics: small units that operate stealthily and cause havoc in larger ones. They are misunderstood as consisting of physically demanding acts. In fact, their special quality comes much less from the character of the troops than from their purpose. They are specially crafted to have a bearing on the outcome of the war—especially on its political issues—out of proportion to the small forces they employ. Such operations can hold or gain allies, influence neutrals to stay neutral or stray from neutrality, help resistance movements in enemy-occupied territory, and introduce sabotage and dissension into the enemy country.

In September 1943 King Vittorio Emmanuele III of Italy constitutionally cashiered his prime minister, Benito Mussolini, and appointed a new one who promptly put his predecessor under arrest and imprisoned him in a mountain fortress. Overnight, Germany lost a major ally and faced the prospect that its enemies would soon have safe passage to the Reich's undefended southern borders. But Maj. Otto Skorzeny landed under Mussolini's prison by glider, with a group of German commandos. Within hours, Il Duce was having a drink with the führer and organizing an Italian collaborationist countergovernment that helped Germany's General Kesselring conduct a brilliant elastic defense in Italy until the end of the war.

Special operations can also be used for strikes deep into enemy territory. During the 1982 Falklands War, Britain sent commandos to sabotage enemy air bases. They had more than a military effect. Their presence demoralized the defenders and created dissension among them. That is why such operations are particularly well suited to the opening phases of a war, against "soft" but vital command and control centers—e.g., the principal U.S. facility for controlling satellites, located within rocket-propelled grenade launcher range of one of California's busiest freeways.

Special operations can be used to establish relationships with foreign forces, to coordinate actions with them, and to gather information from them. Of course, during such operations troops can take and interrogate prisoners and, if they can slip in and out unnoticed, emplace and maintain networks of remote sensors.

Those who make clandestine entry must be capable of combat and able to operate a wide variety of military equipment, teach others how to operate it, and organize foreigners into military units. Each of the U.S. Army Special Forces' twelve-man "A teams" is supposed to incorporate all of the military skills necessary to organize and run at least a battalion of indigenous forces. They are also supposed to be trained in languages and in the political aspects of their work. These "green berets," schooled at the John F. Kennedy Special Warfare School at Fort Bragg, are supposed to bear the brunt of President Kennedy's promise to help any friend or fight any foe for liberty's sake. The Special Forces and their Navy and Air Force counterparts (who make fewer claims of knowing language or politics or of being able to conduct intelligence operations) were never intended to blend into a foreign environment as third-country nationals. Full-fledged capability for special operations would require a cadre of military specialists capable of doing that.

Whether they are helping resistance forces, sowing dissension among the enemy, or influencing third countries, special troops must be able to make genuine political commitments. War, the most constraining of circumstances, makes for the strangest of bedfellows. Only genuinely sympathetic individuals can expect to organize people successfully who are far different culturally during times of high emotion. These people will have their own priorities and idiosyncrasies; and since not everyone can sympathize with, say, both Kurds and dissident communists, a well-stocked special operations department must have staff officers of widely different backgrounds and widely different personal, religious, and political preferences. One of the strengths of the American OSS in World War II was its political catholicity—it sent leftists to leftists and rightists to rightists. As a result, disparate elements all over the world were enlisted to fight on the American side.

Unbloody Conflict in Peacetime

While in the West political warfare has been a pragmatic adjunct to crisis foreign policy and military operations, political warfare was the essence of politics, identical to politics, and the omnipresent engine of politics in the communist world. After the Bolshevik Revolution, mass political action, the myriad actions of fronts, of disinformation agencies, and even of special troops against domestic enemies were part of the normal workings of the Soviet state. At all times, the norm has been struggle and compulsion. Lenin put it this way:

> The dictatorship of the proletariat was successful because it knew how to combine compulsion with persuasion. . . . We must . . . see to it that the apparatus of compulsion, activized and reinforced, shall be adapted and developed for a new sweep of persuasion.[8]

As Vladimir Bukovsky, the Soviet dissident, also observed,

> The Soviet Union is not a state in the traditional meaning of the word, but a huge and well-organized army of ideological warriors, a fortress with hundreds of front organizations, thousands of publications around the world, and with a gigantic budget, perhaps even a bigger one than their military budget.[9]

Soviet policy toward the German Weimar Republic during the 1920s vividly illustrates. On the level of state-to-state relations, the Soviets wooed Germany, Europe's other pariah at the time, into mutually beneficial collaboration. Germany thus was able to evade Allied-imposed arms restrictions by developing its war machinery in secluded regions of the USSR, while Reichswehr officers trained Red Army forces in advanced weaponry. This lasted until Hitler came to power.[10] Yet on the party-to-party level, the

Soviets, through control of the German Communist Party (KPD), secretly worked to overthrow the Weimar regime. On German streets and in Parliament, Nazis and communists collaborated to destroy German democratic institutions. This pattern was paralleled by Europe-wide front organizations pursuing the never-ending Soviet goal of "peace." These logically contradictory campaigns were nevertheless unitary, and were replicated again and again throughout the world, in peace and war, sometimes successfully, sometimes not, until the Soviet Union's death.[11]

Between 1991 and 2003 Iraq's Saddam Hussein reversed the military outcome of the Gulf War. Politics was his "weapon of mass destruction." With it he hampered the Americans' will to deal with him, destroyed what respect the Americans had earned in the Arab world by their awesome display of military force in 1991, and used the United Nations' economic sanctions against him to corrupt officials from Paris to New York. While contriving for his murderous self the image of a humanitarian, he turned some of America's European allies against it, put himself at the head of the cause of Islam in the world despite his bloody anti-Islamic record, and quite simply ended up driving the world's agenda. In the end, however, he wound up facing the gallows because his political virtuosity was not backed by military power.

Saddam understood that since his American enemies had declared victory in the Gulf War without having overthrown him, any attempt they might now make to do it would be a self-indictment of their previous judgment. So he calibrated his challenges to a level high enough to embarrass the Americans, but just below what would make it necessary for them to come get him. Twice he moved troops a few miles toward Kuwait, then as American forces were mobilized and at sea, he played yo-yo with them, pulling back a bit and leading the world in laughter as the Americans went back to the other side of the globe. He hampered and humiliated the UN inspectors searching for his prohibited weapons programs, and called them American spies. The Americans gave substance to the charges by threatening war unless he complied with inspections. Just before the deadlines, he would comply, or seem to. Again, and again. By the time the Americans got wise, they had become objects of contempt in the Arab world and Saddam, a hero.

The Arab world's masses, disgusted with oppressive regimes that aped Western ways, were looking for a symbol of revenge, a savior of their pride. Saddam presented himself as just that. As early as the autumn of 1991, crowds of hundreds of thousands filled the capitals of the Arab world shouting pro-Saddam slogans. Even (indeed especially) the Muslim leaders who had sent military contingents to the U.S. side in the Gulf War hurried to speak of "brother Iraq" (Morocco's King Hassan) and to look forward to working with Saddam (Egypt's President Hosni Mubarak). The Saudi royal family began treating Saddam as someone whom its subjects revered more than their own rulers, and the Americans as more trouble than they were worth. Because of Saddam, the Arab world feared the Americans less and hated them more. By the turn of the twenty-first century his activities earned greater attention on Arab television than those of any other Arab leader. He set the agenda not only for the Arabs but for the rest of the world as well.

Saddam saw that the U.S.-sponsored UN rules that empowered a host of officials to administer his sales of oil were his chance to funnel millions of dollars both to those very officials and to persons in Europe who would become his advocates and would help turn European opinion against America. Cynically, he caused shortages of food and medicine among his domestic enemies, then publicized their suffering and blamed the Americans for it. Clandestinely, his intelligence service trained and sent forth anti-American terrorists. Publicly, he became the chief cheerleader and financier of suicide bombing against Israel.

In the next chapter we will discuss Saddam's relationship to Arab terrorism. Suffice it to say here that regardless of Saddam's relationship to the 9/11 attacks on America, those attacks proved to be on a level high enough to convince enough Americans that undoing Saddam had become necessary. His well-calibrated political war was overcome by military force majeure.

Conclusion

Political warfare may serve as a surrogate for actual war, but it does not work without actual force backing it up. Sun Tzu proposed that the "supreme art of war is to subdue the enemy without fighting." This advice seems to clash with Clausewitz's description of war as "an act of violence pushed to its utmost bounds." But the two conceptions are not contradictory. Here Clausewitz refers to fighting. But fighting is a tool of war, not war itself. Clausewitz's famous dictum that "war is a continuation of politics by other means," which refers to war itself, is quite compatible with Sun Tzu's vision of war. The practical meaning of all this was perhaps best summed up by a Soviet theoretician.

> A state official is offered a choice—to attain this or that political aim, whether to act along lines of peace or with the help of armed violence. . . . [W]hat is important is to select the means which is the most suitable under the given conditions.

This is what it's all about: When war comes, a lot of tools are always lying around or can at least be fashioned. Some are more violent than others. The political art of war consists of judging when and how each can best be used.

9

INDIRECT WARFARE AND TERROR

> The great advantage of indirect warfare is that our en-
> emies cannot answer back. If we ordered our armies to
> capture the oil pumping stations whose pipes run through
> Jordan, Syria and Lebanon and to cut their flow, this
> would unite the entire world against us; but if we sent a
> commando unit to blow up those pumping stations we
> would achieve the same result and the great powers
> would watch us with their hands tied.
>
> GAMAL ABDUL NASSER

STATES AND REVOLUTIONARIES who wage wars indirectly through guerrillas, terrorists, or other third parties with whom they deny connections,
do so because they are incapable of confronting their enemies directly in
strength. Preoccupied as we are with Middle Eastern terrorism at the outset of the twenty-first century, we are tempted to lump together commando tactics, various kinds of terrorism, and the many forms of indirect
warfare. But to understand modern terrorism we must see how it resembles
and differs militarily, politically, and morally from other forms of indirect
and low intensity conflict. Herein we explain how the success of indirect
warfare depends in no small part on the confusion of these very different
things. Then we consider terror as a tool both of indirect warfare and of
revolutionary warfare. We look in general at the causes for which terrorists
fight, and at the states whose indirect weapons they are. Specifically, we
examine secular and religious Middle Eastern terrorism.

Indirect War

Weakness dictates trying to escape responsibility for the painful pressure
one is putting on the enemy, as much as it dictates guerrilla tactics. Surely
the greatest of weaknesses is a regime's own instability. Thus fragile re-

173

gimes, whether superpowers such as was the Soviet Union, or the Mideast's ministates, calibrate their hostilities at low levels. Because they are narrowly based on a political party or on an ethnic/religious minority, such regimes tend to distrust their armies as much as their peoples. They rightly fear that mobilizing for direct war, raising the possibility of foreign invasion, would tilt the internal balance of fear against them. As we shall see, Mideast states are usually so fragile that they tend to use indirect warfare against other weak states as much as they use it against strong ones. But indirect warfare is not just the weapon of the weak.

The tools of indirect warfare include the diplomacy that induces other states to fight on one's behalf. For example, diplomacy was the tool that made Cuba both the object and the subject of indirect warfare for the last forty years of the twentieth century. Under U.S. diplomatic pressure, various countries refrained from normal relationships with the island and contributed to U.S. economic warfare against it. On the other hand, during the same period the Soviet Union's diplomacy (and economic pressure) made the Cuban army into the Soviet empire's main military proxy force in Africa.

The clandestine use of one's own armed forces—what Nasser was talking about—provides some of the benefits of indirect war. Inciting private persons to spread dissent against the enemy's regime—as the United States did to communist South Yemen in the 1980s—or terror among the enemy's civilian population is perhaps the weakest form of indirect war. Nasser knew that if he sent his regular troops on commando raids against Israel's civilian population, Israel would answer with war. So he sent ostensibly private fedayeen to sow terror. They were not as effective as regular troops, but Israel did not answer with war, perhaps because the fedayeen did relatively little damage.

Using any of the tools of indirect war requires some secrecy, or at least a pretext for denying evidence of the responsibility one bears for the attacks and of the benefits one derives from them. But secrecy is not the active ingredient in indirect war. While it may be difficult to know who caused a traffic accident or why, or even who committed a homicide, it is implausible that a people could suffer the onslaught of war and have no idea who is inflicting it on them.

Indirect war succeeds to the extent that the stricken people do not simply answer war with war on the basis of what they know. Whether or not they do is a question wholly political. When Nasser told his officers that Britain's, France's, and America's hands would be tied, he was not suggesting that any shortcoming of facts or understanding would do the tying. Rather, he thought that political impotence would keep the great powers from answering his attacks. In other words, official eyes may not see what real ones see. Acknowledging that one is at war would heighten pressure to do things that the polity may not want or be able to manage.

Political impotence may result from fear, from moral confusion, from leadership that has invested its prestige in policies that would be discredited were the country to acknowledge the source of the war being waged against it, and from internal political divisions. Hence, the success of indirect warfare always depends far less on the attacker than on the ones being attacked.

Closing one's eyes out of fear may well be a healthy response to reality. As Alexander Hamilton argued to George Washington in 1790, Americans, if possible, should have avoided the question of whether to oppose or permit Britain's use of U.S. territory to attack Spanish New Orleans—even to closing their eyes to Britain's unauthorized use. Both approval and opposition would have risked wars that America was likely to lose. Only if Britain's incursion had been blatant should America's honor have outweighed its fear. Hamilton's counsel proved wise in that case.

In many cases however, accepting indirect warfare for fear of near term troubles brings even greater troubles in the long run. Thus in the late 1930s the Czech government declined to acknowledge that the agitations of its pro-Nazi party were simply at the behest of the Reich. Czech President Eduard Benes did not confront Hitler, even diplomatically. Nazi activities eventually weakened the Czechs to the point that they offered no resistance at all to Hitler's takeover of their country. By contrast, Switzerland ordered that the headquarters of the local pro-Nazi party relocate to the German embassy, and held Hitler responsible for the party's obedience of Swiss law. If Germany was going to take over Switzerland, neither proxies nor pretenses would play a part. Similarly, until the mid-1970s Syria refrained from sending terrorists against Israel because Israel would not listen to excuses that terrorists coming out of Syria were somehow acting on their own. Israel would hold Damascus responsible for anything and anyone who came at it from or through Syria.

This brings us to a key point: history, international law, and most counties' domestic laws, as well as common sense, tell us that any government, company, or individual that claims sovereignty or control of any place is in fact responsible for any harm that might come out of that place. Hence, just as water damage to house B from unrepaired pipes in house A are the responsibility of A's owner, so acts of war against country B that come from any place are ipso facto acts of war by the persons who control that place. In 1819 Secretary of State John Quincy Adams made that point in reply to Spain's complaint that Gen. Andrew Jackson had invaded Spanish Florida, captured a fort, and hanged its two leaders. Jackson had done it, wrote Adams, because Spain had not prevented the fort from being used as a base for attacks against the United States. Florida would be returned to

Spain as soon as Spain showed itself able and willing to make sure that no harm would come out of it. Dispelling confusion about this point is the antidote to indirect warfare.

Confidence in the enemy's moral confusion was the basis for the Soviet Union's policy of working through "popular fronts" both within target countries and internationally. "Fronts" consisted mainly of many unwitting or semiwitting individuals (or countries) who agreed with the Soviets on a few things only. But they were led by a few individuals (or countries) who wittingly led the rest into working as Soviet proxies. By infusing their own agents into and among innocent objectives and people, the Soviets often confused their enemies into regarding people who were acting on the Soviet Union's behalf as something other than proxies. Thus beginning in the 1950s the Soviets infiltrated anticolonial movements (among many others) and used them as proxies against Western interests. This tactic successfully fostered moral uncertainty among Americans during the Vietnam War. Was America fighting proxies of a Soviet state whose ultimate target was America, or a bunch of benign, indigenous, nationalist agrarian reformers whom Americans had no right to oppose? The confusion aggravated America's existing political divisions.

Understandably, political figures who have staked their careers and reputations on the foreign policy choices and predictions they have made prefer not to confront evidence that their mistakes have endangered their country. That is so especially where indirect war is concerned. In the late 1930s British Prime Minister Neville Chamberlain had failed to understand that pan-German movements in Vienna, Prague, and Danzig amounted to a Nazi proxy war that portended direct war. Yet when events in mid-1939 proved him wrong, Chamberlain served his country unusually well by acknowledging his error and supporting his chief critic, Winston Churchill, to be his successor. More dismal but more normal was Henry Kissinger. Between 1969 and 1972 he had built his reputation on the proposition that he had so cleverly bound the Soviet Union in a "network of mutually beneficial relationships" that the Soviets would no longer wage indirect war against America. But in October 1973 it turned out that the Soviets had encouraged, supplied, and helped plan the Yom Kippur War, and that they were encouraging Mideast states to embargo oil to the West. A reporter asked Kissinger whether this contradicted his assurances about Soviet behavior. Kissinger replied that if ever he saw anything that contradicted them he would say so. Unlike Chamberlain, Kissinger cast a confusing cloud of political and personal interest over what was happening. This is exactly what indirect warfare requires to succeed.

Partisan divisions are thick optics through which the truths of foreign affairs have to pass. By 1796 bitter experience had taught George Washington how dangerous it is for citizens of any country to form excessive affection or distaste for any other. Americans who followed Thomas Jefferson had fallen in love with their own idea of the French Revolution. Hence they saw nothing wrong with murderous tyrants in Paris, and accused American skeptics, such as Alexander Hamilton, of being British agents. These returned the favor by accusing their counterparts of being proxies in France's attempt to enlist America in its war with Britain. It is indeed difficult to counter the tendency to turn all questions into instruments in the struggle for domestic partisan advantage. Sometimes, as happened in America after 2001, not even a direct attack on the country is enough. Who is responsible for terror attacks against America? Republicans' and Democrats' answers tended to be substantially different but equally scripted for partisan advantage.

Hence the success of any and all tools of indirect warfare depends much less on the attackers' skill at masking reality than on the level at which the damage that the target absorbs outweighs the factors that make for its impotence.

Indirect war is very common. The United States and the Soviet Union fought the Cold War mostly indirectly. (For the pawns involved, however, the warfare was very direct, and the deaths real.) While in the 1950s U.S. forces fought North Korean and Chinese proxies for the Soviet Union and in the '60s and '70s fought Soviet proxies in Vietnam, Soviet troops did not fight U.S. proxies until the United States began supporting the Afghan people's resistance to the Soviets' 1979 invasion of their country. Most of the time however Soviet proxies faced American proxies—in China between 1947 and 1949 the Soviet-supplied army of Mao Tse-tung fought the U.S.-supplied army of Chiang Kai Shek. Throughout Europe in the '40s, '50s, and '60s Soviet-oriented and Soviet-backed trade unionists and politicians fought politically against their American-oriented, American-backed counterparts. In the Congo in 1960 the Soviets' Lumumba fought the West's Tshombe. In Latin America, Soviet and American proxies exchanged coups and counter-coups. Throughout the third world rulers like Cuba's Fidel Castro and Syria's Hafez Assad held power through Soviet patronage. The Soviets built the Palestine Liberation Organization and other terrorist organizations into more than they would have been without it, trained them in Czechoslovakia, and funneled their operatives into western Europe through East Berlin.

In Moscow there was some debate (though not nearly as much as in Washington) about who in any given country was on whose side. But there was little doubt anywhere in the 1980s that the Americans were helping anti-Soviet forces in Afghanistan, Nicaragua, and Angola, and that most third-world regimes were safeguarded by Soviet-trained security services and their anti-Americanism was stoked by the Soviet Union. So why did both sides go through any trouble at all to hide their relationship with their proxies and complain about the troubles that the others' proxies were making for them? Why did they not simply "go to the source"? Because by making excuses, albeit thin ones, they hoped to encourage whatever reticence or timidity might exist on the other side—at least not to strengthen the main enemy by adding insult to injury. In the end, they deemed it safer and more productive to fight indirectly.

None of this is to suggest that proxies are mere automatons, fully in their masters' control. Rather, in most cases the proxy's and the master's interests are intertwined. The point, however, is that the master is the sine qua non of the proxy's involvement. The proxies do the heavy lifting. But the masters offer the essentials: hope of success and material assistance.

Terror

Terror is one of the many tools of indirect and of revolutionary warfare. As well, terror is a tool in direct warfare. Sadly, it is very much part of the arsenal of rulers.

Moral relativism has befogged the commonsense understanding of terror. True, when one army sets about destroying another, it spreads death chiefly in order to spread the terror that actually does most of the destroying. But commonsense usage of the word "terror" implies not what armed forces do to one another, but rather armed men slaughtering helpless, innocent ones. *Terrorism is about terrorizing innocents.* The key concepts for distinguishing terrorism from ordinary military activities are the innocence of the targets and the intention to strike them despite or even because of their innocence. As Thucydides teaches and America's Declaration of Independence states, merely barbarian warfare terrifies because it does not discriminate between combatants, noncombatants, male, female, young or old. But terrorism *does* discriminate; its victims are chosen precisely because they are relatively defenseless and, hence, usually innocent. Terror produces panic by convincing people that mere innocence cannot save them.

Just as the common, pejorative, sense of the word "terror" does not apply to spreading panic among armed enemies, it does not apply to terrorizing enemy governments. After all, striking armies is merely incidental to the purpose of war, namely to affect enemy governments. But are not enemy governments mainly civilian? Are they not innocent? On the contrary. When governments direct wars, they are more responsible than the armies they recruit and direct. Thus, attacks on government offices (Israel's Irgun bombed Jerusalem's King David Hotel, which British occupiers were using as their military headquarters in 1947) or the assassination of enemy officials (a favorite tactic of all revolutionary warriors) or attempts to sink warships (as a bomb-laden small boat did to the USS *Cole* in Yemen in 2000) are mere acts of war just as much when they are carried out clandestinely as when done by artillery, or aircraft.

Under international law, those who do such deeds may be punished as criminals *only* if they do not wear clothing that identifies them as combatants. (They almost never do.) Conversely, armed forces that shoot, shell, bomb, or starve nongovernment civilians (intentionally rather than collaterally) for the purpose of affecting their governments—as did all sides in World War II—deserve the label "terrorist" regardless of uniforms worn and flags flown.

Beginning in World War I all governments betrayed common sense by translating the truth that civilians contribute to the war effort into the nihilistic notion that there are no innocents behind enemy lines. Hence governments began to enforce blockades of food and fuel against entire countries and to use artillery, and later, aerial bombing, against whole cities. According to the twentieth-century understanding of "total war," even children became fair game because they would grow up to be adults, and even their toys became proper targets of blockade because they might raise morale. By crushing civilian morale through pain and fear, so goes the argument, one might undercut civilians' support for their government. Hence killing people previously thought of as innocents became a good thing—as long as they were on the other side. We can call enemies "terrorists" when they spread terror among us. But when *we* spread terror among *them*, we are . . . well, us. It was left to a U.S. Central Intelligence Agency 1978 report to endorse nihilism explicitly: "One man's terrorist is another man's freedom fighter."

Understandably, the great powers' low-grade moral relativism signaled their acceptance of terror in revolutionary warfare against themselves, as well as of terror as a weapon in indirect warfare. Hence in 1970 a United Nations resolution affirmed "the legitimacy of the struggle of colonial peoples and peoples under alien domination to exercise their right to self determination and independence by all necessary means at their disposal." Proponents and opponents understood this as an endorsement of terrorism for causes approved by those who approve them. The UN's Islamic Conference (one-third of the UN's membership) has repeatedly cited this resolution to block any blanket condemnation of killing innocents, and the UN's Commission on Human Rights (with western European states voting in favor) has consistently endorsed the use of "all necessary means" in the Arab struggle against Israel. It is a commonplace in the Arab world that killing Israeli children is permissible not only because they would grow up to bear arms and to occupy Arab land, but also because Israeli civilians' fear for their children tends to weaken their resistance.

The Europeans did not imagine that Arabs in their midst would come to feel that terrorism against Frenchmen, Dutchmen, Spaniards, etc. would be legitimate. In line with this, the U.S. State Department has struggled to differentiate the killing of American civilians, which it calls "terrorism," from the killing of Israeli civilians, which it supposes to be something else, since those who kill Israelis regard them as occupiers. This subjective balancing became more difficult during the post-2003 presence of U.S. troops in Iraq, when persons who claimed to be fighting the U.S. occupation killed American and non-American civilians. When Muslims set off bombs among Madrid and London commuters in 2004 and 2005, Europeans did not understand how they might have encouraged attacks against themselves.

Sowing terror among innocents has always been one of the principal means by which despots convince their subjects that active support is the only possible alternative to violent death. The progressives of the French Revolution were the first, in 1792, to label "terror" their policy of killing innocents to remove potential opponents, forestall opposition, and encourage expressions of support. In 1918 terror became the official, long-term internal policy of a great power—the Soviet Union. By murdering some twenty million innocents and imprisoning tens more millions, Lenin and Stalin meant to kill the biological and socioeconomic bases for opposition, as well as to frighten the remainder of the Soviet population into unquestioning support for their regime. Lenin and Stalin would set arbitrary quotas for people to be killed in each region. People were not killed because they were enemies. The party's terrorist logic labeled the victims enemies because they were being killed. When in 1956 party boss Nikita Khruschev denounced "Stalin's crimes," he made clear that "terrorism" was not among those crimes. No one, he said, could claim the title of communist while rejecting so fundamental a tool of struggle as terrorism.

Of course regimes that live by terror internally naturally tend to use it as a tool of foreign policy as well. The Soviet Union was no exception. Thus it did much to foster terrorism around the world. Its legacy spilled from the twentieth century into the twenty-first.

The Causes and Sources of Terror

Today's terrorism is a combination of indirect warfare and revolutionary warfare. It is anything but "senseless violence."

Terrorists are soldiers of a sort. Though they often grasp their leaders' causes with more passion than understanding, they, more than ordinary soldiers, depend on those causes, are well paid, well insured, and at the end of elaborate logistical chains. For the terrorists' officers, the cause is less any set of abstract beliefs than their political and material bases of support. Indeed most leaders of terrorist groups show a ready versatility of conviction worthy of professional fund-raisers. Thus terrorist chieftains Abu Nidal, Ahmed Jibril, and Yasir Arafat, who began their careers as secular nationalists with deep Soviet connections, began in the wake of Iran's 1978 Islamic revolution to diversify their sources of support by professing a deep Islamic religiosity they certainly did not feel. Even less sincere were the Islamic pretensions of Iraq's Saddam Hussein. He entered politics in 1959 as an assassin in the service of secular socialism. Until the end of his career in 2003 he terrorized Islamic movements at home and practiced terrorism abroad. Remarkably, substantially through that terrorism, he managed to present himself as the world's foremost fighter for Islam. More on that in chapter 15. The point here is that terrorism can be practiced to promote any number of causes, but that the closer one gets to those who define any given cause the more do the interests of the cause tend to merge with the interests of the sources of terrorism—of the regimes that make it possible.

Modern revolutionary war began after World War I in the service of two causes that soon intertwined: socialism and "national liberation." In the 1920s and 1930s Europe was plagued by squads of fascists with black or brown insignia who battled squads of communists with red insignia for the exclusive power to terrorize their countries into "national" or "international" socialism, respectively. In other words, the political violence of those years came from the post–World War I split in the radical wing of the socialist movement. The violence became serious because states embodied the cause of, and served as the base for, each faction. That era's greatest conflict, the Spanish civil war of 1936–39, settled any doubt about the "state sponsorship" of the competing communist and fascist terrors. It was effectively a proxy war between the Soviet Union on one side and Germany and Italy on the other. Each terrorized innocents in its own zone of Spain for the privilege of terrorizing the rest.

After World War II had eliminated Italy's fascist and Germany's Nazi regimes, National Socialism ceased to cause political violence in Europe. The only people who were left to beat, kill, and intimidate others for political causes gave themselves names such as "Red Flying Squad," "Red Brigades," "Red Army," "Red Army Faction," "Proletarian Justice," etc. Such names were no accident. Although these terrorists' causes were not identical with the Soviet Union's they coincided so much that their members got money, training at camps either outside Prague or in the Crimea, and refuge in the Soviet empire when needed. Although at the time European and American leftists hotly disputed these practical connections, documentary proof came after the 1990 reunification of Germany placed East German files in Western hands. Already indisputable, however, was that the Libyan terrorists who blew up a West Berlin discotheque full of Americans in 1985 had come, bombs and all, through East Berlin—hardly a place through which armed foreigners transited without serving government policy. Clearly as well, communist Bulgaria was not a place where a penniless, nonideological, escaped Turkish convict named Mehmet Ali Agca could have stayed at a five-star hotel and emerged in 1981 armed and moneyed to shoot Pope John Paul II—arguably the Soviet empire's most potent enemy—had Agca not been serving the interests of that empire.

Most definitive is the fact that after the Soviet Union's 1991 collapse, revolutionary terrorist groups that called themselves "Red," or "Communist," or "Proletarian" ceased to exist just as surely as Nazi terrorists had ceased to exist in 1945 after the fall of Berlin. By the same token, after the Soviet Union lost control of Eastern Europe, no terrorists any longer trained in or transited Bulgaria, Berlin, Prague, etc. Most interesting, many of the terrorists who had fought under the banner of communist anti-Westernism took a break between 1990 and 1993, and retooled themselves to fit under an apparently new cause, Islamic anti-Westernism. In fact Islamic anti-Westernism is but the latest manifestation of the conjunction of socialist and anti-Western causes—mostly a political movement masquerading as a religious one.

Anti-Westernism emerged in the 1920s as Britain, France, Italy, Portugal, Belgium, and the Netherlands were losing the will to hold on to their colonies in Africa and Asia. The nascent Soviet Union's short-term priority had been to keep the Western powers from attacking it. This it did in part by fostering its part of the aforementioned "anticapitalist" violence on Western streets. But the Soviets also set about mobilizing the entire world against Europe and America. Hence from the very first, the Soviets did what they could to stir up "anti-imperialist" violence. The immediate goal here was to control the anticolonial movements that sprang up as the colonial powers' grip loosened.

The technique was identical to the one the Soviets used in the Spanish civil war: Kill first any and all who are on the side of "national liberation" but who do not submit to communist discipline. Only when you have become masters of your movement should you attack the Europeans. This advice was taken by various "national liberation fronts" (a Marxist term) from Algeria to Zimbabwe, from Indonesia to Iraq.

More difficult to inculcate was the ideological superstructure for doing this. To be sure, Lenin himself had written the canon in 1902, a book titled *Imperialism, the Final Stage of Capitalism*. But its jargon meant nothing to Asians and Africans. Of course ordinary xenophobia fueled anticolonialist movements all by itself. But antiwhite racism did not suit the pale faced men in the Kremlin. So a generation of Marxists worked to produce justifications for vengeance against the West, the most influential of these being Franz Fanon's *The Wretched of the Earth*. It is a simplified, supercharged, and attractive Leninism: since your wretchedness is the imperialists' fault, killing them assures your well-being. Countless semi-educated professors and publicists have translated this cause into their own circumstances, mixing it with native elements. Islamic anti-Westernism is just another of these translations, promoting Islamic piety less than a violent political agenda. There were many translations.

Under the insignia of a globe resting on a pair of submachine guns, the Tricontinental Conference convened in Fidel Castro's Havana in 1968. Its chairman was Achmed Rachidov, first secretary of the Communist Party of Soviet Kazakhstan. Attending were all the world's Soviet line armed movements, from Colombia's Revolutionary Armed Forces to the Communist Party of North Vietnam, to the Palestine Liberation Organization. The point of the conference was straight out of Fanon: Whatever your troubles, regardless of, as we might say today, "where you're coming from," the solution is to help one another shoot up American interests throughout the world.

Each of the conference's attendees combined an international agenda—"anti-imperialism," which required killing Americans and Europeans to drive them out of their part of the world—and a domestic agenda—some kind of "national liberation." This also required killing those locals who stood in their way to power. The practical guidelines for operations accepted by all were contained in the Brazilian Carlos Marighella's *Minimanual of the Urban Guerrilla*, which draws the practical, operational consequences of Fanon's teachings. Thus did revolutionary warfare for socialism and national liberation become a tool of indirect and revolutionary warfare. By the time the Soviet Union died a third of a century later, modern terrorism had acquired a life of its own. Its practitioners had prospered, and its victims had accepted it.

Modern Terrorism In and From the Middle East

Our interest in the fact that America (formerly Europe) and Israel are the foci of so much terrorism in and from the Middle East obscures the equally important fact that terrorism serves indirect warfare among Mideastern regimes and their internal needs more than it does indirect warfare against westerners.

For Middle Eastern regimes, aiding and abetting terrorism against Israel is an *internal* necessity. The Syrian regime consists of Alewites, a sect that most Muslims consider heretical and that makes up only some 11 percent of Syria's population. By ostentatiously hosting and praising anti-Israeli terrorists, the Alewite regime tries to prove itself more Muslim than the Muslims, more Arab than the Arabs. The former Iraqi regime of Saddam Hussein also consisted of its country's smallest religious/ethnic minority, Sunni Mesopotamian Arabs, something over 15 percent of the population. Loud support for killing Jews was something all Iraqi Arabs might approve. Bloodying Jews to drive them into the sea also draws the attention of Palestinians away from the fact that Arab regimes do not allow them to be citizens, buy houses, or intermarry. As for the Saudi regime, financing terrorists both directly and through Syria, pre-2003 Iraq, and Egypt is essential to maintaining its credentials as a proper Muslim outfit, and to induce its radical Wahhabi sect to closing its eyes to the reality that the regime's members lead thoroughly un-Muslim lives. By financing terrorists directly, as well as indirectly through the regimes that harbor them, the Saudis also purchase the political and military protection that they cannot provide for themselves. For Iran, otherwise a stranger in the region because it is Persian and Shi'ite, deployment of its terror group Hizbullah in Lebanon for operations against Israel reinforces its regime's Islamic credentials at home and abroad, and provides leverage in regional politics. *In short, if Israel did not exist, its neighbors would press to invent something like it.*

By working with different terrorist groups, each regime also purchases a sword that it can wield against others. Beginning in the late 1960s Egypt, Syria, Iraq, and Jordan each had their own factions within the PLO. They viewed them less as weapons against Israel than as pawns against one another. By 1970 the Syrian and Iraqi factions so dominated the PLO as to pose serious danger to the Jordanian monarchy. Hence in September 1970 Jordan, with Egypt's support, unleashed its Arab Legion, a Bedouin force, on Arafat's Palestinians. The legion massacred. The Palestinian survivors fled to Syria, which transferred them to Lebanon, where—in addition to everything else they did—they prepared the way for Syria's conquest of that country.

Much of the warfare between rival militias in Lebanon between 1970 and 1990 was terrorist proxy war between Syria and Iran on one side, and Egypt and Iraq on the other, with Saudi Arabia financing all sides. But despite the fact that Egypt was aligned with Iraq in the longstanding violent feud between Iraq's and Syria's ruling Ba'ath parties, Iraq contributed money and operational support to Egypt's radical Islamic opposition, headed by the blind sheik, Abdul Rahman. It also coordinated its longstanding violent and nonviolent efforts against Saudi Arabia with a Saudi dissident named Osama bin Laden.

In the 1990s the special operations branch of Iraq's intelligence service added a new dimension to working with established terrorist groups against other Arab states. It set up a camp at Salman Pak near Baghdad to train individual fedayeen, preferably with Islamic backgrounds, from every Muslim nation other than Iraq in terrorist operations, including hijacking airplanes. An old airplane served as a classroom for that. Iraqi intelligence had long infiltrated and used Baluchi opponents to Iran, just as Iran had infiltrated and used Kurdish opponents to Iraq. But by the 1990s the combination of individual recruitment and ever deeper infiltration of groups tightened Iraq's control over what the terrorists it dealt with would and would not do.

Just which terrorist does what, for and against which regime, depends on who infiltrates whom, and on who provides what to whom. For example, though by the late 1990s Osama bin Laden's al Qaeda had constituent groups with some presence in some fifty countries, despite the fact that most of its fighters were Egyptians, and despite (or because) it was itself heavily infiltrated by Iraqi, Saudi, and Egyptian intelligence, it had deployed the vast majority of its fighters in Afghanistan as part of the ruling ethnic Pushtun Talibans' more or less conventional civil war against the ethnic Tadjik Northern Alliance.

It is difficult to see a direct relationship between the declared goals of Middle Eastern terrorists and what they actually do. Again, bin Laden's al Qaeda illustrates. Its declared top priority is to fight falsely Muslim regimes. Next are regimes that mistreat Muslims. Way down as priority targets are the "little Satan," Israel, and the "great Satan," America. Yet as it turned out, al Qaeda did nothing or near nothing against any Mideast regime, all of which are run by false Muslims and oppress Islamist movements; very little against Israel; quite a bit against America; and an awful lot against good Tadjik Muslims in Afghanistan. Why? The Pushtun Taliban provided al Qaeda a base in Afghanistan, America is a soft target, and the Arab regimes are good at security. Perhaps most important, their infiltrators influence what al Qaeda does. Hence al Qaeda's actions result from a combination of relative hardness of targets, infiltration, and shared interest. The U.S. report on the interrogation of al Qaeda official Abu Zubaydah recounts bin Laden's reaction to cooperation with Saddam Hussein against America. Bin Laden's commitment to destroy the United States was "so strong," said Zubaydah, that he "viewed as an ally" any entity that "hated Americans or was willing to kill them."

AGAINST THE WEST Terrorism became the sole viable mode of warfare for Middle Eastern regimes against Israel and other westerners (Israel being hated more for its Western-ness than for its Jewishness) because all their direct wars against Israel (1948, 1956, 1973, and 1982) revealed the Arabs' military impotence—regardless of numbers of troops or quality of equipment.

The turning against the West of the region's preferred mode of warfare occurred over decades, during which terrorist successes demonstrated Western *political* impotence, and led to ever bolder tactics. Secular groups began it, backed by secular regimes. But by the time of the 1978–79 Iranian revolution, the tide of Islamism in the region had risen to the point that secular regimes—all but Iran's are that—had to pretend radical religiosity though they were actually suppressing religiously based domestic opposition. Supporting religiously based anti-Western terrorism became the most convenient way of doing that.

The point is that terrorism moved ostensibly by religious piety reflects the region's preferred mode of war neither more nor less than does its secular version. Religiously based terrorism became important many years after secular-based terror had succeeded in shaking westerners. It arose as part of a broad Islamist movement directed against the secular regimes of the region more than against westerners.

SECULAR Beginning in 1957 Yasir Arafat, an Egyptian who had entered public life at a Soviet conference in Prague the previous year, headed the Fatah faction of Nasser's fedayeen. In 1964 he gathered around himself some Palestinians unhappy with Nasser's devotion to their cause, took them to Jordan, and formed the Palestine Liberation Organization. His fedayeen's first operation was an attack on an Israeli water-pumping station—no different from the sort of thing they had been doing under Nasser. Soon, however, they began setting bombs in Israel, shooting mortars and rockets into it, and attacking Israeli schoolchildren. After the Arab armies' massive defeat in the 1967 Six Days' War, these tiny successes in drawing Israeli blood made Arafat a hero among Arabs and attractive to their regimes, as well as to the Soviet Union. Emboldened, Arafat began a campaign of airplane hijackings and high-profile assassinations, including that of Jordan's prime minister, Wafsi Tal, on behalf of Egypt and on behalf of the Soviets, of U.S. ambassador Cleo Noel. By 1970 Arafat had set up a state within a state in Jordan, allied chiefly with Syria. Jordan's King Hussein responded by decimating the PLO in September of that year. Its remnants fled to Syria, and Syria transferred them to Lebanon. Thereafter, the PLO's massacre of Israeli athletes at the Munich Olympics, its bombings and mass shootings at airports in Israel and Europe, and its continued airplane hijackings and mass hostage takings, not to mention its creation of a violent ministate in Lebanon, made it into a minipower.

By this time, factions within the PLO had aligned themselves formally or informally with Syria (Abu Nidal) and Iraq (Abu Abbas), as well as with Libya. In a nutshell, Arab terrorism had become a crazy quilt of semirelated groups with shifting relationships to different governments. This complicated matters in Lebanon but made it plausible for Arafat to deny responsibility for some of the most egregious acts. Was he really in charge of Black September, or later, of Force 17, his victims asked? In 1974, shortly after his PLO had murdered twenty six Israeli schoolchildren, Arafat addressed the UN General Assembly wearing a pistol, and was applauded. Until his death in 2004 progressives professed uncertainty about his responsibility for the murderous Tanzim and Al Aksa Martyrs' Brigade.

By 1982 when Israel, allied with Lebanon's Christian factions, made war on the PLO and trapped its fighters in East Beirut, Arafat had already won political victories that overshadowed his military defeats. First, the PLO's mitosis into groups with various names supported by various states in various ways for various purposes, occurring in a Lebanon whose government obviously was not responsible for what happened within its borders, abetted Europeans and Americans who simply were afraid to face the fact that Syria, Iraq, and Libya—all Soviet client states—were making terrorism possible. And so, though the U.S. State Department published lists of states that sponsored terrorism, Europeans and Americans de facto began to regard terror as a set of crimes for which no one but the shooters and bombers was responsible. Thenceforth, antiterrorism would consist of pursuing individuals, as well as of futile security measures at airports.

Second, inability to put a stop to terrorism convinced many westerners that there *just had to be* ways of deflecting the terrorists' wrath, or of getting along with them. Europeans, some Americans, and some Israelis, too, came to believe that if somehow the "Arab-Israeli dispute" were solved, terrorism would disappear. This set off something of a race to see who could discover that Arafat was really a "moderate" who had renounced terrorism and first propose a solution acceptable to the Arabs that would safeguard the proposers from terrorism. As proposals followed one another, the Europeans increasingly put distance between themselves, Israel, and the Americans. Third, the Arabs' anti-Westernism became fashionable in fashionable Western circles.

Hence, as early as 1975, Europeans, led by France, proclaimed themselves "friends of the Arabs," and began supporting the Arab world's demands against Israel. Out of fear of drawing further terror on themselves, Europeans began to release terrorists in their custody. Already in 1972 the German government had released Arafat's terrorists who had murdered Israeli athletes at the Munich Olympics. In 1986 the Italians released Abu Abbas after American warplanes forced his plane to land in Italy. He had murdered a wheelchair-bound American Jew on a cruise ship he had hijacked.

Fourth and arguably most important, Europeans and some Israelis and some Americans began to regard Arafat—and Syria's Hafez Assad and Iraq's

Saddam Hussein—as indispensable negotiators to end terrorism rather than as terrorism's chieftains and beneficiaries. This despite the uncontested presence in Damascus and Baghdad of people who had committed terrorist acts. During the 1980s American officials knew very well that the militias who had killed 240 U.S. marines in Beirut were working for Syria's Assad. But once these chieftains came to be regarded as on the side of progress and peace, they were not to be destroyed but courted. Officially, the Western powers came to believe that terrorists are not the proxies of regimes but rather "loose networks" of "rogue individuals" who operate despite the efforts of regimes.

Hence, European and American officials and media accepted Arafat's 1988 statement that he no longer directed terrorist activities but merely represented the causes for which all Arabs fought. (At roughly the same time Western governments accepted the distinction between the terrorists of the Irish Republican Army, which they called the "military wing," and its "political wing," with which they sought to share political power.) *This granting to the likes of Arafat the contradictory claims that they do not control the terrorists enough to direct them but do control them enough to stop them if they are properly rewarded is the fulfillment of indirect warfare.* And so in 1993 Israelis, Europeans, and Americans granted the PLO a ministate in the Gaza and West Bank territories adjacent to Israel in the expectation that it would contain terror. Yasir Arafat got the Nobel Peace Prize and became the most frequent foreign visitor in the White House. Secular terrorism was paying big dividends. It grew.

Terrorism, religious as well as secular, grew as it did quite simply because Western leaders desperately wanted to believe they could appease it. Thus in July 2003 U.S. Secretary of State Colin Powell said that if Hamas, the PLO's religious rival in terrorism, were to make declarations similar to the PLO's the United States would regard it, as well as the PLO, as a partner for peace. Hamas could then use the same tactic as the PLO, running terrorist operations while denying responsibility for them. In 2006 when Hamas won a majority in the Palestinian parliament, Americans and Europeans rushed to find excuses and intermediaries for doing precisely this. The flow of Western money did not miss a beat.

The progression has no logical end: regimes deny responsibility for terrorist acts by contracting to major terrorist organizations, major terrorist organizations gain the privileges of regimes by imputing these acts to their subsidiaries, and the subsidiaries can earn the privileges of major ones by doing so much terrorism that their victims will beg them to impute it to yet others. Regimes, contractors, and subcontractors can fight the common enemy while pointing fingers at one another: regimes can say that peace can come only if the terrorists' legitimate grievances are satisfied, and the terrorists will be satisfied only when the regimes are. Success depends on the willingness of the targets again and again to raise the criteria for considering one an enemy while lowering the criteria for considering one a "partner for peace."

Meanwhile, however, all regimes throughout the Middle East, especially secular ones, were being challenged by growing religious movements. By the 1980s secular terrorist groups faced a mixture of competition and opposition from religious groups as violent as they.

RELIGION Political circumstances more than religion were responsible for the rise of religious terrorism against both locals and westerners. Since its founding in the 1920s by the Egyptian Hassan al Banna, the Muslim Brotherhood, an Egyptian organization widely imitated throughout the Muslim world, had been in conflict with the elites of Middle Eastern societies. The Brotherhood despised the elites' westernizing ways and envied their relative prosperity. In turn, the elites' progressive elements disdained what they considered the religious simpletons. Both sides united, however, in wanting to rid the Arab world of Western domination. But beginning in the 1950s, after the Brotherhood helped secular, westernizing progressives such as Nasser, the Arab national socialist Ba'ath Party, and the Algerian FLN rid the Mideast of Western rule, they found that the new secular regimes persecuted them more cruelly than either Turkish or Western imperialists had ever done. The Brotherhood fought back with terror of their own.

War between secular Arab regimes and Islamists became the dominant feature of life in the Arab world in the last half of the twentieth century. These regimes' incompetence and corruption compounded the disasters of their socialist socioeconomic policies. Economic life retrogressed. Public education almost disappeared. Welfare became a strictly political tool. The regimes flouted their peoples' moral sense. By default, the mosques became the agencies of the Arabs' mutual self-help, where children could learn to read, the indigent could be cared for, and a sense of right and wrong could be cultivated. From Morocco to Pakistan, the Islamist movements drew society's best young people to themselves. The secular, nationalist, socialist regimes lost whatever legitimacy they had. Bereft of ideas, relying on force and corruption alone, they feared for themselves.

The secular regimes struck hard. In 1979 the Syrian Ba'athist regime destroyed large parts of its third-largest city, Hama, killing some ten thousand, because the Muslim Brotherhood had gained much prominence there. In the other Ba'athist state, Iraq, large parts of the Shi'ite hierarchy had to flee to Iran for their lives as the regime killed Shi'ites by the thousands. Meanwhile Iran was exiling its most active Shi'ite cleric, the Ayatollah Khomeini. In 1981, after Egypt's Islamists killed President Anwar Sadat, several thousand persons associated with the Islamic movement were arrested, and many disappeared. In Algeria, after the National Islamic Front had won national elections in 1990, the governing secular National Liberation Front annulled the results and started a ten-year civil war that consisted largely of terrorism and cost at least fifty thousand lives.

Nevertheless the growing Islamic movements continued to find ways of harassing their countries' ruling regimes from within. Thus for example in 1997 Egyptian Islamists slaughtered a busload of tourists at the Luxor temple complex. Cutting Egypt's revenue from tourism, more than hatred of westerners, motivated this mass murder. But striking Arab regimes proved difficult, and elicited frightful retaliation. Hence gradually the violent parts of the Islamic movements sought to attack their ruling regimes by attacking the westerners who supported them. This is essentially the story of Osama bin Laden: unable to reform the immoral and corrupt Saudi regime, he turned to attacking that regime's main source of support, the United States.

All the region's regimes deal with the growth of Islamism by controlling or repressing it within, while encouraging its violent expression against westerners. That includes even the region's traditional monarchies. In Morocco, Jordan, and particularly Saudi Arabia, the king formally heads the Islamic movement. The first two keep even external Islamist activities relatively well in check. But since one of the Saudi regime's major constituents is the Wahhabi sect, which has done much to redefine Islam as a set of anti-Western activities, the Saudi king's authority over his country's Islamic movement is much more limited. Even less can the traditional rulers of the Gulf deal with a large Wahhabi presence. Like Saudi Arabia they provide ingress, egress, financing, and propaganda (Qtar's al Jazeera television) for terrorist operations abroad in exchange for peace at home.

Since Iran's secular, westernizing shah succumbed to the Islamist movement of the Ayatollah Khomeini in 1979, all the region's regimes, secular ones no less than traditional monarchies, have put on an Islamic face and worked to turn Islamic fervor in an anti-Western direction. In Egypt, which lives in fear of Islamist movements, the endorsement of Islamism is couched strictly in terms of anti-Westernism. In Syria, which fights and fears Islamism more than Egypt, its secular terrorism is couched in Islamic terms. So, in spades, was it in Saddam's Iraq. The result has been that secular terrorists no less than the regimes they serve have presented themselves as servants of Islamic causes. And in fact anti-Westernism has both a nationalist and an Islamic face.

As often as not, secular and religious revolutionary terrorists cooperate. The Ayatollah Khomeini took power in Iran thanks in no small part to the secular PLO, and its even more antireligious sponsor, the Soviet Union. Note that Khomeini's chief lieutenants were graduates of Moscow's Patrice

Lumumba University—established specifically to raise up cadres for secular, anti-Western revolutions the world over. Conversely, the PLO's number-two man throughout its time as an openly secular, pro-Soviet organization, Mahmoud Abbas, alias Abu Mazen, began his career as part of Cairo's Muslim Brotherhood. But just as convergence of political interests have led ayatollahs and commissars to cooperate, divergences of interests have led to clashes. Thus the Iranian ayatollahs' terror tool, Hizbullah, the Party of God, came to blows with the PLO in Lebanon because one of Iran's principal interests, advancing the fortunes of Shi'ites, conflicted with the PLO's agenda. Not even the Soviets could smother the conflict between their allies. In Israel, the PLO's various factions (Al Aksa Martyrs' Brigade, etc.) and the Islamist Hamas terrorize one another as both terrorize Israelis. In short, the struggles and alliances have been political, and terror has been the region's workaday tool for religious as well as for secular revolutionaries and regimes. *Terrorism is the local political currency.*

War and terror tactics are not new to the history of Islam. The relationship between Islam's main branches, Sunna and Shi'a, has been even more violent and less theological than that between Catholics and Protestants in sixteenth-century Europe. The nineteenth-century slaughters of Shi'ites in present-day Iraq by the Saudi Wahhabi heretical sect outdid the worst excesses of its renaissance Christian counterparts. Even so, the practical twenty-first-century redefinition of Islam in terms of anti-Western, specifically anti-American, terror is unprecedented. It cannot be over emphasized that Islamism is a *political* movement sailing under religious colors.

The Scope of Modern Terrorism

The rise of Islamism and the eagerness with which secular terrorists and Middle Eastern regimes adopted religious language ended up confusing the causes of Islam with the causes of those regimes—again, nearly all of which are un-Muslim—and with the un-Muslim cause of anti-Americanism. The violent conflation of Islamism and anti-Americanism has drawn countless recruits to the main instrument of those causes, terrorism. In no way, however, does the role of Islamism make terrorism any less a tool of indirect war or change the role of regimes in indirect war.

Not only are those attracted to fighting for Islam superior in number to those inclined to fight for any kind of secular order. They are also superior in quality. Contrary to popular opinion, they are not semiliterates raised on rote chanting of Koranic verses, but are often technically qualified professionals. More important, while their religious commitment tends to be marginal when they join the movement, it strengthens as they take part in killing innocents. Fervor sweeps away Koranic restraints on behavior toward enemies, as well as it does moderation in personal sacrifice. Hence only after the Islamicization of terrorism in the 1980s did suicide bombings and the use of innocent hostages become important weapons. In the end, labeling "Islamic" all that strikes at the enemy and "infidel" all that does not reduces a complex, transcendental faith to a simple propellant for war. By practically defining Islam in terms of a secular goal war against America, the Islamists diminished their religion's spiritual capital.

Thus the terrorists contend for the future of Islam against the millions of nonterrorist Muslims and the broader Islamic tradition. Not all who join the movement and speak its increasingly Islamic language are moved by faith. On the contrary, by approving secular terrorists who pin Islamic labels on themselves (some of Arafat's very, very secular men called themselves the Al Aksa Martyrs' Brigade), the Islamists have made it hard to distinguish between secularists and Muslims, in practice, erasing the difference.

On the level of indirect warfare, the Islamicization of Middle Eastern terrorism has been an enormous success. The essence of indirect war, recall, is to deflect the victims' attention away from the people who embody the causes of the violence, the people who make it possible—to complicate the question, who's the enemy? As every terrorist from the region professed, sincerely or not, to be fighting for Allah, it was difficult for westerners to avoid the fallacious conclusion that Islam itself, or perhaps only "Islamic fundamentalism," is the enemy, the cause of terrorism.

But in fact terrorists of varying religiosity, while they speak just as loudly of their attachment to Islam, make the very same efforts to dissimulate their ties to the regimes from which they get the things without which any and all terrorist activities would be impossible: money, bases from which to organize, safe havens, and propaganda, as well as living proof that the cause is doing well. Even for suicide bombing, mistakenly supposed to be mere donation of lives to the cause, millions of dollars are necessary for organizing and for, in effect, paying the suicides' families for their services. The money would be useless without permissive environments in which the recruitment can take place. This in turn requires propaganda media that legitimize such things. And of course the organizers need protection against their enemies. Hizbullah is headquartered in Iran and is deployed in Syrian-controlled Lebanon; Hamas cohabits uneasily with the Palestinian Authority in territories granted by Israel, as well as in Lebanon and Syria; and Islamic Jihad is run out of Syria. All these and many more depend on money from Saudi Arabia and the Gulf states. Unknown to many, all of the Palestinian terror groups run on money provided by European and American taxpayers. Can one imagine a cessation of terrorism while such regimes exist? Conversely, can one imagine terrorism were the regimes of the Mideast to police their countries so as to prevent it?

Alas, as the Islamicization of terrorist violence against America made it ever more popular throughout the Arab world, Arab regimes have had less and less choice about supporting it. They are riding a tiger that they have fed, but that has grown to the point that it might eat them were they to try dismounting it. Hence though these regimes are the sine qua non of anti-American terror, it becomes increasingly difficult to describe what they are doing as a war with long-term objectives. Terrorism is indeed a mere tool. But the indirect warfare of twenty-first-century Middle Eastern regimes is no longer a strategy, but rather a succession of stratagems aimed at keeping ahead of a movement that has taken on a life of its own.

10

INTELLIGENCE

> How can any man say what he should
> do himself if he is ignorant of what his
> adversary is about?
> —Antoine Henri Jomini

K NOWLEDGE OF THE enemy's purposes and plans does not guarantee victory. But nothing so enhances your forces or detracts from the enemy's as knowing his plans while leading him to think what you will about your own. History is full of spies who have helped their masters' cause. Throughout the American Revolution, Benjamin Franklin's personal secretary in Paris was a British agent, as was one of George Washington's principal officers, Benedict Arnold. Before and during much of World War II, the Soviet Union had excellent access to German plans through a spy in the German entourage in Tokyo. But history is also full of spies who gain good access and yet so misunderstand the information they gather that they harm their side's cause. According to the Book of Deuteronomy, Moses' spies returned from the Promised Land with overestimates of enemy strength so gross that they disheartened the Children of Israel. By the same token, ill-trained Union spies furnished Gen. George McClellan with exaggerations of Confederate strength that accentuated the general's already excessive caution.

To act on knowledge from spies is almost as big a gamble as acting on no knowledge at all. Such knowledge—Intelligence with a capital "I"—is valuable insofar as it complements intelligence in the ordinary meaning of the word. If a decision maker has to rely on secret information to know who his friends and enemies are, or what his enemy's interests, basic capabilities, and options may be, he is not likely to understand the reports. Nor is he likely to grasp that even the best reports are only part of a picture, and that making sense of partial and uncertain facts is his responsibility alone. An incompetent executive always wants more information and pretends that he can act only on the basis of what Intelligence tells him—that Intelligence, not he himself, is responsible for his decisions. A competent one knows that he must always decide on the basis of less-than-complete knowledge and rejoice at the chance to shape reality through his judgments.

This chapter outlines the principles of intelligence in war. Since whether or not to go to war is always the foremost of questions, it is the natural focus of peacetime intelligence. But because that question is inherently divisive and downright awesome, prewar intelligence is naturally prey to clashes between those who favor the prospective war and those who oppose it, between the timid and the bold. All brandish information that supports their dispositions, and doubt what does not. As often as not, prewar intelligence is grist for political mills. War focuses intelligence on actual operations. This should mean, first of all, humility in the face of the unknown and willingness humbly to make the best of what is at hand. King George VI ended upon such a note in his 1941 New Year's message to the British Empire.

> I said to a man who stood at the Gate of the Year, "Give me a light, that I may tread safely into the unknown," and he replied, "Go out into the darkness and put your hand into the Hand of God. That shall be to you better than light, and safer than a known way."[1]

The purpose of war is to convince the enemy to abandon the aims for which he fights and to place himself at the winner's mercy. But what would bring about such a development in the enemy's mind is not self-evident. The enemy's counsels on such matters are sure to be most guarded. Hence, anyone who fights must pierce his enemy's counsels to learn more precisely what it takes for him to win, and how best to fight. Fighting without good intelligence consists, at best, of campaigns of destruction conducted in the hope that indiscriminate damage to the other side's arms and body will somehow affect unknown pressure points in his head.

For example, perhaps the biggest mistake committed by the Allies in World War II was the policy of "strategic bombing," premised on the false beliefs that (a) enemy soldiers at the front would slacken their efforts if they knew that their homes were being attacked; (b) war production could be crippled; and (c) the Axis governments would decide to stop the war before their societies suffered excessive harm. As we have noted, strategic bombing strengthened morale in the enemy soldiers and did not seriously affect enemy war production. As for inflicting pain upon civilian populations, Italy switched sides in the war without being battered seriously, and Japan's decision to surrender flowed from feelings of helplessness rather than suffering. But Germany's Nazi leaders, though incapacitated, spent their last weeks trying to make sure that their own country's suffering would be a total Götterdämmerung. A better understanding of the Axis governments' relationships with their societies, as well as a better assessment of their military capabilities, clearly would have allowed the allies to employ resources more efficiently.

During the Cold War, American policymakers fought one another fruitlessly over whether the Soviet Union's extensive preparations for sheltering its industry and key personnel in the event of nuclear war meant that Soviet leaders were willing to fight one. The official position of the U.S. Central Intelligence Agency was that they did not, because the Soviets "must realize" that nothing could keep Soviet society from suffering unacceptable damage. But how did the CIA know what the Soviet leadership considered acceptable prices to pay or acceptable risks to run to achieve a goal? It did not know. It supposed. To suggest that someone else "must realize" something that you do not know he realizes is the definition of mirror-imaging—or of whistling in the dark.

Before, during, and ever since the Gulf War of 1991 and indeed after his capture in 1993, the U.S. government was ignorant of what Iraqi dictator Saddam Hussein meant to accomplish, how he thought he would accomplish it, and why he turned down certain courses of action available to him while choosing others. For the same reasons, when the U.S. government invaded Iraq in 2003 it did not have any reliable information on how Saddam planned to deal with the invasion. What was his plan? Why? To fight without such basic knowledge is to ask for unpleasant surprises. And in its occupation of Iraq America got more of them than it imagined.

Fighting with good intelligence means knowing where your enemy's jugular vein is. One extreme case of an operation that made sense only because knowledge of the enemy was thorough and secure was Ho Chi Minh and Vo Nguyen Giap's decision early in the winter of 1968 to commit all Vietcong forces in South Vietnam to a frontal assault against U.S. forces. Because of the Americans' overwhelming firepower, the attack (since known as the Tet Offensive) was doomed to fail with huge losses. And in fact communist forces in South Vietnam never recovered from those losses. Had North Vietnam's prospects for victory depended on those forces, their destruction would have meant losing the war. But North Vietnamese leaders knew their American enemies well enough to bet that the shock of the Tet Offensive would have a decisive effect on America's "effete elite." Their bet paid off because their assessment of America's domestic vulnerability proved correct.

Good intelligence also means knowing your enemy well enough to surprise him—or at least well enough to keep him from surprising you. Thus, competent commanders planning an attack always seek to know what the enemy does not expect. Clearly the main focus of this attempt is to determine where an attack will stand the best chance of success regardless of the physical difficulties. This is why in 1940 German knowledge that the French had not seriously defended the area southwest of the Ardennes Forest made it reasonable for the Germans to push columns of tanks through that inhospitable area. Given the terrain, the French could easily have turned this masterstroke into disaster—if only they had known about it beforehand.

Hence, one of the major preoccupations of any military force must be to guard its secrets. This can be done by concealment or by deception. One of many examples is the Germans' preparation for their May 1918 breakthrough on the Chemin-des-Dames. As large groups assembled for the attack, they moved only by night. When they moved by day, soldiers would instantly turn and march away from the front whenever an airplane appeared. All rolling stock had joints wrapped and muffled against noise. Even horses' hooves were wrapped. Movement by the river was timed to coincide with the croaking of frogs.[2]

Combatants' needs for intelligence vary somewhat depending on whether they are engaged in offensive or defensive operations. In the first two years of World War II Hitler had much less need for intelligence than he did afterward when his fortunes waned. All an attacker need do is to scout out his plan—a simple task. True, the defense can complicate this task by deception or by sowing confusion, thus raising questions as to what its own plans are. But the attacker can deceive and confuse as well. The defender's intelligence task is inherently more difficult. Waiting for the blow to fall, the defender must scout out all the different possible ways by which the attack might come. The attacker is also in a better position to pre-position his spies and observers to keep him supplied with information as the attack develops. The defender, on the other hand, is lucky if his intelligence assets survive the outbreak of war and must shift whatever survivors there are—under enemy fire and according to the enemy's timetable.

For the rest, attacker and defender are in the same boat. During wartime, when governments want to know more about their opponents than before, they tend to classify more information as secret. "Loose lips sink ships" was a popular World War II saying in America, the world's least security-conscious society. Even liberal governments declare areas "off limits" to casual traffic, ask people to curtail casual conversations, and encourage suspicion about those who may be curious. Hence, all information is much harder to obtain. Travelers, magazines, and diplomats become less useful as sources of information. On the other hand, war spawns new sources—troop communications, refugees, prisoners of war, and traitors. Wartime intelligence is driven by the tempo of events. Most information is useful only in relation to the next battle or to the next political ploy. There is not enough time to collect and analyze facts to one's full satisfaction. Leaders must make do with the information at hand. This puts a premium on their ability to interpret sketchy intelligence intelligently, to clarify rather than obscure the fundamental facts. It also produces success for simple deceptive schemes that would not stand up to calm examination. Finally, each side is sure to compromise some of its secret agents because of the urgent need to use them for subversion of the enemy.

Let us now consider the role that intelligence plays in the conduct of war by examining how each of the four elements of intelligence—collection, analysis, counterintelligence, and subversion—function during wartime.

Collection

Although the technology of intelligence collection has changed over the years, its purpose has not. Today's agents do not usually have to travel for weeks, as did George Washington's spies, to report handwritten or memorized secrets. They may use encoded satellite communications beamed from packages that can fit into shirt pockets. But today, as always, agents have the nasty but indispensable job of posing as friends of the enemy, at least long enough to learn the enemy's intentions and his own views of his situation. Today, a military commander who wants to reconnoiter an enemy army does not have to rely on a fast horseman with a good memory. Airplanes or satellites equipped with cameras and electronic sensors are at his disposal. A military commander in the midst of a battle today still wants to know what Napoleon and Alexander the Great wanted to know, namely, what effect they were having on the enemy, where and in what state were the enemy's reserves, and how he was planning to use them. Just as we count tanks rather than chariots, and missiles rather than siege engines, intelligence collection on modern battlefields does not rely on human ears on the ground listening for the beat of hooves. Rather, it relies on picking up the signals emitted by modern weapons. Hence we will consider each aspect of collection, broadly divided into collection by machines and collection by human beings.

Collection by Machines

BATTLEFIELD INTELLIGENCE The primary requirement for modern military intelligence is the timely identification and location of enemy targets.

Nowadays, once a target is identified and located, chances are it can be hit.[3] Most modern weapons (ballistic missiles in silos being a notable exception) either emit or reflect some electromagnetic energy themselves or depend for their direction on other equipment that emits it. Hence, a great deal of tactical intelligence on the modern battlefield consists of intercepting emissions from enemy equipment. These emissions could be an air-defense radar or the radio of an artillery battery or command post. Battlefield intelligence then processes the intercepts to identify and localize the emitters, and forms a picture of the tactical situation. The modern battlefield also abounds with broadcast oral communication—much of it necessarily not encoded. This must be intercepted, quickly translated, and fit into the tactical picture. On the basis of such intelligence, weapons can be assigned almost automatically to attack those emitters, priority being given to the ones that pose the most immediate threat.

Electronic emissions can be collected by a variety of aircraft behind the front lines, as well as by troops on the lines. These collectors can vary in number and differ in level of protection. Processing, however, is the heart of any system, and here there can be no substitute for speed. Ideally, any time a piece of equipment begins to radiate or a military unit reveals its location by going on the air they should be targeted. To accomplish this, tactical processing centers must have linguists to instantly translate the words they hear into information about what is happening and where, as well as reception terminals that interpret various technical sensors. Skilled commanders must then supervise a tactical fire-control network that automatically, or almost automatically, assigns weapons to every enemy unit that is located. Even the best-equipped modern forces can do this sort of thing only approximately. Otherwise the modern battlefield would be the equivalent of a video game. It is definitely not that.

The effectiveness of modern battlefield intelligence depends somewhat on the number, security, and effectiveness of individual collection sensors. But its effectiveness hinges more upon the reliability of communications between the collectors and the processor than upon the processor's efficiency. Some suggest that the weakest link in modern battlefield intelligence is the physical vulnerability of processing centers. Since the entire system ceases to exist if these centers are destroyed, reason suggests that they should be designed for mobility and hardness—even at the expense of capability—and, of course, that they be defended.

RECONNAISSANCE OF THE REAR The mere existence of airborne and spaceborne sensors makes good reconnaissance of the rear theoretically possible—but only theoretically. Actually to see what you want, you need enough sensors to cover the enemy's rear. Even when a war is geographically very limited, as in the Arab-Israeli wars, the Iran-Iraq War that began in 1981, the Falklands-Malvinas War of 1982, the Bosnian Wars of the 1990s, or the Gulf War of 1991 and the Iraq War of 2003, the United States—never mind other combatants—did not have enough aircraft for constant surveillance. The one or two satellites that were available made eighteen revolutions per day and, given the earth's rotation, would scan the war zone about once a day, assuming good weather. That results in rare, fleeting snapshots—not staring eyes. But the snapshots are even rarer in larger wars, or in any war where ocean-going navies are involved. The success of reconnaissance in a world-spanning war would depend largely on the quantity of airplanes and satellites available to either side, *and* on each side's ability to protect or replace its reconnaissance assets. It is technically possible to build large numbers of satellites that carry sensors spanning the electromagnetic spectrum, and to integrate the information from them. This would indeed amount to something like the capacity to stare at any point in the world. But even the United States has hesitated to undertake this large, very expensive task.

Both sides must try to visually scan each other's rear area. We must digress a bit at this point. Not all imaging satellites are created equal. Satellites like the French SPOT operate in relatively high orbits, cover much ground, are relatively cheap, but can barely make out a building. Others, like the American KH-11, fly relatively low, can pick out a duck in a pond, but are terribly expensive and cover relatively little ground. Of course neither can see anything at night or through clouds. Night vision from satellites using infrared cameras is possible and even quite good over relatively small areas. But any satellite that sees through clouds must use radar and hence must be grossly expensive and very limited in coverage. Moreover, to satellite radar reconnaissance, a truck does not really look like a truck, or a house like a house. The blobs need interpretation. Good radar coverage of the oceans, however, is now feasible, since satellites there need only to produce blips from large ships. They can therefore fly high, with relatively cheap, low-resolution radars. All of this is to say that with considerable expense it is possible to give frequent coverage to huge areas with low-resolution imagery, but prohibitively expensive to try to do so with high-resolution, KH-11-type satellites.

It is impractical to try to maintain surveillance of large areas with aircraft. Because they have narrow fields of view, many are needed, especially if they have to shoot their way in. Even when they do not and the area they must surveil is flat and barren—as it was during the Gulf War of 1991—the brevity and infrequency of the time they spend over any given area weighs the odds against them: some four thousand reconnaissance sorties looking for the mobile missile launchers that were hitting U.S. troops and Israeli cities found precisely none.

A score or more of high-flying satellites, however, could do a reasonable job of constant surveillance. To cover any part of the earth constantly, however, requires covering it all. To do so with high-resolution imagery would be both prohibitively expensive and unnecessary, and it would generate so much data as to make all of it unmanageable. So, designers must try to get enough resolution to identify items of interest, but not so much as to overwhelm the system with useless data. Moreover, keeping many satellites in the sky in the face of a determined antisatellite campaign would require successfully shooting down antisatellite devices *and* reserving satellites to replace the ones that would inevitably be lost. A serious reconnaissance effort, then, would be at least in part a contest between the number of replacement satellites and the number of antisatellite weapons each side had stockpiled. In the end, neither side would have full information about the other's rear, and each would have to make the best of what each of its satellites yielded before getting shot down. This is not so different from the way it was in the days when armies relied on expendable second lieutenants as forward observers.

The problems of rear reconnaissance via electronic means are enormous. In wartime, ships—even armies—do not broadcast radio signals while moving in the rear. They either do not go "on the air," and simply *listen* to encoded orders broadcast from national headquarters, or they beam their communications to relay satellites. Land forces would use land telephone lines. This means that various kinds of electronic ears pointed to rear areas may hear nothing, or may hear broadcasts emanating from place X that are normally associated with a particular military unit, while that unit has moved on to place Y. Electronic deception is not a possibility on the battlefield. It is a certainty.

COMMUNICATIONS INTELLIGENCE Communications intelligence (COMINT) is essential in war because it is a primary means of gaining insight into the enemy's intentions. Means of collecting COMINT have increased in importance and sophistication, apace with the growth in communications technology. The growing science of cryptology, however, serves ever less the purposes of those who want access to electronic communications and more those who want to guard such communications. In short, math and computer science have given the code makers lasting victory over the code breakers.

Modern war involves a huge volume of electronic communications. Because volume alone naturally works against security efforts, war, in addition to increasing the likelihood of mistakes, normally produces a lot of valuable COMINT. Moreover, since so much modern communications security depends on complex equipment, especially computers, strikes against enemy forces deep into the enemy's homeland likely reduce the operational readiness of that equipment and result in reductions in the amount and proficiency of encryption. Thus a lot of urgent messages that would be worth protecting would go on the air "in the clear." Although some COMINT is collected by stations on the ground and by aircraft, much of it nowadays is collected by satellites. These are naturally prime targets. (Note, however, that COMINT satellites pick up only *one-half* of conversations.) Each side could expect to suffer and inflict losses on such satellites in a bid to protect its own communications and put the other's at risk.

The problem with communications intelligence, however collected, is that its sources are seldom unknown to the enemy. Hence one seldom knows whether the intelligence is for real or whether the enemy has made any given item available to our collectors to lead us to believe in his preferred version of reality. The U.S. government's preferred approach to communications intelligence is to scoop as much electronic traffic as possible out of the airwaves and then to use massive amounts of electronic processing to pick valuable conversations out of low-grade traffic. But over the years the amount of traffic has grown exponentially, the dwindling proportion of interesting traffic that is encrypted unbreakably has also grown, leaving scarcely any fruits to be reaped by massive processing. Targeting specific telephone numbers has become treacherous because of the massive numbers of cell phones, Blackberries, etc. Besides, when the capabilities for collecting COMINT are as well-known as in our time, the chances of disinformation are inherently high.

Attempts at "mining" vast volumes of data for non-encrypted information can be productive against unsophisticated targets. Thus Italian police who were searching for clues to the 2002 kidnapping of Islamists in Milan sought patterns in the use of cell phones near the time and place of the event. Since the kidnappers–CIA employees–had not followed elementary operational security, the patterns appeared and identified the kidnappers precisely. On the other hand, "data mining" that attempts to follow up "degrees of relationships" between individuals–especially competent ones–who may be scattered around the world in order to discover conspiracies regarding future events multiplies hypotheses with hypotheses and ends up with pretense.

Miniaturization and wireless communications, however, have vastly improved the yield of "emplaced sensors"–bugging. But knowing where to emplace which sensor itself requires much knowledge. In short, modern wartime COMINT is nothing like the straightforward technical problem that it was in World War II.

SCIENTIFIC AND TECHNICAL INTELLIGENCE Only during conflicts as protracted as the twentieth century's hot and cold world wars, when there is
time for countermeasures, does technical intelligence make a difference. In
wartime, it makes little sense to continue trying to figure out the technical
characteristics of enemy weapons. Precise measurements of missile silos
and calculations of the thrust-to-weight ratio of aircraft engines are of little
consequence when war does not allow time for engineering new countermeasures. The exceptions to this include communications and electronic
warfare systems, whose successes and failures depend on instantaneous
changes in computer programs. Nevertheless, a good supply of scientific
and technical intelligence gathered in peacetime is still essential for prob-
ing the meaning of the surprises that are sure to be encountered in war.

The controversy of the early 1980s concerning the Soviet Union's use
of chemical warfare in Laos, northeast Cambodia, and Afghanistan provides a good example of the importance of mere understanding. According
to Sterling Seagrave,[4] thousands of reports by Asians who had been attacked by "yellow rain" falling from Soviet-built aircraft were discredited
in the United States because American intelligence was not aware of any
chemicals previously used in war that would cause the reported symptoms. And, in fact, no such chemicals had ever been used in war. Of course,
American intelligence should have asked immediately what chemicals *might*
have caused the reported symptoms. When Mr. Seagrave asked that question, the correct answer, mycotoxins, was waiting in the library. Collection
of evidence then corroborated library research.

However, any nation must expect that its forces will be confronted by
chemicals, weapons, procedures, frequencies, and so forth not described
in any libraries. To avoid this, peacetime databases must be built imagina-
tively, with an eye to what the other side might do if it really put its mind
to the task.

If a nation's intelligence agencies are on the lookout for the unexpected, and have prepared the databases necessary for understanding the
unexpected, they will be able to ask the right questions to understand
quickly what they are up against and to minimize the surprise. This preparation consists of basic research on the outer limits of certain technologies.
Nothing so cripples understanding of new phenomena as the judgment
that what one has just observed "doesn't fit with anything we know."

Human Collection

In the absence of excellent, consistently available communications intelligence, human agents are the only means of addressing the key questions
of political warfare. What is the enemy really after? Under what conditions

will the enemy decide to cease hostility or surrender? At what point will he think he has won? What will he do if he thinks he's won? Where does the enemy consider himself vulnerable? What and whom does he fear? Is the enemy trying to foment a coup d'état in a third country? If so, is the coup a prelude to the entry of the enemy's troops into the country? If troops do come in, is the enemy willing to make a major strategic commitment to that sector or theater? What do the enemy's allies expect to get out of the war? Under what conditions will such allies desert the enemy? Who are the people in the enemy camp who would likely disrupt the war effort if they were strengthened? Where does the enemy plan to strike next? How does he plan to do it? How does he expect other nations to act? By what means is he managing to purchase embargoed goods? Only well-placed people can answer such questions well.

Let us consider three categories of such people: (a) agents recruited to "stay behind" in enemy-conquered territory or simply to infiltrate through enemy lines, (b) agents in enemy territory, and (c) agents in third countries.

"Stay behinds" must be trained and placed before the enemy's advance. Foresight, humility, and self-discipline are required to realize that the enemy is likely to attack certain areas successfully and to decide to commit resources to find, train, and pay people willing to stay there under enemy rule. For the sake of security, sensitive communications equipment need not be issued until the enemy's move is imminent. Successful stay behinds must be people who would least likely be suspected of being an agent, and who would probably not be included on a purge list. They would probably not be the sort of people one might meet at diplomatic receptions. *Recruitment of such assets would have to be done largely by people with no known connections to foreign embassies. In other words, a truly covert net can only be built covertly.* The speed with which a clandestine stay-behind net could be assembled would depend largely on how thorough were prior preparations.

In his book *Honorable Men,* William Colby describes how, during the 1950s, the United States recruited agents in parts of Europe it expected to be overrun by an eventual Soviet attack.[5] They were to supply invaluable information about the identity and detailed intentions of invading troops as well as to pinpoint any obvious vulnerabilities they might have. Of course that attack never occurred, perhaps because the United States was prepared in this and in many other more obvious ways. But recruitment of stay behinds is prudent in places susceptible to enemy attack.

Agents willing to slip through or parachute behind enemy lines can be recruited from among people who have fled ahead of enemy forces, or among individuals such as students and businessmen who found themselves away from their homes when these were occupied and who wish to return. Also, during an invasion of the enemy territory, any number of people who live there may be willing to bet their lives on the invader's success. Normally, in such circumestances agents are fairly easy to recruit on the spot when the time comes. Their usefulness consists in providing the sort of indispensable basic information about occupied areas that would in times of peace and free movementhave been provided by travelers and newspapers. But since time pressures afford little opportunity to check out the agents' worth, there is always a substantial chance that the agents may be working for enemy intelligence. That is especially so if they offer especially rare information. Thus in 2003, as the United States prepared to invade Iraq, a CIA team built—it thought—an impressive network of hastily recruited Iraqi insiders, code-named ROCKSTARS, who provided many facts, climaxed by the location of a bunker where Saddam Hussein was supposed to be spending the night of 19 March. An agent even located the site by radioing from it as Saddam supposedly arrived. Too good to be true. And it wasn't.

News of troop movements, together with reports of unguarded remarks, can signal the particulars of an impending attack and especially its scope. Even rumors can help target more sophisticated and valuable intelligence resources. The enemy's morale, his concerns, and the weak points of supply lines all can best be signaled by friendly agents behind the lines. Moreover, although intelligence collection and resistance activities theoretically should not mix, collection agents are often involved in partisan activities and can provide valuable links to them. Although communications with such agents is always difficult, the marvels of space-age communications have eased this problem considerably. But one fact is constant: the closer one's victorious troops are, the more and the better the intelligence flowing to them will be.

When wars disrupt normal population-control systems, cause floods of refugees, destroy records, and so forth, they greatly facilitate penetration of enemy territory by intelligence collectors. This is what happened throughout central Europe toward the end of World War II. With proper prewar preparations, confusion can always be used to infiltrate agents under various kinds of cover. The best chance for success lies in using third-country nationals with "cover" that gives them plausible reasons for being where they are. The diplomat, the businessman from a third country who retains good relations with the enemy but who has been recruited to one's own service can potentially be exceptionally valuable in mingling with and reporting the mood of the enemy's ruling class. Communications with such agents could also be less difficult than with other "inside" agents.

Occupation of enemy or third-country territory affords intelligence officers the opportunity to tamper with records of birth, death, and identity. Thus, during Iraq's 1990 occupation of Kuwait, any number of persons disappeared, and the official records of their identities, including finger-prints and photos, were altered to serve Iraqi agents. That is how one Ramzi Youssef, who bombed the World Trade Center in 1993, came to carry the identity of Abdul Karim.

The value of intelligence officers infiltrated into enemy territory is lim-ited. Infiltrated agents who capture a key leader, shake key information out of him, and radio it home are the stuff of movies. It might happen occasionally, but normally such agents try to provide answers to what's happening at a certain location by mingling with locals. They also report on the people's state of mind, levels of nutrition and health—in short, on the valuable things that everybody in the country knows but which an adversary otherwise would not. Of course, the intelligence officers might try to contact native agents who had been recruited before the war but who had somehow lost the ability to communicate. At best, such infiltrators would position audio devices in places where they might pick up impor-tant conversations. But one could not expect them to get close enough to important people to gain information from them. Surely, any activity that does not conform strictly to their cover is very dangerous.

The technical requirements for handling such penetrations would be the same as those for handling agents in enemy territory who had been recruited before the outbreak of war. Except for rare occasions when the agents could come out of enemy territory, communications with them have to be done electronically.

This brings us to the subject of cover itself. Its natural purpose is two-fold: to protect the agent *and at the same time to provide him access* to sources. To the extent that the agent must step outside his cover role to gather intelligence, the cover was ill conceived.

Defectors and prisoners are sources whose temptations are often worth resisting. Like allies, defectors are in shortest supply when needed most—that is, when the outcome looks least favorable—and tend to come when victory is no longer in doubt and they are least needed. There are excep-tions. Germany's Adm. Wilhelm Canaris secretly defected from Hitler and supplied intelligence to the Allies beginning in 1941. But by the time Allen Dulles had advertised his spy shop on Bern's fashionable Herrengasse in 1943, enough high-ranking Nazis feared for their hides that Dulles had more offers of information than he could handle. That is how he became a fabled spymaster.

Regardless of the stage of the war, any and all defectors are inherently suspect. Especially in wartime, all intelligence services send fake defectors and offer "dangles"—too-convenient opportunities to recruit agents who turn out to be doubles. The temptation is to accept the defector as genuine simply because the information he provides is true and seems valuable, especially if it confirms one's own prejudices. Thus, in 1998 the CIA was approached by someone who claimed that he had worked for Osama bin Laden, embezzled money, and wanted to trade information for protection. The defector blamed all recent terrorist activity on bin Laden and exonerated Arab intelligence. The CIA loved it because it confirmed its prejudices. So, absent a rigorous check by one's own counterintelligence—especially difficult to do in wartime—the risk of being led into a trap usually outweighs whatever value the information may have.

Captured soldiers often volunteer information about which enemy units are in action, what they have been doing, and the state of equipment and morale. Further interrogation seldom yields much more. Especially when one is fighting irregulars (or terrorists), there is a temptation to press prisoners for information. But unless some basic conditions exist, such interrogations tend to be counterproductive. The interrogator must know that the prisoner knows the answer to the questions being asked, and he must have a way of knowing or finding out whether the answer he gets is true or false. If the interrogator does not, then pressure or inducement tends to yield the same results: misleading trash and wasted time. The interrogator's own knowledge is his most powerful weapon. Rarely is it even possible to make a case for using torture as a tool for gathering intelligence.

France's Col. Jacques Massu made such a case in the battle of Algiers in 1956. Algeria's National Liberation Front was slaughtering innocents with bombs in restaurants, buses, and marketplaces. The French knew that the FLN was organized as a pyramid of three-man cells. Each person knew only the one above him and the one below. Hence Massu ordered that torture be used immediately to extract those two names from any terrorist caught in flagrante delicto. Such a person was sure to posses the information. Then, when the two named persons were arrested, the accuracy of the original information was checked, and more information was extracted and checked. Thus the French army moved rapidly up the FLN's organizational pyramid. The FLN ceased to exist in Algiers, and the terror ended. Massu thought his actions were just because they were both effective and temporary. In both ways, they were unusual.

More typical was the combination of light physical pressure and bribery with which American forces occupying Iraq in 2003–2004 sought intelligence from persons in their power. Lacking knowledge of who their captives were, having little idea of what the prisoners knew—if anything—possessing only a list of questions to which they did not know the answers, and working through translators, American interrogators humbled and lightly mistreated some captives, while offering bribes to others ("we will pay and they will talk," the general in charge wrote in the *New York Times.*) Both approaches yielded lots of "information" that led to harmful hunts for persons who perpetuated the cycle of ignorance.

The most ancient and effective form of military human intelligence is reconnaissance. Nothing quite succeeds like a squad of special forces inserted into enemy territory to watch, contact dissidents, search enemy facilities, and sometimes kidnap enemy officials for questioning outside the country. Through contact with enemy forces, the reconnaissance teams can gauge their strength. In 2001–2003, as the CIA generated little human intelligence about Afghanistan and Iraq, much of which came from sources whose agendas were not America's, the U.S. Army and Marines sent into both countries teams that returned with firsthand information and live high-level captives.

Human operations in third countries have been and will remain a staple of wartime intelligence. That is because in third (neutral) countries it is possible to approach the enemy's diplomats, to surveil their premises, and to watch them as they carry out their country's foreign policy. Even if enemy diplomats in a third country don't know everything about their country's war aims and plans, their knowledge is sufficient to be worth attention. Moreover, the strains of war might weaken their loyalty. The enemy diplomats' principal friends in third countries are also inviting targets for recruitment or surveillance.

However, preparations for such activities must begin with the assumption that at the outset of war third countries will break diplomatic relations with at least one belligerent party. Of course, they may not. Then, like Portugal, Switzerland, and Turkey in World War II, they become meccas of intrigue. But, if they do break diplomatic relations, they automatically eliminate a country's intelligence presence under diplomatic cover just when it would be most valuable. The only way to avoid such a drastic reduction in one's intelligence presence is to recruit and train a cadre of human collectors who pose as something other than diplomats, and hence who could move about in countries when other officials are not welcome. These people could be international businessmen, journalists, philanthropists, or scholars—indeed, anyone who had a legitimate reason to travel. They could also be permanent residents of the country they are assigned to cover. The alternative to building such networks in peacetime is to face the prospect of having to try to build them hurriedly under harsh wartime conditions.

Liaison with third-country intelligence services is most important, and most dangerous. By definition, third-country intelligence services are likely to have access to people beyond your reach. But two facts cast large shadows over any and all reports from liaison services. First, these services pursue their governments' agendas rather than yours. Second, the fact that they have better access to the enemy than you do necessarily reflects a degree of mutual confidence with the enemy that necessarily undermines your own in them. In other words, if the third-country service knows so much about the enemy, and sympathizes with you, why does it not act decisively on your side? These questions were most relevant in the war on terrorism that the United States waged after 11 September 2001. Lacking human sources on terrorists, the CIA got most of its human intelligence from the intelligence services of Arab countries. To be sure, these services had thoroughly infiltrated the terrorist organizations. But they had done so to exercise influence on them for their own purposes—not to help Americans. Until 2003 the CIA boasted that it got much of its information about the 9/11 conspiracy from one Muhammed Haymar Zammar, who is in custody of the Syrian General Security directorate. The Syrian government gave the CIA what it claimed were Mr. Zammar's answers to the CIA's written questions. But the CIA had no reason to believe that those answers were coming from Zammar rather than from Arab officials who decided what impressions they wanted to give to the Americans.

Similar observations are in order regarding the CIA's "rendition" of terrorist suspects to the "friendly" Arab countries of which they are citizens. The CIA supposes that, under interrogation far more brutal than the Americans might inflict, these suspects would "tell all." Perhaps. But surely the reports of such interrogations will reflect the agendas of governments that may not be as friendly as one might wish.

WARTIME INTELLIGENCE PRODUCTS Intelligence agencies deliver information to policymakers, military commanders, and diplomats in formats designed to be useful in particular contexts, such as in meetings in which bombing targets are picked or on the bridge of a warship. These formatted packages of information are known in the trade as "intelligence products." They may be divided into four categories. First is what we might call static products: descriptions of the military, political, and economic means that are at the enemy's disposal. Foremost among these are the lists of what equipment and manpower the enemy has and how it is organized, called "order of battle" books. They are still called books decades after they became mere computer files. Then there are "books" containing biographies of the people who matter in the enemy's war machine. In addition, there are files on industries and management and labor organizations and records of political alignments, factions, and so forth. Of course these static products require constant updating.

Second, there are dynamic intelligence products. These are reports of troop movements, changes of command, changes in administration and production, and discussions of latest events. Third, strategic products study what the enemy is *capable* of doing in any given functional area (for example, how many tanks or nuclear warheads it can produce) or in any geographic area (how many antiship missiles it can put at the entrance of the Persian Gulf). There are also studies of any given situation from the enemy's point of view, and estimates of what the enemy is going to do. Finally, there are tactical products—reports on how the enemy behaves in specific situations and, occasionally, predictions of tactical moves.

These wartime products are worlds away from the massive peacetime products often known as estimates, which serve as grist for controversies over policies and politics. Wartime products, as we said, should be driven by operations.

In major wars, each part of a government engages in the fighting. Each pays attention to its area of concern and brings unique insights to it. During wartime the operating departments of government, especially the military services, gather more intelligence than usual through direct contact with the enemy and heightened attention to every opportunity to collect it. Consumers of intelligence, such as major military commanders, contribute data to the intelligence product and *insist* on being the final analytic authority on intelligence papers that address matters that concern them. But any "shop" in the government, perhaps only as a hobby, may cultivate outstanding knowledge about an individual, a unit, an industry, or a location. The official source of "all-source knowledge" may lie elsewhere. But in the bowels of some ministry, there may be someone who knows nothing but the proficiency of every Ruritanian pilot who ever flew a plane! The trick in wartime is to channel information so that it flows from the various collectors and consumer-collectors up to some central point where it is integrated with all other relevant information and then down again to those who need it. In practice, information does not flow so neatly.

For Americans, the most poignant example of this occurred during the first days of December 1941. After Army and Navy intelligence had broken Japan's diplomatic code, there was more than enough information in the hands of the U.S. government to have led a reasonable person who looked at it to conclude that Japanese aircraft carriers would strike. But where? When? The CIA's founding myth is that the information was not all where one person could consider it as a whole and render judgment. But on 6 December, Naval Intelligence, which had broken the Japanese code, concluded from all but the last part of decoded messages from the Japanese foreign ministry to its embassy in Washington that the attack would come the following day. The analysts drew the right conclusions and rushed them to individual policymakers.

But these policymakers did not pay proper attention quickly enough. Most of them wanted to wait to see the last part of the message. When that came in, it became as clear to the policymakers as it had been to Naval Intelligence that the Japanese would attack at 1:00 PM eastern standard time. Where on earth would it be dawn at that time? Why, at Pearl Harbor. An hour and a half before the bombs were to fall, the most senior U.S. policymakers faced this fact. All they did was to forward a generic alert—by routine message. No phone calls. Myth aside, America's pre-CIA intelligence services did their jobs. There was no shortage either of information or analytic integration. But those who sounded the alarm did not have authority, while those who had authority were not alarmed. The problem was not one of bureaucratic structure, but of people at the top who failed at their jobs. The CIA, established to prevent a reoccurrence of Pearl Harbor, was supposed to combine expertise with proximity to power.

The CIA represents surely the biggest effort ever made to rationalize the flow of intelligence. The CIA's Directorate of Intelligence—which is in charge of production—is supposed to contain the country's central files for production and analysis, as well as expert analysts in every field of intelligence. Because its analysts have no attachment to any operating department, they are supposed to be dispassionate assessors of truth. Because (theoretically) they work for the president, they speak directly into the ears of power. But from its beginning in 1947 the CIA had preferences for policies even more definite than those of the Departments of State or Defense, and even less restrained by responsibility for decisions, successes, or failures. As the decades passed, the CIA became just another contender in intragovernmental policy struggles for the mind of the president. By 1978 it had staked its claim to exclusive right authoritatively to interpret the world by naming its analytical branch *The* National Foreign Assessment Center (emphasis mine). By the turn of the century, the CIA had extended that claim over the president himself: in the 2004 election the CIA and its political allies held President Bush culpable before Congress and the press for disagreeing with the CIA's judgments about the threats that Iraq posed to America.

The CIA asserts intellectual paramountcy over the president, never mind any other part of government, on the basis of its claim to have more information than anyone else. In the decades before computers became the primary tools for storing and transferring data, when CIA headquarters were the central storage place for intelligence data from all sources, this claim had some plausibility. However, since computers made any analyst in all agencies capable of all-source analysis, the CIA's opinion became no better informed than that of any other part of the government. In wartime, its views are often irrelevant. The military services have tasks to accomplish. They use the CIA information insofar as they find it helpful. They naturally resent attempts to force them to run war according to judgments with which they disagree.

Chaos seems to be endemic to the intelligence business in wartime. The intelligence services that report to the national leadership each have different perspectives and bureaucratic interests. High decision makers influenced either by *their* department's analysis or by central analysis argue against other high decision makers who defend their own department's analysis. Such conflicts are mitigated by the fact that during war bureaucrats are sometimes too busy to fight one another. Modern data-processing systems offer the hope that all centers of analysis and production will work from the same database.

Sometimes in war an intelligence question is so important that it requires a decision binding on all departments. Winston Churchill's resolution of the question of the German air force's strength in 1940–41 is an example of good intelligence management. The Air Ministry, reacting to its own shamefully low prewar estimates, gave a figure for German first-line aircraft about twice the actual number. If that figure had been correct, it would have been good reason for Britain to husband all its aircraft at home and virtually forget the rest of the world during 1941. Churchill, spurred by this and by his own knowledge of German war production, disagreed. The central analytical body, the Joint Intelligence Committee (JIC), knowing the prime minister's view, reanalyzed the evidence. But without fresh insights it only knocked the number down a bit. Churchill then established an ad hoc group under his personal adviser, Professor Frederick Lindemann, which forced the Air Ministry and the JIC to overhaul the basic assumptions behind the definition of air force strength, namely the concept of "first-line aircraft," that is, how many operational aircraft were in each squadron and how frequently each plane would fly a mission. This done, it became possible to reinterpret the signal intelligence data (SIGINT) about the number of aircraft actually on mission at any given time. The Lindemann committee's final figure was very close to the truth. Did Churchill "politicize" intelligence? The point here is that although there had been more than one source of analysis on the German air force, and no shortage of will to please the prime minister, there had been a shortage of insight. The prime minister's personal representative was armed not just with a mandate to come up with a different answer, but evidently also with more ingenuity and honesty than the bureaucracy. Had he not been, Churchill's eventual decision would have produced the wrong result. There is really no alternative, in war as in peace, to checking the parochialism of intelligence agencies by appointing independent bodies to review their work. But they must be really independent. Intelligence agencies are expert at making sure that the only outsiders who will look in on them are really insiders after all.

There is no best or worst way of organizing the flow of wartime intelligence. War tends to decentralize that flow. The top intelligence manager's job may then be summarized as making sure that all the various users receive the intelligence relevant to their missions in a timely manner, monitoring the clashes of views to see whether some kind of national-level arbitration is necessary, and making sure that no single department works on the basis of unchallenged intelligence assumptions.

Practicing and Detecting Deception

The certainty of deception shadows all collection and all production of intelligence about war aims, "statics," strategy, or tactics. Because deception is usually cheap and its success pays enormously, it is always attempted.

In the fall of 1939, for example, Hitler gained a serious advantage over France, Britain, and the Low Countries; finished off Poland; secured his maritime flank in Norway; and secured cooperation from Italy and Russia by dissimulating his war aims as mere German racism. The dictators of Italy and Russia, confident that mere German racism would never drive Hitler to a destructive world war, reasonably figured they could make a few gains (the Mediterranean and Africa, Poland and Finland, respectively) by riding a tiger that was frightening the Western powers. The Western powers continued to hope that if they did nothing to provoke Hitler, the war would continue to be limited to areas that were, had been, or conceivably could be ethnically German. Hence, the war would continue to be a phony war, at least for them.[6] But Stalin and Mussolini, no less than Chamberlain and Daladier, were mistaken. Yet Hitler was not an extraordinarily artful deceiver. After all, his plans for the world had been spelled out in *Mein Kampf.* Rather, during the early part of World War II just about everybody deceived themselves about Hitler's war aims because they resisted believing propositions that, if accepted, would have compelled them to undertake dangerous, uncomfortable actions. Hitler did not have to do much to encourage this massive self-deception.

Even self-interest is not a reliable barrier against self-deception. It was clearly in the interest of most Americans between 1961 and 1975 to keep South Vietnam out of the Soviet orbit. That was the professed goal of four U.S. presidents, two from each party. But this did not keep many Americans from deceiving themselves about the communists' war aims. The communists professed to be working for the same end as the U.S. government, namely the self-determination of the South Vietnamese people. By the time the North Vietnamese, with Soviet help, were overrunning South Vietnam, the elite American press and the U.S. government had accepted de facto that the Soviets and the North Vietnamese were sincere about South Vietnam's independence and that the South Vietnamese people supported them. So strong was this acceptance that it overcame obvious evidence to the contrary. For example, the American press erroneously explained the sight of populations fleeing communist lines for the U.S. side as fear of U.S.

bombing. When the flow of people in the same direction continued, even after U.S. warplanes had left Vietnam's skies and the South Vietnamese air force had been grounded, the widely accepted explanation for why the Vietnamese people fled the communists was that the South Vietnamese were childlike and excitable and did not know themselves why they were fleeing. After the communist victory in Southeast Asia, the spectacle of the communist governments' murder of millions of their own citizens, and the flight of more millions into the sea, convinced some journalists in the West that they had taken part in deceiving their readers about the war aims of the communists. But the fact that such spectacles left many other opinion makers unconvinced is further evidence for the proposition that deception consists in simply giving people even a meager excuse to believe what they would really like to believe anyway.

The most common deception about war aims, practiced since the dawn of time, seeks to convince sectors of the enemy population that they are not the target of military operations, that only their leaders, their policies, their system of government, or their allies are the targets. This line of argument may not be deception at all. In most cases it is wise policy. But in *all* cases it is indispensable. Its absence can only be expected to strengthen the enemy's hold on his people. Thus, the great Russian author, Alexander Solzhenitsyn, chastised the Reagan administration for giving the impression that the United States opposed not so much the Soviet communist regime but historic Russian ambitions. He went on to criticize the American military for making plans not to defeat the Soviet regime but rather to inflict casualties upon the Russian people. The very fact that people of goodwill could characterize American policy as such was a serious indictment of that policy.

Let us turn now to strategic deception. Its purpose is to induce the enemy to deploy his efforts in a way that leaves the main axis of attack relatively undefended. The most common fruit of strategic deception is surprise attack. The most common means of achieving surprise are military maneuvers, attacks announced on axis A that suddenly turn on axis B, and attacks launched under the cover of negotiations for the reduction of tensions.

The United States, the victim of the third kind of deception in 1941, developed elaborate means for detecting surprise attack by ballistic missiles and created a set routine to provide for a near-automatic response. But indications of attack are seldom unambiguous, and are always accompanied by basic technical deception, such as a huge satellite-dispensed cloud of chaff attended by a simultaneous call from the enemy that some technical difficulty has occurred. Transparent as they are, such stratagems gain the first fruit of surprise: time. More common is political deception.

This after all is what covered Japan's preparation for the attack on Pearl Harbor. It is deadly because its main active ingredient is self-deception, eagerness to believe one's own preferred—or feared—version of events.

Thus in 1940–41 the British JIC misinterpreted Hitler's deployment of troops in the Balkans for the invasion of Russia as a preparation for directing the left half of a pincer movement at the Suez Canal. The British understandably saw themselves as Hitler's main target and tried to interpret every move he made in terms of a strategy to defeat Britain. This was not an unreasonable conclusion, given Hitler's plans for a cross-channel invasion in the summer of 1940. But by 1941 the conclusion was mistaken. Hitler helped this self-deception by continuing to rattle a few swords on the channel coast. The point here is that the easiest kind of strategic deception in the course of conflict is a shift away from a strategy that the enemy is aware of and in terms of which the enemy evaluates his intelligence. The deception resides in the enemy's own judgmental fixation and inflexibility.

As for tactical deception, it is easier to implement under modern conditions than ever before, given the mobility of modern military assets and the fact that the performance of military systems often cannot be discerned by technical means of intelligence gathering. Indeed, modern technical intelligence seems to be particularly vulnerable to deception. For example, cruise missiles directed against ground targets must be programmed before launch, and stealth aircraft must have their courses plotted just as carefully, taking into account the location of air-defense radars. The effectiveness of the latter and the safety of the former depend largely on the *angle* from which the radars look at the intruders. Of course, some of the "cruises" and stealths can be targeted on the air-defense sites. But the direction from which they come makes all the difference. Anyone programming cruise missiles and stealths would rely on satellite pictures of the air-defense sites to determine the best angles of approach. But given that the owners of the air-defense sites know that they are being observed by satellite, and given that these sites are mobile, they can move them after passage of an imaging satellite. Or they can simply deceive the satellite by temporarily posing for it in false orientation. Thus any cruise missile or stealth that is programmed to reach its target according to that satellite's data would be flying into a trap. Serbia laid such trap for American F-117 stealth fighters during the Kosovo War of 1999. One was shot down outright, the other damaged.

A similar effect can be achieved in cloudy weather by turning on air-defense radars when an enemy electronic intelligence (ELINT) satellite is in range and then moving the radar. Similarly, by purposely radiating a false, "signature" signal, the enemy may be deceived into thinking that units are armed with a different type of air-defense missile, again setting up a mismatch. The possibilities for such deception are limited only by imagination.

Subversion

As we have already discussed, the exercise of political influence on the enemy is the proximate goal of waging war. Hence, it would be incorrect to think of such political manipulation under the narrow category of intelligence. Nevertheless, intelligence is involved in exercising precisely the kind of political influence that the enemy does not know is being exercised. This kind of influence is popularly known as subversion. Intelligence is involved in subversion in two ways. First, those who are in position—i.e., who have the physical and social access—to gather intelligence are in effect in a position to subvert. Any side that can put people behind enemy lines to gather intelligence can also put people there to subvert. Second, in order to subvert in a competent manner it is necessary to have very good intelligence about a target. In other words, subversion is intelligence-intensive work, and it often uses intelligence people.

Subversion—etymologically, the act of turning from underneath—consists of actions ranging from the spreading of rumors (either true or false), to building up or tearing down the influence of key people or factions in the enemy camp, and possibly to sabotage and assassination. Its distinguishing feature—the "sub" in subversion—is that the actions do not appear to be the work of an enemy. Thus, whereas some injuries rally the victim by focusing its anger on the enemy, the defeats inflicted through subversion confuse the victim as to who the enemy is, and thus further erode the victim's moral energies.

Action of almost any sort is dangerous to spies. Their safety lies in being unobtrusive. Highly placed spies who openly take the side of an enemy power in internal deliberations cast suspicion on themselves ipso facto. Those who "run" spy rings generally resist suggestions that the spies be used for subversion. Yet, because the spies are often the only agents in the "right" places when the need for subversion arises, they must either recruit and run the subverters or become subverters themselves.

Secret agents in the enemy's camp have always been rare and priceless. Usually, unless one has made preparations, the only people on whom one can count in a foreign court are one's own diplomats. In his history of the Peloponnesian War, Thucydides writes of Athenian and Spartan ambassadors who lodged with friends in cities throughout Greece and secretly mobilized groups to influence the host city's government. One of the goriest episodes in that war was the partisan strife in Corcyra, on Corfu, fomented by ambassadors who promised each of the island's factions support that encouraged them to fight one another. During the wars of the Refor-mation, ambassadors did little but stir up court intrigues and partisan warfare. Today, embassies are still the bases of choice for subversion, because diplomatic personnel enjoy both wide social access and almost complete personal immunity. For example, in 1963 American diplomats and CIA officers worked out of the U.S. embassy when they met with South Vietnamese army officers who were plotting against President Ngo Dinh Diem and fomented the coup d'état by assuring them of continued U.S. support. By the same token, in 1986 the Soviet embassy in Aden was the headquarters for a coup d'état—indeed, a mini-civil war in which one faction of the ruling Communist Party seized power from the other.

Perhaps the most complete example of diplomatic subversion was that of Count Diego Sarmiento Gondomar, Spain's ambassador to London at the beginning of the seventeenth century. Gondomar not only induced many of England's leading personalities to accept handsome, secret "pensions" from the Spanish treasury; he also became so close personally to King James I that he was able to steer England's foreign policy. Although Spain, Protestant England's great rival, was in the process of putting down a Protestant rebellion in the Netherlands, Gondomar succeeded in keeping England neutral. Indeed, the king of England even arrested anti-Spanish Englishmen. Compared to this example, Secretary of State Henry Kissinger's grant of a privileged parking space in the State Department's basement to Soviet Ambassador Anatoli Dobrinyin is mild. The former example illustrates an important point about subversion. Subversion is not magic, it is not "brainwashing," and it does not involve "making" people act against their will. No one was ever subverted against his will, just as no one was ever deceived, converted, or for that matter, seduced against his will.

Less dramatic but no less real instances of subversion occur daily in embassies around the world. It is not easy to draw a line between subversion and the customary function of embassies, namely, influencing affairs in the host country through wide-ranging contacts. The distinguishing mark of subversion, however, is choosing not to accept the decisions that a foreign government might make but to attempt to influence those decisions secretly. In effect subversion is warfare waged within a foreign government's decision-making process.

Subversion is also part of the end game of wars—the empowerment of the only people who can actually turn a foreign country around, locals who are already inclined to do so.

Dispatching agents of subversion who magically transform a foreign country is normally the stuff of fiction. Since the dawn of history subversion has relied upon people within a target government or society susceptible to working with, or in parallel with, a foreign power. The foreign power sends operatives who turn the potential for subversion into reality. The Athenian democracy would send words of encouragement to democratic parties throughout Greece, while its rival, oligarchic Sparta, would intrigue with oligarchs. The Soviet Communist Party did not simply send out agents helter-skelter, but rather focused on those persons in foreign countries whose ideas or whose "class" presumably predisposed them to work against the "main enemy," the United States. Nor does any competent government send forth missionaries to convert foreign groups that are not inclined to it. It is difficult enough to convince people to work for the things they want. It is almost impossible to convince people to work for things they do not want. The subverter's art consists in advancing his own agenda by harnessing it to the locals' eagerness to realize their own. Thus, American agents working in Iraqi Kurdistan in the early 1970s did not vaunt the wonders of America or the glories of Iran, but rather their willingness to support a war against the Iraqi Arabs whom the Kurds hated. The American agents who persuaded the H'mong tribe of Laos to fight against North Vietnam would have moved no one with talk of democracy. But they enlisted a nation by showing it the possibility of achieving freedom from its oppressor. It is important that agents, whether they are government employees or people specially engaged for a particular assignment, be able to understand, visibly sympathize with, and give malcontents the necessary tools to act.

To be in a position to subvert, an agent must be credible to those he is trying to influence. This can be achieved by appearing as the representative of a purposeful, powerful foreign country. Or it can mean hiding that fact and appearing as another kind of friend. Whatever guise is chosen, it is indispensable that the agent be trusted as someone who knows what he is talking about and as someone whose counsels are friendly. Thus, in 1986 when President Reagan sent former senator Paul Laxalt to Manila to entice Philippine president Ferdinand Marcos into giving up power, Marcos believed both that Laxalt and Reagan had his interest at heart and that they were in a position to deliver an honorable retirement rather than the gilded cage—and the prosecution—he actually got. Similarly, when various Iranian intermediaries approached the U.S. government in 1985 with the hope of purchasing U.S. arms, they did so as representatives of groups that they said were ready, willing, and able to take certain actions contrary to the regime of Ayatollah Khomeini. They lied but were believed.

The "trick" of subversion, then, consists in knowing what will impel target groups to act, and what will impede them. The subverter must also know what kinds of people or approaches will inspire trust in them and what will alienate them. Often it's a close call. For example, in 1939–40, when the British government sought to enlist U.S. help against Germany, it had to overcome the coolness and even the hostility of the State Department and of Ambassador Joseph Kennedy especially. The British government knew that President Roosevelt favored aid, was hostile to Germany, and was unfriendly to Ambassador Kennedy. British intelligence tapped

Kennedy's telephone and recorded remarks that were pro-German and grossly anti-Roosevelt. The British naturally wanted to share these recordings with the president. But would Roosevelt's tendency to pounce on a chance to squash a disloyal subordinate and push a favorite policy be counterbalanced by unhappiness at having had the U.S. embassy's phones tapped? The British judged that Roosevelt was the kind of man who would put substance over form, and they were correct. They knew their target.

During World War II, the United States preceded its landings in French North Africa in 1942 with agents whose purpose was to secure the noninterference of the French army authorities. The American agents had a lot going for them. The United States was at war with the same Germany that had crushed the French army two years earlier and now occupied Paris. Every Frenchman in North Africa knew that a U.S. victory would liberate France. But American agents had a lot going against them, too. American policy at the time was to work with the Vichy regime, which was ruling France on Hitler's behalf, because the State Department believed that this regime retained the loyalty of most Frenchmen. Thus, the U.S. agents in North Africa tried to split the difference. Though talking loudly of helping to free France from German occupation, they did not work with the allies of Gen. Charles de Gaulle's Free French movement. They avoided attacks on the legitimacy of the Vichy regime and tried instead to persuade its representative in North Africa, Admiral Darlan—to come over to the Allied side. Ambassador Robert Murphy displayed the talents of a world-class diplomat in the service of a self-contradictory policy. On the day of the American landings, the official chargé of the Vichy regime ordered French troops to fire on the Americans and told American agents that he would have to get permission from Hitler's puppet, Pétain, to change sides. American agents failed because they tried to subvert the Vichy government's control of North Africa without really subverting it. Finally, as American troops were landing in force and Frenchmen had to decide whether to risk their lives by fighting them, the fundamentals of the situation asserted themselves. French forces in North Africa aligned themselves under de Gaulle's banner against Germany and the Vichy regime, but not because of American policy, whose brilliant execution was vitiated by ignorant conception.

What will move—or steady—a target group? Who is inclined to be of assistance, and how can they help? These are the intelligence questions that underlie subversion. Without correct answers even technical virtuosity in operations will be counterproductive. Suppose that a country wishes to bolster a foreign regime by weakening its dissident groups. It must know the factions it supports well enough to ensure that strengthening them will weaken rather than merely incite their opponents. For example, during the 1960s and 1970s the United States sought to undergird the regime of the shah of Iran by encouraging it to secularize the country—something that displeased most Iranians, who are devout Muslims. But at the same time, American advisers discouraged the Iranians from adopting the dictatorial measures secularization entails, such as banning the wearing of veils and eradicating or subsuming religious endowments that Mustafa Kemal had undertaken half a century earlier in Turkey. Thus, instead of weakening Islam, the Americans' half measures aroused it. This counterproductive result, which ultimately led to the Islamic Revolution of 1978–79, came as a big surprise for the same reason that it happened at all—ignorant intelligence. U.S. intelligence was not in contact with or intellectually capable of comprehending the religious mentality that made Iran into what it is today. The United States unwittingly helped to subvert those Iranians who were on its side.

Who is on whose side? War naturally narrows the "sides" to two. What will the various people who support a country's enemy do when the immediate danger is over? What can that country do to make sure that they stay on its side in subsequent conflicts? The answers require inside knowledge of the parties involved. Armed with that knowledge, a country can firm up allies and weaken enemies. Machiavelli's favorite example, Cesare Borgia, presents a case in point. Borgia had allied himself with the king of France, Louis XII, and the Orsini family against the Colonnesi family of Rome. He realized that in the long run he lacked the power to manipulate France, so he resolved to have as little to do with it as possible. He knew that the Orsini, though unreliable, were venal, so he showered them with the spoils of war. He also knew that the Colonnesi could be enticed to negotiate for a share of his spoils, but that he could not actually deliver that share without alienating the Orsini. So during the negotiations he assassinated the leading men of the Colonnesi. This left his enemies much weaker and his allies more in his power than ever.

Contrast this with the obtuse way in which the United States dealt with its allies in World War II, by relying on the ones it could not influence and weakening and alienating the ones it could. Not only did the United States place its bets for the postwar order on the Soviet Union, which it could not control, it also chose which political factions to support materially and politically in wartime Europe strictly on the basis of their ability to fight the current enemy, Germany, without regard to their relationship to the Soviet Union. Thus the United States and Britain became largely responsible for the prominent positions that Yugoslav, Italian, Greek, and French communists, allied with the Soviet Union, occupied at the end of the war. By contrast Borgia knew that the Orsini could be bought with material goods. He also knew that to keep them bought he had to kill the Colonnesi. And he was willing to do it. Any country serious about subversion has to have the kind of knowledge and the kind of determination Borgia had. Subversion is a part of war. It is not a cheap substitute for war.

This point is easiest to grasp when one looks at examples in which either intelligence or determination or both are lacking. Unfortunately, the quintessential example is the perennial fascination of the U.S. government with promotion of the "moderate faction" in the camps of its enemies throughout the world. But the term "moderate" begs, indeed hides, all the tough questions. What does the United States want these people to do? What are they disposed to do? What will it take to get them to do it? Is the United States willing to do what is needed to make it work? The term "moderate" is attractive to policymakers precisely because it begs these questions. Thus, unserious policymakers can tinker with foreign situations as fancy strikes them without having to know or commit very much. Presidents from Franklin Roosevelt to George W. Bush have imagined that dictators, whether they be named Josef Stalin, Mikhail Gorbachev, or Yasir Arafat represented the "moderate faction" and that the United States ought to do what is necessary to strengthen them lest "hard-liners" take over. Never mind that the United States has next to no knowledge of who belongs to what faction or what the factions represent (if anything) for the interests of the United States.

Similarly, in the 1980s American policymakers fancied that they could subvert the existing order in Iran and South Africa by supporting, respectively, moderate factions of various secular or self-proclaimed Islamic terrorist organizations or terrorist-supporting governments. Leave aside for the moment whether it makes any sense to call anyone associated with such organizations "moderate," and assume—though this is not the case—that the United States had private, secure knowledge that the people with whom they were dealing were ready to take over their organizations and turn them into servants of U.S. policy. Still, what could the United States do to help these "moderates" achieve that end? The sine qua non of such an accomplishment by the moderates would have been the rather extreme act of killing or helping to kill the "extremists." But surely these "moderates" were not prepared to commit fratricide. If they had, the United States would not have been willing or able to help them do such immoderate deeds. So what could this American subversion have amounted to? Nothing but self-deception.

This brings us to the bottom line on subversion. Subversion is a human activity that cannot be calibrated in terms of money, promises, propaganda, or, indeed, any specific means at all. It consists of somehow inducing human beings to induce others to act in one's interest, wittingly or unwittingly, for whatever reason might lead them to do so. It is not unusual for people to deceive themselves about the reliability of a subversive scheme that they have devised, no matter how competently they have designed it. People being people, no intelligence can foretell who will be one's friends at the time of trial. Machiavelli's rule of thumb, however, has proved valid through the ages: *If one will have good arms, one will always have good friends.*

11

JUST WAR

Love thine enemies.
—LUKE 6.35

CAN IT EVER be right to take part in events that lead to the death of thousands, many of them innocent—never mind to set those events in motion? The answer clearly must be "That depends" . . . let us see on what.

The paragon of justice in our civilization is the Good Samaritan. Christ tells us that a certain traveler was set upon by robbers, who beat him and left him for dead. Priests and scholars saw him as they passed by but moved to the other side of the road. Finally, the Samaritan arrived. He bound the victim's wounds, took him to an inn, and paid the innkeeper to nurse him back to health. Our civilization invites us to imitate this active Samaritan, rather than the passive priests and scholars.

But what would this exemplary Samaritan have done if he had come upon the scene while the violent robbery was still in progress? Would charity have been satisfied if he had watched until the robbers had finished with their victim before moving in to help? Wouldn't the Good Samaritan have attacked the robbers? On the other hand, if the robbers had been so many that by joining the fray he would only have committed suicide, he might have stayed hidden in the rocks. Charity and suicide are two different things. However, if he had been traveling with his own friends, he might have judged the strength of his band against the robbers' before deciding whether it was prudent to ask his friends to join him in war against the robbers.

As for the priest and the scholar, although they did not put themselves out for a stranger, one might surmise that if they had come home from their journeys to find the thieves looting their farms and raping their wives, they would have used all prudent force to put a stop to the evil. Nor can one imagine that Christ would have condemned anyone for using all necessary force—though doing so would involve the commission of some evil—to stop a greater evil from occurring. "Turning the other cheek" is no Christian virtue when it means offering up someone else's cheek or life to be smitten.

Hence, the civilization that has risen on the teachings of Christ has always sanctioned war, providing that sufficiently valuable goods are at stake, that they are seriously enough threatened, that the danger is such that violence is necessary if the goods are to be protected, that there is reasonable chance of success, and that any evils committed in the defense of these goods not outweigh them.

Of course, if all Western rulers who ever contemplated war had made these dispassionate judgments about the justice of their cause, the world would have suffered only a small fraction of the wars that it in fact has suffered. But war happens so often precisely because when men judge their own case they tend to be inspired more by interest, fear, and hatred than by a thirst for justice. Still, not only would the number of wars have been greater without the above criteria, but there would have been no way for third parties and mere citizens to distinguish between Good Samaritans, aggressors, defenders, the prudent, the mad, and the criminal.

Western thought has divided questions of justice regarding warfare into two interrelated sets. One asks whether it is right or wrong to fight for a particular cause in a particular circumstance—*jus ad bellum*. The other concerns whether particular actions taken in the course of a war are right or not—*jus in bello*. Let us examine each set in turn.

Jus ad Bellum

The worth of the goods at stake—human and material—is a necessary element in considering whether it is just to break the peace. But substantially elevating the quality of life for all concerned does not by itself justify breaking the peace. This is because in the Western tradition peace and settled arrangements are themselves of great value. Xenophon tells of the Socratic teacher asking his pupil, the young Cyrus (the Great), what he would do if he came across a small man with a big coat and a big man with a small coat. When Cyrus replied that he would take the big coat away from the small man and give it to the big one, and vice versa, the teacher beat him to drive home the point that although both parties would benefit from the distribution, the big coat actually belonged to the small man and no one had the right to take it away from him, nor the small coat from the big man.

Likewise, Abraham Lincoln, while he had no doubt that Negro slavery was a great evil to be done away with, was determined to do all he could to avoid fighting a war in order to eradicate it. He knew that war would cause death and suffering and might permanently break the U.S. Constitution. He knew that anyone who could turn slaves into free men arbitrarily could by the same token turn free men into slaves. He also realized that no one had the right to dispossess the masters of the property in which they had invested and on which they based their livelihood, and that no one could adequately manage the instant transition of millions of slaves to lives of responsibility. So he sought to arrange laws and public opinion so that the extinction of slavery would happen both gradually and peaceably. When the Southern states resisted these peaceable measures to the point of making war, Lincoln then prosecuted that war at the cost of carnage (Antietam, Gettysburg) for the sake of two worthy goods: the integrity of the United States and the abolition of slavery. The abolition of slavery became necessary both as a measure of war and as a means of eliminating the bone of contention that had led to the war. Lincoln did not issue the Emancipation Proclamation simply because slavery is evil. For their part, the southerners who started the Civil War were not unanimously convinced that slavery was good. Rather, they were defending the only way of life they knew against a threat that, although nonviolent, was just as certain to end that way of life. They broke the peace for this legitimate reason. The fact that the order they were defending was less just than the order they were resisting is important but separate.

The American Founding Fathers, though committed to the proposition that the American form of government was the only one fit for free men, that it was the "new order of the ages" and the future of all mankind, resolved to be at peace with all the despots of the world. A large part of the reason is that they recognized that weak America had no other choice. But as Thomas Jefferson's letter to his friend Thomas Leiper indicated, they looked forward to the day when they would have "a rod to shake over their heads that will make the stoutest of them tremble."[1] Nevertheless, it did not cross the Founding Fathers' minds that the United States would ever fight a world war to "make the world safe for democracy." Who were the Americans to claim the right to force, say, the Chinese to be free? And how could they assume responsibility for making sure that such vast works of cultural revolution would not yield something worse?

Only in the twentieth century, when American leaders had channeled the fervors of their vanishing religious faith into secular pursuits, did they fight wars for "unconditional surrender," to "end all wars," and to "make the world safe for democracy." Perhaps because American leaders valued the earthly goods at stake too highly and lacked prudence in making political strategy, the two world wars left more people under worse governments than before. That contradicts jus ad bellum.

Early America did fight a distant war against North African pirates in order to defend the small but concrete good of unmolested navigation. It also went to war with the Indian tribes and with Mexico to secure for Americans the safe enjoyment of the lands they were settling. Did this good justify breaking the peace? The unofficial war with Mexico over Texas in 1836 and the official one of 1846–48 pose ethically straightforward questions. Mexico laid claim to vast, largely empty lands in North America. It encouraged settlement by English-speaking Americans, and did not warn the Americans that they would have to learn to live under direct Mexican rule. The Americans who poured into these lands preferred to live as they had and to resist Mexican despots. No doubt, the U.S. government was pleased that American settlers in Mexican territory spread the good of the American way of life over the continent. But the U.S. government did not send the settlers and it did not instigate their quarrels with Mexico. When the quarrels came, the U.S. government played no role in the Texans' victory. The war of 1846–48 was different. Mexico's resentment over the independence of Texas made it into an enemy, albeit impotent, and the Southwest border unfriendly. The U.S. government tried to purchase a better border. When Mexico reneged on the deal, the United States made war. Proof that America's conscience about that war was uneasy came when the peace treaty America imposed forced Mexico to accept payment for the largely empty territories that America had seized.

Much less straightforward are the issues surrounding the wars between Europeans and the Indians of the Americas and the aborigines of Australia. The case of the Spanish conquest of America is an exception, because the Spaniards came unambiguously to exploit, enslave, and kill. The conquistadores treated the Indians as they had treated the Muslims they had earlier dispossessed or chased out of Spain—and worse. In all other instances the Europeans did not enslave but sought to work the colonized land themselves. To say that these lands "belonged" to the natives is to use a concept entirely foreign to those natives. At the time, only Europeans, not Indians, bought, owned, and sold land. The "land deals" between European settlers and natives, including the one for some twenty-four dollars for Manhattan Island, were surely examples of different cultures talking past each other. The natives had no idea that the white man intended to have exclusive use of the land or that he intended to stay. Much less could the Indians conceive of making Manhattan into the center of world commerce. On the other hand, the Europeans wrongly expected the natives to behave as Europeans. Add to this the natural preference for one's own way and disdain mixed with fear of peoples so different, and it is not surprising that friction and massacres on both sides fueled wars as cruel as they were unequal. But where did justice lie?

Violent and nonviolent conflict alike were less the result of decisions that can be judged just or unjust and more the consequence of events that flowed naturally—and tragically—out of the proximity of irreconcilable human differences. In general, both the natives and the Europeans believed, correctly, that they were endangered and fought in defense of their ways. But because the civilization of the Europeans was superior in its capacity to accomplish things, it attracted the natives and thus destroyed their ways far more efficiently than did violence.

In most wars, fighting for particular goods is never as urgent as fighting for identity or interest. Which of the two princes claiming kinship to the deceased king shall rule? Will the Burgundian peasant pay his taxes to his duke, or to the agent of the French king? Will Venetian or Genoese ships carry the bulk of silk and spices from the East to Europe? Will the French or German flag fly over Strasbourg? Will the Italian peninsula be ruled by various French- and German-speaking princes or by an Italian-speaking king? Thus stated, these "goods," for which the majority of wars in our civilization have been fought, do not begin to justify breaking the peace. Yet, things are not so simple.

The various parties in former dynastic struggles were not morally equal (although in most cases they were not as unequal as they thought). Who would deny that it was just to raise an army against the mad and murderous Richard III? Surely anyone who lived at the time when Cesare Borgia appointed Remirro d'Orco to terrorize and "pacify" the city-states of Romagna would have been able to make a case to the Duke of Milan (who was not a nice guy) and to the Council of Venice—Borgia's opponents at that time— that it was their moral duty to send an army to end this oppression. In our time, few would dispute that the Tanzanian tyrant Julius Nyerere acted justly when he sent his army to help depose Idi Amin, the cannibal tyrant of neighboring Uganda. Few outside Western universities dispute that deposing the Iraqi tyrant Saddam Hussein was good and just. But were these just actions justified by their results? Were the motives of those who acted pure? Did they have to be?

There is no doubt that the various kings who gradually turned France into a unified state broke the peace and destroyed a relatively benign medieval order to do so. But the moral arguments that supported their actions cannot be easily dismissed. For hundreds of years English armies had been crisscrossing the land, causing much grief. Perhaps the principal reason they had been able to do so was the autonomy the Duke of Burgundy and other nobles enjoyed. Moreover these nobles found much of their fun in life by fighting each other over insults, real or imagined. Thus, the kings who made war to subjugate their nobles saw themselves as farsighted defenders of the peace. Human nature being what it is, however, the kings then raised armies for bigger quarrels abroad, quarrels usually without moral significance.

The Genoese's and the Venetians' greedy wars over seaborne trade followed directly from clashes between individual merchants in foreign ports or between rival argosies at sea. These in turn were fueled by envy and the desire to reduce commercial competition. Ships' captains would return home to both cities, demand protection, and assure their fellow citizens that without it the city's economy would wane and everyone would starve. Fight, they would say, or watch the enemy starve your family. Only wisdom, prudence, and fortitude made war between these two cities sporadic rather than constant.

But what happens when people of one race, language, or religion are being ruled by people of a different race, language, or religion? Is it then not just to break the peace in order to change an unjust status quo? In fact, the wars of the nineteenth century, were fought on the premise that the answer to this question is yes. But common sense requires distinctions. On the one hand, there was Muslim Turkey's rule of Christian Greece. Each year until the eighteenth century, Turkish troops would exact from Christian communities a "tax" of their best boys. These would be taken away from their families forever and brought up as Muslim janissaries in the service of the sultan. Some would be castrated and employed as eunuchs. The only argument against waging war to topple this system was not whether the end was just, but whether there was a reasonable chance of success. The reasonable likelihood of success is a sine qua non of jus ad bellum. Human life is not to be hazarded lightly.

On the other hand, Austria's rule of Lombardy in the eighteenth and nineteenth centuries provides a contrary example. It is true that the prince spoke German and the subjects spoke Italian. But Milan was governed about as well as Vienna. The Italians who lusted for war with Austria adhered to the nationalistic (and neo-racist) tradition in which good government is no substitute for government by one's own kind. The wars of the Italian Risorgimento were not especially bloody. Then again, they affected the moral tone of government on the peninsula little, if at all. And within two generations, Milan would be governed by modern Roman standards—distinctively lower than Viennese.

The extreme example of nationalist-racist reasoning applies to the British dominion in India. In 1919, after a British officer had put down a riot in

Amritsar (some say there was only an incipient riot) at the cost of 317 lives, the British viceroy, Viscount Chelmsford, objected on moral grounds. Previously, the British had had no qualms about killing people by the hundreds in order to suppress mobs swiftly, reasoning that if they did otherwise, the Hindus, Muslims, Sikhs, Tamils, Dravidans, Afghans, and other groups of the Indian subcontinent would kill each other by the millions and the British by the thousands. In fact, the governor's 1919 prohibition of further such suppression, motivated by his sincere view that British rule in India was not morally defensible, opened the floodgates. During the 1920s and 1930s, as British units gradually withdrew from enforcing order in India, thousands died in interracial rioting. When Britain finally withdrew in 1947, the ensuing intercommunity violence uprooted perhaps one hundred million people and claimed uncounted millions. The carving out of Pakistan in 1947 and the bloody secession of Bangladesh from Pakistan in 1970 did not end the intercommunity violence. The massacre of 1919 looms large in historical consequence, but imperceptible in quantitative comparison with what continues to happen in the area.

Nationalism is the most widespread excuse for war in our time. From Algeria to Indonesia people have convinced others to break the peace to take power in the name of their "kind." The notion of self-determination grew during the eighteenth and especially the nineteenth centuries and became somewhat associated with the idea of democracy. But in practice, few of those who have started wars in the name of nationalism have turned out to be democrats. Nor does democracy guarantee or even imply fair treatment of minorities. For example, had nineteenth-century Americans followed Stephen Douglas rather than Abraham Lincoln and adopted a utilitarian attitude toward Negroes, the United States would not thereby have ceased to be a democracy. Indeed, the scope of popular choice would have been even wider. Douglas was "pro-choice" on slavery, and argued that Lincoln would restrict the scope of private and public choice on the matter. Lincoln did not dispute that. Rather, he argued that a good democracy should not have certain choices.

Because race and nationality are morally neutral concepts, no argument can be made that any suffering is justified simply to give power and glory to one race or nationality. Indeed, any such argument would seem to be a good definition of injustice.

Another frequent justification for war is the fulfillment of obligations to others. World War I is often assumed to have started because of a system of alliances, and the accepted cause of World War II was Britain's commitment to Poland. But in fact, few break the peace simply to keep their word. Nor can the moral worth of a personal commitment weigh in the balance against the horrors of war. So in fact, when leaders take their followers to war pursuant to a promise, the real reason is whatever led to their making the promise in the first place. Pieces of paper do not cause war.

Perhaps the most common excuse for war is self-defense. If an army is marching toward one's home, one will naturally prepare to prevent armed men from roaming the streets as conquerors. Common sense says that conquerors can and often do take and destroy anything they want. Protection of the normal, decent order of a community is among the worthiest goods that may be safeguarded by war. And indeed, a high percentage of those who have fought wars throughout the ages have done so because enemy armies were bearing down on them and they feared what would happen if they did not fight. The right of individual and collective self-defense is explicitly recognized in Article 51 of the UN Charter as the only justification for going to war.

But many more people throughout the ages have taken up arms while deceptively citing this fear. Still others have feared honestly, but mistakenly. Surely, leaders of aggressive states often try to convince their peoples that their attacks are really acts of defense. The German military surely succeeded in doing this in World War I. How does one evaluate the moral worth of preemptive attacks? In June 1967, hostilities had begun with a preemptive Israeli strike against Egyptian and Syrian airfields. But Egypt's media were full of threats to wipe the Jewish people off the face of the earth. Israel had merely beaten the Arabs to the punch. Dayan was correct, and Israel's attack was defensive, just as the U.S. Navy would have been acting defensively had it been able to attack the Japanese aircraft carriers that were moving into position to strike Pearl Harbor without waiting for their bombs and torpedoes to hit. The governing fact here is that the peace is broken by whoever makes the decision to break it. If the party that is to be attacked learns of this decision and strikes out first, its action cannot be called an act of aggression.

Perhaps the most common excuse for breaking the peace has been this claim that the other side was about to attack. The fact that most of these claims have been false does not negate the fact that some have been true, while others have been authentic cases of misperception.

Yet not even a clear victim of aggression, like the United States after Pearl Harbor, Hitler's declaration of war, or the attacks of 11 September 2001, can escape the questions: What are our war aims? Are these aims just? What are we fighting to achieve? Do we have a reasonable plan for doing so? As we have seen, one of the characteristics of war is that people redefine their aims, and sometimes their character, in the course of the fighting. A country may at first attempt to simply protect itself. But what then? Perhaps the rarest outcome of any war is the reestablishment of the *status quo ante bellum.* Hence, the moral quality of a country's goals necessarily changes as one's goals change.

For example, while the causes for which Britain and the United States entered into World War II—essentially self-protection against attack from Hitler and Tojo and, incidentally, reestablishing the rights of lesser nations from Poland to the Philippines—were just and achievable, by the end of the war U.S. aims had changed to making the world safe for the UN system. For the sake of this new "good," which required above all accommodating Stalin, the United States and Britain committed a variety of injustices—including abandoning the immediate goal for which several of the Allies had entered the war, namely, protecting Poland. Thus, at the end of World War II the United States and Britain were fighting on an ostensibly much higher, but actually much lower, moral plane than that upon which they had fought at the beginning.

The ends in themselves, however, justify nothing. Violence will not suffice if the fight is hopeless or if there is another way to achieve just goals.

During the Peloponnesian War, for example, the representatives of the neutral city of Melos were besieged by the much stronger Athenians, who sought to occupy their land and enlist them in an alliance. The Melians tried to dissuade the Athenians, until the latter defined the dialogue by declaring, "The strong do what they can, while the weak suffer what they must." At that point, was it right for the Melians to wage a hopeless fight? The Melians' goals were morally unexceptionable: to be left alone in an honorable neutrality. But fighting could not bring peace—only death. The Melians fought. As a consequence, their men were put to the sword and their women and children were sold into slavery. Surely the Melians' just ends did not justify their decision to resist, because the resistance was hopeless and out of proportion to the Athenians' demands.

Just ends and the absence of peaceful alternatives do not justify breaking the peace unless a plan has been reasonably formulated to bring success. For example, many have noted that between 1937 and 1941 the United States, together with the British and Dutch empires, so restricted Japan's access to raw materials, especially oil, that Japan was forced to choose between war and economic strangulation. But even if one accepts this theory, one is still compelled to agree that the Japanese never formulated a war plan to achieve anything. They knew that they could conquer the Philippines, Indochina, perhaps Singapore and Malaya, and perhaps put a big dent in the U.S. Pacific Fleet. But what could they expect after that? How could Japan compel Britain and, above all, the United States to let it retain any portion of its gains? The Japanese navy estimated the U.S. overall potential advantage over Japan at ten to one. Japan could scarcely think of conquering Hawaii, much less California or Washington, D.C. Nor did Japan build submarines and distribute its troops in the Pacific in order to form a strong defensive perimeter that would tire the United States and force it to negotiate. It simply struck out ferociously to the very limit of its reach. And then it awaited disaster. If for no other reason, Japan's war was grossly unjust because it stood no chance of success. But note well: As President Roosevelt and Secretary of State Cordell Hull forced Japan into its fateful choice, they presented no plan by which Japan could buy raw materials and sell its products—only demands that Japan give up its empire. Though just in a sense, these were not the stuff of peace.

Under President Reagan, the U.S. government repeatedly argued that the cause of the anticommunist guerrillas in Nicaragua, Angola, and Afghanistan was just. Hence, said Reagan, it was also just for the United States to publicly associate itself with those causes and to send them some aid. But to achieve what? President Reagan never seriously addressed the question of what results could reasonably be expected from any given kind of association and any given level of aid. The United States never formulated any plan by which it could have caused these forces to win in any sense of the term. Over a period of years the United States consciously refused to supply these forces with the kinds and amounts of supplies that would have allowed them to make a serious try for victory. Nor did the United States ever consider isolating Nicaragua's and Angola's communist governments from Soviet supply routes by air or sea blockades. Indeed, throughout the struggle, the United States maintained an embassy in two of these three countries under communist regimes, recognizing them as the legitimate governments of their peoples. President Reagan's domestic opponents had more than a rhetorical point when they berated him for in effect making war against legitimate governments. Arguments for their illegitimacy were ready at hand, and Reagan sometimes voiced them. But his official acts contradicted them.

Thus, granting that the causes of the anticommunist sides in these civil wars were just and weighty and that there was no alternative to war, one could still conclude that U.S. involvement on their side was unjust because it was not done as part of a plan reasonably calculated to bring about a new peace. The purpose of war is not to fight and die, or to temporize among contradictory lines of policy, but to win a peace worth winning. By 1990, however, as the Soviet Union died, so did the communist governments of Nicaragua and Afghanistan. Ex post facto, some argued that U.S. actions, by indirectly putting pressure on Moscow, had brought freedom indirectly to Managua and Kabul. Perhaps. But since events surprised all, no one argues that this outcome had been anyone's plan.

In 2003 the U.S. government invaded Iraq because, according to some, its regime was as brutally unjust as any in history. Similarly, some justified war against Afghanistan's Taliban regime because of its inequitable treatment of women. President Bush articulated a vision of the peace that would justify these military campaigns: transforming the Middle East from a place of violent, corrupt dictatorships, of cultures of mutual exploitation and victimhood, of anti-Semitism and anti-Americanism defined as religion, into one of liberal democracy, free economies, honesty, and religious tolerance. But the injustice of a state or way of life does not automatically translate into justification for war against them. As we shall see, President George W. Bush also gave very different principal definitions of the U.S. cause: protection against Iraqi weapons of mass destruction, Iraq's involvement in terrorism. Regardless of their worth or accuracy, however, the justice of war on behalf of any or all these causes depended on the existence of a reasonable plan for achieving a peace the goodness of which would outweigh the inevitable evils of the war. Great hopes can even be noble in and of themselves. But they can be just only when accompanied by reasonable plans for their realization.

Jus in Bello

Whereas the question of whether it is just to enter into a given war in a given set of circumstances is complex, the matter of just behavior in the course of war is governed by simple, straightforward rules. Alas, those rules are rarely observed, because even when war does not spring from hate, it inevitably engenders hate. As various exceptional leaders throughout history, from Nicias in the Peloponnesian War to Douglas MacArthur in World War II, have shown, it is possible not to succumb to hate's temptation to simply inflict pain on the enemy. But the sad fact is that the longer a war lasts, the more likely hate will drive it to irrational ends and unjust means.

The general rule is that the means used to fight the war must not outweigh the good that victory might bring. In other words, the means must not be allowed to dishonor the ends. The point of the rule is that the enemy in war is not so much a set of persons—much less whole peoples—but rather a set of evil intentions. It is imperative to defeat these intentions without hate. This rule of public life is identical to the private commandment to hate the sin while loving the sinner.

The specifics of the rule are that one must make reasonable efforts to spare noncombatants from harm and, indeed, that the harm inflicted in order to achieve the worthy ends of the war, even upon combatants, must be as minimal as possible. The rules boil down to *discrimination, economy,* and *mercy.*

Discrimination

Discrimination means that armed forces should fight armed forces and not ravage the enemy's countryside, cities, or economy. While "starving out" an army is permitted, blockades of whole countries, such as the ones that kept food from Germany in World Wars I and II, have traditionally been considered unjust means of warfare because they do not discriminate between combatants and noncombatants. By the same token, it has been a traditional rule of Western warfare that when an army takes possession of a city with the intention of using it as a fortress by which to fight another army, both armies must allow the civilian population of the city to depart in an orderly manner. This is what Gen. Charles George ("Chinese") Gordon and his enemy, the Mahdi, Mohammed Ahmed, did before fighting the final battle of Khartoum in 1890. In other words, the corollary of the rule that armies may not make war on cities full of civilians is the rule that armies may not hide behind civilians.

Both the French and German armies respected this rule with regard to Paris during World War II. But in the battle of Leningrad the Soviet Union violated that rule, with disastrous results. The German army besieged the city. But on the northeastern side Leningrad has access to the rest of Russia through Lake Ladoga, which remained in Soviet hands. In the winter, good truck roads crossed the frozen lake, and ferries plied it in the summer. The Soviets could have let the civilians depart at any time. Instead, to maintain the fiction that the city was functioning normally, they prevented the population from leaving. And they gave inadequate supplies to the population that they were forcibly keeping in harm's way. As a result, almost a million civilians, kept on a minimum diet of as little as one hundred grams of black bread per day, died of starvation and disease.

Discrimination above all means not intentionally harming civilians. Yet intentionally killing civilians is precisely what the United States did in World War II. The policy of strategic bombing, which meant the outright murder of millions, had become routine long before 1945, established by the same President Roosevelt who at the outset of World War II had written to all combatants asking them not to bomb cities. American and British bombers had leveled much of urban Germany and Japan well before 1945. Hiroshima was picked as a target for the atom bomb according to criteria laid down by James B. Conant, later Harvard's president: a factory complex full of workers, surrounded by closely packed workers' housing. Eighty thousand died. Upon Soviet request, the United States also carried out the most destructive raids of World War II, against Dresden, specifically to kill civilians who were fleeing the advancing Soviet armies. In a little over twenty four hours, 135,000 people perished.

Why did this happen? In general, the Roosevelt administration was overcome by hate, an irrational and unjust desire to punish rather than to win, by a millennialist streak, and by a demagogic desire to show the American people that the relatives of those killing their relatives were being killed. In the specific case of Dresden, Roosevelt simply killed at Stalin's request. This, along with Roosevelt's delivery to Stalin—and certain death—of millions of prisoners of war and displaced persons, was a peace offering to Stalin intended to reassure him of America's commitment to friendship in the postwar era. U.S. officials called this "Operation Keelhaul." There is no clearer example in history of two sets of murders—Dresden and Operation Keelhaul—executed to achieve the same end. One was undertaken to cement an alliance in war, and the other as a peace offering. But murder delegitimizes peace just as much as it delegitimizes war.

The essential expression of both the practical and the ethical problem of warfare is "Whom shall we kill and why?" As the American nuclear targeters who tried to make concrete Robert McNamara's plan for killing 25 percent of the Soviet population discovered, random killing of an enemy population stands little more chance of winning a war than a monkey at a typewriter has of tapping out a novel. The craft of the military leader is to cause death and destruction in the manner most likely to prevent the enemy from effectively continuing the fight. Even shooting as many simple soldiers as possible all along the line—imposing attrition—is such an inefficient, uncertain, and slow means of winning a war as to be immoral. Certainly the specialized weapons, strategy, and training developed in the history of war have been designed expressly to concentrate the killing at key points. Killing those whose death is most likely to stop the killing is not only more ethically defensible but also more effective militarily.

Taking this point to its logical conclusion, it is clear that the higher the rank of the persons killed, the more likely they are to be carriers of the purpose that is the legitimate target of hostilities. Hence, the most discriminate, economical, effective, and moral act in World War II surely would have been the killing of Adolf Hitler. The conclusion that follows runs counter to the conventional wisdom that has grown up recently about war, namely that among its worst features is the assassination of individuals. But what could be more just *and* economical than that those who are most actively engaged in promoting a particular end should be the targets of those who oppose that end? What could be more unjust than going out of one's way to spare the leaders while targeting the poor draftee—or, worse, his hungry family at home? No doubt leaders, or those who fancy themselves as such, have a stake in defining war as a kind of chess game in which the opposing kings (and their staffs) are never taken, while they coolly maneuver their bloody pawns. But the common sense of mankind and the Western tradition of just war reject this.

The high tide of this foolish reasoning may have come during the Vietnam War. The CIA ran a project, code-named Phoenix, to identify secretly and to kill clandestinely the leaders of the Vietcong infrastructure in South Vietnam. The numbers killed under this program ran into the hundreds. When the program was disclosed, editorials in the leading liberal dailies of the Western world denounced it as the epitome of immorality. The chief complaint was that the people killed were identified as enemies without the benefit of trial. In other words, the killings were insufficiently discriminate. So far the critique, though excessive, is soundly based. No doubt, without attorneys and impartial juries (or for that matter, with them) it is possible to mistake someone's involvement in an enterprise. Personal vengeance, mistaken identity, and misleading circumstances skew judgment. Assignment of individual responsibility is always imperfect. But the critique misses the point. Surely the people killed under Project Phoenix were far more carefully chosen than the rank-and-file Vietcong who fell by the tens of thousands on the battlefield. Did the moralists who attacked Project Phoenix mean to assert that the rank-and-file Vietcong, many of whom were draftees, should have been killed while their leaders were spared? They certainly did not say this. The moralists were not advancing a particular view of justice; they were blaming the U.S. government for being on the side they opposed. The U.S. government, for its part, did not force a serious debate by asking the moralists, "Whom do you suggest that we kill in order to end this war?"

If there had been a debate rather than a shouting match, the moralists' answer would have boiled down to: We oppose this killing precisely because it begins to strike at the heart of the anti-U.S. forces in Vietnam—forces we want to see succeed. Of course, the critics of Project Phoenix were not eager to talk about who they wanted to see win the Vietnam War, so they used expressions of moral outrage to batter the United States while partially hiding their anti-U.S. partisanship.

To expose and counter this, the U.S. government's position would have had to boil down to: We want to kill these people because killing them is the quickest, most effective way to win the war. But if Presidents Johnson or Nixon had argued this, one might well have asked them, "If you are really interested in winning this war quickly, at the lowest cost in lives, while killing only those who most fully embody the purpose you are trying to frustrate, why then don't you bomb or invade to destroy North Vietnam's politburo?" But the U.S. government was not interested in victory, and it did not want to explain why it was not. Thus, it was uncomfortable explaining why it was killing anyone at all. So both sides, each for their own reasons, avoided a debate that would have been enlightening.

For similar but somewhat reversed reasons the U.S. government and its critics in the mid-1980s avoided debating the morality of assisting the Afghan mujahedeen's efforts to assassinate Soviet officials in that country. The same moralists within the U.S. government who had opposed the Phoenix program were aghast that the Afghans were using U.S. weapons for assassinations, and argued internally that U.S. assistance to the Afghans violated an internal government prohibition against assassination. As in the Vietnam War, they were unwilling to suggest that it would be better to shoot enemy draftees while sparing communist officials. But this time they were also unwilling to oppose U.S. involvement in the war entirely. So they did not argue the matter in public. On the other hand, since the U.S. government was again unwilling to consider the topic of victory, it once again welcomed the chance not to debate the matter.

The U.S. government did not have such an easy time in 1986 avoiding the question of whether it was (or should have been) trying to kill Libya's dictator, Muammar Qaddafi. In 1981–82 official Washington accepted intelligence reports to the effect that Qaddafi had dispatched "hit teams" to kill the U.S. president. During the following years, the United States gathered incontrovertible evidence that Qaddafi had ordered or sponsored a series of murderous acts against U.S. and European citizens culminating in the bombing of a Berlin discotheque frequented by Americans. The United States launched a strike by a squadron of FB-111 bombers against Qaddafi's headquarters. Qaddafi was not killed, but about one hundred of his men were. A baby girl described as his daughter was also reported killed. The president and the secretary of state categorically denied any intention of killing Qaddafi or of overthrowing his government. What, then, one may ask, was the point of bombing his headquarters? Did the United States intend to kill the one hundred Libyan soldiers and the baby girl? If so, why? And if not, then who had the U.S. government intended to kill and to what end? The U.S. government's official explanation that it had struck at the "infrastructure" of Libyan terrorism did not dispel doubts about the government's moral sense or about its competence.

The proposition that leaders should be spared the consequences of war, then, is a product less of moral and practical reasoning than of the contemporary lack of willingness (or perhaps capacity) to think through difficult questions.

Further evidence of this came between 1991 and 2006 as the U.S. government struggled with Iraq's Saddam Hussein, the Palestinian movement's Yasir Arafat, and Osama bin Laden. During the Gulf War of 1991 the official U.S. view was that the Iraqi regime and its head, Saddam

Hussein, were not the problem that had brought a half million U.S. troops to the Persian Gulf, and hence ought not to be their target. Rather, the problem to be solved was Iraq's invasion of Kuwait. In subsequent years, the consensus changed. Many problems in the Gulf would continue as long as Saddam stayed; so he had to go, alive or dead. Hence he became a political as well as a military target. Notably, during the same period the U.S. government came to the first half of the same conclusion about Arafat. Whereas he had once been seen as the key to peace he was now seen as the obstacle. But the United States not only did not make him a target. It prevented Israel from targeting him. About bin Laden, there was never a doubt. He had to be killed.

Leave aside the matter of culpability for killing Americans. All three had done it. Ask, rather, what good it would have done to kill any of them. The answer is that, just as it makes no sense, in terms of justice and effectiveness, to exclude killing top leaders, neither does it make sense simply to kill just them. That is because rarely is any single individual responsible for what his country is at any given time. Effective leaders lead regimes. Regimes make countries what they are. Regimes are the problem, and hence the just targets. But killing regimes takes a lot more than killing the top man—indispensable though that may be. In sum, killing anyone is justified only as part of a reasonable plan to reap the fruits that make the war worthwhile.

The most shocking case of lack of discrimination in warfare is terrorism. Indeed, it is precisely the willingness to target noncombatants, rather than enemy officials, that qualifies one for the label of "terrorist." The terrorist may argue that his ends are very worthy, that given his relative weakness he cannot afford to fight with the enemy's armed forces, and that hence he is compelled to kill those who cannot defend themselves. By detonating bombs in marketplaces or machine-gunning airports, bus stops, and schools, he may argue, he can force the enemy either to give in to his demands or take self-destructive measures in an effort to establish security. But the terrorist is wrong. He does not *have to* fight. Indeed, if the only means at his disposal are the intentional harming of innocents, the Western tradition says that he must not fight. Nothing in Western tradition sanctions the intentional as opposed to the collateral (unintentional) harming of innocents. Of course, most terrorists come from outside the western tradition and openly intend to tear it down. This does not change the character of their acts. Much less does it warrant the judgment that there is no moral difference between striking innocents and sparing them or that innocence is a matter of opinion.

By far the largest acts of nondiscrimination in modern history have been committed by governments. During World War I, the German government enslaved—there is no better word for it—four hundred thousand civilians in occupied Belgium and France and deported them to Germany to work. Conditions were so harsh that one in ten died. By World War II, the practice of enslaving occupied populations had become almost normal and had acquired a deadly twist: the slaves were literally used up and their remains recycled. By deriving maximum work for minimum food and shelter until the slaves died, the enslaving power both increased war production and freed itself of potential trouble in the future. In World War II, Germany, the Soviet Union, and Japan together may have enslaved thirty million human beings, perhaps two-thirds of whom had their lives sucked out of them. Needless to say, the Western tradition judges that if this is what it takes to win a war, then winning is absolutely not worth it.

Mercy

Mercy is a duty not only toward noncombatants but to enemy combatants as well. No one can set out precisely beforehand how much violence, how much killing, will be required to cause an enemy to stop resisting, and how much restraint it will be possible to exercise. But the rule of the West has been that one should not to go beyond what the battle against combatants requires and that as soon as resistance stops one should show mercy.

The issue of mercy chiefly concerns prisoners of war. The traditional Western teaching is that as soon as an enemy is wounded, lays down his weapons, or otherwise ceases to pursue the purpose of the war, he ceases to be an enemy to be killed and becomes someone to be treated in a brotherly fashion. This is more easily taught than done. An enemy may have just finished killing a soldier's friends. Because of him the soldier will have suffered fear, privation, exposure, fatigue, and pain. Hatred and the desire to kill the enemy have helped sustain the soldier in battle. What should compel him to reverse his violent feelings just because the enemy is wounded or has surrendered, just when the occasion is at hand to satisfy them all? Only the Western tradition of the just war, inspired by Christianity.

In the West, the incidence of this difficult, demanding mercy has been remarkable. In the best of times regarding these matters—the wars between King Louis XIV of France and Queen Anne of England—prisoners of war were often released to return home on "parole," that is, in return for the promise that they would not fight again in that war. But alas, in their fight against American rebels, the British mistreated their prisoners unto death. As late as World War I, the German army picked up French Capt. Charles de Gaulle, severely wounded on the battlefield, and provided him with conditions under which he not only recovered but wrote a book while giving a course on military history to his fellow prisoners. Even under Nazi influence, the German army of World War II lapsed only occasionally from its proper treatment of *Western* prisoners of war.[2] American troops, for their part, might well win the prize as the group by which one would most enjoy being captured. Any number of German (not to mention Italian) POWs shipped to the United States during World War II fell in love with the country. Lt. Hans Sennholtz of the Luftwaffe, for example, became an honorary citizen of the town in New Mexico where his prison camp was located. Upon repatriation he applied for U.S. citizenship, returned to the United States, and taught economics. He was one of about 5,000 (out of 375,000) Germans held in the United States who overcame legal hurdles to immigrate to the land of their captivity.[3]

But the lot of most prisoners in most wars is one of cruel abuse and death. It is noteworthy that the great abuses have not resulted from overflowing passions on the battlefield, but rather from policy and culture on the homefront. The greatest act of cruelty in Thucydides' Peloponnesian War was the imprisonment of the entire Athenian expeditionary force in the Syracusan quarries. There, without even the capacity to dispose of their comrades' corpses, much less their own excrement, the Athenians suffered all the worst things that can possibly befall men.

The crusaders and the combatants in the religious wars of the sixteenth and seventeenth centuries did not believe that the rules of war applied to infidels or that they had any obligation to keep their promises to infidels. Under this misunderstanding, tens of thousands of prisoners were put to the sword. Another common error was committed by General Santa Ana at the Alamo. In order to encourage surrender, he set a deadline after which surrender would no longer be accepted. Then he sounded the *deguelo*, the order to slit the throats of all who were wounded or captured. Perhaps just as famous is Shakespeare's rendition of Henry V's warning to the people of Harfleur:

> The gates of mercy shall be all shut up,
> And the flesh'd soldier, rough and hard of heart,
> In liberty of bloody hand shall range
> . . . mowing like grass
> Your fresh-fair virgins and your flow'ring infants.
> If not, why, in a moment look to see
> The blind and bloody soldier with foul hand
> Defile the locks of your shrill-shrieking daughters;
> Your fathers taken by the silver beards,
> And their most reverend heads dash'd to the walls, . . .
> (*King Henry V* 3.3.10–37)

But encouraging surrender is no excuse for killing harmless human beings. The point of war is supposed to be the peace of the living, not of the dead.

Totalitarians, however, do not understand this. If they have any concept of peace at all, it is indeed the peace of the dead. Because they fight wars to extinguish enemy classes or races or religions, they embody the opposite of mercy. While German generals treated prisoners on the western front well, they boasted that they had reduced their Russian prisoners of war to "eating each other." The survivors had the life sucked out of them through slave labor.[4] Of course, those who survived this ordeal were handed over to Stalin at the end of the war; he then had them killed because they had committed the crime of surrendering in the first place! The Soviets, for their part, also efficiently "used up" their millions of German POWs. The most typical, though far from the biggest, act of deliberate totalitarian cruelty was the Soviet Union's murder of fifteen thousand Polish officer prisoners in the Katyn Forest (and in two camps) in order to deprive Polish society of its leadership. Even if the totalitarians' ends had been noble, such means would have wholly discredited them.

The behavior of Japanese troops in World War II toward all their captives demonstrates another sad fact. Some people simply get satisfaction by making others suffer. The Japanese were not out to exterminate any class or race. They simply went out of their way to kill, rape, maim, starve, and humiliate. Southeast Asia will remember them for a thousand years. When this Asian style of warfare blends with the totalitarian style, there occurs the treatment that American POWs received in Korea and Vietnam. Now, the Western tradition, codified in the Geneva Convention, states clearly that not only are prisoners to be left unharmed, but they also may not be compelled to act against their country or to be used as hostages in any way. Yet these two Asian communist regimes literally "used up" a significant proportion of its American POWs by torturing them into making statements injurious to their country's war effort and turning them into pitiable objects that should be ransomed in a hurry. In the end, North Korea and North Vietnam let out of captivity only those they had not crippled or disfigured. The others may be dead. Or they may be held as amusements to confirm their captors' peculiar kind of self-esteem.

In our time, Islamic terrorists have kidnapped innocents precisely to perform "demonstration killings" upon them. By beheading them and then broadcasting the videotapes thereof, the terrorists show the helplessness of their enemies to save the victims, exhibit their own confidence in their cause, and make a powerful argument that no one is safe from such a fate unless their ambitious demands are met. This of course is the polar opposite of civilized warfare—and is done not by savages, but by persons who know better.

How do civilized warriors deal with the merciless? Gen. Douglas MacArthur's court-martial condemnation of Japanese general Yamashita to the gallows provides an example. Yamashita had not actually ordered Japanese troops to inflict deadly brutalities on American prisoners in what became known as the Bataan Death March of 1942. But as commanding general of those troops, Yamashita had had it in his power to instill civilized habits on them. He failed in his duty to the civilized profession of arms and justly swung at the end of a rope.

Proportionality and Punishment

As if jus ad bellum and jus in bello were not concepts difficult enough in themselves, the Western tradition also holds that for a war to be deemed just, there must be a reasonable proportion between the ends sought and the means used, even when these means are just and necessary in themselves. Clearly, there can be no strictly defined rules. Rather, the rule is that one must constantly ask: Is this worth it? Would any reasonable man unaffected by the passions of the moment think it worthwhile to go through all of *this* for *that?*

Who is to judge? In practice, the victors often punish the vanquished. But all men can exercise their judgment at all times. The just war tradition aims less at prescribing the punishment imposed by winners than it does to forming the consciences of the combatants. The attempts to enforce the laws of war after World War II show why.

The trials of the German leaders at Nuremberg were problematic above all because the Soviets were among the judges. The Soviets' only claim to judgeship was that they were winners. If nothing else discredited the Nuremberg trials it was Molotov helping to hang Ribbentrop for the offense of having joined him in signing the Molotov-Ribbentrop Pact that started World War II. Moreover, the Allies had weakened their moral basis for judgment because they intentionally bombed civilians. If Germany and Japan had won, they would have had a good case for hanging Generals "Hap" Arnold and Ira Eaker of the U.S. Army Air Corps, as well as Roosevelt, for breaches of jus in bello. Of course, Ribbentrop would have hanged Molotov for breaches of jus ad bellum. But that would have been no more ludicrous than what actually happened. In sum, the flawed attempt to apply ethical guidelines as if they were criminal laws brought undeserved discredit upon those guidelines.

Justice and War in the Nuclear Age

How can there be proportion between ends and means if the means of war happen to be inherently disproportionate wreckers of the planet? The question carries its own answer. But the premise of the question is wrong. For better or for worse, nuclear weapons are not necessarily disproportionate tools any more than are fire and sword. With nuclear weapons, as with all others, the primordial question remains, whom should we kill and why?

As we have seen in chapter 7, there is no basis for the speculation that the widespread use of nuclear weapons would alter the world's climate or significantly poison the environment beyond the areas where they were employed for more than a few weeks. Nuclear weapons certainly do inflict collateral damage. But the effects of nuclear weapons, both direct and collateral, are finite and calculable. Moreover, these effects vary widely according to the design of the weapons and how they are used. Thus, to speak about the ethics of using nuclear weapons as if there were no difference between a one-kiloton enhanced radiation weapon delivered precisely on tanks attacking a town and a one-megaton weapon delivered on a square mile of high-rise apartments makes no sense. Nor will it avail to overlook such distinctions by declaring that any use of nuclear weapons by anyone will lead all parties to disgorge their stocks of them onto residential areas while neglecting rational military uses. Clearly, it is no more likely—and it may be less likely—that people will jeopardize their own interests when nuclear weapons are used than when other kinds are involved. The destructiveness, the justice or injustice, the relative mercilessness of any war never depended on the weapons available to the warriors. Rather, it depended on what was on the warriors' minds. The issue, then, is which uses of nuclear weapons, or any other weapons that self-interest may inspire, are more just and which uses are less just.

This question, like all the others regarding *jus in bello,* is logically dependent on the reasons why the combatants may be fighting, which falls into the domain of *jus ad bellum.* It so happens that nuclear weapons became prominent during a time when the "issue" dividing the great powers of the day was as important as any that ever set nations against one another. The Marxist-Leninist objective of the Soviet Union, emblazoned on buildings in every city and taught in every school, was the destruction of every noncommunist regime on earth. The official position of the Soviet Union was that it would have been desirable for other "ruling classes" to give way to the new order peacefully, but that this could not be expected. The shadow of the Soviet Union's military power was the only hope for peace and the only assurance of victory. This victory would have involved physically eliminating the people who had helped mold the former society, and then doing away with religion, emplacing a new history on the lips of adults and in the minds of schoolchildren, and instituting compulsory public obedience to Marxism-Leninism—regardless of the leadership's private unbelief. The declared objective of the U.S. government, and of the North Atlantic Alliance, and of all noncommunist governments, was that none of this would come to pass. And it didn't. Nuclear weapons had much to do with the struggle.

From the point of view of the Soviet Union, the question of justice with regard to nuclear war was framed in Lenin's words, "Justice? For what class?" In other words, with or without nuclear weapons, the most just course of action was the one that best advanced the interests of the vanguard of the world's proletariat, the Communist Party of the Soviet Union. The end justified the means by definition. But nuclear weapons never were efficient, discriminatory tools for physically eliminating the class enemy. That would have been the job of commissars.

How did the Western tradition confront this? Though it recognized that frustrating the Soviet objective was worth killing and dying for, it also rejected the notion that ends justify means. So the ethical question for the West with regard to nuclear weapons depended in large part on whether one could devise ways of using nuclear weapons that would bring about victory while causing no more harm than was proportionate to the good achieved and the evil avoided.

The great problem in the West, however, was that utopian hopes and fears regarding nuclear weapons obscured the moral dimensions of practical choices with regard to nuclear weapons. Recall: with nuclear weapons, as with others, the question is, whom do we shoot and why? Few realized that the question whether to nuke Moscow was meaningless in practice. Where in the modern Moscow area's fifty miles by fifty miles (twenty-five hundred square miles), would one have put our four- to ten-square-mile circles of destruction? Were we after the population? If so, which sector? Industrial plants? Which ones? The military? But the Moscow area had perhaps three hundred distinct military targets. The moral significance of such questions was no smaller than their military significance. Surely, the fact that a person happens to live in a place that is both heavily populated and unprotected does not make him a carrier of the evil purpose, the negation of which is the legitimate purpose of war. So, simply killing those who can easily be killed is doubly unjust. It is terrorism of the stupid kind.

As soon as one begins to ask which sectors of the population—other than simply the ones who are most accessible—ought to be the targets for one's nuclear weapons, the focus of the discussion turns squarely to the central question of jus in bello with regard to any and all weapons, that is, how to achieve victory while causing, and allowing, the least possible harm.

In practice, nuclear weapons, just like other kinds of weapons, always cause collateral damage. How much they cause depends, and will always depend, on how they are targeted. Certainly the collateral damage in a nuclear attack on a missile field in Siberia would have been much below the civilian devastation that resulted from the U.S.-British iron-bomb raids on the ball-bearing plant in Schweinfurt during World War II. Of course, the ideal means of completely disarming an opponent of his nuclear arsenal without collateral damage is to intercept that arsenal in flight. Thus antiaircraft and antimissile systems are the most discriminating, most effective, and least harmful means of combat in the nuclear age.

After the Soviet empire's demise, India, Pakistan, and North Korea acquired nuclear weapons, Iraq almost did, and Iran is on the brink of doing so at this writing. Since none of these countries or any of the others that might join the nuclear club in the twenty-first century seems the least bit interested in using these weapons other than as tools of mass destruction, any discussion of justice in their use of them is meaningless. Whether brandished by states or used in indirect warfare by ostensibly private terrorist organizations, nuclear weapons would be tools of terror. The threat of massive retaliation is even less appropriate for dealing with nuclear terror than it was in dealing with the Soviet Union's military nuclear threat. In war, it is essential to begin by identifying the enemy: Who or what do I have to kill or destroy to get rid of my problem? Surely nuking millions of innocent Muslims will not end the possibility of nuclear terrorism among us. Nor can nuking a prospective nuclear power's nuclear program necessarily stop it. Where there is a will, a plenitude of available technology will find a way. No, in the twenty-first century as in the previous ones, neither peoples at large, nor weapons themselves are the authors of evil. Regimes are. The problem of just war in the nuclear age is the same as it has been in every other age: a problem of regimes.

PART III

How Wars End

12

MAKING PEACE

Both parties deprecated war; but one of them would *make* war rather than let the nation survive; and the other would *accept* war rather than let it perish. And the war came. . . .

. . . [W]ith malice toward none; with charity for all; with firmness in the right, as God gives us to see the right, let us strive on to finish the work we are in; to bind up the nation's wounds; to care for him who shall have borne the battle, and for his widow, and his orphan—to do all which may achieve and cherish a just, and a lasting peace, among ourselves and with all nations.

—ABRAHAM LINCOLN

PEACE IS THE PRODUCT of war. It comes when at least one of the parties to the war changes its commitment to the kind of peace for which it was fighting, enough so that *it appears* that mutual satisfaction can occur without further violence. The loser asks for the armistice in the hope of cutting his losses. He hopes that success will not embolden the winner to demand even more, and to do even more damage. At the very least he gives up his quest and claims. Perhaps he pays a ransom. Often, he gives up his means of self-defense as well. The winner, for his part, rather than paying the price to force every last man on the losing side to fight to the death, accepts just the essence of what he was after. In exchange for the surrender he gives certain assurances.

Contrary to the belief of many, finishing off a war is even more painful and problematic than starting one. That is because the cessation of hostilities is fraught with the possibility—even the likelihood—of betrayal. The winner fears that the loser may just be gaining a respite to prepare for more war, while the loser fears that as soon as he lays down his arms the winner will fall on him and destroy him all the more easily. Either or both fears may be well grounded. In peacemaking, precisely as in warmaking, everything depends on intentions, capacity, skill, and luck.

Regardless of the outcome, ending a war involves some kind of agreement between the winner and loser. The immediate consequences of the capitulation depend on how the agreement is carried out, which in turn shapes the kind of peace that follows. Let us look in turn at negotiations, at the various consequences of capitulation, and at several kinds of peace.

Negotiations

Since surrendering an army, a cause, or a nation is a complex matter, negotiations are almost always necessary. Yet thinking of negotiations as the harbinger of peace is at least premature and often mistaken. When two sides meet to negotiate an armistice, each side's intentions are still not obvious, even in the clearest of circumstances. Gibbon, for example, tells of the meeting in 410 CE between Alaric, king of the Goths, and the ambassadors of a Rome whose armies had ceased to exist. The Romans demanded a fair and honorable surrender. If Alaric refused this, they said, he would have to confront a warlike people who would sell their lives dearly. Alaric knew that the Romans were blowing smoke, and he quickly blew it away. He laughed, expressing "his contempt for the menaces of an unwarlike populace, enervated by luxury before they were emaciated by famine." He made it clear that he wanted to sack Rome. "The ministers of the Senate," says Gibbon, then "presumed to ask in a modest and suppliant tone, 'If such, O King, are your demands, what do you intend to leave us?' 'Your lives,' replied the haughty conqueror."[1] The Romans knew perfectly well that once they opened the city gates, the Goths would be able to take their lives as well, and even more easily. But they correctly decided that under the circumstances the best chance of saving their lives lay in appeasing Alaric.

Sometimes there is even less to negotiations than that. In 1945, especially after Hitler's death on 30 April, the German high command was frantic to surrender to the Western Allies. Any man who surrendered to them, they reasoned, was a life saved. By contrast, any man who surrendered to the Soviets was a life likely to be lost in captivity far more painfully than in battle. However, the policy of the United States, enforced on Britain and France, was that only "simultaneous and unconditional" surrender of German forces on all fronts would be accepted. Nevertheless, in the final weeks U.S. commanders from sergeants to generals were not about to waste the lives of their men killing Germans who wanted to lay down their arms. Thus, Allied forces were accepting the surrender of countless individual German military units, "capturing" millions of willing prisoners, and moving into Germany virtually without opposition. Meanwhile in the east, Germans resisted Soviet forces as best they could or moved westward to surrender to the Americans. Grand Admiral Doenitz, on whom authority had fallen after Hitler's suicide, and the German military representatives at General Eisenhower's headquarters in Reims, France, tried to prolong talks to allow this process to continue. Finally, threatened with the prospect that the West would stop accepting military surrenders, the Germans signed a general cease-fire that included an order for all German troops, including ones facing the Soviets, to stay where they were. The Germans had gotten the most they could from the negotiations under the circumstances.[2]

The most common fear among those who are about to lay down their arms is: Will the winner now slaughter us? As we have mentioned, this sort of thing is all too common, even when the winning commanders try to prevent it. For example, on the evening of the Battle of Waterloo some Prussian troops bayoneted disarmed French soldiers. Negotiations, however, can do little to ease this fear or to prevent slaughter. At most they can serve to provide a clearer picture of the winner's intentions. But there is no insurance. In the end, armistices are acts of faith, good or bad.

Often, however, there is much more to negotiations than protecting lives and easing the transition to peace. That is because the disparity of power is seldom so great as to really convince the loser that he has lost, or the winner that he has won. Often, the very process of negotiation is part of political warfare, a direct attack on the enemy's nerve center that does not so much ratify the verdict of arms as contribute to it—or even substitute for it. The outstanding examples are the protracted "peace" negotiations between the United States and various communist powers and the late-twentieth-century phenomenon known as "peace processes."

By 1951 the military situation on the Korean peninsula was clear. The United States had so much firepower that any Chinese offensive across the front on the 38th parallel could only result in mass slaughter of Chinese troops. But the political situation in the United States was not so clear. Because of conflicts between those Americans who wanted to eliminate communism and were willing to widen the war and those who wanted to get along with it and were yearning for peace, the United States had decided that it did not want to advance beyond the 38th parallel. This is why the Chinese negotiators used the negotiations to reinforce American reluctance to wage a decisive war. They continued to fight in a way that could not be militarily decisive but that would pile up casualties the Americans could only regard as meaningless. They did not attempt a breakthrough. This, in addition to exposing their troops to slaughter, might have forced the United States to reassess its policy of not conquering North Korea and not supporting a challenge to the newly established communist regime in Peking. Instead, the Chinese launched local attacks to cause American casualties. In fact, about as many Americans died in Korea during the negotiations as before the start of negotiations.[3] The longer this process continued, reasoned the Chinese, the likelier it was that the Americans would give them "peace" terms under which they could eventually win the war. Thus, the Chinese negotiators harshly raised points of protocol, charged the Americans with every imaginable wrongdoing, used the suffering of American prisoners of war as a lever, and demanded everything from territorial concessions to a say in the future of South Korea.

However, in 1953, after the Eisenhower administration took office on a platform of "rolling back" communist influence worldwide, after Stalin's death put Soviet support in doubt, and after the Chinese government was informed that B-29 bombers armed with atom bombs were warming up in Japan, the Chinese quickly agreed to formalize the status that had existed since 1951.

During 1965–73 the government of North Vietnam wholly learned the lessons of Korea, while the U.S. government mostly forgot them. The United States fought the Vietnam War for two objectives: to achieve a negotiated settlement with North Vietnam and to "let South Vietnam choose its own form of government." These objectives were mutually contradictory for the most part and not obviously related to the U.S. national interest, because each sprang from competing attitudes about communism among Americans. Since North Vietnam's sole objective (other than the survival of its regime) was to take over the South, the U.S. government could achieve both of its objectives only by defeating North Vietnam and threatening the communist regime there. But the U.S. government's internal divisions made it difficult to contemplate this. Thus, the U.S. government's eagerness for negotiations amounted to an incipient preference for agreement with North Vietnam over the independence of South Vietnam. This had been clear since 1968, when the United States first stopped its already very limited bombing of targets in North Vietnam in order to "signal" its good faith and to entice North Vietnam to the negotiating table.

Because North Vietnam knew that the U.S. government valued negotiations not so much for what they could bring about in Southeast Asia as for the sake of reducing its own internal tensions, it came to the table with the intention of turning the U.S. government's preference for an agreement into an active abandonment of South Vietnam. Thus, because the United States would be reluctant to carry out any military act that might break them off, the negotiations assured North Vietnam that the war would drag on indecisively. North Vietnam was quite content with that, precisely because the United States could not be. Thus, between 1968 and 1972, the Vietnam negotiations followed the Korean pattern.

In December 1972 the newly reelected Nixon administration brought the negotiations to a climax by seemingly retracing the steps the United

States had taken twenty years earlier in Korea. It resumed and drastically changed the pattern of bombing in North Vietnam in a way that augured the collapse of the regime. Instantly, as in Korea, the complexity that had bedeviled the negotiations vanished, and North Vietnam agreed to all American demands. But there was a vital difference between the Vietnam and Korea negotiations: the nature of the American demands. In Korea, the United States had held off the Damocles' sword in exchange for the enemy effectively giving up the fight. The U.S. Eighth Army has remained in Korea to guarantee that result by threatening war against the North Korean regime if it should renege. But in Vietnam the price for withholding doom was simply to allow the United States to withdraw from the entire area with a semblance of honor—that is, the return of some, if not all, U.S. prisoners plus a "decent interval" between America's withdrawal and North Vietnam's final, victorious offensive.

It is impossible to know in retrospect how North Vietnam would have reacted to the Americans' final act of pressure in the negotiations had the United States meant to enforce the terms of the agreement, forcing North Vietnam to give up the objectives for which it had fought the war. At the time of the Nixon bombing campaign of December 1972, North Vietnam *could not have been entirely certain* that the United States had abandoned its commitment to South Vietnam. *Conceivably* the United States might have insisted, as it did after signing the Korean armistice, that its adversary abide scrupulously by the agreement. But the balance of political forces *within* the United States in 1973 was very different from what it had been in 1953. Whereas the United States had left the Eighth Army in Korea as a living pledge, in 1972–73 the U.S. government advertised that American combat troops would not return to Vietnam no matter what happened. So why would North Vietnam not have been in a hurry to sign a piece of paper that relieved it of an immediate threat, made it much less likely that the threat would ever return, and portended the achievement of all its war aims? Hence, through negotiations, the winner surrendered to the loser. This was one of the rare instances in which what happened at the negotiating table was out of proportion with what was happening on the battlefield. However, the outcome reflected very accurately the results of a decade of political struggle among Americans.

The experiences of Korea and Vietnam show unmistakably how silly it is to regard negotiations as anything but part and parcel of the war effort. The American leaders' blind faith in compromise and their unwillingness to realize that any agreement with an enemy is meaningful only insofar as it is based on both a willingness and an ability to continue fighting (recall Lincoln's words, "to finish the work we are in") can only be characterized as fundamental ignorance about the fundamentals.

The whole point of negotiations at the end of a war, just like negotiations prior to or during a war, is for each side to determine what the other side is and is not willing to kill and die for, to relate that to what one's own side is willing to kill and die for, and then to make a deal with the other side to advance one's own interests as best one can. In fact, at the outset of negotiations one does not know whether the end of the war is at hand because one does not know the other side's intentions. As the examples of Korea and Vietnam show, it is possible to influence an opponent's intentions by and during negotiations. But the chief means of doing this is to somehow drive for victory. Absent this, one is really negotiating one's own defeat.

The clearest example of this is the negotiations held in 1988 between the United States and the Soviet Union over the future of Afghanistan. Immediately after the Soviet Union invaded Afghanistan in 1979, the United States began to supply arms to the many Afghan resistance groups that sprang up. Until 1986, when the United States began to supply serious antiaircraft missiles to the Afghans, the Soviet Union regarded the U.S. effort as the mere irritant it was. But in 1987, faced with a reasonably well-supplied resistance, the Soviet Union began a diplomatic effort to end U.S. supplies to the Afghans. The Soviets proposed to withdraw their troops in exchange for the cessation of aid to the Afghans. Did the Soviets intend to stand by and watch the destruction of the Afghan government they had created? The principal American negotiators did not ask. They *assumed* that the Soviets had decided to give up their war goals. They *assumed* that the Soviet objective in the negotiations was merely to lessen the resistance's military pressure during their withdrawal so that the Afghan mujahideen would not chase Soviet troops back to the Soviet border.

Instead, the Soviets insisted on a commitment that the United States cut off aid to the mujahideen. Everything else in the negotiations was nebulous except that. The American negotiators hardly noticed that the Soviets were making no commitments to stop helping their Afghan puppets. The Soviets made sure that the relationship with their Afghan clients would continue, while the relationship between the Americans and *their* Afghan clients would be broken. The U.S. negotiators eagerly accepted these terms. Because the U.S. Congress objected to cutting off the Afghans while the Soviets maintained their commitment, the U.S. negotiators reluctantly made a unilateral statement that the United States would maintain "positive symmetry" in the aid going to both sides in Afghanistan. Nevertheless, the flow of antiaircraft missiles to the resistance stopped immediately. In sum, the Pakistanis and the United States gave up much of what had pressured the Soviets into negotiations. If the Soviets had ever been tempted to give up control of Afghanistan, the negotiations must have persuaded them otherwise. At any rate, Afghanistan's Soviet proxy regime survived the fall of the Soviet Union itself by a year. In sum, the Afghan negotiations were not the end of the war, but a very effective operation of the war.

Negotiations also offer tempting opportunities to winners. In the Peloponnesian War, for example, the Athenian navy cut off a substantial Spartan army on the island of Sphacteria. Both sides agreed to a truce for peace negotiations, during which time the Athenians would allow food to reach the trapped Spartan forces. The Spartans gave up some ships as collateral on condition that they would be returned at the end of the negotiations. But the Athenian assembly voted against the peace proposal, in part because now that the ships were in their hands they could safely break the truce deal and thus deprive the Spartans on the island of any hope of escaping captivity or death. The Athenians figured correctly that once the Spartans on the island had surrendered, Athens would be in an even better bargaining position.

Indeed, it seems that "peace" negotiations, one of the parties to which is not being slaughtered or starved, or is not about to be, tend to be themselves acts of war aimed at changing the balance of power.

Nowhere is the importance of intention clearer than in what have come to be known as "peace processes"—protracted negotiations between undefeated antagonists. Peace processes exist where there is war rather than peace, and where it is by no means clear whether any of the parties prefers peace to war, or what, if anything, it may be willing to give up in exchange for what. The point of these affairs has been hopes on each side that the process might change the political balance of power within the other side. Meanwhile, the more competent side has sought to trade its *promises* of concessions—things inherently insubstantial—for the other side's concession of actual things that, once given, cannot be taken back easily. The prime example has been the peace process between the Arab states and their Palestinian proxies on one side and Israel on the other since 1967. Other prominent processes have involved the Protestant and Catholic factions in Northern Ireland, as well as the government of Colombia and the Marxist, cocaine-purveying Revolutionary Armed Forces of Colombia (FARC). U.S. diplomats invented peace processes and have sponsored them unceasingly, without ever attempting to ensure that any resulting agreements will be adhered to.

The essence of the Arab-Israeli peace process has been the proposition that Israel might cede some or all the land it captured in the 1967 Six Days' War to "the Palestinians" (which ones is not clear) and to Syria in exchange for the Arab states' cessation of terrorist war. This process has involved two generations of American and Israeli diplomats, and has con-

sisted of countless "plans" and "road maps" for a "solution." The culmina-
tion of the process began in 1993 when Israel agreed to establish the PLO
as the semi-sovereign authority over most of the territories it had occupied
in 1967. It, the United States, and the European Union financed the Palestinian Authority and even armed its police. But the PLO never gave up its
claim to all of Israel (its maps and textbooks do not acknowledge Israel's
existence) or to the right of descendants of Palestinian refugees to claim
whatever parts of Israel they wish. In 2000, backed by Arab states, Palestinian organizations of all stripes used the land, money, and weapons
granted to them by Israel to launch an all out war against it. This seems to
have interrupted, not canceled, Israeli and American, not to mention European, enthusiasm for the peace process. Understandably, the various Arab
states and warlords are eager for further negotiations to produce even more
favorable conditions for the next step in their war.

Similarly, in Colombia the peace process led the government to grant
the FARC effective sovereignty over about one-fourth of the country in exchange for the promise of a better attitude in further peace negotiations.
The FARC used that grant of peace to make war more efficiently. In Northern Ireland, the British government's grant of government ministries to the
Irish Republican Army in exchange for its promise that it would disarm led
to the IRA's acceptance of the ministries and to the declaration that it had
put its weapons in safe places. Where these were was nobody's business.
The point is that peace processes grant opponents things that deprive them
of whatever incentive for peace they might have had. In international relations as in personal ones, it is always prudent to ask, "But will you love me
tomorrow?"

One of the most notable aspects of peace negotiations involving greater
and lesser powers is that the greater power may sacrifice the interests of
the lesser power. For example, using Spartan captives as a bargaining chip,
Athens induced Sparta to restore the Macedonian city of Amphipolis to
Athenian rule. Had Sparta not welched on the deal, the pro-Spartan party
in that city would have perished. Similarly, in 1938, when Stalin perceived
that Britain and France were going to sacrifice Czechoslovakia to Hitler, he
promptly ordered the end of Soviet involvement in Spain and ordered the
world's communists to sabotage the anti-Hitler side in the Spanish civil
war (and, incidentally, to blame the defeat on Trotskyite treachery). This
meant the death of thousands of Spanish leftists, but it enabled Stalin both
to husband his forces and to seek a rapprochement with Hitler. In the same
year, Britain and France doomed thousands of their Czech allies to death
when they negotiated peace with Hitler for their own interests at the price
of letting Hitler have his way with Czechoslovakia unopposed.

The Munich negotiations, at which Britain and France handed the

Sudeten region of Czechoslovakia to Hitler, are worth special notice because although the Munich betrayal on the surface seems to resemble Stalin's betrayal of the Spanish republic, in fact it was much less intelligent. Whereas Stalin's cruelty was meant to achieve a reasonable objective, Britain and France's cruelty was the result of mere incompetence and cowardice. The British and French asserted (and perhaps believed) that while they had led the Czechs to give up the security of their own fortresses, they had given the Czechs something even more solid: international guarantees of the little that remained. But what remained of Czechoslovakia after Munich was much harder to defend. When Hitler invaded in 1939, the Czechs found it impossible to defend themselves, and Britain and France found it impractical to help. George F. Kennan—then U.S. ambassador to Prague, reacted with an excess of equanimity and a dearth of common sense when a Czech Jew he had known sought refuge from the Nazis at the U.S. embassy and, finding none, went out, in Kennan's words, to "face the music" alone. This shows the foolishness of inducing an ally to give up military power in exchange for guarantees that the reduction of military power manifestly render less credible.

Any small power drawn into peace negotiations with a big-power sponsor is well advised to keep its hands firmly on its weapons. However small its armaments, they are nevertheless more real than any promise could ever be. In early 1988 the Nicaraguan *contras* forgot this. In their wholehearted attempt to win support from a divided U.S. body politic, they agreed to forgo U.S. weapons, to observe a cease-fire, and to respect an ambiguous understanding between the American and Nicaraguan governments. They thus ceased to be important in Nicaragua. Because they let American politicians off the hook, they ceased to be important in the United States as well. When in mid-1988 they turned to the White House to request arms once again, their request was not even forwarded to Congress. The fact that they won the elections of 1990 proved less important than the fact that the Sandinistas remained armed while they were not. They forgot the maxim that only he who has good arms is likely to have good friends.

Rarely do negotiations between two undefeated antagonists end rather than advance the struggle. Yet sometimes it happens. This was the case with the Peace of Ghent in 1814 which ended the war of 1812 between the United States and Great Britain. Great Britain thought it had ended the Napoleonic Wars at Waterloo, and did not want to pour greater effort into a sideshow war in North America. By 1814 Great Britain had long since given up the hope of reconquering its wayward American colonies. Since Britain's only transatlantic objective in the War of 1812 had been to safeguard Canada, why should it have fought on? Britain wanted to turn to peace in Europe and to empire in India. The United States was even more eager for peace. The war had not gone well for the United States. And now that Napoleon was cooped up on the island of Elba and Britain had nothing more to worry about in Europe, the war could only go worse. Canada had proved difficult to conquer. Why should America continue to go after frozen northern lands while superior western ones were there for the taking? The United States wanted to turn westward as much as Britain wanted to turn eastward. These peace negotiations succeeded because both sides recognized that they had better things to do than fight each other.

Nothing "greases" peace negotiations like the appearance of a greater enemy, or of larger fish to fry. In 1968, soon after the Soviet invasion of Czechoslovakia, and concurrent with the buildup of Soviet forces on the Chinese border to forty-five divisions, Mao Tse-tung decided to end all hostilities with the United States. When American officials met with Chinese leaders to arrange President Nixon's visit to China, they found warm welcomes, no complications, and reassurances that China was not interested in seeing the United States lose in Vietnam. There were forty-five reasons why China wanted to get close to the United States—each consisting of some ten thousand nuclear-armed Russians!

Most of the time, however, negotiations concern the mere modalities of capitulation. The conditions for stopping the fighting may be very different from the conditions of peace. That is not only because, as we have just pointed out, treachery almost always plays its part, but because the circumstances in which armistices are decided are too hurried, too beset by immediate problems, to grapple with the most important issues. Also, minds change as the capitulation itself changes the relative power of the belligerents.

Thus, in 1918 the German government surrendered while its armies were still on foreign soil and had not lost the power to resist because it believed that the Allies would be governed by President Wilson's Fourteen Points, the thrust of which was the promise of a nonvindictive peace. Yet at the Versailles Peace Conference the Germans were forced to sign full responsibility for the entire war and to agree to pay a "blank check" of reparations later set at an astronomical 132 billion gold marks—certainly a vindictive peace by the standards of the day! Treachery had not been intentional. President Wilson simply was not able to fully resist British and French public opinion that demanded harsher and harsher terms. By contrast, when Robert E. Lee handed his sword to Ulysses S. Grant at Appomattox Courthouse in 1865, ending the Civil War, Confederate officers were allowed to retain sidearms and horses and enlisted men their mules for plowing. No one would have expected from this courtly capitulation that the aftermath of that war would become harsh enough to pollute American life for a hundred years. But then no one could have foreseen the death of Abraham Lincoln and the rise of radical Republicans who "waved the bloody shirt."

Let us now turn to the subject of capitulation.

Capitulation

The immediate consequences of the cessation of hostilities range from the benign to the infernal. Let us descend the steps into the hell of defeat.

In the best of circumstances, the defeated nation is compelled to relinquish its objectives. When Lord Cornwallis surrendered to General Washington at Yorktown in 1781, the defeated armies marched out between files of American soldiers with full military honors as bands played sad tunes, as if to say, "Sorry, old boy." Most Americans loyal to Britain had long since gone to Canada, and calm came to both countries. King George III, ashamed of the defeat, briefly considered going back to Hanover, his German kingdom, but soon thought no more of it. Almost the same happened in 1982 when Britain fought Argentina for possession of the Falkland Islands. Argentina's troops on the islands surrendered and were promptly put on ships for home. The Argentines turned against the government that had led them into the war, blaming it more than they blamed Britain. The British had no hand in this at all. No Argentines were lynched in Britain, and the Argentine upper classes retained their Anglophile customs. There were no embargoes or blockades, and the Argentines' famous beefsteaks were as thick as ever.

Even merely abandoning political purpose, however, may bring great suffering to individuals. When France gave up its effort to hold on to Algeria (even though, by 1961, it had militarily defeated the Algerian rebels), it had to absorb, within a year, refugees from Algeria amounting to about 5 percent of the population of metropolitan France. The people of metropolitan France continued their march to prosperity as if nothing were happening. But the refugees had to start from scratch. These refugees were Algerians both of European stock, known as *pieds-noirs*, or of native stock, known as *Harkis*. All had to leave homes, farms, and businesses, lucky to escape with their lives and start life over with only the clothes on their backs. For about five years they caused political trouble in France, and even a quarter of a century later, though well integrated into French life, they remained an identifiable voting bloc.

In the second-best set of circumstances, the defeated state not only gives up its objectives but, as a condition of stopping the fighting, gives up its form of government as well. This was what happened to Germany after World War I. Germany was not occupied, except briefly for the Rhineland

and the Saar. But the Allies had made it clear that they were out to do away with the monarchy, which their propaganda depicted as responsible for the war. The German military reasonably thought that a civilian government could get a better deal under President Wilson's Fourteen Points. Not incidentally, General Ludendorff also wanted civilians, rather than military leaders, to take public responsibility for the humiliation that Germany was to suffer. The humiliation and the economic privations came, and so did the German public's loathing for those civilians whom it wrongly supposed had betrayed its country by capitulating.

Even though most of Germany was not occupied, it was disarmed and at the mercy of vengeful Allies. When Germany had trouble paying reparations, it faced the threat of invasion. Once, under Prime Minister Poincaré's policy of "hands on the collar," French troops marched into Germany to collect commodities because the German government had decided to pay with money rendered worthless by inflation. The price of this resistance, though, was the pauperization of any German with liquid assets. Also, the Allies had not been quick to remove the blockade that had literally starved Germany. The debauching of the German mark further retarded the resumption of normal food imports. As a consequence, Germany stayed hungry into the mid-1920s, with irreparable harm to the bodies of individuals and poison to the body politic.

In the aftermath of World War II the Soviet Union chose not to occupy Finland, and the Finnish government remained nominally independent. But every Finn knew that the price of displeasing the Soviet Union would be occupation by Soviet troops—a disaster that every Finn wanted to avoid. The price of avoiding it was high. Finland could have no independent foreign policy and could not publicly criticize the Soviet Union, which the Finns loathed as much as feared. The Finns also had to pay heavy reparations, delivering to the Soviets percentages of Finnish products as part of unequal trade agreements. They did not starve; but the weight of their relationship with the Soviets kept them from being as prosperous as other Scandinavian peoples.[4]

These first two sets of circumstances—in which the defeated country relinquishes war objectives or changes its form of government—are like a pleasant antechamber opening onto the far worse ills found in the hell of capitulation. The difference between the first two circumstances and the others is the fact of foreign occupation.

In the third set of circumstances, the occupation is deliberately benign. This is what happened to Italy and Japan after World War II. Here and there a foreign military governor may rule more justly and have the people's interests more at heart than any previous domestic ruler. But the very fact of foreign occupation means that the dislocation of previous patterns of doing business is piled upon the destruction that the victorious armies caused prior to the capitulation. Uncertain about what will and will not be allowed, eager not to get into trouble they won't be able to get out of, and frightened of the arbitrary power of armed foreigners who are not subject to domestic courts and who are accountable only to *their own* superiors, most occupied peoples shun large-scale economic activity at a time when such activity is especially vital. This, added to the normal dislocations of war, almost always brings hunger and all the diseases of body and soul that follow hunger.

Italy and Japan were fortunate that the American occupiers for different reasons regarded the civilians as innocent. The occupiers prosecuted only a handful of former government leaders and from the beginning did not try to make themselves substitutes for civil authorities. General MacArthur, who made it clear that he was the absolute dictator of occupied Japan, did not disband the Japanese civil administration and did not destroy the nominal authority of the emperor. He made sure that public blame was assigned to those who had led Japan to war and left no doubt that their militaristic way of life would henceforth be unprofitable. At the same time, he encouraged rather than impeded the revival of normal life. He also did not exact reparations.

Italy benefited from the occupiers' immediate sympathy—and food supplies. Nevertheless, the immediate postwar years saw both Italians and Japanese afflicted with diseases of malnutrition such as rickets and enlarged thyroids. During this period, survival and advancement came most directly from a person's ability to ingratiate himself with the occupiers. This brought to the fore some of the most distasteful elements of society and tended to diminish the occupiers' respect for all the locals. Almost a generation had to pass before Italian and Japanese statesmen could deal with the Americans on the basis of equal and mutual respect. For some people, however, the occupation meant the permanent loss of self-respect— such as the women who gave in to the temptation to prostitute themselves to foreign soldiers in order to feed their families.

The fourth category of circumstances involves all of the above ills, plus an occupation force that regards its job as cleansing the defeated society of the main element responsible for the war, punishing it, and exacting reparations. This was the lot of those parts of Germany lucky enough to be occupied by the Western Allies after World War II and of the American South after the Civil War. It is difficult for Americans to imagine hunger in fertile Georgia. But the Union invasion of 1864–65, like most invasions, seriously disrupted planting for two years. In many cases, seeds and livestock had been burned or eaten. And so, *Gone With the Wind*'s Scarlett O'Hara wept hungrily over a meager radish in her antebellum mansion while Yankee carpetbaggers swarmed over the land backed by military governors, buying up everything of value for practically nothing and monopolizing or taxing all attempts at economic resurgence. Meanwhile, the South's natural leaders were being jailed or banned from public or economic life because of ties to the rebellion, and former slaves were being urged to commit outrages against their former masters. This was enough to turn the South away from the gentlemanly leadership of the likes of Robert E. Lee to that of the Ku Klux Klan.

In post–World War II Germany and Austria, pitiful groups of women, children, and old men picked through rubble for rags and scraps of wood as the occupiers looked on sternly and put off definitive decisions about their future. During the two winters after the surrender of May 1945, the urban population of Germany lived virtually without heat and on the ragged edge of starvation. Mortality rates rose, and people lacked the basic nutrients necessary to dig out of the rubble and rebuild their lives.[5] For two years after the war it seemed that the country was on a downward spiral: the people were too weak to produce enough to keep from getting weaker. The victors' efforts to break the spiral did not help. For example, German coal was needed for reparations and for foreign exchange. So the miners had to be fed enough to work. But the miners were forbidden to take any of the food home to their starving families. As Konrad Adenauer, a leading German personality of the time (later to become chancellor), shivered in an unheated hotel, fully clothed and wearing an overcoat under the blankets, he thought that his people might perish.

The German economy was reduced to barter and to the use of cigarettes as currency. But the black market at least was honest. The biggest deals—the competition for the occupiers' favor, which alone could ensure food—were made by accusing one's competitors of having been Nazis. This was prostitution far less honest than that of the poor frauleins who ate by it.

The Western occupiers were not malevolent, but they were confused. They knew that they were supposed to transform the defeated society. But they did not know how they were supposed to do it. Were they going to try to turn it into a bucolic backwater, as called for in U.S. Secretary of the Treasury Henry Morgenthau's punitive plan? Would the country be transformed into a Fabian socialist experiment, as the newly elected British Labour government wanted? Meanwhile, the occupiers, who themselves would not govern, would not allow any but local authorities to govern, and then on the shortest of leashes. And so the western zones of Germany, short of everything, including able-bodied men, and swollen with some fifteen million refugees and deportees from the Soviet-occupied eastern zones, marked time. Their suffering was relieved only by charity food parcels sent from abroad. Nevertheless, as the year 1947 passed, the American, British, and French military governments, lacking any design to exploit or impose, gradually let the Germans choose liberal-minded rulers. Even though the military government officials warned the infant German economic ministry that its plans for ending rationing and for a free market would be ruinous, they stepped aside. The "economic miracle" followed immediately, and Germany was reborn. Massive American aid to Germany, without which recovery would not have been as spectacular as it turned out to be, began in 1948. When the Soviet Union started to loom as a serious threat to the United States, American leaders quickly began to see Germany not as a defeated enemy but as a possible asset. It is a rare and lucky loser whose conqueror quickly finds another enemy and starts considering him a potential ally!

The U.S. occupation of Iraq shows what can happen to a people caught among a conqueror that combines confused objectives with ambitious policies, its undefeated regime, and its own divisions. Concern for the welfare of Iraqis was one of the reasons why the United States decided to depose their dictator in 2003. But the U.S. government could not agree within itself to which Iraqis it should hand the government of their country. Nevertheless it was determined to transform Iraqi society radically. The United States sought to bring freedom and self-determination, but at the same time to maintain a unified Iraq regardless of what its residents wanted. This forced the country's major ethnic and religious groups, which feared one another, to fight one another for power. The resulting troubles were much aggravated by the remnants of Saddam's regime, which the United States had not eradicated and whose murderous offensive brought about a destructive response from the U.S. occupation forces. Thus political mismanagement turned good intentions into instruments of strife, and aid more generous than any conqueror had ever given to any vanquished into an instrument of misery.

The fifth ring in the hell of capitulation is much more common. Because the winner is out to punish, exploit, and radically reform the defeated society, the occupation brings far worse than the privation and degradation mentioned above. Compare Solzhenitsyn's accounts of the entry of Russian troops into East Prussia in World Wars I and II. His novel, *August 1914*, describes invading Russian troops filing into neat little German farming communities. A colonel would get off his horse, meet with the Burgermeister, and arrange to camp in areas where the troops would cause the least amount of damage. The Russian officers would line up outside the barbershop and then go window-shopping. In 1945, however, the invading Soviet troops had heard Ilya Ehrenburg's call to "break the racial pride" of German women by raping them. How lucky were the women on the western front who could choose whether to prostitute themselves for bread! As one can read in Solzhenitsyn's poem "Prussian Nights," the rule on the eastern front in World War II was first to rape, then to torture and kill.[6] The poor civilian wretches caught by Russian troops endured almost the worst that mankind could dish out, including mothers watching their children bayoneted by the men who then raped them. A couple of weeks after conquering an area, the Soviet authorities would put a stop to the semi-spontaneous orgy of blood by conspicuously hanging a few of their own soldiers. This sort of thing was not much different from the routines of other barbarian armies throughout history.

After the semi-spontaneous killing came the programmed killing necessary to transform society. Throughout Eastern Europe, "class enemies" and "enemy classes" were rounded up, shot, or sent to the gulag. Religious leaders, landowners, members of conservative and social-democratic parties, and former military officers were wiped out. They were not accused of war crimes. They were killed not because of anything they *did*, but because of who they *were*. At Yalta, only Winston Churchill's resistance prevented agreement on Stalin's proposal to execute all German military officers in all zones of occupation. Nevertheless, the Soviets had their way wherever the Red Army ruled. Millions who were not killed were enslaved. The Soviet Union took part of its war reparations in the form of civilians shipped off to forced labor in fields, mines, and factories. Meanwhile, Soviet authorities took everything in Eastern Europe that was not nailed down, and much that was. Whole factories were dismantled and shipped eastward.

Imagine, then, the life of ordinary families in such circumstances. Some of the men have been killed in battle, the women raped, and the children brutalized. Home and possessions are gone, someone in the family has been deported. Everyone is on the edge of starvation. Everyone is at the total mercy of the occupier and his friends. The possibility of deportation hovers over everyone. The clear and present prospect of violent death drives one to do anything to get on the right side of the occupiers, and hunger drives everyone to do anything for a scrap of food. The new order that the occupier wishes to impose has one shining attraction: any kind of normalcy must be preferable to this living hell.

This is the standard consequence of capitulation in civil wars fought over what one might call lifestyles, or of capitulation in civil wars caused by rebellion. Surely the capitulations in the civil war that followed the Bolshevik Revolution in 1918–21 were of this kind.[7] Indeed, the mass deportations were so large as to place them close to the horrors of the sixth category. The capitulation at the end of the Spanish civil war of 1936–39, however, unquestionably falls into the lesser reaches of that category, with 70,000 executions and perhaps 170,000 expulsions and deportations.[8]

The surrender of Cuba's military to Fidel Castro's insurgents during Christmas week of 1958 did not fit into that category at all—at first. At first it was a joyous party on both sides. Cuba's dictator, Fulgencio Batista, had not had a large following. He had been a small-time thief, and his few henchmen had left with him. The war had been neither destructive nor particularly bitter. Only a handful of killings were carried out during the first weeks after the capitulation. But after the society had been disarmed and Castro's control had been consolidated, Fidel Castro's persecution of "class enemies" became so harsh that perhaps 20 percent of the population fled and perhaps another 5 percent were enslaved directly. This, along with hunger and yet uncounted executions, was the price the Cuban people paid for being reformed into a communist society.

The immediate price that South Vietnam paid for surrendering to communist North Vietnam was higher. Out of fifteen million people perhaps two million threw themselves into the sea on anything that would float in order to escape the fate that befell perhaps three million of their confreres: forced labor in "new economic zones" or in "reeducation camps." Under these circumstances the distinction between outright execution and slow death brought on by forced labor or forced transit or a "trail of tears" into exile is not terribly meaningful.[9]

The most definitive example of what happens to rebels who surrender, however, is what happened to the army of the Streltzy, a class of merchant-warriors who were hereditary servants of the czars, and who rebelled and then surrendered to Peter the Great of Russia in 1712. All were tortured. All but a few were executed. The very luckiest had their heads chopped off. Most were hanged in front of their wives and children, because Peter, the great modernizer, wanted the crowd to heed the lesson. The unlucky few were broken on the wheel in Red Square and left to die slowly, cursing the good fortune of those who had been dispatched quickly.[10]

The pit of hell differs from the above only quantitatively. A vengeful occupier may want simply to extinguish the enemy's society or to reform it so radically that huge chunks of it—say, a third or more—will die. From 1915 to the early 1920s Turkish troops slaughtered the Armenian minority living in eastern Turkey. Armed resistance ended quickly. But the slaughter went on and on. Babies were cut out of pregnant women and stuck on bayonets. Rape and torture usually preceded murder. But the really big killing was done by confiscating food. Perhaps three million people died. This was the same technique that the Soviet government used to eliminate independent farmers in the Ukraine in the 1930s. Perhaps ten million starved to death.[11]

All major genocides are carried out primarily by starvation. The Chinese Great Proletarian Cultural Revolution may have killed fifty million people.

Disruption of planting and harvesting, combined with forced migration into areas bereft of food, accounted for the majority of deaths. Starvation played an unusually small role in the holocaust that struck Cambodia between 1975 and 1979 in the aftermath of the Cambodian government's surrender to the Khmer Rouge. After all, food grows exceptionally easily in Cambodia, and it is exceptionally difficult to create an artificial famine. The Khmer Rouge, however, performed radical surgery on society. Cities were emptied. Even amputees in hospitals were forced to crawl. They then killed everyone they could identify as, or imagined to be, professionals or tainted with Western culture, mostly by beating.

Contemplating the consequences of such surrenders, it becomes possible to understand the otherwise incomprehensible Roman saying that death on the battlefield is sweet.

The degree of severity following a surrender depends on the character of the winning troops, the level of their discipline, the amount of hatred that has been built up during the war, and above all the policy pursued by the winner.

One might wonder what would happen if the United States were to surrender after some future conflict. One must keep in mind that for some two generations the staple of intellectual discourse in much of the world has been to ascribe America's prosperity to its alleged exploitation of the rest of the world and to blame America for the world's ills. Thus there would be no shortage of peoples from around the world eager to take part in an occupation of America, both to taste its delights and to punish its people. Moreover, these occupying peoples might well come from traditions inured to cruelty.

The Several Kinds of Peace

As was said before, just about everyone wants peace. But human shortcomings, both intellectual and moral, lead most people to imperfect understandings of peace. Let us now look at the several kinds of peace that men try to establish through war.

The Peace of the Dead

The prophet Isaiah warned the Jews, "Your country is desolate, your cities are burned, strangers devour it in your presence, and it is desolate, overthrown by strangers." A half millennium later, in AD 70, this prophecy was realized a second time. The Romans dealt with the Jews almost as sternly as they had dealt with the Carthaginians in 146 BC—and for the same reason. Both peoples had been irritants for too long, and the Romans had become convinced that they could not live in peace as long as either continued to exist.

After the Romans had come to this conclusion, there was nothing the Carthaginians could do about it. In the decades before BC 146, Carthage tried mightily to convince Rome that it would never threaten it again. It gave Rome its finest young men as hostages. It entered into unequal arms-control agreements by which it dismantled its navy. It restricted the size of its army and paid tribute. But nothing would do. Even the most innocent things convinced the Romans that Carthage had to be destroyed. Once, when Cato returned to Rome from a trip to Carthage, he showed the senate a fruit he had picked there. The fruit had not yet rotted. This dramatized how physically close Carthage really was. Cato's fruit helped convince Rome not to rest in peace until every Carthaginian man had been put to the sword, every woman and child sold, every stone knocked off every other stone, until the plow had been drawn over the city and salt had poisoned the earth. Rome's troubles did not end in 146 BC. Indeed, many argue that Rome's moral decline began in the ease that followed this third and last Punic War. But after 146 BC, no Roman lost a night's peace over the Carthaginian threat ever again.

As for the Jews, the Romans did not destroy Jerusalem quite as thoroughly as Carthage because they had never feared it as much. Nevertheless, after AD 70 the Romans believed that their peace would never be troubled by Jews again. What a mistake! Within a generation, Rome's biggest *internal* prob-lem was what to do about the *ideas* that had been spread by the followers of a crucified Jew, Jesus. So, by the time the Romans had carried out what they thought was the final solution to the Jewish problem in AD 70, it was already too late to impose the peace of the dead. The next two centuries saw Christ's church first disturb, then divide, then conquer the Roman Empire.

Our point here is that for good or ill, the peace of the dead is a peace of sorts. But even in the rare instances when one can kill off all of one's enemies, their deaths do not necessarily bring peace because people do not have only biological families. Love, hate, and commitment to a cause need only a few living carriers and sometimes travel well with no living carriers at all. Most important, after 146 BC, internal corruption rather than external enemies made it impossible for Rome to enjoy even the peace of the dead.

Of course, the power of ideas depends on their quality. When one's enemy rules with no ideas—for instance, a Latin American dictator such as Cuba's Fulgencio Batista during 1953–58—he is as good as dead the moment he gives up power. But ideas, even crazy ones propounded by a South American dictator, can outlive their carrier. Juan Peron between 1943 and 1955 preached that the nation owes every citizen a living. Two generations after his death, and almost three generations after he was first overthrown, several movements still under the banner of Juan Peron's name do not leave Argentina in peace.

Other, more serious ideas are even more immune to death. Machiavelli was not the first to notice that while it is possible to extinguish people, fire and sword cannot extinguish memory. A conqueror will never have peace to the extent that he fails to come to terms with the ideas that sustained a defeated enemy. If he stumbles, the ideas will raise a nation of enemies to overwhelm him just as surely as if their ancestors, whether biological or ideological, had risen from the dead. This is certainly what undid Soviet rule in Poland. Between 1944 and 1950 the Soviets killed many in Poland whom they thought might lead opposition to them. But they did not kill the very notion of an independent Poland, and they could no more kill Christianity than could the Romans. And so in Poland, as elsewhere, the Communist Party of the Soviet Union enjoyed, for a while, a precarious kind of peace—the peace of the prison.

The Peace of the Prison

Communist countries were unique in history in that, like prisons, they made it a serious crime to try to leave their borders, and those borders, like prisons, were fortified to keep people in rather than to keep invaders out. The wall that cut in half the city of Berlin was only the best known of these fortified borders on land and sea, from Hong Kong to Havana.

This, too, is a peace of sorts. Both the jailer and the prisoner are at rest because both know what is expected of them. History is full of captive nations—the Jews in Babylon, the Tibetans in China, the Greeks in the Ottoman Empire, and countless others who have been conquered by empires but did not lose their identity, their memory of past glories, and the hope of future ones. For both the prisoners and the jailers, peace is neither more nor less than the policy most convenient at the moment. Although both agree on the behavior appropriate for the current balance of power and may even agree not to change it given the circumstances, neither has any illusion that they have any good in common. The imperial power exacts what it can, and the subjects give what they must. Each fears and hates the other.

The peace of the prison can be terribly stable, however. Most peoples throughout history, especially in the non-Western world, have lived as the subjects of empires. When Columbus discovered the Indies, he found a relationship between the Carib and the Arawak tribes that resembled the dealings between humans and semidomesticated animals: the Caribs would catch Arawak boys and fatten them until they ate them. The girls were breeding stock. Apparently it had not occurred to either tribe that their roles could or should be different. Understandably, the Arawaks did not like what was going on. But no one remembered it ever having been different. Even when such people remember having had other masters, the only question that has meaning for them is *which* master they shall have in the future. For example, the various Central Asian peoples, the Kazakhs, and the Uzbeks have been reasonably content to be part of the Mongol Empire, Tamerlane's empire, the Ottoman Empire, and the Russian Empire. They have always retained their identity while being passed from master to master.

Observers from Alexander the Great to Machiavelli have noted that such empires, while they appear solid, are actually quite brittle. If the master is defeated in a major battle the peace between him and his subjects is broken. If the subject people do not instantly take out their grievances against the master's officials, at the very least they will stop obeying them.

The peace of the prison is even more precarious when it involves people who have known freedom or when the idea of freedom has somehow entered their heads. It is easy for a superior military power to threaten an inferior with annihilation and carry out its threat. But it is far more difficult for the superior power to know *what to demand* as the price for its restraint.

When the Western Allies faced the problem of achieving victory over Germany in 1919, all too few thought of the obvious: Since nobody was proposing to draw the plow Roman-style over the land and impose the peace of the dead, was it conceivable that Germany could be indefinitely held down by force? Was it not probable that the effort to hold it down would stimulate its people to rise up again? The Allies of 1919 did the most thoughtless thing possible. They imposed a prison regime for the people of Germany while neglecting any effort to change their minds. Their simplistic dogma—monarchy equals war, democracy equals peace—blinded them to the fact that war and peace are in the hearts of men and in the preferences of society, and not found in legal institutions. Thus, Germany between 1919 and 1939 will remain a textbook example of how an ingenious people used every bit of elbow room in its prison to reestablish its independence and power vis-à-vis nonoccupying conquerors.

The prison that the Soviet Union established for the conquered peoples of Eastern Europe in 1945 was incomparably more binding than that established by the Treaty of Versailles. Nevertheless, as time passed the Polish, Hungarian, Czech, and other subjects wiggled more and more room for themselves until at last in 1989 they broke free. That is because while the Soviets succeeded as no one else in modern times in establishing the peace of the prison, they failed to establish a peace based on cultural conquest. While they monopolized power and privilege as few ever imagined possible, they failed to establish legitimate authority. Having failed to root out civil society totally, and being enemy strangers to it, communist regimes could not keep it from growing even as they decayed. Every truck driver, every cleaning lady, knew that the Marxist rhetoric that attempted to justify communist rule was wrongly subordinating Christians to atheists, working people to party hacks, decent people to corrupt ones, Europeans to Russians. More and more of those who served the regimes became ashamed of doing so. More and more people paid no more than the lip sevice they needed to pay to survive. The moment that they began to suspect that they might not be shot for walking away, they did so.

The Peace of Cultural Conquest

"France," Charles de Gaulle correctly tells us in the opening sentence of *La France et Son Armée*, "was made by strokes of the sword." But the various provinces were not united by force alone. Today the struggles between the Île de France, Brittany, Burgundy, and Provence are mere episodes of ancient history because the kings of France and subsequent regimes made Frenchmen out of all whom they conquered. France's literature, music, architecture, and administration trained the provinces to forget what once divided them more definitively than the sword alone could do. Burgundy will never fight France again because it ceased to exist as something even possibly willing to do that. In fact all successful conquerors draw the conquered unto a human ideal that they personify. Just as France came together in the seventeenth century behind the ideas of Descartes, the music of Rameau, and the administration of Vauban, a century earlier the Habsburg empire had embodied the ideals of the Christian warrior Ignatius of Loyola, and the British empire of the eighteenth and nineteenth centuries held its subjects less through force than through the culture of Eton and Oxford.

Thus was Douglas MacArthur's cultural conquest of Japan after 1945. Like all wise conquerors who want their achievement to outlive them—or who merely want not to have to play the jailer—MacArthur set about making his subjects *like* what had happened to them. This is difficult but not impossible to accomplish. Rather than destroying Japanese culture, MacArthur *turned* it toward emphasizing another aspect of itself, commerce. Discipline, Japan's outstanding cultural trait, could find at least as satisfying an outlet in trade as in war. MacArthur discredited one facet of the Japanese way of life, accredited another, allowed exponents of the new order to root themselves in power, and then faded from the scene. It is possible that someday Japan will turn its disciplined soul back toward war. But for a halfcentury it has turned away. No one can make anyone else change his mind, but MacArthur used the power and prestige of his sword to persuade Japan to *want* to choose his way.

Alexander the Great, the Romans, and later, to a lesser extent, Napoleon followed their military conquests with cultural ones. They brought to conquered lands a superior way of life, and the conquered for the most part seized the chance to take full part in it. In the second century BC elites from Persia to Egypt were proud to argue with one another in the Greek language and thought patterns that Alexander had brought, and to forget the traditions of Babylonians, Hittites, Persians, and Pharaohs. Two centuries later, the same peoples, plus Gauls, Celts, Germans, Iberians, and Jews could say, *"Cives Romanus sum"* ("I am a Roman citizen") along with the Jewish apostle Paul, who proudly claimed the full protection of Roman law. Soon thereafter the Roman Empire was itself conquered. But today the descendants of the Gauls and Germans, not to mention the descendants of the Goths, Franks, and Longobards, who reconquered them, think in the categories, worship the God, and speak in the terms that the Romans taught them. Indeed, Machiavelli shrewdly noted that while the barbarians were riding up and down the Italian peninsula seizing things, they were naming their sons Peter, Paul, Matthew, Mark, Luke, and John. In this case, those who were conquered militarily accomplished a far more lasting cultural conquest. But our point is more general: only such accommodation can bring a peace more genuine than the peace of the prison, whichever the direction in which cultural accommodation occurs.

"Our ancestors, the Gauls." Such words, read aloud in perfect French by classrooms of black children in northern and western Africa testified to the peace that followed France's nineteenth-century conquests there. A century and a half after those conquests Frenchmen and French-speaking Africans had more in common with each other than French-speaking Normans and Saxons did two centuries after the Norman victory at the Battle of Hastings in 1066. The Ivory Coast's Felix Houphouet-Boigny was a proud member of France's intellectual elite, and Senegal's Leopold Senghor had earned France's highest academic laurels at the same *Lycée* as its president, Georges Pompidou. But by the turn of the twenty-first century, though much of Africa was still francophone, native culture had pushed France aside, crowds were shouting for French blood, and France's armed forces did not even try to defend the old orders.

We do not mean to imply that cultural accommodation occurs primarily in the direction of the culture that holds military supremacy. To the extent that it occurs, the process is a combination of both force and reason. Its result, however, regardless of who changes the most, is that both sides come to refer to the same standards of behavior and hence recognize a common good. It is no accident that Africa was abandoning French culture just as France itself was.

Cultural conquest requires sincere commitment to standards. Consider by way of contrast the efforts of the Soviet Union and of generations of Islamic conquerors. No modern imperial power paid more attention to cultural matters than the Soviet Union. No less than France, it imposed the study of its own language on conquered peoples. It also imposed the study of Marxism-Leninism on all categories of people—from workers required to attend indoctrination sessions to schoolchildren who had to learn basic grammar and arithmetic by manipulating only communist symbols. Moreover, advancement in Soviet-conquered societies was strictly regulated by the Communist Party. Nevertheless, the communist elites' hypocrisy was so patent, so clear was Marxism-Leninism's denial of the very possibility of a good common to any two individuals, that despite all of communism's cultural efforts its conquests stood and fell with the peace of the prison.

Islam did not have to try so hard. It is true that it gave conquered rulers no choice but to proclaim the One God or die. But in accordance with the Koran, Islamic conquerors allowed ordinary infidels to live undisturbed as second-class subjects. The muezzin atop one of the minarets of a mosque would call people to forsake their former ways of life and follow the law by which the new Muslim rulers lived. Millions responded, and the Muslim conquest of northern and coastal Africa, as well as much of southern Asia, became solid. Conquest by Islam succeeded because it represented a good shared by both conqueror and conquered. By contrast, modern Muslim rulers' obvious hypocrisy, as well as the hypocrisy inherent in modern Islamists' redefinition of the faith in terms of political struggle, reduce the range of Islam's cultural influence to that of its temporal power.

Thus, we conclude that cultural conquest, although it may contain various admixtures of force and love, nevertheless always produces a kind of tacit agreement between the winners and losers that, whatever happened in the past, things now are more or less as they should be. This is remarkable testimony to the power of real peace, if given time, to heal wounds and to justify even the victory of unjust causes.

The Tranquility of Order

Whether agreement between winner and loser to live life on a mutually satisfying basis comes at the time of a peace treaty, long afterward, or, tacitly, in the absence of a treaty, only such an agreement can be the basis of peace among men living and free. As we mentioned at the beginning of this book, it is impossible to define peace because peace is a kind of satisfaction, and different people can be satisfied in different ways. Saint Augustine, knowing that war is the struggle for different conceptions of peace, summed up the matter by saying that peace is "the tranquility that comes of order." No one can mistake this as including the peace of prison. By "order" Augustine meant something far more solid.

> The peace of the body lies in the ordered equilibrium of its parts; the peace of the irrational soul, in the balanced adjustments of its appetites; the peace of the reasoning soul, in the harmonious correspondence of conduct and conviction; the peace of body and soul taken together, in the well-ordered life and health of the living whole. Peace between a mortal man and his Maker consists in ordered obedience, guided by faith, under God's internal law; peace between man and man consists in regulated fellowship. The peace of a home lies in the ordered harmony of authority and obedience, between the members of a family living together. *The peace of the political community is an ordered harmony of authority and obedience between citizens. . . . Peace in its final sense is the calm that comes of order.*[12] [Emphasis mine]

The classical tradition had taught Augustine that different people have different capacities for participating in the order of nature. So, just as there can be no perfectly ordered human body, or any perfectly ordered family, or for that matter, any perfectly ordered polity, there can be no perfect order among polities. Perfect peace, the perfect tranquility that comes from perfect order, exists only in the City of God. On earth, an approximation of the right order, whether of the body or of the polity, would have to be sought in finite, imperfect circumstances.

Again, this does not mean that all earthly solutions are equally good. Quite the contrary. The order of the City of God was to be the standard by which all earthly solutions would be judged. Approaching this harmony, he argued, is perhaps man's deepest natural desire. "According to the poor limits of mortal life, in health, security, and human fellowship," peace is "the loveliest of all lovely things on earth" because it allows men to partake of all other lovely things, both temporal and eternal.[13] But Augustine knew that God guarantees not the achievement but only the longing for peace and the freedom to pursue it—wisely or unwisely.

For Saint Augustine, only one thing was certain. Any peace established on earth, in addition to being imperfect, would last only as long as it was defended. As the French philosopher Etienne Gilson has commented, "[T]he only force capable of preserving a thing is the force which created it."[14] But alas, the force that creates peace—victory in war—is typically inclined less to creating a harmonious order than to satisfying the victor's passions.

Assume for a moment that the winner of a war wants to establish a peace as just and stable as possible. What would he have to do? Both history and common sense point to the need to avoid two extremes. On the one hand, the winner must not fail to consummate the victory, to make sure that the issues of the present war have been thoroughly resolved and that at least *that* particular set of troubles will not arise again. Thus although Abraham Lincoln had been willing, even eager, to guarantee slavery in the Southern states in order to avoid war, he was determined, once war had started, that it should end with the elimination of its principal cause. Americans might clash again. But it would not be over slavery.

By the same token, the winner also should not fail to retain the military power necessary to enforce the settlement and to guard the new order against the new and different threats that will inevitably arise. A country that thinks of the finished war as the last and the settlement as the beginning of a costless tranquility is setting itself up for another war, which it will lose. On the other hand, it should not dare to impose a peace so harsh as to preclude the loser from reconciling himself to the new order. To forget Churchill's dictum "in victory magnanimity, in peace goodwill" is to throw away the fruit of peace for the sake of which the war was fought.

Is it possible to avoid these extremes? Often it is possible, but never in the same way twice and never to the same extent twice. Sometimes it is not possible at all. Everything depends on the nature of the vanquished foe, how well the victor understands it, and how competently the victor deals with it. In 1945, for example, there was no shortage of Americans who believed that the Japanese people were unfit partners for a harmonious world order. And indeed, the Japanese had shown quite enough cruelty, dishonesty, and fanaticism for a reasonable case to have been made that only the peace of the prison or of the dead was possible for them. But some saw the possibility that the humiliation of one side of Japanese culture together with the promotion of another would produce a different Japan. This possibility was made into reality. But, under less skillful direction than Douglas MacArthur's, it might not have been. Given the wrong set of incentives, it might not endure.

In our time, Israel has repeatedly defeated Arab attempts to destroy it. Israelis would dearly love to establish an arrangement under which they could live in the land of the Covenant in peace. Although Israel has defeated Arab armies and crushed countless mobs, it has not been able to gain leverage over the politics of Arab nations and turn them away from their goal: the elimination of Israel. In Israel's case the exceptions prove the rule.

In 1967 Israel captured the Sinai Peninsula from Egypt, the Golan Heights from Syria, and Jordan's lands west of the Jordan River. Since that time, the seemingly obvious path to peace has been Israel's return of the lands in exchange for the Arabs' genuine acceptance of Israel's right to exist in peace. But with the exception of Egypt, which traded a halfhearted peace treaty for Israel's (demilitarized) return of the Sinai, the Arab states for their own reasons have continued to mobilize their citizens to annihilate Israel and assassinate those among themselves who want otherwise. Pointedly, Egypt's leader, Anwar Sadat, was assassinated for having made peace. So, as Arabs in the occupied territories seethe with hatred of Jews, and any Arab who might disagree fears for his life, what can Israel expect were she to withdraw to less defensible borders in exchange for paper promises of peace? This seems to be a case where the peace in the hand, though it be the peace of the prison (and of the garrison) is better than the one in the bush, which might well turn out to be no peace at all. The U.S. State Department has repeatedly urged Israel to "take chances for peace." But the other side of the chance is defeat in war—and at whose hands!

The Arab-Israeli struggle is the clearest example in our time of an unconsummated war—a *bellum interruptum*. When the issues that gave rise to a war have not been resolved and when one side has not given up its objectives it is dangerous to think the war is over. In 1919 the German people never came to terms with their defeat and were not averse to resuming the fight when they could.

Why then would anyone have kind words for a bellum interruptum? Because by disregarding or denigrating the very idea of victory, by declaring that stopping the fighting is more important than who wins, one avoids difficult questions such as which side is right? And on what or whose basis is peace to be built? Hence, the formula familiar to contemporary Americans: the adversaries must go to the bargaining table. They must arrange a cease-fire or an agreement to limit certain kinds of weapons, and possibly interpose unarmed "observers" and inspection teams. Create a committee where the two sides can charge each other with violations, award the mediator the Nobel Peace Prize, and hope that *somehow,* even though the peace process did not resolve the questions that set the belligerents to killing each other, those questions will fade away after the killing has stopped. But this familiar formula for bellum interruptum constrains only those who wish to be constrained, while the other side licks its wounds and prepares for an honest-to-goodness victory. The bellum interruptum usually is a smart tactic for one side and a stupid one for the other.

Happily, this is not always so. It is conceivable that the half-century "time-out" enforced by the United States in the war between China's Communists and Nationalists may have allowed bases for peace to develop that had not existed before. For more than a generation beginning in 1949, while Nationalist China (Taiwan) was integrating itself into the world economy and even moving toward being that most un-Chinese of things, a democracy, mainland China seemed to retain a particularly harsh and isolated brand of communism. But in the 1980s mainland China began to change. It of course remained a tyranny, but by then the tyranny appeared not so different from what China has long known. Moreover, that tyranny was surely loosening and opening itself to the world. Most important for the future, it seemed that Marxism-Leninism had sunk very shallow roots in China after all. By the turn of the century, then, despite harsh political declarations and continued military preparations, a harmonious relationship between the mainland and Taiwan had developed de facto and it was no longer inconceivable that it would last. Time had moved on.

But this sort of thing cannot be *counted on* to produce peace. Time can be counted on only to kill the current generation. Ordinarily, in the world of the living the tranquility of order can only be built by intelligent choices backed by victorious arms. Given good choices and good arms, time and the amnesia that may accompany it can be allies in achieving both victory and peace while minimizing bloodshed. Abraham Lincoln, for example, sought to head off the looming Civil War by allowing time to settle the issue of the war, namely, whether the United States should be all free or all slave. To safeguard peace, Lincoln wanted to reassure slave owners that he would strenuously oppose anyone trying to deprive them of their slave property. Nevertheless, slavery would not be allowed to expand, and every incentive would be given to slave owners to sell their slaves into freedom. Capitalist economics, as well as the moral weight of a nation in which slavery would have been a shrinking backwater would finish off the "peculiar institution." If the Southern states had agreed to let time run under these circumstances, Lincoln's peaceful victory would have come about. But the South started the Civil War precisely because time would have been working against it.[15]

PART IV

Wars of Our Time

13

OUR SMALL WARS

Superpowers don't do windows.
JOHN HILLEN

THIS BOOK'S PREMISE is that each kind of peace is the result of some war, whether waged or prospective. Our premise is also that force amounts to war only when it is reasonably aimed at producing some peace. In our time as in others the fortunes of peoples have been decided by the management of force. Who is willing to kill and die for a cause? How wisely does he decide at whom to shoot? Which side is better at evaluating its enemy? Which is the most effective tool to employ in any given situation to gain one's peace?

The biggest intellectual splash of 1989 was made by Francis Fukuyama's article (later, his book) "The End of History." It argued that now, once and for all, mankind had settled its quarrel about how to organize society in favor of liberal democracy. Deprived of the controversy that had been its main engine, argued Fukuyama, history would stop. Without serious causes, so would wars. In fact, though, it seems that in 1989 history switched to fast forward, that its mainsprings have not changed, and that its events continue to illustrate the principles of conflict. Along with Michael Howard we believe that upon hearing of the demise of war the prudent man will make sure his bomb shelter is in good repair. The more one neglects the fundamentals of force, the likelier it is he will have to relearn them the hard way.

Just as the previous two generations' time began with the end of World War II, our time began with the revolutions of 1989–91—when the fall of the Soviet empire brought forth a set of problems peculiar to us. This section discusses some contemporary situations in which the conduct of war or management of force has made a major difference in the kinds of peace under which various peoples live.

There has been little proportion between the number of casualties and the significance of any conflict in history. Most of the conflicts of our time have not been perceived as wars at all—except of course by their participants. Certainly as the United States and other Western powers got involved in them they did not treat them as such. And yet the memorable lesson they teach is that whenever a conflict involves killing, or takes place under the specter of deadly force, all the principles of war apply. The following chapters, which deal, respectively, with the Gulf War of 1991, the Iraq War of 2003, and the War on Terror of 2001 show that commitment of massive means is no substitute for the subordination of means—of whatever dimension—to well-crafted ends.

The Soviet Empire

Our first example concerns the (largely bloodless) war of 1989–91 between the Soviet empire and its own people. While the peoples understood what was happening and won, the Soviets realized too late that they stood to lose—and they lost. The Western powers turned out to be big winners, despite themselves.

Between 1989 and 1991 the empire's subjects, sensing its disinclination to use force decisively, broke the peace of the prison they had endured. In a nutshell: Stalin had killed by the millions. Khruschev had killed by the thousands. Brezhnev by the hundreds. But Gorbachev and his East European subordinates killed only by the tens, while courting the people's favor. Under those conditions, any opening that became available to the peoples, any failure to plug it, would spell quick disaster.

In July 1989 the Hungarian government, under the "liberal communists" Imre Pozgay and Gyula Horn, began to dismantle the fences and death strips on the Austro-Hungarian border and publicly ordered its guards henceforth not to shoot people who were trying to leave the country illegally. We argue that one of the kinds of peace between an empire and its subjects, the peace of the prison, exists because both the jailer and the inmates see no better way at the time. But when any part of the prison's wall goes down, the balance of expectations is upset, and that peace comes to an end. Hungary's opening of the iron curtain destabilized East Germany first. For all the empire's inmates but the Germans, the iron curtain's barbed wire, mines, dogs, and watchtowers were only the first barrier. Even if they crossed it, Western governments might well repatriate them. Or they might remain stateless. But any East German who got out was by law automatically, instantly recognized as a full citizen of West Germany with full benefits.

So Hungary's border opening broke the peace between the East German regime and its subjects. East German tourists in Hungary were the first to defect. Then East German tourists in Czechoslovakia crossed to Hungary and left. Then East Germans went to Hungary just to leave. By October about a quarter of a million had left—almost 2 percent of the population. This both emboldened and empowered those East Germans who remained. They took to the streets chanting, "We are the people, we want to stay." The implication was clear—"Change the government, or we too will go." The government, looking at a fast-emptying jail, opened all the gates including the infamous Berlin Wall, betting that the inmates, having full freedom to come and go, would not leave permanently. But this of course brought about a new and very different kind of peace between the rulers and the ruled. The peace of the prison became a truce to permit the jailers' surrender.

Poland, East Germany, Czechoslovakia

The jailers of the captive nations of Eastern Europe opened the gates. They would even let the captives run the prison a bit. But they kept the guns firmly in their own hands. They forgot that guns are useful only if they are used.

In Poland, Gen. Wojtiec Jaruzelsky, the man who had run the "war against the people," offered the people a deal: he would legalize Solidarity, the political organization the Polish people had built up against the regime, and allow it free elections in which Solidarity would win every seat. But in exchange, Jaruzelsky and his communist associates would retain exclusive control of the armed forces, the police, foreign relations, and the transportation system that ensured Soviet military supply lines in Eastern Europe. The Polish people did not fear these retained powers—let us see why.

In East Germany, when huge public demonstrations followed the opening of the Austro-Hungarian breach in the iron curtain, Communist Party chief Erich Honecker reportedly ordered his security forces to open fire on the demonstrators à la Tienanmen Square. But the dominant faction of the leadership countermanded the order because it knew that Soviet military power would not back up the crackdown. And so the East German Communist Party tried to follow the most recent Polish example and set up a Polish-style "national round table"—a kind of internal peace conference that also served as an interim government.

As in Poland, the party did not think it was negotiating a surrender.

Without shooting, it meant to play to the hilt its greatest remaining asset, the sole possession of weapons. As crowds surged around the officers of the security forces, Hans Modrow, the new prime minister, a man reputed to be an archmoderate by the Western press, warned the people that "where there are weapons there are limits" and "the guns must remain in the right hands." Alas, for the overwhelming majority of his countrymen, the root of their troubles was that for the previous forty-five years the weapons had been in precisely the wrong hands. As 1990 opened, the communists had changed their name and denied their ideological heritage—but they controlled the army, the ministries of the interior, the police, and the foreign ministry. *But guns that do not shoot prove useless.*

In Czechoslovakia, angry crowds started assembling in Prague's Wenceslas Square after the Communist Party had collapsed in East Germany. Within days the East German scenario was repeated in Czechoslovakia—but with a difference: the noncommunist leaders who became part of the coalition government with the communists publicly demanded the removal of Soviet troops from the country and set about gaining a share of control over the police and armed forces.

In these countries, the conflict took place by political means alone solely because of political decisions as to the use of force on the Soviet side alone.

The Baltics, Georgia, Azerbaijan, Ukraine, et al.

The Soviet Union's military reticence abroad was due primarily to political troubles at home so serious that they posed a choice between open warfare against the people and the outright overthrow of the Soviet regime. Anti-Russian, anticommunist, anti-Soviet demonstrators demanded essentially the same things in Catholic Lithuania as in Muslim Azerbaijan: in the name of religion, language, culture, history, economic well-being, and so forth, let us no longer be ruled by these Russian communists. *The Soviet government did not crush these internal threats for the same reasons it did not let the ones in Poland and other places be crushed: It had excessive faith in its possession of guns despite its unwillingness to use them.* It also suffered from internal divisions about what its relations with the people should be. In short, it was not united in the realization that it was at war.

In May 1989, in Georgia's capital, Tiblisi, a special unit of Soviet troops attacked a crowd with lethal chemicals and sharpened shovels. The number of casualties is in dispute, but the political effect was indisputable. Soviet officials tried to shift responsibility. The move was widely denounced in the Council of People's Deputies, as well as by senior officers of the regular army. This signaled to other dissidents that they were not likely to be treated with the same harshness. Hence by the end of 1989 Gorbachev's threats of "blood" did not prevent the Baltic states from electing national fronts, which declared their intention of seceding from the Soviet Union. Then, in January Gorbachev withdrew the threats. Common sense suggested that when the Baltics seceded, Georgia would follow—which it did.

The word "empire" means maintaining the peace of the prison. The Soviet Union called itself a multinational workers' and peasants' state. Marxism-Leninism was the only possible justification for its existence. In reality, the Soviet Union had always been held together by force. But that force was exercised by a party that explained what it did in Marxist terms. Then, in the mid-1980s, for a variety of reasons, the leadership of the Soviet Communist Party stopped speaking the language of Marxism-Leninism with conviction. At the same time, it stopped killing its enemies the moment they raised their heads. By 1990 the empire appeared to its subjects at once divided at the top, unsure of what it was about, no longer to be feared, naked—an invitation to millions eager to avenge uncountable hurts.

Only military force could have saved the Soviet regime. Yet if the regime had called on the troops to save it from its own people, it would thereby have left behind what remained of its political character. And would the troops have obeyed? We ask the primordial question: what if they gave a war and no one showed up? Regimes live and die by their capacity to call on troops who are ready, willing, and able to defend them. In January 1990 the Soviet regime called in army reserves to bolster forces sent to suppress an uprising in Azerbaijan; it had to cancel the mobilization because common people objected—as did the generals of the regular armed forces.

This book highlights the essential role of special troops in the Soviet military system—whether in the Ministry of Defense, the KGB, or the Ministry of the Interior. Their function was primarily to do "dirty work," such as shooting demonstrators, that regular troops would not do, and to ensure the regulars' loyalty by controlling their communications channels, ammunition, and the like. Soviet "special troops" of various kinds numbered almost 750,000. For seventy years the "special troops" system, under control of the KGB, prevented any hint of "Bonapartism," a takeover of the revolution by its armed forces analogous to Napoleon's coup, in the Soviet Union. Hence the KGB had been the party's "Sword and Shield." But in August 1991, when the regime called on the KGB's ultra-special Alpha Force troops to attack the Russian parliament, which was in the process of seceding from the Soviet Union, the Alpha force refused, perhaps out of fear of the regular armed forces many of whose men thought of themselves more as Russians than as Soviets.

At least the Russian regime did not lose as badly as the Rumanian one had at Christmas 1989.

Rumania

In Rumania, a private in the Securitate, a secret police cum special military force, was paid more than a university professor and lived like a king compared to his counterpart in the army. In December 1989 Rumania's communist dictator Nicolae Ceaucescu ordered the regular army to drown in blood a small incident of resistance in the ethnically Hungarian border city of Timisoara. The army obeyed reluctantly, killing hundreds and perhaps thousands. But there were reports that soldiers who hesitated to shoot were themselves shot by the Securitate. This angered the regular army critically.

The spark for the explosion that followed was provided by a few students who joined a crowd that had been mustered to hear Ceaucescu speak from his balcony. The students booed, the booing caught on, and the dictator stepped back inside. He was still very much in power. He would make a phone call, and the square beneath the balcony would be filled with bodies. But within minutes, whether by prior arrangement or not, regular army units that had been called to the square had joined the crowd. All that remained for Ceaucescu was a panicky attempt to escape. Three days later, as his Securitate fought for their own lives, regular soldiers vied for the privilege of joining the firing squad that emptied its guns into Ceaucescu and his wife.

Machiavelli points to the fate of the Emperor Caracalla. Because he managed to retain the loyalty of the vast bulk of his army he was not undone by his "unprecedented" savagery and ruthlessness or by having executed "much of Rome's populace and all of Alexandria's." Rather, Caracalla perished because "he executed with disgrace a brother of that Centurion [who eventually murdered him] and continued to threaten the surviving Centurion daily, even though he kept him on as his bodyguard." The lesson is clear: tyranny is a permanent state of war. In war, the prime requirement for survival is drawing a deadly line between yourself and those who have reason to hate you. The communists lost sight of this, and they lost everything.

The West's Role

The Western powers proved clueless about the events that were producing total defeat for their enemies and total victory for themselves. Victory came despite their best efforts.

Ever since the 1950s NATO's planners had feared the numerical superiority of Soviet (and Eastern European) forces. This fear reasonably increased in the 1970s when the quality of Soviet military equipment came to equal that of NATO, while Soviet numerical superiority continued to mount. Until 1989 NATO planners could only dream of a central front on which they would enjoy numerical equality. But when the political roof fell in on the Warsaw Pact in 1989, the Soviets became eager to fulfill NATO's dreams of parity. A great deal? Yes—for the Soviet Union.

By the end of 1989 the peoples of Eastern Europe had acquired a voice and reached a consensus universal and unequivocal regarding Soviet troops in the region: They must leave. All of them. Right away. The Soviet Union's response was to say the number and kind of Soviet troops in each country would be determined by "international agreement." The Soviet line was, "The Americans and the rest of NATO want us in your country, too. We and they are negotiating parity for the sake of peace. If you object, the West will join us in regarding you as enemies of peace." But that impressed Poles, Czechs, and other East Europeans not a bit. Forty-four years of Soviet occupation had taught them that they had no enemies but the Soviets themselves.

U.S. persistence in the goal of parity, however, was surprising, because the rise of democracy in the region offered a result far better than parity, a far more secure guarantee against Soviet attack than any arms-control agreement could possibly be: namely, a total absence of hostile troops. A fortiori, the ultimate guarantee against Soviet attack would be the disappearance of the Soviet Union itself. But by August 1991 the Ukranians were joining the Balts and the Georgians, and the Russians themselves, in rejecting the Soviet Union. President George H. W. Bush stood in the central square of Kiev and told the Ukranian people to seek their future in a flourishing Soviet Union. They did not listen. While Western officials dealt with Soviets as partners, the Soviets' subjects eliminated them as enemies.

The West's Wars

Panama

Uncertainty about whether to deal with someone as an enemy or just as a bother was behind the biggest U.S. military operation of the 1980s, the invasion of Panama.

Ever since 1981, when the U.S. attorney in Miami obtained a grand jury indictment against Panama's dictator, Manuel Noriega, for drug trafficking, and especially after 1988, when Noriega flaunted his defiance of Panama's voters by refusing to recognize the winner of the presidential elections, the U.S. government had felt justified in publicly pressing for his ouster. But to oust an armed ruler who does not wish to be ousted requires violence, that is, war. But war requires killing, and the U.S. government found it more morally defensible to stand by while Noriega killed than to associate itself with any killing undertaken to stop *his* killing. This logic reached its pons asinorum in October 1989. A group of Panamanian military officers led by a Major Giroldi told the U.S. government that they would overthrow Noriega and asked the United States to block Noriega's special forces from coming to his rescue. On the night of 3 October, the plotters seized Noriega in his headquarters and asked the U.S. command to come and take him away. But not only would the United States not do that, but U.S. forces had blocked only two out of the three streets leading to Noriega's headquarters. So Noriega's reinforcements got through and the plotters were killed.

The most noteworthy part of the episode was the appearance on U.S. television of Secretary of Defense Richard Cheney, National Security Adviser Brent Scowcroft, and Chairman of the Joint Chiefs of Staff Colin Powell. They all said that no American, from the commander of the U.S. Southern Forces in Panama to themselves to the president of the United States, had decided either to help the coup succeed or to let it fail. Why block any streets at all, then, never mind only two? Upon hearing that there would be a coup, U.S. forces had blocked those two roads because doing so lay within the forces' mandate with regard to the canal. To do more would have meant involvement in a coup in which General Noriega might possibly have been killed, and none of these high personages could defend *that*. They did enough to interfere, but not enough to prevent their enemy's enhancement and their country's embarrassment.

During October, November, and most of December, this episode strengthened the public's long-standing perception of the Bush administration as the gang that couldn't shoot straight, led by an arch wimp. Then Panamanian soldiers killed one American and roughed up two more—something that was happening every other week somewhere in the world. The Bush administration, shocked à la Claude Rains, sent two divisions after Noriega, employing the Army, the Navy, the Marines, and even the newest stealth attack airplane. They had to defeat and disarm the entire Panamanian army and police before Noriega sought refuge in the Vatican embassy. Some six hundred Panamanians (half of them civilians) and twenty-three American servicemen were killed.

This book argues that assassination is often the most morally defensible of any lethal act in warfare—as well as the most effective—and that the contemporary American aversion to it is an attempt to evade responsibility for identifying the enemy and choosing the best way of dealing with him, and above all for explaining why certain objectives are worth killing and dying for. We believe that the U.S. killing of six hundred, after having recoiled at the thought of being involved in possibly killing one, is a textbook example of incompetence.

Somalia, Bosnia, and Kosovo

Because the purely military elements of Western, and especially American, involvement in the wars of Somalia (1992–94) and the dying Yugoslavia (1991–99) were so relatively small, the flawed thinking that guided those involvements is all the more evident. Both were intended to be instances of "Missions Other Than War" (MIOWs for short) that ended up with lots of people dead and not much accomplished. Somalia reveals as nonsense the notion of humanitarian relief in the face of armed force, while Yugoslavia (first Bosnia, then Kosovo) highlights even more starkly the necessity for seriousness whenever guns are involved.

SOMALIA In 1991 drought reduced harvests in Somalia; but the main reason for the mass starvation that existed was that the Somali people's various armed clans heightened food shortages by fighting over what little food there was. From the very first, the problem consisted mainly of armed men, not nature. Hence the solution could not consist of engineering or administration. The choice had to be between war and letting the problem solve itself. But few thought this way, and even fewer asked the other questions, enumerated in previous chapters, that one should ask about any war.

In April 1992 the UN passed its first resolution on Somalia, pursuant to which the United states and others made available some twenty-eight thousand tons of food, delivered to Somalia mainly by Pakistani troops under the UN flag. The armed clans, however, forced the Pakistanis to pay protection money for the food convoys and often looted them anyway. On 9 December, again as part of the UN operation Restore Hope, U.S. forces landed in Somalia to protect food convoys and to disarm the clans. In so doing, U.S. and allied forces were supposed to maintain impartiality among the clans. U.S. forces were to accomplish their mission not by making war on any clan or on all clans, but rather through political dialogue, psychological operations, and humanitarian activities such as building roads, bridges, schools, and hospitals, etc.

Given their assigned role, it almost seems strange that the allied forces took guns at all. The explanation—and the core problem with MIOWs—lay in the U.S./UN definition of "peace enforcement" missions: They are to be undertaken only when both parties to a conflict agree to a cease-fire, to have "neutral" monitors of that cease-fire, and to guarantee the safety of those monitors. In return, the enforcers pledge not to use force. One might almost ask why peace enforcement should be necessary at all, since it seems intended strictly for places where peace already exists. Nevertheless the Nobel Prize committee awarded a collective Peace Prize to UN peacekeepers in 1988.

In Somalia, however, the absence of peace set the tone. After a clan had held a group of Pakistanis prisoner for two days, UN secretary general Butros-Ghali urged the Security Council to inject more forcefulness into the operation, while aiming it at what it considered the root cause of the problem—not any set of persons but anarchy itself. Note that defining the enemy as abstractions, whether "anarchy" or "terrorism," dispenses with the bother of having to decide at whom to point one's guns. Hence the UN's resolution, which would take effect in May 1993, called for "Rehabilitating political institutions and the economy, promoting political settlement and national reconciliation"—by force, if necessary. It was not made clear how that could be done without making war on some if not all of the clans. Obviously, the new mission was a threat to all of them.

Mostly it threatened the largest of the clans, led by Mohammed Farah Aideed. He was no mere marauder, but the first of the region's feudal barons. As such, he had better relations with the other clans than did the Americans and their allies. The UN commissioners who were in charge of the operations and, not incidentally, in friendly contact with Aideed's chief competitors, decided that bringing Aideed to heel was the key to success in Somalia. But the means they chose, halfhearted attempts to disarm his militia and prohibiting him from certain parts of the country, could not possibly achieve that. All they did was put UN troops in trouble. On 5 June 1993, a company of Pakistanis suffered twenty-four killed and fifty wounded when they attempted to enter an arms warehouse. This set up the United States/UN at war with Aideed.

But what was the point? Eliminate him, and his clan would raise up another leader. Eliminate his clan, and others would be empowered thereby. Eliminate all clans? But the country consisted of little else. And the means? Any serious military campaign would have had to attack the powers of the clans, killing thousands of militiamen—who spent most of their time as civilians—intermixed with their families. Then, something like full-fledged colonial rule would have had to be established. No one was prepared to do that. Merely to try intimidating the clans one would have had to move among them safely. That required tanks. The U.S. Army contingent asked for them, but was told, no, we do not want to cause the war to escalate. And so the entire Somalia operation came down to having the U.S. antiterrorist Delta Force, Task Force Ranger, hunt down Aideed. Aideed had his troops stage provocations in various places. UN forces would respond. Delta Force would take the chance to pounce. But Aideed would be gone before it got there.

The climax came on 3 October. A Somali CIA agent who later turned out to have been working for the other side (as CIA agents so often do) assured the Americans that Aideed would be at a certain place at a certain time. In midafternoon, the elite of the U.S. Army conducted a perfect vertical assault, rappelling from helicopters—right into a massive ambush. Two helicopters were shot down. By the time a rescue force arrived at about 2:00 the following morning, eighteen Americans had been killed and their bodies had been dragged through the streets. President Clinton withdrew American troops in disgrace.

The military postmortem was easy. The mission had morphed from humanitarian assistance to the transformation of a society. Placing soldiers in danger and restricting their ability to use artillery and aerial bombing had compromised their ability to protect themselves. No tanks had been provided. Above all, there had been an imbalance between the ends, both grandiose and fuzzy, and the measly means.

BOSNIA AND KOSOVO For most of the 1990s the U.S. government illustrated in slow motion in the Balkans what it had shown already in the Gulf War, that commitment of vast resources does not make up for a mission ill conceived and on behalf of which one is not wiling to suffer casualties, or even to inflict them.

Yugoslavia, one of the congenitally dysfunctional offspring of the Versailles settlement of 1919, had really been an empire of Serbs over Croats, Slovenians, Bosnians, Macedonians, Albanians, and Montenegrins, held together by a communist dictatorship. Starting in the summer of 1991, as communism fell and nationalism rose throughout Eastern Europe, first the Slovenes and Croats, then the Bosnians and Macedonians and, years later, the Albanians, broke free of communism—and especially of the Serbs. The separation was bloody. Its terms were set by war between armies and between peoples. As soon as the fighting began, the governments of Europe and the United States, as well as the UN, intervened politically and militarily to stop it. In Bosnia the killing ended in 1995. In Kosovo, in 1999.

To what extent the interventions altered the outcome is not clear. It is indisputable, however, that by seeking peace while avoiding the question whose peace, and by making threats and promises they failed to back up, the interveners lengthened the process. The interveners were indecisive because they were not willing to impose their own peace by war or to help any of the contenders impose its own. Each of the contenders was sacrificing for something. Since the interveners were not fighting for anything, they would sacrifice nothing.

On 25 June 1991 Slovenia and Croatia declared independence from Yugoslavia. The Yugoslav army attacked Slovenia directly. But since Croatia was nearly as strong as Serbia (Croats in the Yugoslav army had defected to their ethnic homeland), the rump Yugoslav army fought it indirectly by transferring arms and personnel to Serbs within Croatia who had been skirmishing with their Croat neighbors. By late summer both new republics were independent de facto. Germany recognized them in December. At the end of February 1992 Bosnia, too, declared independence. Here, as well, Yugoslavia—now effectively Serbia with Montenegro tagging along—made war indirectly turning one hundred thousand troops in the Bosnian region over to the Bosnian Serb military. Thus the Serbian army in fact was the bulk of the Yugoslav army merely relabeled. Quickly it captured some 70 percent of Bosnian territory.

Serbia had already lost the illusion that it might continue to rule Croats and other peoples under the label Yugoslavia. The war would be about how much real estate the Serbs, Croats, and Muslims each would end up with and how few persons of the other ethnic groups would be left on any given piece of land. In January 1993 former U.S. Secretary of State Cyrus Vance and former British Foreign Secretary Lord Owen came up with a plan for peace in Bosnia, namely, to divide the country into ten provinces, each covering an area where one of the ethnic groups dominated. None of the groups was happy with the plan because each wanted to draw the boundaries more favorably to itself. Among potential interveners the argument was made that the various former Yugoslavs should be left alone to fight out their differences. But the consensus opinion was that the international community should force peace. But whose peace should they seek? Whose cause should they support? The interveners refused to choose sides, but firmly decided that they themselves would not use force.

The international community's members had different levels of interest and clashing preferences. All were more interested in the safety of the people they sent than in achieving any result. The United Nations was least interested in results, Europeans a bit more, and Americans another bit more. But among the Europeans, France was pro-Serbia, while Germany was pro-Croatia. The Russians were outright partisans of the Serbs, while the Americans had a soft spot for the Bosnian Muslims, as did the Turks. These differences diluted the collective commitment to stopping the slaughter of innocents. Then again, the closer one looked the fewer innocents there were. People of one group who had been driven from their homes would take the first opportunity they found to drive folks from another group from *their* homes.

Hence it is not difficult to understand how, say, a French officer in charge of a company escorting the deputy prime minister of Bosnia on 8 January 1993, when stopped at a Serbian checkpoint, stood by as a Serb soldier walked up to the minister sitting in the French car, put a pistol to his head, and fired. Or how Dutch troops guarding the UN's declared "safe area" of Srebenica watched as Serbian troops massacred perhaps four thousand of the refugees whose safety they were supposed to guarantee. But by what means were they to deliver that guarantee? At their trial in the Netherlands, the officers argued that their orders from the UN did not clearly direct them to make war. They were correct. Indeed, they might have been brought to trial if they *had* made war.

The role of the interveners grew throughout the war, impelled by American public opinion. Because the Americans came to demand it, the NATO alliance became more active, effectively taking over the undefined task of observers that had belonged nominally to the UN. Gradually also, this increasing American involvement reversed a neutrality on the part of NATO and the UN that had benefited the Serbs most of all. In a nutshell, until well into 1994 the interveners' role, beyond lots of impotent talk, consisted of enforcing an arms embargo on the whole of Yugoslavia. This was very much to Serbia's advantage because it owned most of the Yugoslav army's stockpiles while other combatants—with the partial exception of Croatia—were lightly armed at best. Real neutrality would have consisted of lifting the embargo. The most vocal anti-Serbs pressed the international community, and above all the United States, to "lift" the embargo and "strike" the Serb armies from the air. Eventually the United States lifted the embargo clandestinely and unilaterally, and led NATO into striking.

Sarajevo, Bosnia's capital, was the news focus of the war. The Serbs besieged it in March 1992, and regularly shelled marketplaces, schools, and other public places. The televised horrors of the siege led to the UN's dispatch of the inappropriately named UN Protection Force, or UNPROFOR. It protected nothing and forced nothing. As for NATO, since July 1992 its ships had monitored the arms embargo (but not enforced a blockade) and since October had monitored the airspace over Bosnia. In March 1993 NATO first authorized its pilots to fire—but only to protect UNPROFOR if it was under attack and asked for help. The UN did not ask because UNPROFOR itself was not under attack—only under constant threat of attack from the well-armed Serbs. A year later, NATO authorized its pilots to attack Serb artillery that was hitting civilians in Sarajevo—if the UN asked. It did not ask. U.S. aircraft had enforced a no-fly zone over Bosnia since April 1993, but they first struck in April 1994 to protect French UN forces when they came under attack near the UN designated "safe area" of Gorazde. France had asked.

The intervention began to change character in mid-1994 following an international outcry over a Serbian mortar shell that killed sixty and wounded two hundred in a Sarajevo marketplace. NATO threats of "lift and strike" led the Serbs to promise to stop shelling Sarajevo, and to remove artillery from the area. In August, when the artillery was found still in the area, one U.S. strike sufficed to get it removed. In November U.S. planes struck again in retaliation for antiaircraft fire and for continued Serb strikes against Bosnian civilians.

The Serbs retaliated. "Peacekeepers" like UNPROFOR, are always potential hostages in no-peace zones. In November the Serbs captured four hundred of them as hostages, against NATO enforcement of its demands. The Serbs did not release them until June 1995. Meanwhile, they reintroduced artillery around Sarajevo and began shelling again. In April a U.S. airplane carrying relief supplies to Sarajevo was hit, and aid flights stopped. The Serbs expected that the UN would hold back NATO. They were correct. The U.S. response consisted of an air strike against Serb ammo dumps near Pale. It was a "show of force" advertised as such, hence a show of weakness. Further emboldened, in July 1995 the Serbs carried out their boldest offensive of the war, overrunning the UN "safe area" and carrying out the most conspicuous mass slaughters of the war.

This brings us to the strategy of the war's two sides and to the war's decisive phase.

Serbia's war had been indirect: The bulk of its army had taken a new identity as the army of the Serbs living in Croatia, but mostly of the Serbs living in Bosnia. Augmented by militias from those populations, it sought simply to "cleanse" as much Bosnian territory of non-Serbs as it could. In the southeastern parts of Croatia where Serbs lived, there was no action because local Croats had been largely chased out at the beginning of the war. So the Serbian army was largely in Bosnia. The Serbian high command did not worry about having to protect the Serbian heartland around Belgrade because the West was proving feckless and the Croats did not have enough weapons for a serious offensive. Besides, the Croats had used up much of their ammunition in 1991, and the embargo was preventing them from restocking. So the Serbs' strategy was simply to take more land and then to make peace.

The Bosnian Muslims were in a bind. Largely unarmed and kept that way by the arms embargo, they were forced to hope that the UN would save their lives and NATO would stop the loss of their lands. Besides, they were also fighting the Bosnian Croats for the lands that the Serbs had not taken. Whatever help the Muslim world was sending amounted to a drop in the bucket. About the only thing that the Muslims managed to do for themselves was to stop fighting the Croats in 1993 and to ally with them against the Serbs in local battles. But the tide was against them. Their main weapon turned out to be their suffering, broadcast to the world. This produced ever more action on NATO's part, but nothing decisive, at least directly.

In a nutshell, the Bosnians and Croats who wanted to defeat the Serbs could not do so because of the UN arms embargo, while NATO would not, in part because no UN resolution authorized war. In 1994 the United States reacted to the pressure created by images of Bosnian suffering and NATO impotence simply by ignoring the UN arms embargo—clandestinely. By arranging for Croatia to rearm itself, the United States indirectly waged war on Serbia.

By mid-1995 Croatia was ready. On 28 July it launched a major offensive toward the southeast. Its objective was twofold. First it would drive Serbs out of the Slavonian provinces from which they had chased Croats in 199–92. (Some one hundred eighty thousand Serbs sought safety in the Bosnian Serb areas.) Then Croatia would secure victory by driving its army to the routes between Serbia and Bosnia, thereby cutting off the Serbian army from its supplies. On 10 August, after the Croats had taken the key to those routes, the town of Knin, Serbia, was in extremis. The Serb areas of Bosnia were now crowded with refugees, Belgrade could not help them, and the Serb army was trapped. If the Serb army tried to go forward and take more land, it would soon run out of supplies. If it tried to fight its way back east, its tough fight might be hopeless were NATO aircraft to enforce the no fly zone over Bosnia. The decisive blow had been struck.

In what was perhaps the war's most counterproductive move, Serb artillery hit Sarajevo massively on 22 August. This provided an excellent excuse for what many Americans wanted to do anyway, cripple the Serb army with air strikes and make it impossible for it even to try fighting its way out of the trap it was in. So between 30 August and 11 September NATO planes reduced the Serbs to asking for a truce.

There followed nearly three months of talks, ending in the Dayton accords of December 1995, the point of which was that all ethnic groups would stay where they were and there govern themselves, although individuals had the right to return to their homes (but only theoretically). In terms of territory, this was little different from the Vance–Owen Plan of some four years and thousands of dead earlier. But on top of that the accords called for a purely fictitious central Bosnian state. In reality, Bosnia would govern only the largely Muslim areas, whereas the Serb areas were Republika Srpska, and the Croat areas were equally independent. There were three armies. But nominally, they were all part of one Bosnian state. This allowed Americans and NATO to tell themselves that they had saved Bosnia.

As regards politics and territory, the interveners could not have done more for Bosnia, and they might have served it better by doing less. But by late summer 1995 the interveners had military options vis-à-vis Serbia that, if exercised, would have prevented much greater problems looming in Kosovo. Simply, they could have demanded the radical reduction of the Serbian army or they could have reduced it by bombing or by closely supporting the Croatian army. Had they done any of these things, Serbia would have been unable to cause NATO the trouble it did in the Kosovo crisis of 1998–99. But the interveners did nothing. And the Kosovo War ensued.

Kosovo was a province of the Yugoslav republic of Serbia, not a republic itself. But it was more alien to the central government than any of the other republics because its historic, ethnic, and religious differences with the Serbs were deeper. Kosovars are not just Muslims. They are Albanians, not Slavs. Since they live on the site of the Slavs' greatest defeat at Muslim hands in 1382, the Serbs regard them as descendants of those who beat them. They hate and despise them. And they oppressed them more than they did the Bosnians. In 1989 Slobodan Milošević abolished whatever autonomy Kosovo had enjoyed heretofore. He built his popularity among Serbs on baiting Kosovars.

Hence, it was no surprise that Kosovo declared its independence from Yugoslavia when the Slavic republics did. Throughout the Bosnian War, Belgrade had more urgent problems to worry about than Kosovo. Meanwhile, the Kosovars were preparing themselves for the onslaught that would come. Among them there arose the Kosovo Liberation Army, essentially people who started doing to the Serbs what the Serbs had been doing to the Kosovars, and would soon do in even greater quantity.

Kosovo, even more than Albania, is of little interest to NATO, much less to the United States. But since both had proved unable to resist the temptation to react to images of brutality from Bosnia, it was clear they would not resist the images that would come from the inevitable conflict in Kosovo.

In the spring of 1998 Serbia's Slobodan Milošević, with the cheers of his people, cracked down on Kosovo. Hundreds died and hundreds of thousands were chased from their homes, as often by their Serb neighbors as by Milošević's Interior Ministry. Milošević wanted to eradicate the KLA, cancel any thoughts of independence on the part of the Kosovars, and expand the Serb areas in the province to make them more dominant. NATO diplomats moved in immediately, threatening air strikes unless Milošević ended the violence. In October he agreed to do so and accepted the presence of two thousand NATO military observers in Kosovo—provided they were unarmed. By January the observers were in place, the violence had resumed, and the observers were looking like the hostages they were in fact. So NATO negotiated the presence of a two-thousand-man rescue team in nearby Macedonia ready to rescue the observers.

The failure of this agreement led NATO to demand another one at a February-March conference at Rambouillet, France, that would disarm Serbs and Kosovars and be enforced by armed NATO peacekeepers. Knowing that Milošević would reject disarmament, the KLA accepted it and thereby committed NATO to its side of the war. Now NATO had no alternative but to strike in order to force at least some concessions.

Available to NATO for this campaign were some four hundred aircraft and seven ships that fired cruise missiles. The attacks that began on 24 March 1999 increased gradually in intensity. Gen. Wesley Clark, the operation's commander, said that its objectives were to "disrupt, degrade, devastate, . . . destroy" Serbia's armed forces. But reminiscent of the air war on North Vietnam, the planes and cruise missiles hit only one sector at a time. The military results were not brilliant. Initial claims that one hundred aircraft, four hundred artillery pieces, one hundred fifty tanks, and two hundred fifty armored personnel carriers had been destroyed proved wrong. The Serbs had proved apt at camouflage and deception. Moreover, NATO pilots were ordered not to fly below fifteen thousand feet. This contributed to their safety but degraded accuracy.

The most significant effect of the military bombing campaign, however, was both to rally Serb public opinion behind Milošević and to convince him that the bombing was not doing much damage. This emboldened him to get rid of the Kosovo problem once and for all. He ordered his army and Ministry of the Interior to cleanse most of Kosovo of Albanians. This was ethnic cleansing on a big scale. In response to these horrors NATO started bombing government targets in downtown Belgrade, bridges and factories in civilian areas, and oil-refining facilities. The latter proved most debilitating of all. Support for Milošević evaporated. Milošević had to agree to what he could no longer prevent, namely, the deployment of a NATO peacekeeping force in Kosovo beginning 12 June.

NATO did not stop the violence, never mind achieve a multiethnic Kosovo. In fact it helped to win the war for the Kosovars in general and the KLA in particular. Nearly all the eight hundred thousand Kosovars who had been ethically cleansed returned, to cleanse out about half the Serbs who remained in Kosovo. There would not be much of a future in Kosovo for any Serb. The Muslim world did not so much acknowledge that westerners had saved Muslim lives, as it acknowledged the fact that westerners had involved themselves in the Balkans in a way that avoided getting any of themselves killed.

In the Balkan wars of the '90s the Europeans and Americans did not eliminate any threat to themselves. They interfered in periodic changes within the region's balance of power. They earned the hate of those whom they helped to defeat, and the contempt of those who they helped to win. They established no peace because they did not win any war.

14

THE GULF WAR OF 1990-91

It is magnificent, but it is not war.

FRANCE'S ATTACHÉ AT THE BATTLE OF
BALAKLAVA, 1856

THE WAR IN THE PERSIAN GULF in 1990–91 illustrates again the principles of warfare set forth in this book. The Gulf War's most remarkable features were the mismatches between the two sides' political objectives, military capacities, and strategies. Despite the eye-catching new weapons on the battlefield, this war turned on the political-diplomatic decisions of the top leaders, George Bush and Saddam Hussein. Seldom in the history of war have both sides been so close to victories of such vastly different kinds, only to have their leaders throw them away with a single political decision. Saddam Hussein's Iraq invaded Kuwait on 2 August 1990, for purposes that we still can only speculate about a decade and a half later. President Bush, having decided that the invasion threatened American interests, deployed half a million troops against him. By 23 February 1991, Saddam Hussein had had opportunities to withdraw his troops to safety on his side of the Iraq-Kuwait border and still achieve all he had set out to gain. Instead, he exposed them to pointless destruction. Then, on 28 February, when American and allied troops had almost destroyed the regime that threatened American interests, George Bush stopped the troops, leaving Saddam's regime, and the threat, intact.

Between 17 January 1991 and 28 February 1991, the U.S. armed forces routed and nearly destroyed the Iraqi army in one of the most one-sided events in the history of war. Of the more than half a million Americans who were in the war zone for half a year, 125 were killed in action, fewer than the normal mortality rate for a similar civilian population, while Iraqi deaths were uncountable. Nevertheless the fighting did not resolve the issues of the war; it only clarified them somewhat, in retrospect.

Purposes and Objectives

War is essentially a clash of purposes; only incidentally does it become a clash of arms. From the U.S. point of view, the Gulf War was a clash between the long-standing U.S. policy of opposing the hegemony of any state over the area that supplies much of the world's oil exports and the attempt by Iraq's dictator, Saddam Hussein, to establish such hegemony. The rush of diplomatic and military maneuvers following Iraq's invasion of Kuwait on 2 August 1990 served to obscure these purposes and complicated each side's understanding of exactly what it was doing. Hence, to understand the fundamental clash of purposes we must first consider the long buildup to the war as well as the material and political conditions of battle. We will then examine the battles of the Gulf War, including the contributions of the most remarkable weapons, and finally, the cessation of the fighting and the reshaping of the struggle for hegemony in the Persian Gulf.

Iraqi Purposes

Modern Iraq, a fragment of the Ottoman Empire's demise after World War I, is a small-scale empire. Sunni Arabs make up less than 20 percent of Iraq's population and are located around the capital, Baghdad, in the central valley of the Tigris and Euphrates Rivers. Less than 25 percent of the population is Kurds, an ancient Caucasian mountain people who live along the northern borders. Over half of Iraq's population is made up of Shi'ite Muslims—a few of whom are Persians rather than Arabs—who live in the southern part of the country. In 1932 Britain used its mandate from the League of Nations to give power to a Sunni Muslim king of a Hashemite Arab family (which Britain also set to rule Jordan and Syria). Since then, Iraqi governments have been by, of, and for the Sunni Arab minority. Moreover they have been tumultuous. In 1958 Nasserite national socialists overthrew the monarchy. Starting in 1968, the Ba'ath Party continued a chain of secular military dictatorships whose only purpose seems to have been the dictators' aggrandizement. No ruler of modern Iraq has died a natural death. Since the early 1970s Iraqi dictators have been fueled by high prices for the roughly 3.5 million barrels of oil per day that Western companies pump from Iraqi soil. Roughly one-third of the income from that oil (some twenty billion dollars per year under Saddam) brought the fourth largest stock of military equipment in the world and a world-class secret police system to control the population. Thus, modern Iraq became an increasingly powerful weapon in the hands of men whose politics, both at home and abroad, are those of empire.

In the 1970s Iraq's dictators sought to extend their control over neighboring Iran's oil-rich province of Kuzestan. To this end they harbored the Iranian shah's domestic nemesis, the Shi'ite Ayatollah Khomeini. In 1979 Khomeini overthrew the shah without Iraqi help, but his government looked shaky at home and was a pariah in the world. Hence, Iraq's Saddam Hussein launched what he thought would be a quick war to wrest Kuzestan from Iran. This, the Iran-Iraq War, turned into eight years of bloodletting that yielded insignificant territorial changes.

The Iran-Iraq War, however, filled Iraq with money from the Sunni Arab monarchies of the Gulf, especially Kuwait (afraid of Shi'a power emanating from Iran) and with all manner of support from both the West, which considered Iran an international outlaw, and the Soviet Union, for which Iraq was an ally with access to the Persian Gulf. The U.S. government provided satellite imagery, granted some two billion dollars worth of commodity credits and the liberal transfer of technology, and turned a blind eye on Saddam Hussein's sponsorship of anti-American terrorism. The Soviet government, for its part, regarded Iraq as a natural enemy of the Arab states that were allied with the United States. It supplied the bulk of Iraq's armed forces and actually ran its communications system in exchange for hard currency. German, French, and Italian companies profited from supplying Iraq with the infrastructure of high-technology weaponry, including chemical weaponry and nuclear materials. When, in 1981, Israel bombed Iraq's French-built nuclear reactor to forestall the threat of Iraqi nuclear weapons, the world, led by the United States, expressed nearly unanimous outrage—against Israel. By the end of the war with Iran in 1988, Iraq was bristling with modern armaments and fairly secure that, whatever it did in the region, no outside power would challenge it.

The end of the war, however, found Iraq deeply in debt to Kuwait and Saudi Arabia. These and other regimes in the Persian Gulf, though they do not lack military hardware, are impotent because they lack the capacity to mobilize their peoples. Iraq's dictator, Saddam Hussein, settled on a policy of intimidating them to raise the world price of oil, making it easier for him to repay his debts. Later he demanded that his creditors forgive his debts outright.

Saddam's intimidation was also political. Throughout the war with Iran, Saddam had portrayed himself as the champion of all Arabs against the Persians and of Sunnis against Shi'ites. He had always been the most intransigent of all Arabs against the Jews (not sharing a border with Israel made this cost-free). But beginning in 1988 Saddam also posed as the champion of the Arab man-in-the-street by charging that the rich Arab regimes of the Gulf were stealing the wealth that rightly belonged to all Arabs, and perhaps even all Muslims. For good measure, this most irreligious of politicians accused the Saudi, Kuwaiti, Bahraini, Omani, and other princes of being lax in their duties as Muslims. Saddam's very stridency, backed by his military prowess, caused the Arab masses throughout the Gulf, especially the rootless Palestinians, to take him at his word. They did so regardless of the well-known fact that he himself was an atheist who persecuted Shi'ites and even some Sunnis, lived luxuriously, and had used his country's oil wealth for his own purposes without doing anything for the Palestinians.

Saddam's proximate purpose was to overawe a widening circle of Arab states and thus persuade them to do his will. With a diverse population of only seventeen million, he could not conquer and administer the vast territories of the Gulf, defenseless though they were, never mind the rest of the Arab world. But by making a grisly example of what happened to people who resisted him, he could become the "emperor" of the Gulf, foremost among the Arabs, the man who could set the world price of oil. He had good reason to believe that the United States would not intervene against him. U.S. presidential envoys had come to pay him homage. He was a recipient of U.S. intelligence, and his intelligence service enjoyed the confidence of the CIA. He knew that the U.S. government wanted him to be the champion of U.S. interests in the Gulf and was willing to pay him to be that. On 25 July U.S. Ambassador April Glaspie capped off a long series of official American obsequies (including official apologies for some Americans who had called him a brutal dictator) by stating that the United States had "no opinion" on conflicts between Arabs. Even after the United States intervened following Iraq's invasion of Kuwait, Saddam Hussein repeatedly stated that the intervention would not be decisive.

Saddam's approach to hegemony rested on solid bases: his own control over his people and their wealth, the political and military weaknesses of the rich Arab regimes, the Soviet Union's support, and the United States' apparent disinclination to involve itself decisively in the area.

American Purposes

The U.S. government's path to the Gulf War of 1991 began in October 1956, when it sabotaged Great Britain and France's military attempt to secure their contractual rights in the Suez Canal. Thereafter, much to the U.S. government's chagrin, Britain gave up all its responsibilities "east of Suez." The U.S. government realized that the Arab regimes of the region had neither the political nor the military wherewithal to defend themselves and the oil wealth beneath the sands. Hegemony over the Persian Gulf could give a local dictator power over the world economy. It could have given the Soviet Union a major advantage in the Cold War. The United States, however, had no desire to replace Britain as the protector of the Gulf, so it strove to build Iran into the area's "pillar of stability." The United States invested much in Iran's shah, even acquiescing to his leadership in raising oil prices in the 1970s.

When the shah collapsed in 1978, the United States confronted the possibility of a nightmare scenario. Iran's new anti-American, fundamentalist Islamic regime, possibly with Moscow's support, would intimidate or conquer the weak but wealthy regimes of the Gulf. The world price of oil would be set by enemies of the United States. U.S. Japanese and European allies would have to satisfy this local tyrant or his Soviet backers to get their essential oil supplies. This would be the end of the United States as a world power. To exorcise this specter, President Jimmy Carter enunciated a doctrine according to which the U.S. government would fight to preserve the stability of the region, and he established a central command at McDill Air Force Base in Florida to plan for such a contingency. This command would fight the Gulf War of 1990–91.

Through the 1980s, however, this nightmare scenario receded into the background because Iraq and Iran were fighting a war that incapacitated both. The U.S. government did not then see Iraq as a possible threat that was temporarily being held in check. Instead Iraq was becoming the new "pillar of stability," the United States' latest chosen "regional partner," which could and was supposed to play the role that U.S. foreign policy assigned it. Hence the United States invested almost as much in Iraq as it had in Iran despite mounting evidence that Iraq's dictator had no intention of playing the role of "regional partner." The day before Iraq invaded Kuwait, U.S. Assistant Secretary of State John Kelly testified before Congress that Iraq was a force for peace and stability in the region.

The U.S. government's nightmare scenario of the 1970s was realized when Iraq invaded Kuwait—only the devil was an Arab rather than a Persian. However, the invasion changed the grand design of U.S. policy only slightly. Within hours of the invasion the U.S. government realized that none of the Gulf states would even express objections, never mind resist ulterior Iraqi pressures, unless the United States provided the military muscle to back them up. So the Iraqi bid for hegemony would succeed unless the United States directly caused it to fail. It did not.

This meant that the entire U.S. policy in the region since 1956—to promote stability strictly by doing the bidding of local surrogates—had failed. Nevertheless, the United States hoped that a coalition of regional powers

(Saudi Arabia, bolstered by Egypt and Syria) would claim the role of pillar of stability. In September 1990 Secretary of State James Baker described this new ideal arrangement as akin to NATO, the North Atlantic Treaty Organization, a view that was promptly ridiculed in the U.S. press as "GULFO." To achieve this the United States would need to change Saudi Arabia from a protectee to a protector, make the Egyptians and Saudis stop loathing one another, and turn the Syrian and Egyptian governments into something other than each other's mortal enemies. Cooperation in war against Iraq, reasoned U.S. policymakers, would lower the height of these hurdles.

The U.S. government's purpose in the Gulf was conditioned by President George Bush's intense desire to act not so much as the representative of his country but as that of a "new world order." Ever since the days of President Franklin Roosevelt, the U.S. foreign policy establishment had dreamed that the United States and the Soviet Union together would lead the world to resolve its conflicts through international law. This dream, embodied in the United Nations, was never realized. But in 1990 the U.S. foreign policy establishment's ruling dogma was that the rise of Mikhail Gorbachev in the Soviet Union had made the Soviet regime willing and able to play the role that American idealists had traced for it during World War II. So, as George Bush confronted Saddam Hussein in the Persian Gulf, he deemed the process of having the United States act in concert with the Soviet Union to be more important than the actual results in the Gulf.

George Bush bent U.S. plans, to a lesser extent, to accommodate other allies, like Syria. Interestingly enough, the states that had contributed the most to the U.S. effort in the Gulf—Britain, France, and Italy—did not ask the United States to alter its purposes, while those whose contribution to the war effort was purely symbolic or even counterproductive—the Soviet Union, for example—demanded compromises that precluded serious consideration of the U.S. government's intentions toward the Iraqi regime.

Last but not least, the U.S. government sought to stay out of trouble with the American public, which, it (mistakenly) believed, was disposed to undercut vigorous military action abroad, as it had in the Vietnam War. Hence the U.S. government portrayed its objectives as modest and even regarded detailed discussion of what they might be as a threat in itself. Hence the Bush administration opposed senators who wanted to declare war. In addition, George H. W. Bush did not like explaining things to others, perhaps even to himself. A dozen years later, another President Bush had the same penchant. These several factors converged to complicate the setting of priorities among the U.S. government's purposes in the Gulf.

This book argues that the only reliable guide through the fog of war is an understanding of one's own purposes and from those purposes a reasonable deduction of objectives, so that one can clearly say, "If we can manage to do this and that, then we will have gotten what we wanted, and the whole effort will have been worth it." Our point is that while understanding purposes and objectives does not guarantee victory, failing to understand them virtually guarantees defeat. At crucial points in the Gulf War, Saddam Hussein seemed to have forgotten what he was after. But the United States never decided in the first place.

Objectives

Given their different purposes, the two parties to the Gulf War had to achieve different objectives in order to win. Saddam Hussein invaded Kuwait. Almost immediately—days before the United States decided to intervene and weeks before significant numbers of U.S. troops arrived—that is, long before they met any obstacle, never mind faced any threat—his forces dug into defensive positions. There is no evidence that Saddam ever planned to invade Saudi Arabia. On the contrary, during August and most of September, his fresh, well-supplied, million-man, armored army might have tried to overrun the few thousand lightly armed U.S. forces that had taken defensive positions in the Saudi desert. And he knew that because new U.S. troops were flooding in by the tens of thousands every week, any offensive military plans had best be executed quickly. But Iraqi troops never stopped digging in. Saddam obviously figured that he had already met all the military objectives he needed to achieve his long-term purpose—whatever that might have been.

Did Saddam think that victory meant holding on to Kuwait, while giving it up meant defeat? The evidence is ambiguous. Saddam Hussein divided Kuwait into two parts. He annexed to Iraq's Basra province the northeastern edge, including much of Kuwait's oil wealth and the two islands that control access to the mouth of the Tigris and Euphrates Rivers. The Iraqi army treated inhabitants of these areas relatively well, and caused no physical damage. The rest of Kuwait Saddam called "the nineteenth province of Iraq." Every other province has a name. This one only got a number. Worse, Iraq's Republican Guard looted and destroyed this part of Kuwait. It is reasonable to conclude that Saddam meant to give up the "nineteenth province" at some point, but to keep the oilfields and the islands.

The physical control of any part of Kuwait, however, was not essential to Saddam's purposes. Of course, being able to keep some territory taken by force majeure would have enhanced Saddam's intimidating image. But the brutal demolition of a neighboring state and the prospect that he could repeat this at will were the essential parts of that image. This image, not

Kuwaiti territory itself, would give Saddam a big slice of the revenues of the Persian Gulf and the leadership of the Arab world. Thus by August, victory was Saddam's to lose.

The U.S. deployment first of a quarter million, then of a half million troops to the Persian Gulf gave Saddam the chance to achieve yet another objective: to pose as the world-class Arab leader who had stood up to mighty America. This image would have magnified his real and growing military power (Iraq was close to manufacturing a nuclear bomb) as well as his political assets.

Saddam Hussein's objectives in the crisis, therefore, did not require further military action. He would achieve his objectives simply by allowing his several images to grow. Time was on his side. The Persian Gulf was his home. The Americans could not and would not stay long. After they left, the region's leaders would have to treat him as the winner. It mattered little how he might get Bush out of there. The point was to get him out. This could be done easily enough without fighting.

What would George Bush have to do to win in 1990–91? Simply put, he would have had to eliminate Iraq as a contender for regional hegemony—quickly and definitively—in a way that would have discouraged others who were similarly inclined. The United States could not be expected to deploy a half million troops to the other side of the globe on a regular basis.

The complexity of President Bush's purposes—the "new world order"— complicated U.S. objectives. The Soviet Union, long allied with Saddam Hussein, would have no part in trying to overthrow him. Syria thought it unseemly for a non-Arab country to interfere in the affairs of Arab Iraq. Moreover, Syria, like Iraq, was ruled by the Ba'ath Party. Saudi Arabia, home of Sunni Muslim orthodoxy, craved the overthrow of Saddam but feared the domination of Iraq by Shi'ites. Also, Bush did not want to be accused of assassination, an anti-Arab attitude, imperialism, or getting "bogged down" in the Gulf. Bush wanted victory, but there were no military objectives that could win him victory without overthrowing the Iraqi government, upsetting Iraq's internal power balance, undoing the Ba'ath Party, or killing its leader—none of which things he was willing to do. Hence he took America into a war in which none of these things would be done.

The first U.S. objective, drawing a "line in the sand" to protect Saudi Arabia (hence the operation's title, Desert Shield), was obviously self-defeating. The United States could protect Saudi Arabia against a triumphant Iraq only for as long as it could maintain the "line in the sand"— practically, a matter of months. Adoption of that objective is prima facie evidence of incompetence. The second objective, the liberation of Kuwait, addressed the Iraqi threat only tangentially. In response to this objective, Saddam could have withdrawn his troops behind the Kuwaiti borders at any time and said to the Americans, "You've got what you want. Why don't you go home, you imperialists!" Hence some Americans sought to interpret this objective broadly. Within the White House there was no shortage of hopes that, in the course of a fight with Iraq, the United States could smash the Iraqi armed forces as well as Iraq's capacity for nuclear and chemical warfare. But the Soviet Union, and others with a narrower interpretation, agreed only to add to their demands of Iraq words such as "reparations," "punishment of war criminals," and "regional stability" that were too vague to authorize U.S. troops to accomplish any such things. Because publicly declared U.S. objectives never went beyond the liberation of Kuwait, Saddam fought the war with the inestimable advantage of being able to call a halt any time that the course of events threatened his vital interests. He never did.

In short, the U.S. government never formulated a set of objectives that, if achieved, would have satisfied the purposes for which it entered the war. Rather, while official Washington fluctuated between various formulations of war aims, the U.S. armed forces' preparations to win the battle against the Iraqi armed forces became objectives in themselves. In the end, the logical link between what the U.S. government wanted in the Gulf and what the U.S. armed forces did there remained as tenuous as that between winning battles and winning wars.

The Material and Political Conditions of Battle

Kuwait and much of southern Iraq are flat desert (the marshy part was hardly involved in the battle). The desert imposes certain conditions on battle: hiding is very difficult; supply lines are exceptionally important, long, and exposed; weapons of all kinds find their marks more easily; engagements are quick and destructive; and airpower is dominant. Indeed, the very notion that airpower could be decisive was developed by Italy's Gen. Giulio Douhet the first time the airplane was ever used in battle, in the Libyan campaign of 1912. While the so-called airpower theory (see chapter 6) has been misapplied to a variety of circumstances, it is fully valid for the desert context in which it was developed. And while the invention of precision-guided munitions has multiplied the effectiveness of airpower everywhere, in the desert, PGMs have magnified airpower exponentially.

The desert devalues the holding of territory, rewards maneuver, and makes the destruction of the enemy force or its supplies the natural focus of battle. There is no need, therefore, for an army to defend its ground against an attacker if it can withdraw along its own supply lines and then, when the attacker's momentum is spent, quickly turn astride the enemy's lines.

If, however, an army controls the air, what its opponent does hardly matters. If the opponent chooses to attack, the army can withdraw while its airplanes destroy the opponent's exposed troops, armor, and supplies. By attacking, the opponent trades security for the dubious pleasure of advancing over useless territory while being decimated from the air. If, on the other hand, the opponent chooses to shield its men and equipment in bunkers, the army need only use airpower to deprive him of food, water, munitions, coordination, and hope. Little by little, bombs will dig out the bunkers and those in them. Most important, if the enemy digs himself into the sand while others control the air, he makes himself irrelevant except to that spot of sand.

Iraq put a large, well-equipped army in and around Kuwait: 12 armored and mechanized and 14 infantry divisions, totaling some 540,000 men and 4,280 tanks, including 500 excellent Soviet T-72s. Iraq's artillery, including 100 South African G-5 field guns, outranged and outclassed anything the United States had.

The superior range of artillery, however, is irrelevant when that artillery is exposed to attack from the air. So it was with Iraq, whose five hundred combat aircraft, including excellent Soviet MiG-29s and French F-1s, were at an insurmountable disadvantage vis-à-vis the U.S. air forces. America's air-superiority fighters—the Navy's F-14 and the Air Force's F-15—were as good as or better than the Iraqis' best; Iraq's air-superiority fighters were outnumbered; and more important, the United States could direct its fighters to the most advantageous positions for intercepts, because only they had aircraft with airborne warning and control systems (AWACS), which can fly far behind the lines, protected by the fighters to which they give the edge. Iraq could not even protect its limited, ground-based capacity to guide interceptor aircraft, its "ground control interceptor (GCI) radars," which were smashed by American cruise missiles and other aircraft at the outset of the war. Indeed, because it was always clear that Iraq's radars would be the war's first casualties, it was always clear that the United States would quickly gain control of the air—with everything that implies in the desert.

On 2 August 1990 the United States had no combat troops or planes in Saudi Arabia. By February 1991 the United States had 541,000 men and women, organized into ten Army divisions and three Marine divisions, including about twenty air wings, more than one hundred combat ships, and many other units. America's combat equipment included 1,200 M1A1 tanks, 270 Apache attack helicopters, 1,800 assorted tactical aircraft, including 44 F-117 radar-evading fighter-bombers and 2 squadrons of old but heavy-lifting B-52 bombers. No list could do justice to the massive amount of American equipment and to the existence of a high-technology solution for almost every imaginable combat task. Each U.S. armored division in combat needs 555,000 gallons of fuel and 5,000 tons of ammunition per day. All other armies make do with far less. The logistical feats of the U.S. armed forces in the Persian Gulf in 1990–91 dwarfed those of the U.S. troops Vietnam, which in turn dwarfed those of U.S. forces in World War II, which far outdid anything that any other nation had ever done to supply its fighting forces. *War, American style, means the extra-superabundance of things.* The Americans had rocket-propelled, exploding ropes that detonate land mines ahead of troops, fuel-air explosives, and huge plows for clearing minefields on land (but alas, nothing with which to clear sea mines under fire). They had food, health care, and amenities on a truly American scale. For each of the roughly half million Americans on the ground in the area of operation, the U.S. government transported nineteen tons of cargo!

Not least of the material conditions of battle were the time and safety that the United States had to assemble and order all that material into a war machine. Iraq never made a serious attempt to disrupt the Americans' rear. Thus, even while civilians in Baghdad and the Iraqis in their bunkers in Kuwait had been deprived of safe drinking water because of air assault, Americans were snacking at hamburger and soda stands in the desert and setting up makeshift football stadiums for recreation. Finally, the Americans' material advantages were magnified by their ability to deploy out of sight of Iraqi aircraft, whereas all of Iraq's dispositions took place under American surveillance—a case of one material advantage, airpower, compounding others.

The deployment of Iraqi forces was both a material and a political condition of battle. In Kuwait itself the forward fortifications were filled with poorly fed, armed, and trained draftees who were motivated primarily by threats of death for desertion. Behind them were Iraq's regular forces, ranking somewhat higher by these measures. Behind them were the Republican Guard divisions—the best-trained, best-equipped, highest-paid soldiers, drawn from families with a personal stake in the fortunes of Saddam Hussein. Saddam's idea was for the people of Iraq to bear the brunt of any fighting while those loyal to the regime would gather the glory and, ultimately, retain the capacity to control Iraq on its dictator's behalf. Saddam Hussein's overriding political priority was the survival and prominence of those who were ready and willing to kill fellow Iraqis for his sake.

Nevertheless, Saddam's deployment was a gamble—in strictly military terms, a bad one. Iraq deployed its troops in deeply bunkered positions, obviously expecting heavy bombardment from the air. But by digging the flower of the army into the Kuwaiti sands, *where they would be immobi-*

lized by U.S. airpower, the Iraqis took the chance that these troops would become irrelevant to any move that U.S. troops might make against the regime in Baghdad, or to any U.S.-backed revolt by Iraqi Kurds or Shi'ites. *Iraq's troop deployments in Kuwait made sense only given the assumption that the United States would take the most inefficient of all possible approaches to the conflict—to focus on Kuwait rather than on Iraq itself.* Saddam often mentioned U.S. political constraints, and could only have been impressed by George Bush's promise to the Iraqi people that he would not interfere in their internal affairs. In other words, Saddam Hussein had his own political priorities straight, and bet on George Bush not having *his* straight. Saddam's bet paid off. However one might fault Saddam's judgment, Bush's, Cheney's, Scowcroft's, and Powell's were worse.

The politics of America's involvement in the Gulf were on two levels, the public's and the politicians'. During August, September, and the first half of October 1990, the American people strongly supported sending troops against Saddam Hussein. By mid-October, however, both the American people and the troops themselves started to suspect that their leaders had no plan, that the commitment was pointless and endless. Support for the whole affair plummeted. It picked up again once President Bush set a deadline of 15 January 1991 for Iraq to remove its troops from Kuwait. When the fighting actually started, on 17 January 1991, political support sky-rocketed and remained high for the duration of the fighting.

The political perceptions of President Bush, his advisers, and Congress were muddled. Their political calculations stressed the United Nations, the Soviet Union, the Arab states, and the U.S. experience in Vietnam twenty years before. These considerations, however, while they loomed large in the minds of some American elites, evidently meant almost nothing to the average American. By February 1991 no public opinion poll recorded fewer than 80 percent of respondents in favor of killing Saddam Hussein or overthrowing his government. The difficulties that American leaders had in setting objectives came from their own minds, not from the American people. President Bush feared it might be bad politics to ask Congress to approve the use of force in the Persian Gulf, and when he did, the Democratic Party thought it would be good politics to oppose the request. Both were mistaken. Congress approved the request, and the Democrats suffered politically for having opposed it.

Both material and political factors combined to give the U.S. government the broadest possible latitude. It could do whatever it wanted to win. Saddam, however, could win only if the United States, despite having both the political and military power to overthrow his regime, chose to pursue another objective. Since its enemy had no political or military weaknesses, Saddam could rely only on the muddleheaded thinking of its leaders.

Winning the Battle

Iraq's leaders had no military strategy. In fighting the Americans, their tanks and planes would only be destroyed; in no imaginable way could they serve a useful military purpose. The usefulness of any survivor would begin after the Americans' eventual departure for home. In the meantime, Iraqi airplanes would stay in their bunkers and not challenge the Americans' control of the air. If and when this became unsafe, Saddam would send them to a friendly neutral country (in this case, Iran), just as he had sent them to Jordan at the low point in the Iran-Iraq War. As for the tanks, the old ones would be cannon fodder. The war would have to stop before the new ones were destroyed. The war would have to be won by George Bush's inhibitions. There was no other way. Whatever its flaws, this was a strategy to win the war according to Saddam's lights—as best we can surmise.

The U.S. government's military strategy was summed up by President Bush's top military adviser, Gen. Colin Powell, when he said, "First we are going to cut it off, then we are going to kill it." The remark, specifically about Iraq's Republican Guard, applied to all Iraqi forces in Kuwait and southern Iraq. This, however, was a strategy for winning a battle, not a war. The U.S. government's political objectives, to maintain the coalition of states supporting the use of force against Iraq, did not amount to a war-winning strategy either. In fairness, George Bush thought that the "new world order" was the primordial end, and that building the widest possible coalitions was the proper means to that end.

The U.S. government struck Iraq at 2:30 AM, 17 January 1991. Apache helicopters flew long and low to destroy Iraqi early warning radars, thus clearing the way for American cruise missiles and aircraft to hit targets in the Baghdad area by surprise. During the first day, Allied forces flew seventeen hundred sorties and lost three aircraft to ground fire—below the accident rate for exercises. During the first day of the bombing campaign the allies bombed primarily "command and control" targets—radars, communications facilities, and headquarters, but also airfields and antiaircraft sites—making it even easier to wreak further destruction later. The first day's targets also included Iraqi facilities known to be used for the manufacture and storage of chemical weapons, as well as buildings where materials for Iraq's first nuclear bomb were being readied. These were hit immediately so that even if Saddam had decided to stop the war, they would not be in his arsenal for years to come. Finally, the first day's targets included some thirty launch sites for Iraq's Soviet-supplied SCUD-B surface-to-surface missiles—Iraq's sole and feeble means of striking out beyond artillery range.

On the second day of the war, after Saddam fired the first of eighty-one SCUD missiles at Saudi Arabia and Israel, the allied air forces began to devote a disproportionate number of sorties to seeking and destroying SCUDs. These massive efforts largely failed. Iraq launched SCUDs until the last day of the war. Although about sixty were intercepted by U.S. air-defense missiles (hitting the missile bodies so close to the targets that the warheads fell on them anyway, leading critics to claim that the intercepts never happened) the SCUD turned out to be Iraq's most effective offensive weapon, causing twenty-eight American deaths. But this was not close to being significant.

The bombing campaign progressed to include Iraq's modern infrastructure: the electric grid, water systems, roads and bridges, and trucks. Then U.S. Navy and Air Force planes methodically destroyed the Iraqi armed forces by collapsing their bunkers. The Republican Guard divisions got particular attention from giant B-52 bombers, each of whose raids covered a square kilometer. The bombing had cut the Iraqi army into pieces and was killing it piece by piece. But how fast?

During much of February a sterile debate took place in the United States over whether the bombing had degraded Iraq's combat effectiveness by 50, 30, or 10 percent. The answers bandied about depended less on differing damage assessments made from photographs than on subjective evaluations of how Iraqi soldiers had been affected by reduced rations of food and water and by their helpless confinement under fire. Most of all, the assessments depended on subjective views of how effective Iraqi units might have been originally. But surely their effectiveness would always have depended on the quality of their opponents. Given what the United States was preparing to hit them with, Iraq's armed forces might not have made a good show even at full strength.

The essence of U.S. tactics, the AirLand Strategy, which originated in the late 1970s to deal with Soviet forces in central Europe, consists of minute coordination among tanks, artillery, infantry, helicopters, and fixed-wing planes. The idea is for units to move and shoot so that they cover each other, and so that the enemy never has a chance to meet any of them directly. But AirLand was designed to work against a numerically superior, electronically sophisticated enemy who would be fighting for control of the air in a foggy, semiforested environment. In the desert, against an enemy semistarved and cut off, totally lacking airpower and mobility, numerically inferior, AirLand would be little more than a live-fire exercise. The Americans could count on being on top of the Iraqis with one weapon or another from beginning to end.

The so-called ground war began on 23 February 1991. After the war the main allied thrust, carried out by three divisions of the XVIII Army

Corps and two divisions from Britain and France, was innovative. It swept far to the west of the main Iraqi fortifications in Kuwait and hit the Republican Guard divisions from the side near the southern Iraqi city of Basra, cutting off their retreat. But to outflank enemy forces through rapid movement is a time-tested tactic. It usually produces maximum disorganization of the enemy at a minimum of casualties by avoiding bloody frontal assaults. In this case the maneuver shattered the Iraqi army at the cost of a dozen American lives.

It is important to note, however, that U.S. forces also performed _frontal_ assaults that turned out to be just as shattering and resulted in an equally low number of U.S. casualties. The reason is that the Americans' ability to fire accurately on a target from fixed-wing, then rotary-wing aircraft, stopping only when the target is already at the mercy of tanks or infantry, turned out to be more important than the direction of the attack. Because the Americans were able to suppress enemy fire, they were able to deal with minefields and fortifications as if these were engineering problems rather than military ones. Moreover, airpower had already produced one of the major benefits of an enveloping attack, namely, that of cutting off the enemy.

On the other hand, one of the main benefits of large, enveloping maneuvers, trapping the enemy, was utterly lost when President Bush unilaterally ordered a "temporary" cease-fire on 28 February 1991. Airpower had pinned down the Republican Guard, the AirLand attacks had flushed it out, and the fastest, best-supplied, armored flanking maneuver in history had trapped it. But Bush's decision saved it by letting it escape.

Inexplicable Decisions

It is possible to chronicle, but not to explain, both Saddam Hussein's decision to refuse the Soviet Union's offers to end the war in a way that would have left him the winner and George Bush's decision on 28 February 1991 to declare victory unilaterally and thereby to deprive himself of it.

Each decision, however, had to do with the Soviet Union. By continuing to supply Iraq's military with about a dozen daily cargo flights between 2 August 1990 and 15 January 1991, Gorbachev exercised only minimal military influence on the battlefield. Yet he exercised great and almost decisive political influence throughout the conflict by helping convince George Bush to accept Soviet blessings for U.S. actions in exchange for a pledge that Bush would do nothing of which the Soviet Union disapproved. Thus, in September Bush set the liberation of Kuwait as the U.S. government's maximum goal. Thereafter Moscow's propaganda outlets held him to it by continually accusing the United States of "going beyond" this goal. Immediately prior to the start of U.S. hostilities on 15 January 1991, Gorbachev offered to support Saddam's claims in the region in exchange for Iraq's withdrawal from Kuwait. On 23 January 1991 Soviet Foreign Minister Bessmertnykh convinced U.S. Secretary of State James Baker to restate publicly that the United States would cease hostilities as soon as Saddam announced that Iraqi troops were leaving Kuwait. Between 15 February and 23 February 1991, the Soviet Union publicly offered to guarantee the integrity of Saddam's government and its immunity from sanctions and to support its agenda, if Iraqi troops would leave Kuwait. President Bush's ultimatum to Iraq on 22 February differed from the Soviet offer only in timing and tone. Had Saddam complied, the Iraqi army would have stood on Kuwaiti and Saudi borders more formidable than ever because of its Soviet shield, while the half million Americans would have been transformed from a projection of force into an impotent laughingstock. And yet Saddam refused to move. We still have no idea why.

The four days following 23 February 1991 were ones of unalloyed triumph for American arms. Iraqi soldiers crawled out of their bunkers to hug the knees and kiss the hands of their American captors. A few of the Republican Guard fought as best they could against an overwhelming enemy, while the majority joined the hordes of Iraqis fleeing madly either to their homes or to American lines. This was far more than a military rout or the disintegration of an army. In fact, a substantial part of the Iraqi people was delighted to be relieved of Saddam's yoke and eager to take up arms against him. By the fourth day, it seemed that those Iraqis who were intent on toppling Saddam would encounter little opposition, because the allied armies had cut off all Iraqi forces in the vicinity of Kuwait. Baghdad lay 150 miles—less than a day's drive—away.

The two lightly armed Republican Guard divisions in Baghdad, bereft of air cover, could not have put up a fight against the allies. Moreover, gripped by panic, they might well have killed Saddam to save themselves. So Bush could have pushed on to Baghdad to topple Saddam or to cover those who would do the toppling, or just to see whether someone would thereby be encouraged to do so. Or he could have offered safety to those Iraqi troops who stopped in their tracks—effectively eliminating the Iraqis trapped in the south and subverting those elsewhere who Saddam would order to fight the rebellions. Instead, Bush simply declared victory.

Ironically, even as Bush was effectively handing Iraq back to Saddam, he encouraged the Iraqi people to try to overthrow him. Why would Bush encourage attempts to do something that he was making impossible? Some have suggested that Bush was intrigued by the thought of limiting the war to one hundred hours, a round figure. Others suggest that Bush did not want to see the low number of U.S. casualties rise even incrementally.

Whether or not these were Bush's reasons, it makes no sense for anyone to limit a war for reasons such as these, or to take actions that work against each others' logic. Nor is it mercy to avoid new casualties at the cost of making vain the sacrifices of those already fallen. Bush's own explanation was that once Kuwait had been liberated, the job had been done. Subsequent events showed that the job had not been done.

Ending the War

The aftermath of the fighting had two stages. During the first, everyone in the region believed that the U.S. government retained the will to bring down Saddam Hussein. The second stage began when everyone realized that the United States would not do it and that it was irrevocably withdrawing the capacity to do it.

In the aftermath of the cease-fire, Iraqi Shi'ites in the south and Kurds in the north rebelled against Saddam's government. The United States declared that any Iraqi aircraft or helicopter that flew against the rebels would be shot down. The absence of air cover weakened the Iraqi army both physically and, perhaps most important, psychologically. By contrast, the rebels felt they had the wind in their sails. By roughly 8 March 1991, the rebellion had taken Iraq's second city, Basra, the capital of the Shi'ite south. In the north, Kurdish rebels quickly evicted the army from all of Kurdistan, including the oil cities of Kirkuk and Mosul on its edge.

Had the United States continued to deprive the Iraqi army of air cover, its local commanders might have struck deals with the rebels, and its senior officers in Baghdad might have moved against Saddam. The United States could have augmented the anti-Saddam forces by releasing prisoners of war as individuals, with their weapons, rather than turning them over to the Iraqi government. If the United States had simply decreed a nationwide cease-fire ("Any troops that move will be bombed") there would have been a de facto partitioning of Iraq, and each of the three parts would have had bargaining power vis-à-vis the others. Instead, the U.S. government let the Iraqi government use all its power to put down the rebellions. Thus ended the first stage, during which the United States could have reaped the fruits of victory.

Beginning after about 15 March 1991, as American troops were being withdrawn, Saddam Hussein crushed the rebellions, defiantly reestablished himself as a point of reference in the region, and made it impossible for the United States to benefit from its military success. By the rule "I slaughter, therefore I am," Saddam reestablished his authority at home and some of the regional prestige that he had lost in the military rout. The Republican

Guard, having escaped the Americans through no merit of its own, took out its rage on Shi'ite and Kurdish civilians. They shelled them and rolled over them, raped and murdered so genocidally as to send millions fleeing for the nearest border. The borders nearest the Kurds were snowy mountains, where they died at the rate of up to one thousand per day. President Bush had claimed a great moral victory, but Saddam's conspicuous carnage seemed to show that this victory had made things worse. The Bush administration equivocated. It extended humanitarian aid to the refugees under U.S. military protection, while doing its best to withdraw that protection as soon as Saddam—and the refugees—would allow that to happen without embarrassing the president before American voters.

As time passed, the fundamentals of the situation became unmistakable. UN peacekeeping troops soon replaced Americans in town after town. Within hours of the Iraqi secret police tightening its grip on an area, pro-Saddam posters would appear on the walls, and ordinary people would refuse to be seen with reporters. Saddam himself soon appeared before dutifully cheering crowds, firing his pistol in the air and yelling, "Listen, Bush!" At the very least, Saddam had retained the power to embarrass George Bush and to make American people ask, "What did we win, anyway?"

That question was underlined by the Saudi and Kuwaiti governments. Far from exhibiting gratitude at having been saved, their racially haughty attitude toward the "inferior" Arabs of Egypt instantly drove Egypt out of the role of surrogate protector of the Gulf that American policy had traced for it. Also, when the U.S. government asked the Saudis to take the lead in eliminating the Arab world's state of war with Israel, the Saudis responded by adding another hundred American companies to the list of those whom Saudis boycott because they do business in Israel. The Saudis eliminated their subsidies to the Palestine Liberation Organization for a few years. (When George Bush's son became U.S. president, the Saudis persuaded *him* to subsidize the PLO directly.) Immediately the Saudis increased their subsidy to Syria, which used it as a basis for redoubling its anti-Israeli animosity and for virtually annexing Lebanon. Then, of course, the Saudis cut production of crude oil enough to cause the price to rise roughly to the level of August 1990, before Saddam's occupation of Kuwait was challenged. One reason why they had to be aggressive on oil and Israel, explained the Saudis, was that Saddam had renewed his propaganda to the Arab masses, charging Saudi Arabia with being a tool of the Zionists and the Americans. Eventually, in the mid-1990s the Saudis resumed their subsidies of Iraq.

Thus the Gulf War was a desert storm indeed—blowing the sands around, but changing nothing.

Intelligence, Morality, and the Sense of War

President Bush certainly had the military means and the political latitude to achieve a different outcome. What was missing? Strategic intelligence was certainly inadequate (by contrast, the closer to the battlefield, the better U.S. intelligence was). For reasons that this book explains and that apply around the world, U.S. intelligence did not have agents in Iraq to report on Saddam Hussein's intentions. Nor did strategic communications intelligence supply any hard facts about either Saddam's intentions or any coordination between Iraq and the Soviet Union. So the United States fought a war without hard knowledge of what the enemy was after. Moreover, American intelligence analysts drew the wrong conclusions from circumstantial evidence—that Iraq would not attack Kuwait, that it would attack Saudi Arabia, that it would not attack Israel, and that the Soviet Union was on America's side, to mention just a few. Against a major league enemy, such lapses of intelligence are usually fatal.

Nevertheless, lack of information cannot be blamed for President Bush's failure to focus American military power on Saddam and his regime rather than on Iraqi forces in Kuwait. Events themselves made clear that Saddam's plans for hegemony rested on his long-term control of his country, and that politics would be his chief wapon of mass destruction.

No doubt, President Bush and his entourage lacked a sense of moral proportion when they insisted, truthfully, that they had no intention of targeting Saddam Hussein "or any individual," while at the same time they were killing Iraqi soldiers by the tens of thousands, plus uncounted civilians who happened to be in the wrong place at the wrong time. The only justification for killing people in war is that they somehow embody the evil purpose the war is being fought to defeat. But draftees—not to mention civilians—embody the purposes of war hardly at all, especially under dictatorships. The practical rule of justice and effectiveness in war is to target the officers and spare the subordinates. By contrast, American forces killed thousands of people who meant little or nothing to the issue of the war, while sparing the one man who meant everything.

Hence Bush and his entourage unjustly served a just cause. Justice in war depends not only on the cause and on the proportionality of means used to ends sought, but also on the existence of reasonable plans for achieving good ends. Various accounts of the Bush administration's decision making, however, show that these high officials never considered the long-term consequences of heavily damaging the Iraqi army while leaving Saddam's regime intact. They realized that their predecessors in the Vietnam War had failed both morally and practically when they sent soldiers into harm's way but did not let them win. This time they let them "win" by beating the hell out of the army in front of them. But Bush and his entourage failed to determine what, if anything, they were winning. And so, they lost and stored up a worse war for America.

This is more than a failure of moral imagination. After all, no sooner had American troops come into contact with Iraqi civilians and prisoners of war than they were almost swept into a spontaneous rebellion against Saddam. At that point, President Bush made a considered choice to save the Iraqi regime, threatening the lives of Saddam's opponents and devaluing all the sacrifices he had imposed on Americans and Iraqis alike. Bush acted in part to assuage the Saudis and Soviets who, for vastly different reasons, wanted to maintain the Iraqi mini-empire. Bush hoped that the fighting had sufficiently weakened Saddam (and had sufficiently strengthened international cooperation) to allow international economic sanctions and embargoes henceforth to contain Iraq, and he hoped that the Saudis and the Soviets would do their part to help.

Surely, though, the war did not end when U.S. troops withdrew. Instead it moved into the shadowy channels of international commercial intrigue, arms-control agreements, and terrorism—fields in which the United States showed far less prowess than on the battlefield.

"No one," wrote Carl von Clausewitz in his book *On War,* ought to start a war "without first being clear in his mind what he intends to achieve by that war and how he intends to conduct it." This book argues that war is less the shooting of guns than the designation of objectives. The most important act in any war is to formulate one's objectives. To fight battles, even brilliantly, on the basis of ill-considered objectives is to build castles on sand.

15

TERROR AND IRAQ

Forgive them, for they know not what
they do.

                                    JESUS CHRIST

O<small>N 20 SEPTEMBER 2001</small>, after nineteen men had crashed three airliners in America, killing some three thousand innocents along with themselves, President George W. Bush told the Congress that America was at
war. The enemy was terrorism. But making war against an abstract noun
that refers to a tool of war is, literally, nonsense. Operations of war can aim
only at human beings. But which ones does it make sense to kill or constrain? The meaning of any war depends upon the answer to that. So what
could a war on terror be?

Bush said that the war would "bring the terrorists to justice." But since
the terrorists of 9/11 died in the act, as do many if not most of their sort,
America's war could not be against them. Moreover, if the war were to
consist of pursuing surviving perpetrators, it would be but a police drag-
net, not a war at all. More important, how could the capture of yesterday's
perpetrators shut off the supply of tomorrow's?

Bush also indicated that in this war America would make no distinction between terrorists and those who consort with them. And indeed people
aplenty exist who inspire, recruit, supply, benefit from, and harbor terrorists in countless ways. The war could and should be against them. But just
what relationship with terrorism qualifies any of them as the enemies whose
demise would yield victory in America's war? And of what would victory
consist? No U.S. official attempted an answer. Such answers might be bet-

320 AR: ENDS AND MEANS

ter, or worse. But without any answers the war was to be fought in a fog of fantasies.

Nevertheless, millions of soldiers, sailors, and marines have acted. Over two thousand have died in action while killing more than ten times that number. The military holds some five hundred captives and the CIA some three dozen. There is no public evidence that any of them have done harm. But it is self-evident that their incarceration has not diminished terrorism. All major U.S. military operations have been successful. Yet the U.S. government continues to tighten security measures. No one speculates whom else Americans should kill or capture to be safe from terror.

On 20 March 2003 the United States attacked Iraq. By 9 April Baghdad was in U.S. hands. By 13 December so was Iraq's dictator, Saddam Hussein. What did this have to do with eliminating terrorist attacks against Americans? For the better part of a year Bush had built support for a war to eliminate Iraq's weapons of mass destruction. On 21 October 2002 he had implied that if Iraq's regime rid itself of such weapons, it would not be America's enemy. Yet when the invasion took place, it did so on other grounds, under the label Operation Iraqi Freedom—its ostensible purpose being the liberation of oppressed Iraqis. Later, after no stocks of weapons of mass destruction had been found, President Bush described the operation as the central front in the war on terrorism. Yet his administration never decided between the CIA's conclusion that there was little relationship between Iraq and anti-American terror, and the Defense Department's view that Iraq and kindred regimes are the essence of it.

Later yet, as President Bush campaigned for reelection in 2004, he argued that America's strategy for ridding the world of terrorism was to change the culture of the Middle East. Yet while history records victorious wars that have forced cultural changes on the losers, it knows of none in which the winners have won by changing the enemy's culture. Meanwhile, Senator John Kerry, the alternative to Bush in the 2004 election, argued that it had been wrong to make war on Iraq and promised victory in the war on terror. But since he argued that the war should consist solely of killing those who have committed terrorist acts and of tightening domestic security, what could victory have meant? By 2005, as various Iraqis fought one another, Americans were caught in the middle.

In sum, neither Thucydides nor Machiavelli nor Clausewitz would have recognized any of the above as war. In their tradition, this book has argued that mere violence does not make a war. And yet the events of 11 September 2001 were part of a war against America that had begun perhaps two decades before. In chapter 9 we described the tool of war called terrorism and mentioned who has used this tool against America in indirect warfare. Our task herein is to describe how the U.S. government has actually conducted what it calls "the war on terrorism," as well as the war in Iraq and, in parallel, to contrast this conduct with the principles of warfare.

Is There a War?

Terrorist acts had been killing Americans since the 1970s. But only after 9/11 did the U.S. government recognize them as part of a war. Since 1990 terrorism has been carried out in part by people and organizations that had done the same things during the Cold War (Yasir Arafat, Abu Nidal, Saddam Hussein). Their condemnations of America acquired an Islamic overlay but otherwise changed little. The Islamist movement joined this war after 1980, and its involvement has been mushrooming since 1990. But, the Islamists, like the secularists, live and act within states whose regimes do not tolerate countercurrents. States and regimes enable this war at the very least. At worst, they wage it.

However, while the U.S. government condemns "states that support terrorism," and information about who embodies what cause and where they do it is common knowledge, the United States is reluctant to impute responsibility for any terrorist act to any state. As our discussion of indirect warfare pointed out, various fears and internal interests contribute to this reluctance. Hence while United States officials in the 1980s talked of terrorism in terms of "state sponsorship," in 1993 the United States officially took the position that terrorist acts are the responsibility not of states but of "shadowy networks." Necessarily, this has focused intelligence about terrorism on the perpetrators, officially assuming that states and regimes—with the exception of Afghanistan's from 1996 to 2001—may be faulted only for insufficient zeal in pursuing them. But the images and the casualties of 9/11—iconic buildings utterly destroyed, thousands killed, tens of thousands running for their lives, traffic clogged as people fled America's cities—looked too much like war to call what was going on anything else. George W. Bush did not change the position that terrorist acts are not the responsibility of the states whose causes they further and from which they come. America's war would be against shadowy things.

Who Is the Enemy?

On 12 September CIA director George Tenet told President George W. Bush that Osama bin Laden had been responsible for the previous day's events, "game, set, and match," on the basis of broadcast statements on the part of his associates expressing glee at them, as well as because he had become an icon of anti-American violence. But countless other Arabs who had contact with the perpetrators and who had previous involvement with killers of Americans expressed similar glee. One can only wonder what a U.S. trial of bin Laden on the charge of responsibility for 9/11 would have been like. More to the point, imputing to bin Laden the role of artificer in chief of terrorism tended to identify the phenomenon with one man and his "shadowy network" and to focus the war on them. The absurdity of this became clear as he disappeared, most of his associates were killed or captured, and terrorism increased.

Obviously, in cases where the perpetrators sacrifice their lives, the identity of those who piloted the plane, set the bomb, or pulled the trigger is irrelevant to the question, who's the enemy? The ulterior question—who else is responsible?—overlaps "who's the enemy?" only partly, if approached in legal terms. The trigger pullers will have had relationships with any number of persons and will have been inspired by others whom they never even met. Arguments could be made that any such persons made possible the terrorist act in question. But in civilized courts of law, "conspiracy" is difficult to prove, and rightly so. How much contact or help makes any person responsible for another's act? How closely tied to the act in question must such help be? How does one argue, much less prove, that any such person even knew what the trigger puller was going to do? And if one argues that person A inspired person B to kill, one had better have documents or witnesses that detail the time, place, and manner of incitement to kill person X rather than Y. In war, however, such questions obscure the main point.

The fruitful line of wartime questioning begins with, what is the problem of which we wish to rid ourselves? And then moves to, who personifies that problem? As in math, the importance of any factor can be judged by factoring it out. After who or what is killed or destroyed will we be rid of our problem? *That* is the enemy.

American political discourse on this war has not proceeded along this line. Some identified bin Laden with a larger phenomenon they call "fundamentalist Islam." This would mean that the more strictly someone adheres to Islam, the more seriously he takes his religion, the more he becomes America's enemy. According to the notion that "fundamentalist Islam" is the problem, "moderate Islam" is the solution, the enemy would be Islamic religious seriousness itself. Only superficially different is the U.S. government's official position that despotism—lack of democracy—in the Middle East causes poverty, ignorance, disease, and political and religious extremism, including especially the exclusion of women from public life. Because all these things make for terrorism, the argument continues, the enemy is the culture of the region. And since that culture is fundamentally Islamic, the enemy that the U.S. government ends up identifying is the application of Islamic principles to life.

And if the physical enemies are individuals who are overly serious about their religion and unduly in tune with the dominant culture of Middle Eastern regimes, then the war must consist of destroying Islamic networks, making Islam less serious, and building democracy on an anti-religious basis. Wisely or not, the U.S. government in fact has conducted the war against these enemies. Note that such a war is, as the Vietnam War was, less an exercise in military strategy than in sociology. The results seem to indicate that it is bad sociology.

The War

It is a troublesome fact that, since the late 1960s and with increasing severity in our time, a variety of people have killed Americans, hijacked American aircraft and ships, and otherwise made Americans' lives less safe and less free. Ending this terror, and thus restoring Americans' safety and freedoms, is the natural, logical purpose of this war. But the war declared after 9/11 has not proceeded logically. This is in part because, as is often the case in indirect warfare, the U.S. government is unwilling to recognize that things it thinks and does make it vulnerable.

Americans below middle age have never known a time when they could stroll onto airplanes or into public buildings without passing through metal detectors, when policemen were not menacing paramilitaries, when one did not have to prove one's identity at every turn. That time began to end circa 1966, when American leftists drew attention to their causes by hijacking airliners at gunpoint and forcing them to land in Havana. Cuba's dictator, Fidel Castro, supported their common anti-American cause by refusing to extradite them. The U.S. government chose not to exercise its right to threaten or make on Castro a war that would have eliminated the hijackers' impunity. Instead, in 1972 it prohibited the general public from carrying weapons aboard airliners. The age of metal detectors had begun. Moreover, rather than encouraging passengers to resist hijackers, government rules required passengers to put up no resistance to them, even to assume whatever "body position" the hijackers required, while "breathing deeply." Just as the government would not make war on Castro, it would not single out domestic leftist radicals for special attention. Instead, it would treat the general population as a problem and begin restricting its freedoms.

By 1969 Arab fedayeen, who had been killing only Israelis, began to hijack airplanes carrying Europeans and Americans as well, and to hold the passengers hostage—and kill some. Beginning in 1976 and led by Israel, Western governments developed specialized military hostage-rescue teams—again, trying to deal with the manifestations of indirect warfare without the inconvenience of forcing rogue governments to adhere to international law. Thus, when Uganda's Muslim dictator Idi Amin (who was a cannibal in addition to being a murderer) held hostage the passengers of an airliner hijacked by Arabs, no civilized government thought to do more than just to rescue them.

By 1980 terrorists adapted to the existence of rescue teams, ceased to take masses of hostages to public places and moved to kidnapping individuals and hiding them or killing them. Lebanon was the ideal place in which to do this, because its government did not control the country and thus could not be held responsible. In fact, Syria was in control of Lebanon (and remains so at this writing). But after 1982, when Syria and its partner Iran firmly controlled Lebanon, Western governments chose not to hold either of these governments liable for the terrorist acts taking place in and originating from that country. The U.S. response to the 1983 bombing of U.S. Marine barracks in Beirut was to leave Lebanon to Syria—the likeliest sponsor of the bombings.

America's involvement with Iran and the Khomeini revolution of 1979 added much fuel to the war and broadened its scope. Since 1953, the United States had supported, guided, and identified itself with the Iranian shah's secularizing reforms. Not surprisingly, the Muslim resistance to those reforms took on an anti-American character. When the victorious Khomeini forces took over the U.S. embassy in Tehran—a classic act of war—the United States did not answer with war, but suffered the imprisonment of its diplomats for over a year. The Paris daily *Le Figaro* summed up the world's feelings on the matter with the headline "Open Season on Americans." Most important, Khomeini's success in humiliating America on behalf of Islam invited all Muslims to join in the hunt.

In sum, the United States treated the acts of war it suffered in Beirut and Teheran and elsewhere as though they had been something else. The consequences proved that pretending that acts of war have not taken place aggravates their seriousness.

During the 1980s also, Western governments chose not to hold Iraq responsible for its terrorism (in 1982 the Reagan administration winked and took Iraq off its list of states supporting terrorism) because Saddam Hussein was making war on Iran. At least someone was doing it! This, U.S. officials believed, created a diplomatic opportunity to turn Arab countries into partners for a general peace. This belief was even stronger with regard to the Palestine Liberation Organization, which, as we saw in chapter 9, had pioneered modern anti-Western terrorism. The experts were sure that a general resolution of conflicts with the Arab world—paramount among them the Arab-Israeli conflict—was possible and would end terrorism without need for war.

Iraq's Saddam Hussein evidently read U.S. diplomacy differently, as an indication that the United States would not or could not oppose his aggrandizement in the region. Hence in 1990 he invaded Kuwait and put himself in a position to coerce Saudi Arabia. Though the invasion would have been bad for U.S. interests, there was nothing particularly anti-American in Saddam's move. President George Bush sent in some half million U.S. troops, who ejected Iraq from Kuwait and destroyed much of Iraq's infrastructure, but intentionally left Saddam's regime in power—the latter as part of a larger diplomatic strategy in the region.

U.S. officials believed that, with U.S. troops in Saudi Arabia and the Gulf states, the comprehensive settlement of the Mideast conflicts that generate terrorism was more likely than ever. But if there is anything that stimulates war more than failing to answer war with war, it is making war in a half-baked manner. *Troops that attack inspire fear and respect. Troops that sit inspire contempt and become targets.* Indeed, the Muslim world saw Saddam's survival of America's massive effort of 1990–91 as proof of America's impotence. It saw America's continuing presence in the Arab world—with talk of reforming Arab social customs—as an insulting assault on Islam. The Gulf War also redefined Saddam's role: no longer simply one bandit among many, now he was the avenger of his people, the champion of the Muslim world's grievances against America and Israel, as well as (unlikeliest of all for a vehement atheist) the leader of a holy cause.

The year 1993 saw the massive revival of terrorist activities and their refocusing against the United States. The main difference between these terrorist acts and former ones was the degree of support they enjoyed throughout the Muslim, and especially the Arab, world. For the Arab media, terrorism against America quickly became the truest expression of Islamic piety. The Arab media had been anti-Western since the late 1950s. But a decade of propaganda from Iran, now joined by Iraq and multiplied by the satellite TV stations al Jazeera and al Arabya; a decade of unanswered terrorist successes; Saddam's missiles raining on Israel as Palestinians danced on their rooftops; Saddam's skillful leadership, including his financing of suicide bombings and his blaming of the United States for the privations of Iraqi children—all bolstered by Western appeasement—whetted Arab appetites for American blood in the name of Allah.

The U.S. response was to push Israel harder to make a settlement at the same time to try to draw Arab states into closer cooperation against individual terrorists. In 1993, under the U.S.-sponsored Oslo agreement, Israel granted the PLO a ministate in the West Bank and the Gaza strip, complete with army and police. Instantly, this became another base for Hamas, Islamic Jihad, et al., and a source of endless clashes with Israel, which fed Arab TV with endless images of funerals at which America was denounced as the culprit. Thus, as the 1990s proceeded, the dynamics of the confrontation between the United States and the Arab world (including the burgeoning Arab population of western Europe) moved in the same fateful direction, America focusing ever more on individual terrorists while whole regimes, peoples, and even a civilization were becoming ever more belligerent.

The U.S. government's view of what it was facing was shaped by its own decision that terrorists were individuals acting without the help of specific regimes and certainly not on their behalf. Since the CIA had no direct sources of information about terrorists and relied substantially on information it got from the intelligence services of Arab governments, the U.S. view of those governments' roles in terrorism came in substantial part from those governments! *Not surprisingly, America's list of enemies turned out to be the same as that of secular, Sunni, Arab governments.* The first of these enemies was the Islamist movement. America should help the secular regimes fight the common Islamist enemy (and, theocratic, not incidentally Shi'ite, Iran as well). Thus was America set on a collision course with Islam. The second enemy was Osama bin Laden's al Qaeda. Thus America would chase individuals whose lives and deaths meant nothing. Because it accepted the terrorists' Islamic disguises at face value, it failed to fight political enemies while multiplying religious ones.

Thus did the United States deal with the 1993 attempt to topple the World Trade Center. The first clue "who done it" was that Mohammed Salameh, the man who had rented the van that had carried the explosives, whose associates had deserted him without a dime, returned to the rental office to claim his deposit. He was a very religious Palestinian with a slight mental handicap, who apparently had been drawn into the plot to be left holding the proverbial bag. Much the same is true of two others involved, Nidal Ayad and Bilal al Qaysi. Two Egyptians, Mahmud Abu Halima and Ibrahim el Gabrowny, had longstanding terrorist connections. The latter possessed Nicaraguan passports in his name, apparently from a batch of blanks that the Nicaraguan Sandinistas had given to Saddam's regime and to other Soviet-line movements. Abdul Rahman Yasin arrived in the United States and returned to Iraq on his own Iraqi passport. The bombing's mastermind, however, came to America on an Iraqi passport as Ramzi Youssef and left on a Pakistani passport as Abdul Karim, ostensibly an ethnic Baluch residing in Kuwait. New York's Pakistani consulate granted Youssef/Karim the passport on the basis of Kuwaiti identity papers—which carried his photo and fingerprints—that turned out to have been altered during Iraq's invasion of Kuwait.

After the bombing, Youssef/Karim fled New York for Baghdad. In 1995 he and other associates were arrested in the Philippines when bombs they were planning to set on U.S. airliners exploded accidentally. They had been frequenting bars—behavior very unusual for Muslims, especially fundamentalist ones. From all this, the U.S. government concluded somehow that the bombing of the World Trade Center had been a criminal act by Islamic extremists, not an act of war by the Iraqi government.

Similarly, the U.S. government accepted at face value reports from Arab intelligence services that Islamic extremists had perpetrated the 1996 attacks on the U.S. Air Force barracks in Saudi Arabia, the 1998 bombings of U.S. embassies in Africa, and the 1999 bombing of the USS *Cole*. However, when U.S. officials sought to question the sources of the reports, the Saudis either refused outright or said the sources had been beheaded.

The United States dealt similarly with the facts surrounding 9/11. The mastermind, in U.S. custody since 2002, seems to be a Baluchi man who calls himself Khalid Shaik Muhammed. He claims to be, and the U.S. government believes him to be, the uncle of the Baluch Abdul Karim, who, according to this account, only claimed to be the Iraqi Ramzi Karim Youssef. He worked with him on the 1993 attack, and, with Youssef, was planning to bomb the airliners in the Philippines in 1995 when the bombs went off. The year after, Muhammed took refuge with bin Laden (whom he had never met) in Afghanistan. The money for both attacks on New York, as well as for the Philippine operation, came from another of Muhammed's "nephews," one Ali al Ammar Baluchi. Nevertheless, Muhammed claims, and the U.S. government officially believes, that 9/11—in detail, money, fake passports, and all—was the work of Osama bin Laden in Afghanistan's caves.

The U.S. government might have asked, given this "family's" supposed role, how much sense it makes to impute responsibility to bin Laden. After all, factor out bin Laden, and this "family" still seems to have had everything it took to pull off 9/11. The government might have found it unlikely that a single family without a motive or independent resources would be at the center of vast enterprises—and it might have asked whether bin Laden or an Arab state actually provided those resources. It might have asked whether Youssef is really Youssef or whether he is Karim or someone else, whose uncle (if anyone's) Muhammed might be, and what in fact the relationships between the members of this "family" are. It might have wondered where the 9/11 hijackers had learned the sophisticated navigation techniques they used, or where they learned to turn off the airliners' transponders—since these things were not taught at the U.S. flight schools the hijackers attended. Then it might have investigated the role of Iraqi intelligence in all this—considering the Arab regimes' practice of indirect warfare, and the role that infiltration of various groups plays in that practice. It might have asked whether, in the real world, private groups really work around professional intelligence services or whether professional intelligence services work through private groups. But the U.S. government has done none of these things, primarily because the CIA people formally in charge of such things do not like the conclusions to which such questions lead. This may explain in part why the U.S. government has not presented any evidence about any of these matters in any forum (e.g., a courtroom) where it might be challenged.

Vain Fighting

On 11 September 2001 crashing airplanes set off a war in Washington. Although this war would involve plenty of shooting abroad, its decisive operations, like those of the Vietnam War, would take place in Washington. The two sides in this war represent longstanding, clashing views of the world, of America's role in it, and of America itself. They are not so different from the factions that fought each other over Vietnam. Some four years after the start, each side has succeeded in preventing the other from implementing its vision of policy coherently. The result has been a set of operations compromised from conception and not aimed at victory.

The character of the U.S. war became evident within days of 9/11. As news of the crashes reached the Arab world, only its top officials abstained from public celebrations. Dancing in the streets marked a victory for what had become a popular Arab, and even a Muslim, cause. Meanwhile Americans were mourning not just their dead, but also what most believed was the permanent exchange of America's free and easy way of life for one of "security," friskings, and identity checks. Retiring U.S. senator Phil Gramm said that he did not want to change the way he lived, rather preferring to change the way *they* live. But would U.S. officials even try to turn the tables, to make mourners of revelers and vice versa? There was virtually no discussion of that, or of whether the war President Bush was declaring was against anything other than individuals who would be "brought to justice." Instead, there began an endless series of inconclusive debates about discrete measures and general principles, but nothing that would connect principles with measures—no strategy for victory.

Without argument, President Bush accepted the CIA's "game, set, and match" judgment about bin Laden despite his unarticulated feeling that Saddam Hussein was "probably behind this in the end." He ordered the military to provide a set of military options for inflicting pain on the terrorists. Meanwhile, defense officials pointed out that the problem of terrorism went beyond bin Laden, and argued for bringing about "regime change" in the region, while the State Department warned that only if the mission were restricted to al Qaeda would it be acceptable to U.S. allies. The president put the question aside then, where it has continued to haunt operations. What passes for strategic discussion has oscillated between two poles, "We must do something serious" and "We must disturb the status quo as little as possible." Rather than choosing between contradictory approaches, President Bush would choose both—and get the benefits of neither.

The military's first option was to use cruise missiles against a set of targets in Afghanistan. The second option added other targets that would require only aircraft, while the third added "boots on the ground." It took a week of deliberations to figure out that the destruction of the entire target set would have doubtful relevance to anything, and would amount to "pounding sand." Hence there would have to be "boots on the ground."

But what would these American "boots" do? Some time between 26 September and 3 October the Bush team realized that only an Afghan government could rid Afghanistan of bin Laden's "Afghan Arabs." Hence the United States would have to overthrow the Taliban regime. However, since the State Department wanted to avoid alienating Pakistan, the United States would try to do it without coordinating its attacks on the Taliban with the Northern Alliance, the Taliban's rival in the ongoing civil war, which Pakistan opposed. This contradictory set of purposes led the United States to use the first two weeks of its attack for target strikes that amounted to "pounding sand." Only at the end of October, when the futility became embarrassing, did the Bush team coordinate its air strikes closely with the Northern Alliance's ground attacks. Quickly the Taliban ceased to exist, and the victorious Afghans simply sold their surviving Arab allies to the Americans. Mission accomplished. But so what?

This question haunted the Bush team's celebrations. It would be implausible to declare victory in the war on terror. Even if U.S. forces managed to find bin Laden and to track down every band from the Philippines to Liberia that had ever associated with him, terrorists were as likely to strike America after the Afghan campaign as before. The U.S. government was not about to rescind any of the security measures it had imposed on the American people. But these were mostly irrelevant to the American people's safety. The hijackings had succeeded only because passengers had believed that passivity would keep them safe. Now that they knew the opposite, no hijacking could succeed. Hence passenger security was nonsense. But American society as a whole was beyond protection. Even more than in Israel, nothing conceivable could stop the bombing of school buses or malls or the sniping of cars on highways, much less suicide attacks. The Department of Homeland Security and the Transportation Security Administration urged Americans to be wary of everyone in general and of no one in particular. But the self-evident reason why no major terrorist attacks had taken place in America is that no one had tried them. The war had a whiff of unseriousness.

Moreover, the war so far had proceeded on the fiction that the whole Arab world was as determined as the United States to stamp out terrorism. In answer to an attack on America by Arabs for Arab causes, the United States had overthrown a regime on the Indian subcontinent that meant nothing to those causes. Something else would have to be done.

To Iraq, or What?

The continuing electoral controversies of 2004 notwithstanding, there was no viable alternative in 2002–2003 to preparing to invade Iraq.

The argument that the alternative was a bigger, better search for bin Laden is unsound above all because he was never the source of anti-American terrorism, of its money, or of its organization. Nor was he its inspiration. Searches of his whereabouts in Afghanistan turned up no trace of the kind of "terrorism command central" that the CIA had imagined. A better argument can be made that bin Laden has been dead since November 2001 than that he is alive. All leads to him proved unfounded. The tapes that purport to be his were never wholly credible and had grown increasingly less so. No one claims to have seen him since the Taliban's collapse. Perhaps his associates, rather than let him be handed over to the Americans and become dangerous to everyone with whom he had ever dealt, disposed of his body. Thus, he would haunt the Americans forever.

The argument that diplomacy could have persuaded Arab regimes to rid themselves of terrorists, that they could turn terrorism off, tacitly acknowledges that they do in fact turn it on. This argument's practical trial occurred in 2002 when Saudi regent Abdullah promised the Arab world's cooperation in fighting terrorism in exchange for more American pressure on Israel. In his own kingdom, Abdullah was unable (or unwilling) to shut off the flow of Saudi money to terrorists and did not pretend to try to prohibit the teaching of religious extremism and anti-Americanism. How could he have coerced other Arab regimes to do what he could not, or would not, do at home? As for Iraq, although few in 2002–2003 imagined the scale on which Saddam Hussein had bribed high-ranking personages in the UN organization, in France, Germany, and Russia, it was already perfectly clear that these countries, for whatever reason, were utterly opposed to containing whatever he might wish to do.

If U.S. diplomacy could not shut off threats from Iraq, surely it could not coerce any Arab regime that was equally ill disposed but had done less to earn America's animus. And if it were able to, the war on terror would have to tiptoe around the very loci and causes of terror while trying to police their edges. And since this could not cut down the onslaught of terrorists on America, the United States would have to concentrate on passive security at home—a losing proposition.

The Bush team did not reason this way. Simply, it grasped what it might have grasped before—that the Afghanistan operation was about one remote terrorist base and that the public would demand that something be done to get at the sources of terrorism. These are in the Arab world. Iraq was simply the best target there that anyone could think of.

The problem was that the Bush team did not consider seriously what problems Iraq posed for America, that is, what Iraq's part was in America's troubles, and hence what, precisely, the U.S. armed forces would do in Iraq. Instead, its yearlong deliberations were driven by the desire to formulate its objectives in terms that would appeal to domestic and foreign opponents of U.S. action, as well as by the conflicts between the State Department and CIA on one side and the Pentagon on the other. The result was to send troops with objectives that were neither fish nor fowl and that changed with the changing balance of forces in Washington.

Would the objective be "regime change"—overthrowing Saddam's regime—as the Pentagon advocated, or would it be "disarming" Iraq, as the State Department and CIA preferred? And just what might the invasion of Iraq have to do with fighting terrorism? The CIA sought to discourage the invasion. Hence it publicly cleared Saddam Hussein of connections with terrorism—on the basis of no direct knowledge. On the same basis, it provided plenty of judgments that Saddam possessed weapons of mass destruction. If the president could be induced to seek only Iraq's disarmament, perhaps the UN could convince him (if Saddam agreed) that inspections would satisfy America's concerns. The president made a cleverish strategic choice: he would state that the U.S. objective was "disarmament." This would diminish opposition from the Left in America and abroad. But since Saddam was untrustworthy and disarmament could be achieved only by his overthrow, the result of American policy would be "regime change." It was too clever.

Beginning in September 2002 the Bush team tried to gain support from the UN, France, Germany, and Russia for a decision that it insisted it had not yet made to invade for the sake of "disarmament" and that would depend on their support. By February 2003, predictably, opposition from these quarters as well as from America's left of center had increased, while support from America's right of center had declined. Worse, the team's preoccupation with whether to invade and with packaging the invasion for the news media had preempted resolution of intramural conflicts about what U.S. forces should do once they got to Iraq.

For example, although all agreed that Saddam would be removed from office, few asked seriously what U.S. forces would have to do to change the regime because most confused "regime" with "government" and identified "government" with "Saddam." U.S. troops entered Iraq with silly decks of fifty five playing cards bearing the photos of high government officials. In fact, regimes are much more. They are the persons who set society's tone, its habits, who enjoy its best fruits, who make it what it is. In Iraq the regime consisted of the ruling Ba'ath Party, which was coterminous with the elite of the country's Sunni Muslim minority—a bare minimum of some two thousand people, most of them unknown to Americans. Would U.S. forces try to eradicate the regime by de-Ba'athifying the country and removing the Sunni minority from its privileged position? The Defense Department said yes. State and the CIA said no. The president said yes at first, no later, and later yet, yes again—perhaps, but only a little. By late 2005 it was no again.

As well, State and Defense disagreed about what U.S. forces should do in Iraq and for how long. The Pentagon's preference was to train a cadre of Iraqi exiles who would accompany the invasion and to whom the United States would convey power. United States forces would leave quickly, and these Iraqis would deal with their own country's deep problems. State and CIA disliked the Pentagon's exiles. They had favorite exiles of their own, whom they wanted to install *after* the United States had pacified and rebuilt the country. At first Bush backed the Pentagon, then he backed State.

Worst, these preoccupations and conflicts obscured the war's primary focus: what would the United States have to do in Iraq to make its invasion into an event that would eliminate or at least cow all those who make terrorism possible? We do not know of any high-level discussions of this question. They may have been precluded by President Bush's conviction that the birth of democracy in Iraq would so strengthen decency and discourage indecency in the region that its regimes would no longer employ terrorists or be hospitable to them. At any rate, what the United States might have done in Iraq to coerce the region's other regimes must remain a matter of speculation, because it did not do anything.

The Iraq War

As late as 10 April 2003 the White House spokesman said of Iraqi weapons of mass destruction, "That is what this war is about." But President Bush had begun in February tentatively to reintroduce into public discourse the link between Iraq and 9/11, as well as the expectation that "regime change" in Iraq would transform the Middle East. But on 19 March, Bush called the invasion Operation Iraqi Freedom. And once the guns began firing, any and all objectives depended on collapsing armed resistance.

The Iraqi armed forces fought without operational plans or central command and control, never mind a strategy. Saddam's inner circle had decided to abandon the regime well before the battle began. As to why this was so, U.S. intelligence can only speculate on the basis of what happened once the occupation began.

Secretary of State Colin Powell had squeezed out of Bush a key concession: if Saddam "disarmed," America would claim victory without shooting, and the regime could stay in power. Like his father, Bush would look good in the short run. Saddam would win in the long. Yet Saddam did not make that diplomatic move or any other. Saddam knew better than the Americans how little his weapons of mass destruction were the basis of his influence in the world. Weeks or months before the battle, he ordered not just their destruction or transfer, but also the chemical decontamination of the instruments involved in their manufacture, even as he was looting one billion dollars in currency. He abandoned his own regime on his own terms. We know not why.

As the well-advertised date approached for the beginning of the well-advertised American bombing of "leadership targets" and "military targets," the target palaces and ministries had become empty, meaningless bomb sinks. Preprogrammed strikes in and around Baghdad between 22 and 24 March, by some thirty-four hundred cruise missiles and aircraft sorties were supposed to "shock and awe" the Iraqi regime into collapse. But the leadership had already abandoned the military. Triggering the strikes through Iraqi double agents who fooled the CIA into fooling the president into believing that Saddam could be killed by bombing a certain house, the Iraqi dictator covered his own escape. The intelligence battle was the only one Saddam chose to fight. He seems to have won it. Key to Saddam's intentions were some ten thousand "fedayeen Saddam," the black-clad criminals whom his son Qusay had organized after the 1991 Gulf War to terrorize the country back into submission. Fear of them froze Iraqis at their posts. The fedayeen accounted for most of the American casualties by fighting disguised as civilians or by feigning surrender. They formed the core of the insurrection that, during the subsequent occupation, would take twenty times as many American lives as during the invasion.

The U.S. Third Infantry Division, the U.S. First Marine Expeditionary Force, and a brigade of British Royal Fusiliers moved northward from Kuwait. Other U.S. units, including the 101st Airborne Division and various special forces, were dropped or airlifted onto oil fields, airfields, and bridges and into northern Iraq. The movement of troops not preceded by artillery barrages or air strikes was made possible and prudent by the fact that between Baghdad and Basra and Kuwait, there was little to hit. Rapid advance could secure bridges and oil fields intact. Besides, American forces could count on unchallenged, near-instantaneous air cover. *Not one* Iraqi aircraft would challenge the Americans. So some eighty thousand U.S. and British ground troops drove some fifteen thousand vehicles of all kinds some one hundred miles into Iraq in the first thirty-six hours. Regular Iraqi units surrendered on sight.

Moving north past the cities of Nasiriya and Najaf, the Americans encountered what the press called heavy, unexpected resistance. But on the heaviest day of fighting, 23 March, only thirteen Americans were killed—most after a unit of cooks and mechanics had taken a wrong turn. The next largest group of casualties occurred when some fedayeen feigned surrender and then fired. The rumor that Iraqi resistance stalled the drive to Baghdad was nonsense. The only pause was caused by a sandstorm.

By 1 April, when marines advancing from the southeast and the Army from the southwest moved against the Republican Guard around Baghdad, four days' work by U.S. aircraft (along with massive defections) had "degraded" three guard divisions to perhaps a third of their strength. Two American divisions drove through the remnants in four main columns—some forty miles of combat in a little over three days. Some twenty thousand American combat soldiers drove through a somewhat greater number of Iraqis—perhaps fifty thousand men fighting each other with the deadliest of weapons—at the cost of fewer than fifty Americans killed. The final U.S. combat death toll was 124. Iraqi soldiers who had surrendered walked toward Baghdad in civilian clothes. This was not Stalingrad.

On 9 April, as U.S. troops eliminated resistance in Baghdad and toppled Saddam's statues to universal cheers, the Bush team's indecisions began to haunt the operation. At that moment, the only U.S. interest in Iraq itself was that it be ruled by persons hostile to anyone hostile to America. Machiavelli's prescription for running conquered territory is to arm your clients while disarming the rest. The conqueror's local clients have the knowledge and the motivation to drown the former regime's roots in blood. But the Bush team had clashing ideas on who was on America's side in Iraq. The State Department wanted Iraq to be governed by former Ba'athists. The Department of Defense wanted it to be governed by anti-Ba'athists. And so Bush counted on rival Iraqi claimants along with their respective U.S. sponsors agreeing on a democratic process for sorting things out. This was nonsense. America had deployed a massive force without that discernment between friends and enemies that alone makes sense of force.

Meanwhile, thousands of Sunni Arabs in central Iraq, the body and beneficiaries of Saddam's regime, did not believe they had been defeated—because they had not been decimated. And so they fought. The Americans were not going to defeat the Sunni-Ba'athist forces, and they were prohibiting the Shi'ites and Kurds whom the regime had oppressed from doing so. They had every intention of reestablishing themselves in something like the old regime. The Americans were perfect targets. They would respond to attacks by searching out the individuals responsible—answering war by policing, rather than by making war. Iraqi infrastructure was easy to hit, as well. Under these conditions, the Sunni insurgents could prove that the country would be governable only if they received at least some of the privileges that had been theirs under Saddam.

And so Iraq's main oil export line to Turkey was sabotaged. Attacks on southern oil fields cut oil deliveries in half. Electrical lines were cut, towers toppled, stations damaged or destroyed. A total of 111 sabotages in the year following the invasion prevented the Americans from turning the lights back on. Insurgents captured foreign workers and killed some to cause their countries and companies to stop doing business with the U.S. armed forces and reconstruction effort. In the face of the Americans' inability to either protect their citizens or intimidate the kidnappers, several countries gave in. By slaughtering some five Iraqi policemen or other officials per day, and a dozen or more U.S. soldiers per week, the insurgents made clear that no official of any government of which they did not approve would be safe.

At this point the Bush team might well have grasped that the fighting in Iraq was mainly among Iraqis over their own privileges. But by now, unconsciously, the mission had morphed. Disarming and pacifying, rebuilding, unifying, and preparing the country for democratic elections producing the oxymoron of an Iraq at once democratic and unified—a model for the region—had become ends in themselves. The United States was stuck between impossible ends and inadequate means. No number of troops would suffice.

The combination of U.S. troops' power, ignorance, and lack of offensive mission eventually led them to behave in the classic manner of occupation forces—that is, counterproductively. Since the summer of 2003, U.S. troops had been barging about Iraq, combing through people, and taking away some 250 per week. Already military intelligence officers believed that between 70 and 90 percent of the inmates "had been arrested by mistake." One study said that 55 out of 57 inmates had no intelligence value. When it became clear that the interrogation of captured Iraqis was yielding little intelligence, one Stephen Cambone, the undersecretary of defense for intelligence, decided that the military police in charge of the prisons should dispose the prisoners to talk by stressing them in various ways. His decision had all too predictable consequences. First, of course, intelligence thus gathered led to wilder goose chases because interrogees say what their interrogators want to hear. Second, it confirmed that the surest way to corrupt any army is to assign it to occupation duty. Third, the Americans' slight mistreatment of Iraqi prisoners gave a gloss of legitimacy to the insurgents' beheadings and burnings of Americans and those who worked with them.

In March, April, and May 2004, publicity about prisoner abuse helped fuel an insurrection that overcame what remained of American officials' resolve to carry through their plans for Iraq. The crisis began when Sunni insurgents in Fallujah, a city of 250,000 west of Baghdad, lured four American private security guards into an ambush. After dismembering and burning them, they hung their remains from a bridge for the world's TV cameras to see and to dare the U.S. Marines to do something about it. The marines moved into the city with bombers, AC-130 gunships, and artillery. Meanwhile, to give Sunnis the impression that he was evenhanded, U.S. viceroy Paul Bremer announced a warrant for the arrest of Moktada al Sadr, a young Shi'ite cleric who was agitating against the American occupation. The announcement led to riots by Shi'ites in the Baghdad suburb of Sadr City. The Army attacked the Sadr militias in the south-central Shi'ite cities of Karbala and Kufa and the holy Shi'ite city of Najaf.

Hence vast elements of two communities that had been at odds, people whom Americans had come to liberate, had united against them. Iraqis who had enrolled as policemen and been hired on as workers simply switched sides. Indeed it appeared that the four security guards who had been burned in Fallujah had been led to their deaths by their employees or by Iraqi police. There was not and would never be a way for Americans to guard against infiltration of their workforce or of the security forces they were training—none. The entire U.S. design of benevolent tutelage over Iraqis eager to learn, grateful for help, and readying to take over policing their country in cooperation with America had turned out to be an illusion.

Now, following the State/CIA blueprint, and the advice of their favorite Iraqis, the Bush team agreed to suspend the attack on Fallujah, and effectively granted the insurgents control of their main areas of operations. Then it transferred nominal sovereignty to those Iraqis. The prime minister would be Iyad Alawi, the CIA's paladin of several unsuccessful coups to establish "Saddamism without Saddam." Nominally, the U.S. government's objectives remained: keep Iraq united despite the divisions between Shi'ites, Sunnis, and Kurds, establish democracy, and rebuild the country. In practice these boiled down to enabling the holding of national elections in January 2005.

Immediately, however, it became clear that the political and ethnic divisions among Iraqis had their own dynamic, and that Americans were caught in the middle.

Right after taking "sovereignty" in June 2004 the Alawi government let it be known that its solution to the problem of Fallujah was to entice its Ba'athist elements into closer relations with the government. As well, the Alawi government planned to recommission Republican Guard officers as the core of a new army and to reconstitute the old regime's intelligence services. This, along with its assignment of emergency powers to itself, raised further suspicions among Kurds and Shi'ites, who feared that the Americans were helping the Sunnis to reestablish their tyranny. Only the promise of elections kept the Shi'a majority from forming their own insurgency. But the Sunnis saw elections as a threat to be fought. More and more Sunnis supported the insurgency. By late summer and fall 2004 their region of the country, north and west of Baghdad, was in full-blown insurgency. Neither the government nor the Americans could venture into Fallujah, Ramadi, and similar places. Key roads were off limits. Unless something were done, elections would be impossible in central Iraq.

The U.S. military had always resented the Bush team's decision to grant effective sovereignty to the insurgent areas of central Iraq. By fall, the military got clearance to reverse it physically and psychologically. The tactical objective was the city of Fallujah, to kill or capture the insurrection's leadership and radically to reduce the number of its fighters. The well-advertised November attack well-nigh leveled Fallujah. Some one thousand Iraqis (Mostly Sunni, many of whom were Ba'athists, with a 5 percent admixture of foreigners) died resisting the Americans, and another six hundred were captured—at the cost of forty Americans killed in action.

But of course the insurgency's leadership had long since escaped with the bulk of its forces. It implemented a new military strategy: instead of taking and holding small cities, it would melt into large ones. It concentrated especially on the northern city of Mosul. This had been a largely Kurdish city until Saddam expelled many Kurds and replaced them with Sunnis. Since Saddam's fall, the Kurds had been reclaiming it. Now the Sunnis wanted to make sure that in an eventual separation or regionalization of Iraq, Mosul would remain theirs.

In addition the insurgents continued to hit Americans along the roads, to cause casualties and restrict U.S. movements. By mid-November Americans had given up traveling to and from the airport except by helicopter, and even that was becoming more perilous. The insurgents' widespread, untrammeled killing of Iraqis also spread a sense of inevitability. The U.S. military was attempting to keep the insurgents on the run, and the insurgents were doing the same. By the end of 2004 the U.S. military was not fighting a war but simply coping with the costs of an occupation.

Finally, U.S. officials realized that the insurgents' offensive was about Iraqi internal politics. Sunnis knew that the ballot box would reflect the other groups' distaste for them. *The insurgency was, at heart, the beginning of a Sunni war against a presumed Shi'ite Iraqi government.* To counter that, U.S. officials, along with the ex-Ba'athists they had appointed to the interim government, tried to lure the Sunni population into cooperation with unspecified promises of special privileges. This of course angered the Shi'ites and Kurds. The Shi'ites were angered further by the government's, the Sunni Arab world's, and the Americans' accusation that they were part of an Iranian conspiracy to alter the balance between Sunnis and Shi'a throughout Islam by establishing an Iranian-style Shi'ite theocracy in Iraq. Rather than calming the country, U.S. officials were rubbing salt in old wounds.

Any Iraqi government that emerged from the elections would act against the core interests of one or more of the country's main groups. Inevitably, the outcome of the 2005 elections reflected the facts of Iraqi life: the Shi'ites and Kurds, together with some 80 percent of the population, voted for parties committed to their joint interest in never again being ruled by the Ba'athists and Sunnis as well as to the passion of each group to govern itself. Their majority was heightened further by the Sunnis' violent boycott of the election. The assembly that resulted from the election named a committee that wrote a constitution tailored to ensure these interests.

If one had reasoned that the U.S. government, for whom Iraqi democracy had become the war's declared objective, would have regarded the expression of the people's will as fulfillment of that objective and supported it as being in its interest, one would have reasoned logically. After all, the Sunni Ba'athists were America's only Iraqi enemies. But the U.S. government was not pursuing democracy any more logically than it had pursued anything else in Iraq. It spent the remainder of 2005 trying to set aside the majority's expressed interest in de-Ba'athification and loose confederation. As the constitution was being drafted, U.S. diplomats acted as proxies for the Sunnis' and Ba'athists' interests while the U.S. military continued trying to find persons among them with whom they could exchange concessions for a slackening of the insurgency.

The aforementioned events of the spring of 2004 had led the U.S. military to conclude that the U.S. government would not let it do what was necessary to defeat the insurgency, and hence that it did not want to ruin itself trying. In 2005 U.S. forces ran search-and-destroy missions against insurgent strongholds near the Syrian border that were reminiscent of the war. U.S. troops clashed with Syrian troops that who protecting the substantial flow of fighters into Iraq. The U.S. ambassador in Baghdad as well as military officials publicly complained that the insurgency was being run from Syria. Nevertheless, just as the U.S. government a generation earlier had not attacked the governments of North Vietnam and Cambodia as they were funneling enemy forces into South Vietnam, the U.S. government now treated Syria as a "sanctuary."

The mantra had become that Iraq's problems did not have a military solution, and a political one had to be found. One high-ranking officer told *Time* magazine that the United States hoped to find an Iraqi equivalent of the Northern Ireland IRA's Gerry Adams—never mind that Adams, like Arafat and other terrorist chiefs, had purchased ever greater concrete power with never fulfilled promises of moderation. The senior U.S. military yearned to wash its hands of Iraq.

De facto, the U.S. government's war aims in 2006 were twofold. The president wanted to begin withdrawing U.S. troops before the 2006 congressional elections, under cover of some kind of political deal between Iraqi factions that seemed to augur peace. The State Department and CIA, the agencies that defined and pursued the deal, were committed strongly to a unitary, secular Iraq the political tone of which would be set by the Sunnis—enough at least to be acceptable to the Sunnis of Saudi Arabia, Syria, Egypt, etc. But as the U.S. government squeezed small concessions from the Shi'ites and Kurds, the Sunnis demanded ever more.

The Sunnis' argument consisted of some eighty terrorist attacks per day. During one week in September 2005, Sunni suicide bombers killed two hundred Shi'ites. As the holy month of Ramadan began, they bombed a Shi'ite mosque, an act akin to bombing churches at Christmas. The U.S. government's reaction was to worry lest the Shi'ites and Kurds answer war with war. It noted that the governments of Sunni Arab nations did not disapprove of the campaign against the Shi'ites. But the State Department had the same priority as these states, namely, that Iraq as a whole remain part of the Sunni Arab bloc. But of course Iraq's majority saw only enemies in that bloc. So, although American soldiers continued to stand guard against and occasionally to be killed by Sunni Ba'athists, the U.S. government's position in Iraq was ever more self-contradictory, and ever less tenable. Having ceased to wage war in Iraq, the U.S. government had become an obstacle to the peace most of its people wanted.

The most positive development of 2005, especially after the majority of Iraqis reaffirmed their orientation by ratifying their constitution in October and electing their permanent assembly in December was the U.S. government's growing recognition that it could not force Kurdish and Shi'ite politicians to accept deals opposed by their constituents, and hence that it could not appease the Sunnis. Hence it began to dawn on the U.S. government that the better part of wisdom, as well as of valor, might be truly to let Iraqis decide how they would live. This would mean that the Kurds and Shi'ites would deal with the Sunnis as they thought best. This became the default solution by 2006, as U.S. troops began to withdraw.

Speaking strictly of Iraq, one might even say that the United States won the war of 2003–2006. After all, the war removed the virulently anti-American government of Saddam Hussein and, despite the best U.S. efforts, the vast majority of Iraqis were determined to uproot its regime in most (but not all) of the country. It was difficult to imagine the Shi'a and Kurds tolerating anti-American terrorists in their zones—chiefly because they would fear for themselves. No, the "unified" Iraq that the United States was leaving behind was not much more unified than the Bosnia whose troubles the United States had tried to fix a decade earlier. Nor was the new Iraq such as to please Saudis, Turks, or Syrians. But although all this vexed the U.S. State Department, none of it was bad for America. On the negative side, Iraq's Sunni areas—in the likely case that the Kurds and Shi'a would leave them autonomous—were likely to be under Ba'athist influence and allied to Ba'athist Syria. Then again, the U.S. government had not made war on the Ba'ath Party. Also very much on the negative side, the supply of anti-American terrorists had increased, and Iraq's Sunni areas, in communion with Syria, would funnel them into the world. But again, in 2003–2004 the U.S. government had been unwilling to carry out—or to allow others to carry out—the small-scale slaughter that would have subjugated these areas. Much less had it been willing to fight Syria. And so, in sum, while the war of 2003–2006 removed a big part of one of America's problems in the Middle East, it left a smaller part more energized and merged with the larger problems of the so-called war on terror. To these we now turn our attention.

Back to the Main Point

After three years of mis-focusing America's power in Iraq, America's predicament vis-à-vis the world's terrorists had worsened. America would have to rethink and restart the war from a position less advantageous than it had on 9/11.

Invading Iraq could have been a decisive move in a war to eliminate terrorist attacks on Americans. Once the governance of Iraq had been turned over to Saddam's enemies and Saddam's regime—among them the "intelligence" and "security" personnel who had made possible so much terrorism in the world—had suffered the inevitable ensuing carnage, America would have had one less major source of terrorism to worry about. More important, the example of America's enemies delivered into the hands of their domestic enemies would have sobered the rest of the world's sources of terrorism. Most important, America could have used the prospect that it might undo Syria's regime as it had undone Saddam's to force it as well as others that engender terrorism to choose between stepping aside and being crushed. The Middle East would have been transformed all right, though not exactly in the way the Bush team imagined. But the first step was not taken, and the managers of U.S. foreign policy proved downright disinclined to use the leverage of military victory in Iraq to force changes of behavior in other regimes.

Coercive diplomacy translates military success into victory by showing foreign governments that it is better for them to adjust themselves to the reality created by one's military success than to suffer whatever the winner chooses to inflict. In the aftermath of America's military success, the Syrian, Palestinian, and Saudi sources of terrorism were not subjected to U.S. coercive diplomacy because the U.S. State Department had a different agenda. It presented to these governments proposals that differed only cosmetically, if at all, from those of years prior, effectively telling them that they need not be concerned with what America could do to them as a result of its military success. Predictably, these governments took this as further reason for contempt of America.

After April 2003 the world's only other Ba'athist regime, Syria's, surely among the top three purveyors of terrorism, and the source of the only weapons that had killed U.S. Abrams tanks in Iraq, lived exclusively among rocks and hard places. American forces controlled the Mediterranean to the west and Iraq to the east. On Syria's northern border is Turkey, which it fears most of all and which can destroy its livelihood by flood or drought. On the south is Israel, which can destroy its army as easily as America can. Any of these alone can defeat it. Politically, Syria was isolated. "Ba'ath" had become a dirty word, even in France. Syria was in the legally indefensible position of being the occupying power in Lebanon. Syria's regime—consisting of the tiny Alewite minority despised by Muslims—stood on shakier ground than even Saddam's had in Iraq. U.S. diplomacy was positioned optimally to make Syria offers that it could not refuse.

But as Syria cowered, Secretary of State Powell did not demand the freedom of Lebanon or even the arrest and consignment of thousands of known terrorists. He turned over a list of known Iraqi escapees about whom he asked for information, requested that Syria close some terrorist headquarters, and praised its dictator for having been "helpful . . . in our global war against terrorism." Syria's Assad gave Powell contemptuous assurances. The following day his newspaper, *Al Ba'ath,* made all of them conditional on America taking Syria's side against Israel. Reporters who telephoned the terrorist offices in Damascus found them open for business. In 2004 evidence that the Iraqi insurgency that was bleeding the U.S. military was being run out of Syria became undeniable. George W. Bush asked Syria for its help.

Yasir Arafat's mini-terrorist regime in the West Bank and Gaza Strip was even more vulnerable. Arafat had supported Saddam Hussein's invasion of Kuwait and had run his campaign of suicide bombing against Israel with Saddam's money. Now America had crushed Saddam's regime. Meanwhile, Arafat had discredited himself and his movement by acts of terrorism and corruption so egregious that even Hillary Clinton had been forced to distance herself from his cause. Only George Bush, and he tenuously, was holding Israel back from utterly destroying it. Again, it was difficult to imagine America making the Palestinian Authority an offer it could refuse.

But the State Department (and the CIA) had never abandoned their support of Arafat's Palestinian Authority. Their stock-in-trade had been the "peace process," by which Israel gave Arafat land, autonomy, and money in exchange for promises of peace. Arafat's stock-in-trade had been to pocket concessions and to use terrorism to demand more. Notwithstanding 9/11, State argued that good relations with the PLO were necessary for America's war on terrorism. State did not require the Palestinian Authority to stop acts of terror, only to declare that it was trying. Instead of taking the U.S. military victory in Iraq as warrant for making nonnegotiable demands on the PLO, or for simply allowing Israel to annihilate it, George W. Bush's diplomacy used the occasion as an opportunity to help it reform by turning over some fifty million dollars in U.S. taxpayer funds. The Palestinians responded in their usual manner, with more bombings followed by official denials, and demands for more concessions lest more terrorism follow. In 2005 after Arafat died and was replaced by his deputy Mahmoud Abbas, the United States turned over another twenty million dollars to service its hopes about the PLO. After the PLO rival, Hamas, won the 2006 elections in the Palestinian territories, the Bush team combined public warnings that it would cease to firance the Palestinian Authority with private efforts to make sure that it would not lack for money. For U.S. foreign policy, the battle of Iraq might as well not have happened.

It is no exaggeration to say that the problem of international terrorism is an extension of the features of Saudi Arabia's royal family, including its intertwining with the extreme Islamist Wahhabi sect, the family factionalism based on different harem lines, and generalized corrupt, moneyed, impotence. For nearly a half century, U.S. policy has moved heaven and earth and overlooked much to keep the Saudi regime from collapsing. But after 9/11, Americans came to realize that a large amount of the money that pays for international terror directly, and indirectly through spreading Wahhabism, comes from the wealthy families that make up the Saudi regime. Using the leverage of military success in Iraq to make upon the Saudi regime demands essential to America's war on terror might well hasten that regime's death from its congenital ills. Despite the argument that the stability of a regime of the world's chief inspirers and financiers of terrorism is not good for America, the State Department (and oil interests) easily persuaded President Bush to continue betting on Saudi stability.

In sum, although there is no doubt that the U.S. government very much desires that acts of anti-American terrorism disappear from the earth, it is just as clear that this desire has not overcome either the U.S. government's habitual relations with Arab regimes and sympathy for their causes, or its late twentieth-century unseriousness about war.

The Main Point

This book has shown that although the paths of war are often devious, essence of war is straightforward: identifying the enemy whose demise will rid you of your problem, and then doing to him whatever it takes to make sure that he will never make problems for you again.

The problem that manifested itself on 9/11 is that for many Arabs and other Muslims inured to terrorism, anti-Americanism has become a cause célèbre. For anti-American terrorism to cease, that cause must be defeated and discredited.

Causes are embodied in human beings who live and thrive in institutions. Causes live through people, and with them they die. What stripped Nazism of awe and made it into a dirty word, and what transformed communism from the icon of millions into the butt of jokes? Quite simply, the fall of regimes in Berlin and Moscow, the demise of their capacity to sustain material offensives and to propagandize their creeds, and the humiliation of their leaders. Arab regimes embody the causes of terrorism. They are its al Qaedas, its real bases, complete with television stations, secure bases for organization and recruitment, money, and sovereign refuge. Terrorists and their causes live by, for, and through these bases. They will disappear only when their bases do.

At the very least, a war that aimed at shutting off the supply of terrorists would aim at doing away with the things that generate them. Causes exist in people's minds, and minds are formed by school curricula as well as media. In the Arab world, such things are the creatures of regimes. Terrorists are produced by textbooks like those of the Palestinian Authority and Saudi Arabia, which make the racism of the Nazis look mild. Their media use the deaths of terrorists to recruit new ones. The al Jazeera television network tells the Arab world that the U.S. government itself masterminded 9/11 to give itself a pretext for attacking the Arab world. In short, the fact that millions of Arabs cheer when American blood is drawn, and that drawing it has become a cause for thousands, is possible only because of the cheerleaders. Hate, as the old song says, has to be very carefully taught. And it is. Without that culture of hate, the recruitment of terrorists, especially "suicidists," would not be possible. Factor out these media, and terrorism would be most unusual because it would make little sense. A serious war on terrorism would ensure that nothing broadcast or printed in the Arab world incited terrorism.

Note as well that neither any "radical" cleric nor any member of his family, neither any "radical" politician nor any member of his family, nor any Arab journalist who celebrates suicide bombing has been known to sacrifice his life in an act of terror. Yet those clerics, politicians, and regime stalwarts are the ones who pay for, glorify, and arrange the sacrifices. Their weapon of mass destruction is political. They are the living, undying sine qua non of suicide bombings, the "effective causes" of terrorism. It follows that suicide bombings and similar acts will continue as long as their effective causes are alive and act without fear for their lives. Factor *them* out, and few if any terrorist acts would happen.

Hence a serious war on terror that aimed to kill these "effective causes" would demand that the societies ruled by these chiefs sort themselves out. Those who did not distance themselves sufficiently from such leaders would suffer the rough Roman justice of war.

Can anyone imagine terrorism were Arab regimes not awash in oil money? Conversely, can anyone imagine that Arab terrorism will cease as long as they are? The U.S. government's war on terrorist financing has investigated suspect Arab "charities" and has stopped the flow of a few million dollars from a dozen sources. It has not confronted the fact that the regimes' constituent families support terrorism financially in uncountable ways. More important, the U.S. government and American elites have not begun to face the hard fact that they themselves have provided unearned cash for Arab regimes to dispose of in the form of direct subsidies and of oil royalties to regimes that do not keep it out of terrorist hands. Saddam Hussein's use of the UN Oil for Food program to feed his regime as well as terrorist activities reminds us of the basic economic fact that money is fungible. And this fact says that a serious war on terrorism would have as its goal to deprive Arab regimes with any connection to terrorism of funds from any source whatsoever. Financial deprivation of the enemy is a sine qua non of war. Paying oil royalties to Arab regimes, and even financing the PLA while fighting terrorists financed by those very monies is counterintuitive.

America's war, while espousing the end of ending terrorism, has not considered the means by which incitement to terrorism may be stopped, regimes whose members finance it deprived of money, and their leaders killed and discredited. The United States does not enjoy peace because it did not fight, much less win, a real war. In fact, the U.S. government would rather live with the current level of terrorism than adopt means proportionate to its ends. But since without such means there is no way to control the level of highly motivated, well-organized, well-financed terror, a rising level may one day force Americans to take seriously the question that King Archidamus asked his Spartans—"What is to be our war?"

There is an art to war, an art we have sought to explain in these pages.

Its essence lies in making day-to-day decisions in light of the fact that the purpose of war is victory and that any action that deviates from that purpose leads to defeat. In other words, the primary requirement of this art is concentration of the mind, not to say single-mindedness.

Our purpose here has been to describe the ways in which exemplary winners and losers have struggled for differing kinds of peace. Our reflections mean to inform our students and fellow citizens that everything we do that influences the foreign policy or the defense posture of the United States will have a bearing on the outcome of our struggles for our peace. Our reflections do not prescribe recipes for conducting any particular struggle. We do not rule out any means. Circumstances arise in human affairs in which even normally disastrous measures are required. But the very purpose of these reflections has been to redirect thoughts away from arguments over recipes and toward the stark fundamentals of peace and war. What can possibly satisfy the enemy? What means does he have of ensuring his own satisfaction? How much do we value our own kind of peace? What, then, do we have to do to make sure that it prevails? These fundamentals deserve our single-minded attention. Our civilization, following Augustine, prizes the tranquility of order. But for us to see war as anything but the other side of the coin of that tranquility is to misunderstand it, to suffer it, and ultimately to lose it.

NOTES

Introduction

1. For example, as of 1990 Syria, with fewer than ten million people, had over 2,500 tanks, while the United States with 250 million had fewer than 12,000. The Syrians had eight times as many tanks per capita as Americans. Indeed, Syria had about as many tanks as West Germany, which had six times Syria's population. Nor is Syria unusual. South Yemen had only two million people, but 450 tanks.

2. See James L. Payne, *Why Nations Arm* (London: Basil Blackwood, 1989), pt. 1, chap. 3.

3. Ibid., pt. 1, chap. 1.

4. R. J. Rummel, "War Isn't This Century's Biggest Killer," *Wall Street Journal,* 7 July 1986, 12. Rummel's numbers are 119.4 million people killed by governments, 35.7 million people killed in war. The number of people killed by governments does not include those executed for nonpolitical criminal acts, nor does it include deaths from either the Soviet famine of 1921–22 or the Chinese famine of 1958–61, both of which were caused in large part by forced collectivization and state planning of agricultural production. See also Antony Sutton, *Western Technology and Soviet Economic Development,* 3 vols. (Stanford, CA: Hoover Institution Press, 1968–1973).

5. Numa Denis Fustel de Coulanges, *The Ancient City* (Garden City, NY: Doubleday, 1956), bk. 3, chap. 1. Originally published in Paris in 1864.

6. Saint Augustine, *The City of God* (Garden City, NY: Image Books, 1958). Augustine writes in bk. 19, chap. 13 that "the peace of the political community is an ordered harmony of authority and obedience between citizens."

7. The Prophet Mohammed's injunctions about war and peace, including the jihad (holy war), were stressed by Iranian Shi'ites in the Iran-Iraq War. For the faithful, *jihad is the means of separating the people of para-*

dise from all others. The prophet said, "Jihad is necessary for you even if you prohibit it. . . . God buys property and life of the faithful in exchange for Paradise, for they fight and kill and get killed for God. . . . One hour of jihad is better than sixty years of worship." See Sepehr Zabib, *The Iranian Military in Revolution and War* (London: Routledge and Kegan Paul, 1988), 139–40. See also Bernard Lewis, "The Language of Islam," *Encounter* (May 1988), 39–45; and Daniel Pipes, *In the Path of God* (New York: Basic Books, 1983).

8. For a classic Hindu text on war, see Kautilya's *Arthasastra,* trans. R. P. Kangle (Bombay: University of Bombay Press, 1960). For a Chinese text on war, see Sun Tzu's *The Art of War,* trans. Samuel B. Griffith (Oxford: Oxford University Press, 1963).

9. See Frederick Engels, *The Origin of the Family, Private Property, and the State* (New York: International Publishers, 1942); and Karl Marx, Critique of the Gotha Programme (New York: International Publishers, 1972).

10. Thucydides, *The Peloponnesian War* (New Brunswick, NJ: Rutgers University Press, 1975), bk. 2, 79–81. The passage includes and follows the account of the revolution in Corcyra.

Chapter 2

1. F. E. Adcock, *The Greek and Macedonian Art of War* (Berkeley: University of California Press, 1957), 2.

2. Quincy Wright, *A Study of War* (Chicago: University of Chicago Press, 1942), 1261–83.

3. See Donald Kagan, "The Pseudo-Science of 'Peace,'" *The Public Interest* 78 (Winter 1985): 43–61. See also Bruce Bueno de Mesquita, *The War Trap* (New Haven: Yale University Press, 1981).

4. Henry Ashby Turner Jr., *German Big Business and the Rise of Hitler* (New York: Oxford University Press, 1985).

5. James Payne, *Why Nations Arm* (London: Basil Blackwood, 1989), pt. 2, chap. 9.

6. Such sentiments animate those who seek to introduce peaceable sentiments into educational curricula and to eliminate instructions, content, or behavior suggestive of combat in order to induce exemplary peaceable behavior in children. Several years before Pearl Harbor, Eleanor Roosevelt urged American toymakers to "turn their attention from tin soldiers, cannon, tanks and battleships and other warlike toys and make instead armies of foresters and farmers and mills with modern workmen" (Jason Berger, *A New Deal for the World* [New York: Social Science Monographs, 1981], 7). Disputes on this matter are revived in the pre-Christmas buying season every year.

7. See Reinhold Niebuhr, *The Irony of American History* (New York:

Scribner, 1952), 84–86.

8. See Michael Howard, *War and the Liberal Conscience* (New Brunswick, NJ: Rutgers University Press, 1978), ch. 1 and 2.

9. Ibid., 29–30. See also Felix Gilbert, *To the Farewell Address* (Princeton: Princeton University Press, 1961).

10. The victims of this "classicide" until the mid-1950s were chiefly, but not exclusively, Russian and Chinese victims of Stalin's and Mao Tse-tung's purges. The blood baths in Indochina, which followed the Vietnam War in 1975, bear witness that this form of peacemaking knows no boundaries. That *economic* theories can be more brutal in their logic than other modern ones is ironic. They are a truly dismal science, indeed, graveyard socialism.

11. Payne, *Why Nations Arm*, pt. 2, chap. 8.

12. Geoffrey Blainey, *The Causes of War* (New York: Free Press, 1973), 133.

13. Ibid., 141–42. The pathetic young protagonist of Theodore Dreiser's *American Tragedy*, Clyde Griffiths, exemplifies such a man. Having elaborately plotted the murder of his pregnant girlfriend, at the critical moment his will fails, yet he accidentally drowns her.

14. During the above-mentioned Russo-Japanese War, the commander of a Russian navy ship sailing from Murmansk on its long voyage to the Far East mistook a fleet of British fishing vessels for hostile Japanese warships and shelled them, causing many casualties. A real accident! This "Dogger Bank Incident," as it was called, briefly jolted but scarcely harmed Anglo-Russian relations. British policy already was moving strongly toward detente with St. Petersburg for reasons of state. However, had such an accident happened a generation before or after, it easily could have been a casus belli.

15. Carl Schmitt, *The Concept of the Political,* trans. George Schwab (New Brunswick, NJ: Rutgers University Press, 1976), 27–29.

16. Plato, *The Republic,* trans. Harold Bloom (New York: Basic Books, 1968), 147–52.

17. Schmitt, *Concept of the Political,* 30–33.

18. Winston Churchill, *The Second World War* (Boston: Houghton Mifflin, 1948), 1: 667.

19. See Patrick Glynn, "The Sarajevo Fallacy," *The National Interest* 9 (Fall 1987): 30.

20. Ibid.

21. Quoted in Martin Gilbert, *Winston Churchill: The Wilderness Years* (New York: Macmillan, 1981), 267.

22. Regarding Roosevelt's state of mind see Robert Dalleck, *Franklin Roosevelt and American Foreign Policy 1932–1945* (Oxford: Oxford University Press, 1979), 316. Ironically, the war in the Pacific started in Japanese surprise and ended in American surprise, the bombing of Hiroshima and

Nagasaki.

23. *Abraham Lincoln's Speeches*, compiled and edited by L. E. Crittenden (New York, 1895), 19.

24. Gilbert, *Winston Churchill*, 267.

25. See Charles de Gaulle, *Memoires de Guerre* (Paris: Plon, 1954), vol. 1, ch. 1 and 2.

26. See Paul B. Henze, *The Plot to Kill the Pope* (New York: Scribner, 1985).

27. Among Mr. Ramadan's twenty books are *Western Muslims and the Future of Islam, To Be a European Muslim,* and *Islam and the West.* He has published some seven hundred articles. A citizen of Switzerland, the francophone Mr. Ramadan is the grandson of Hassan al Banna, the founder of the Muslim Brotherhood. His anti-Americanism made him a darling of European intellectuals. He was invited to a prestigious U.S. academic post in 2004, but his visa was disapproved by the Department of Homeland Security.

Chapter 3

1. Quoted in Isaiah Berlin, *Russian Thinkers* (New York: Penguin Books, 1984), 60–62.

2. Bruce Catton, *Terrible Swift Sword* (New York: Doubleday, 1966; New York: Washington Square, 1967), 429.

3. Hans Mark, *In Search of the Fulcrum* (Berkeley: Institute of International Studies, 1988), 65–66.

4. U.S. Department of Defense, *Soviet Military Power: 1988,* 109–16, and *Annual Report to the Congress for Fiscal Year 1989,* 29–34 (Washington, DC: U.S. Government Printing Office, 1988).

5. Carl von Clausewitz, *On War,* ed. and trans. Michael Howard and Peter Paret (Princeton: Princeton University Press, 1976), 579.

6. This is particularly true of military surprises, such as Pearl Harbor, which have inspired a rich literature. Some of its post hoc wisdom resembles the old adage about locking the barn after the horse has been stolen. See Roberta Wohlstetter, *Pearl Harbor: Warning and Decision* (Stanford, CA: Stanford University Press, 1962). See also Klaus Knorr and Patricia Morgan, *Strategic Military Surprise* (New Brunswick, NJ: Transaction Books, 1983). New sophisticated surveillance technologies, at least for the superpowers, lessen the risk of certain forms of surprise attacks, but they are vulnerable, delicate, and especially subject to deception. Therefore, they increase rather than decrease uncertainty.

7. Ingenuity can compensate for C^3 inadequacies. During the 1984 Grenada invasion, a U.S. Army unit was briefly trapped by enemy fire,

without communications to request support from offshore naval forces. Its commander cleverly placed a call through to Fort Benning, Georgia, with a personal AT&T credit card. Help was forthcoming. This sort of thing happens frequently in warfare but one cannot count on it. That is the unpredictable nature of warfare.

8. Western strategic theorists since the 1950s, envisioning future great-power wars, have directed their attention to constraints and limitations. These compunctions, however, were not shared by Soviet strategists. While the Soviets were quite concerned about the uncertainties of war, they tended not to be paralyzed by them. The standard Soviet view was expressed by Marshal V. D. Sokolovskii in his authoritative work, *Soviet Military Strategy* (New York: Crane, Russak, 1975): "It is entirely clear that both gigantic military coalitions will put out massive armed forces in a future decisive world war; all modern powerful and long-range means of combat, including multi-megaton nuclear-racket weapons, will be used in it on a huge scale; and the most decisive methods of military operations will be used" (187–88).

9. *Standard Encyclopedia of Southern Africa* (Capetown: NASDOU, 1975), vol. 11: 44.

10. See Georges Fauriol and Eva Loser, *Guatemala's Political Puzzle* (New Brunswick, NJ: Transaction Books, 1988).

11. Albert Speer, *Inside the Third Reich* (New York: Macmillan, 1975), 220–21, 320.

12. Ibid., 225–28.

13. Edward Teller, *Better a Shield than a Sword* (New York: Macmillan, 1987).

14. David E. Sanger, "U.S. Chooses Martin Marietta for Simulation of 'Star Wars,'" *New York Times,* January 23, 1988.

15. Robert McNamara, "Speech to the Democratic Party Convention of 1964, Washington, DC, 17 August 1964," *Vital Speeches of the Day* 30, 10.

16. Alexander Orlov, *Handbook of Intelligence and Guerrilla Warfare* (Ann Arbor: University of Michigan Press, 1963), 10. Orlov, a general in the NKVD (one of the earlier incarnations of the KGB, the Soviet intelligence agency) originally wrote this book in the 1930s as a textbook for the education of Soviet military officers and party cadres. After he defected to the West, he rewrote it from memory.

17. See *Transcript of Defense Secretary Laird's News Conference,* Washington, DC, Monday, November 23, 1970 (U.S. Information Service, Press and Publication Branch, Document no. 70–125). See also the *New York Times,* 29 November 1970, 1; *The Economist,* 28 November 1970, 14–16; and the *Washington Post,* 24 November 1970, 1.

18. Winston Churchill, *The Second World War* (Boston: Houghton Mifflin, 1948), 3: 393.

19. Niccolo Machiavelli, *The Prince* (New York: Penguin Books, 1962), chap. 7.

Chapter 4

1. Roy P. Basler, ed., *Collected Works of Abraham Lincoln* (New Brunswick, NJ: Rutgers University Press, 1953), 6: 409.

2. Winston Churchill, *The Second World War* (Boston: Houghton Mifflin, 1948), 1: 311–14.

3. Edward Luttwak, *The Pentagon and the Art of War* (New York: Simon & Schuster, 1984), 86.

4. Ibid., 17, 44–45, 55, 153, 271.

5. Annual Report of the Chief of Staff, U.S. Army, for the fiscal year ending 30 June 1933.

6. Charles de Gaulle, *Memoires de Guerre* (Paris: Plon, 1954), 1: 427.

7. B. H. Liddell-Hart, *History of the Second World War* (New York: Putnam, 1971), 622–28.

Chapter 5

1. See Hitler's plan, "Operation Barbarossa," quoted in Winston Churchill, *The Second World War* (Boston: Houghton Mifflin, 1948), 2: 559–89. See also B. H. Liddell-Hart, *History of the Second World War* (New York: Putnam, 1971), 141–70.

2. Hart, *History of the Second World War*, 639–59.

3. The geometric formula for calculating how far away the horizon is from any given altitude is $z = (2Eh)1/2$, where E is the earth's radius and h is the altitude above the earth.

4. Arthur H. Westing in E. W. Pfeiffer, "The Cratering of Indochina," *Scientific American*, (May 1972), 20–29. By the end of 1971, the United States had dropped six million tons of bombs on Indochina, three times the tonnage dropped by air forces in all theaters of World War II. Some 3.6 million tons of these bombs had been dropped on South Vietnam. See also Phillip B. Davidson, *Vietnam at War, the History: 1946–1975* (Novato, CA: Presidio Press, 1988), 589.

5. Churchill, *Second World War*, 4: 732. See also Albert Speer, *Inside the Third Reich* (New York: Macmillan, 1970), 247–51.

6. U.S. Department of Defense, *Soviet Military Power* (Washington, DC: U.S. Government Printing Office, 1985), 40–41.

7. U.S. Naval Institute, *Proceedings, The Maritime Strategy* (Washington, DC: U.S. Government Printing Office, 1986).

8. Churchill, *Second World War,* 2: 182.

Chapter 6

1. A. A. Sidorenko, *The Offensive,* trans. and published by the U.S. Air Force (Washington, DC: U.S. Government Printing Office, 1971) 24.

2. Winston Churchill, *The Second World War* (New York: Houghton Mifflin, 1948), 2: 46.

3. Ibid., 289.

4. Frank C. Carlucci, Secretary of Defense, *Annual Report to Congress, Fiscal Year 1989* (Washington, DC: U.S. Government Printing Office, 1988), 29–34.

5. Ibid., 55.

6. See John Lehman, "Rebirth of a U.S. Naval Strategy," *Strategic Review,* Summer 1981, 9–15; Thomas Wilkerson, "Two if by Sea," *U.S. Naval Institute Proceedings,* November 1983, 34–39; and James L. George, *The U.S. Navy: The View from the Mid-1980s* (Boulder, CO: Westview Press, 1985).

7. Michael M. McCrea, *U.S. Navy, Marine Corps, and Air Force Fixed Wing Aircraft Losses and Damage in Southeast Asia, 1962–1973* (Arlington, VA: Center for Naval Analyses, 1976).

Chapter 7

1. Bernard Brodie, ed., *The Absolute Weapon* (New York: Harcourt Brace, 1946).

2. Ibid., 80. See also Richard Pipes, "Why the Soviet Union Thinks It Could Fight and Win a Nuclear War," *Commentary* 64 (July 1977): 21–39; also Brodie's editorial letter of reply in the September 1977 issue, 6–7) and Pipes's rejoinder (20, 22).

3. Daniel Graham, *Shall America Be Defended?* (New Rochelle, NY: Arlington House, 1979), 38.

4. Samuel P. Huntington, *The Common Defense: Strategic Programs in National Politics* (New York: Columbia University Press, 1961), 298.

5. Samuel Glasstone, ed., *The Effects of Nuclear Weapons,* U.S. Atomic Energy Commission (Washington, DC: U.S. Government Printing Office, 1961), 135. One thousand feet from the center of a one-kiloton blast, the peak overpressure is ten pounds per square inch, enough to blow away frame houses but not enough to kill unprotected human beings except by means of flying debris.

6. U.S. Department of Defense, *Soviet Military Power,* 8th ed. (Washington, DC: U.S. Government Printing Office, 1985), 55.

7. Ships are seriously damaged or sunk by overpressures exceeding ten pounds per square inch. This means that a ship cannot allow a cruise missile with a warhead of twenty kilotons to get closer than about four thousand feet. Larger warheads require a greater keep-out range. See Glasstone, *Effects of Nuclear Weapons,* 255.

8. "As I have explained . . . in previous years, this question cannot be answered precisely. . . . I would judge that a capability on our part to destroy, say, one-fifth to one-fourth of her population and one-half of her industrial capacity would serve as an effective deterrent. . . . It is precisely this mutual capability to destroy one another, and conversely, our respective inability to prevent such destruction, that provides us both with the strongest possible motive to avoid a strategic nuclear war" (Robert S. McNamara, *Annual Report to Congress for Fiscal Year 1969* (Washington, DC: U.S. Government Printing Office, 1968), 47, 49).

9. McNamara later described his thinking most concisely in his *Statement of Secretary of Defense Robert S. McNamara before the Senate Armed Services Committee on the Fiscal Years 1969–73 Defense Program and 1969 Defense Budget* (Washington, DC: U.S. Government Printing Office, 1969), esp. 47–50.

10. Pipes, "Why the Soviet Union Thinks It Could Fight and Win a Nuclear War." See also Frank C. Carlucci, Secretary of Defense, *Annual Report to the Congress, Fiscal Year 1989* (Washington, DC: U.S. Govern-ment Printing Office, 1988) 28, esp. last paragraph.

11. Leon Sloss and Marc Dean Milot, "U.S. Nuclear Strategy in Evolution," *Strategic Review* 12 (Winter 1984): 19–28. See also Albert Wohlstetter, "Bishops, Statesmen, and Other Strategists on the Bombing of Innocents," *Commentary* 75 (June 1983): 15–35.

12. David S. Sullivan, *The Bitter Fruit of SALT: A Record of Soviet Duplicity* (Houston: Texas Policy Institute, 1981). In 1974 Kissinger responded to a reporter's question at a press conference saying, "What in the name of God is strategic superiority? What is the significance of it operationally, politically, militarily . . . at these levels of numbers? What do you do with it?" (32).

Chapter 8

1. Paul Smith, *On Political Warfare* (Washington, DC: National Defense University Press, 1988), 1.

2. *United States Foreign Broadcast Information Service Daily Report: Middle East and Africa,* 7 October 1981.

Libyan President Qadaffi used Sadat's death to threaten other less radical, less pro-Soviet Arab leaders in a statement over Tripoli radio: "The sound of the bullets [that] resounded firmly and courageously in the face of Sadat this morning was in fact saying 'this is the punishment of those who betray the Arab nation; this is the punishment of those who betray the martyrs'" (Q2). "After this day, whoever dares to sign an agreement of capitulation with the enemy, in Egypt or elsewhere, the Arab nation will be laying in wait for him" (Q3). "His end will be the end of anyone who follows the path of treason and treachery, the end of King Abdallah, Wasfi al-Tall and Sadat, the path of treason . . . which Sadat called the march of peace" (Q4). "It is the right of the progressive forces to assume authority and to restore Egypt to its progressive socialist march, the anticolonialist front" (Q5). "Death always to the traitors" (Q9).

Syrian radio reports followed in the same vein, threatening moderate Arab leaders and praising the Soviet Union. "Today, it is Sadat's turn; tomorrow, it will be [King] Husayn, afterward Saddam Husyan and Numayri until all traitors are wiped out for good from our Arab homeland." (H1) ". . . [P]articularly in our Arab region, the friendly Soviet Union constitutes today the most important guarantee of the march of freedom in the world at large" (H2). "The U.S. road forced Sadat to concede the Palestinian issue, the pan-Arab issue and to play the role of serf to U.S. imperialism in the Arab homeland, Africa and Afghanistan" (H3).

Baghdad radio drew parallels between Sadat's assassination and the downfall of the shah of Iran, using both as examples of the fate that will befall those leaders who cooperate with the United States in the quest for peace in the Middle East. "The death of Sadat is an eloquent historical lesson which once again confirms that those who betray their people and nation believing that they can continue their traitorous behavior forever are greatly deluded no matter how long they remain" (E1). "The Egyptian Army will not become the region's policeman as Sadat planned with the United States after the disappearance of the Shah of Iran" (E2).

On the same day that Algerian President Chadli Benjedid signed a protocol with the secretary general of the Spanish Communist Party, Algiers radio also described Sadat's murder as the inevitable fate of those leaders who seek peaceful coexistence with Israel and cooperate with the United States. "Sadat betrayed Egypt and the Arab cause and entered into an alliance with Zionism and imperialism against the Arab nation. The action taken today by certain men of the armed forces to eliminate Sadat was an inevitable consequence in the confrontation of the regime of treason" (QI).

3. Georgi Arbatov and other members of the USA-Canada Institute in Moscow frequently visited the United States and were widely received by the press and other media. The institute reported directly to the Central Committee of the Communist Party.

4. Joseph Finder, *Red Carpet* (New York: Holt, Rinehart, Winston, 1983), 292–314. See also Steve Munson, "Armand's Story," *The National Interest* 9 (Fall 1987): 98–103.

5. Herman Rauschning, *Hitler Speaks,* as cited in Allan Bullock, *Hitler: A Study in Tyranny,* rev. ed. (New York: Bantam, 1961), 188.

6. Quoted in Albert Weeks, ed., *Soviet and Communist Quotations* (Washington, DC: Pergamon-Brassey, 1987), 313.

7. Harry G. Summers Jr., *On Strategy: A Critical Analysis of the Vietnam War* (Novato, CA: Presidio Press, 1982), esp. pt. 1. Summers recounts a conversation he had with a North Vietnamese general after the American withdrawal. "You know you never defeated us on the battlefield," said the American colonel. "That may be so," said the North Vietnamese general, "but it is also irrelevant" (1).

8. V. I. Lenin, *Collected Works* (New York: International Publishers, 1927).

9. Vladimir Bukovsky, "Peace as a Political Weapon," in *Soviet Hypocrisy and Western Gullibility* (Washington, DC: Ethics and Public Policy Center, 1987), 9.

10. Gustav Huger and Alfred G. Meyer, *The Incompatible Allies: A Memoir-History of German–Soviet Relations 1918–1941* (New York: Macmillan, 1953), 241.

11. The use of combined political warfare operations may sometimes be crudely overdone. A huge Soviet-inspired propagandistic "peace campaign" in western Europe against the NATO installation of intermediate-range nuclear forces miscarried in the 1980s when there was a backlash against its crudities from Western public opinion. See Alex R. Alexiev, "The Soviet Campaign against the INF," *Orbis* 29: 2 (Summer 1985): 319–50.

Chapter 10

1. Quoted in Tom Shachtman, *The Phony War: 1939–1940* (New York: Harper and Row, 1982), 129. King George's source for these moving words was an obscure book by Minnie Louise Haskins, *The Desert,* published in 1908.

2. B. H. Liddell-Hart, *Thoughts on War* (London: Faber and Faber, 1924).

3. Frank Barnaby, *The Automated Battlefield* (New York: Free Press, 1986).

4. Sterling Seagrave, *Yellow Rain* (New York: M. Evans, 1981).

5. William Colby, *Honorable Men* (New York: Simon & Schuster, 1978).

6. Shachtman, *Phony War.*

Chapter 11

1. Thomas Jefferson to Thomas Leiper, 12 June, 1815, in *The Works of Thomas Jefferson,* ed. Paul L. Ford (New York: Putnam, 1905), 2, 477–78.

2. "Only 4 percent died among the 260,000 British and American prisoners captured by the Germans" (Ronald H. Bailey, *World War II Prisoners of War* [Arlington, VA: Time-Life Books, 1981], 4).

3. Arnold Krammer, *Nazi Prisoners of War in America* (New York: Stein and Day, 1979), 256, 266.

4. "Of 5.7 million Russians taken prisoner, 3.7 million died in German hands" (Bailey, *World War II Prisoners of War,* 122). Eight hundred thousand Russians (prisoners and émigrés), especially Cossacks and nonSlavic minorities, fought with the Nazis as the Russian Liberation Army (128). Most of these were killed when they were forcefully repatriated to Russian authority. Altogether, only a small number of those Russians who were taken prisoner in World War II ever returned to their homes.

Chapter 12

1. Edward Gibbon, *The Decline and Fall of the Roman Empire* (New York: Heritage Press, 1946), 2, 975–76.

2. Robert Murphy, *Diplomat Among Warriors* (Garden City, NY: Doubleday, 1964), ch. 5–6. The German military authorities at Reims believed that they were acting as representatives of their government, while the Allied military authorities there contended that the Doenitz government did not exist and that in any case they did not make deals with the German government but were merely accepting the unconditional surrender of the German armed forces. This position, however, contained a contradiction: the Allies were demanding from the German high command an order for a simultaneous cease-fire on all fronts, clearly a political act.

3. Max Hastings, *The Korean War* (New York: Simon & Schuster, 1987). "1,319,000 Americans had served in the Korean theater, and 33,629 did not return. A further 105,785 were wounded. Forty-five percent of all U.S. casualties were incurred after the first armistice negotiations with the Communists took place" (329).

4. DOR Sekretariatet et al., *Economic Growth in a Nordic Perspective* (Copenhagen, 1984). The gross domestic products per capita in U.S. dollars at current prices and exchange rates in 1960 were $1,200 for Finland, $1,400 for Norway, and $1,800 for Sweden

5. Konrad Adenauer, *Memoirs: 1945–1953,* trans. Beate R. von Oppen (Chicago: Henry Regnery, 1966). "Statistics showed that in March 1946 men weighed on the average seven kilograms below normal. Their weight

had sunk to 9.1 kilograms below normal by June—that is thirteen percent below normal weight—while the inmates of old people's homes averaged as much as twelve kilograms or twenty percent below normal. . . . More than fifty percent of the pupils in our elementary class that was tested in the spring had tuberculosis. . . . While there had been 11.8 deaths registered per thousand inhabitants in 1938, the number was already up to 15.1 in April 1946 and had risen to 18 by June 1946 (58–59)."

6. Aleksandr Solzhenitsyn, "Prussian Nights": A Poem, trans. Robert Conquest (New York: Farrar, Straus and Giroux, 1977).

7. John J. Dziak, Chekisty (Lexington, MA: Lexington Books, 1980), 19–39. See also Richard Pipes, The Russian Revolution, vol. 1 (forthcoming). See also Robert Conquest, Harvest of Sorrow (Oxford: Oxford University Press, 1987). This is the definitive account of the artificial famine in the Ukraine that broke resistance to communist collectivization at the cost of perhaps 10 million lives.

8. For a good account of the aftermath of the Spanish civil war, see Stanley G. Payne, The Franco Regime: 1936–1975 (Madison: University of Wisconsin Press, 1987). Franco's Nationalists executed 70,000 to 72,000 Republicans from 1936 to 1950, almost exactly equal to the number of Republican executions of Nationalists during the civil war (217). In addition, Spain lost approximately 162,000 Republicans to permanent exile (220). However, Payne notes that conditions undoubtedly would have been worse had the Republicans triumphed under the communist hegemony created in 1937–38. He adds that Franco's was the second most clement resolution to any revolutionary civil war in the twentieth century, the resolution of the Greek civil war of the early 1950s being the most clement.

9. See Jacqueline Desbarats and Karl D. Jackson, "Political Violence in Vietnam: The Dark Side of Liberation," Indochina Report, no. 6. (April–June 1986): 22–28, especially; and Richard M. Nixon, No More Vietnams (New York: Arbor House, 1985), 86–88, especially.

Casualty figures are always tricky. In this case two baseline numbers exist. In 1978 Vietnamese premier Pham Van Dong claimed to have released over one million people from reeducation camps, lending weight to claims that far more than that number went in. Also some 600,000 Vietnamese who fled by sea reached safe haven, and enough bodies and wreckage have been found to support the estimate on the order, only one out of two boat people survived the sea. Desbarats and Jackson limit themselves to estimating actual executions. They estimate 320,000 reports and divide that number by an arbitrary factor of four. But in such situations, execution is the least of the causes of death.

10. The name Red Square, which existed at the time of Peter the Great, is not an allusion to communism. The Russian adjective "red" sometimes

means "beautiful." See Michael Glennon and John L. Moore, eds., *The Soviet Union* (Washington, DC: Congressional Quarterly, 1982), 4. It is also true that the square's centerpiece is a structure on which beheadings took place, from the spouts of which red blood flowed into the square.

11. See Conquest, *Harvest of Sorrow*, 309–11.

12. Saint Augustine, *City of God* (Garden City, NY: Image Books, 1958), 456.

13. Ibid., 458.

14. Etienne Gilson, in Saint Augustine, *City of God,* 34.

15. Roy P. Basler, ed., *Collected Works of Abraham Lincoln* (New Brunswick, NJ: Rutgers University Press, 1953), 2: 461.

BIBLIOGRAPHY

Arendt, Hannah. *On Violence.* New York: Harcourt, Brace, and World, 1970.
———. *The Origins of Totalitarianism.* New York: Meridian Books, 1963.
Aron, Raymond. *The Century of Total War.* Garden City, NY: Doubleday, 1964.
———. *Clausewitz: Philosopher of War.* Englewood Cliffs, NJ: 1984.
Augustine, Saint. *The City of God.* Garden City, NY: Image Books, 1958.
Blainey, Geoffrey. *The Causes of War.* New York: Free Press, 1973.
Bozeman, Adda. "Statecraft and Intelligence in the Non-Western World." *Conflict* 6 (1985): 19.
Brodie, Bernard. *War and Politics.* New York: Macmillan, 1975.
Carr, Edward Hallett. *The Twenty Years' Crisis, 1919–1939.* London: Macmillan, 1946.
Churchill, Winston. *The Second World War.* 6 vols. Boston: Houghton Mifflin, 1948–1953.
———. *The World Crisis.* New York: Scribner, 1923.
Clausewitz, Carl von. *On War.* Ed. and trans. Michael Howard and Peter Paret. Princeton: Princeton University Press, 1976.
Cohn, Norman. *Pursuit of the Millennium.* New York: Oxford University Press, 1970.
Cox, Richard. *Locke on War and Peace.* Washington, DC: University Press of America, 1982.
Craig, Gordon. *The Politics of the Prussian Army.* Oxford: Clarendon Press, 1955.
Creasy, Edward S. *Fifteen Decisive Battles of the World.* New York: Dorset, 1987.
Crozier, Brian. *A Theory of Conflict.* London: Hamilton, 1974.
de Gaulle, Charles. *Memoires de Guerre.* Paris: Plon, 1954.
Deane, Herbert. *The Political and Social Ideas of Saint Augustine.* New York: Columbia University Press, 1963.

Dulles, Allan W. *The Craft of Intelligence.* New York: New American Library, 1965.

Earle, Edward Meade, ed. *Makers of Modern Strategy.* Princeton: Princeton University Press, 1943.

Erasmus, Desiderius. *The Complaint of Peace.* Trans. Margaret Mann. New York: Garland Publications, 1972.

Feierabend, I. K., and Betty Newhold. "The Comparative Study of Revolution and Violence." *Comparative Politics,* April 1973.

Fischer, Fritz. *Germany's Aims in the First World War.* New York: W. W. Norton, 1967.

Fitzgibbon, Constantine. *Secret Intelligence in the Twentieth Century.* New York: Stein and Day, 1977.

Fuller, J. F. C. *The Conduct of War, 1789–1961.* London: Minerva, 1968.

Fussell, Paul. *The Great War and Modern Memory.* London: Oxford University Press, 1975.

Gilbert, Felix. *To the Farewell Address.* Princeton: Princeton University Press, 1961.

Gilbert, Martin. *Winston S. Churchill: Road to Victory, 1941–1945.* Boston: Houghton Mifflin, 1986.

Glynn, Patrick. "The Sarajevo Fallacy: The Historical and Intellectual Origins of Arms Control Theology." *The National Interest* 9 (Fall 1987).

Godson, Roy. *Intelligence Requirements for the 1980s: Intelligence and Policy.* Washington, DC: National Strategy Information Center, 1979.

———, ed. *Intelligence for the 1990s.* Lexington, MA: Lexington Books, 1989.

Grant, Ulysses S. *Personal Memoirs.* 2 vols. New York: 1885–86.

Grotius, Hugo. *Prolegomena to the Law of War and Peace.* Indianapolis: Bobbas Merrill, 1957.

Hinsley, Francis Harry. *British Intelligence in the Second World War.* New York: Cambridge University Press, 1979.

Hobbes, Thomas. *Leviathan.* Ed. Michael Oakeshott. Oxford: Oxford University Press, 1957.

Howard, Michael. *War and the Liberal Conscience.* New Brunswick, NJ: Rutgers University Press, 1978.

———. *War in European History.* London: Oxford University Press, 1976.

Huntington, Samuel P. *The Common Defense: Strategic Programs in National Politics.* New York: Columbia University Press, 1961.

———. *The Soldier and the State: The Theory and Practice of Civil-Military Relations.* Cambridge, MA: Harvard University Press, 1957.

Iklé, Frederick. *Every War Must End.* New York: Columbia University Press, 1971.

Johnson, Paul. *Enemies of Society.* New York: Atheneum, 1977.

————. *Modern Times.* New York: Harper and Row, 1983.

Kagan, Donald. "World War I, World War II, World War III." *Commentary,* March 1987.

Kahn, David. *The Codebreakers.* New York: Macmillan, 1967.

Kahn, Herman. *On Thermonuclear War.* Princeton: Princeton University Press, 1960.

Kautilya. *Arthasastra.* Trans. R. P. Kangle. Bombay: University of Bombay Press, 1960.

Kecskemeti, Paul. *Strategic Surrender: The Politics of Victory and Defeat.* Stanford, CA: Stanford University Press, 1959.

Keegan, John. *The Face of Battle.* New York: Viking, 1976.

Kissinger, Henry. *A World Restored: Europe after Napoleon.* Boston: Houghton Mifflin, 1973.

Krebs, Richard [Jan Valtin]. *Out of the Night.* New York: Alliance, 1941.

Lefever, Ernest W., ed. *Ethics and World Politics: Four Perspectives.* Washington, DC: Ethics and Public Policy Center, 1988.

Lenin, V. I. *Collected Works.* New York: International Publishers, 1927.

Liddell-Hart, Basil. *Strategy.* New York: Frederick A. Praeger, 1962.

Lincoln, Abraham. *Abraham Lincoln's Speeches.* Comp. L. E. Crittenden. New York: 1895. Includes his first and second inaugural addresses and his letter to Mrs. Bixby.

Luttwak, Edward. *The Grand Strategy of the Roman Empire.* Baltimore: Johns Hopkins University Press, 1976.

————. *The Pentagon and the Arts of War.* New York: Simon & Schuster, 1984.

————. *Strategy: The Logic of War and Peace.* Cambridge, MA: Harvard University Press, Belknap Press, 1987.

MacArthur, Douglas. *Reminiscences.* New York: McGraw Hill, 1964.

Machiavelli, Niccolo. *The Prince and Other Works.* New York: Penguin Books, 1962.

Mahan, Alfred Thayer. *The Influence of Seapower in History.* New York: Hill and Wang, 1957.

Mao Tse-tung. *Selected Military Writings.* Beijing: Foreign Language Press, 1963.

May, Ernest. *Knowing One's Enemies: Intelligence Assessment Before the Two World Wars.* Princeton: Princeton University Press, 1984.

Murphy, Robert. *Diplomat Among Warriors.* Garden City, NY: Doubleday, 1964.

Nef, John. *War and Human Progress: An Essay on the Rise of Industrial Civilization.* Cambridge, MA: Harvard University Press, 1952.

Nicolson, Sir Harold. *The Congress of Vienna.* New York: Harcourt, Brace, 1946.

————. *Diplomacy.* Oxford: Oxford University Press, 1955.

————. *Peacemaking, 1919.* Boston: Houghton Mifflin, 1933.

Niebuhr, Reinhold. *The Children of Light and the Children of Darkness.* New York: Scribner, 1944.

————. *Moral Man and Immoral Society.* New York: Scribner, 1960.

Nixon, Richard. *The Real War.* New York: Warner Books, 1980.

Orlov, Alexander. *Handbook of Intelligence and Guerrilla Warfare.* Ann Arbor: University of Michigan Press, 1963.

Orwell, George. *Homage to Catalonia.* New York: Harcourt Brace, 1956.

Osgood, Robert E. *Limited War: The Challenge to American Strategy.* Chicago: University of Chicago Press, 1957.

Osgood, Robert E., and Robert W. Tucker. *Force, Order, and Justice.* Baltimore: Johns Hopkins University Press, 1967.

Paret, Peter, ed. *Makers of Modern Strategy.* Princeton: University of Princeton Press, 1986.

Payne, James. *Why Nations Arm.* London: Basil Blackwell, 1989.

Pike, Douglas. *PAVN: The People's Army of Vietnam.* Novato, CA: Presidio, 1986.

Preston, R. A., S. F. Wise, and H. O. Werner. *Men in Arms: A History of Warfare.* New York: F. A. Praeger, 1962.

Ramsey, Paul. *The Just War: Force and Political Responsibility.* Washington, DC: University Press of America, 1968.

Richardson, Lewis. *Statistics of Deadly Quarrels.* Ed. Quincy Wright and C. C. Lienau. Pittsburgh: Boxwood, 1960.

Schmitt, Carl. *The Concept of the Political.* Ed. George Schwab. New Brunswick, NJ: Rutgers University Press, 1976.

Seabury, Paul, and Patrick Glynn. "Kennan: The Historian as Fatalist." *The National Interest,* Winter 1985–86.

Smith, Adam. *The Wealth of Nations.* London: George Routledge, 1893. (See esp. bk. 5, chap. 1, pt. 1: "Of the Expense of Defense.")

Smith, Paul A., Jr. *On Political War.* Washington, DC: National Defense University, 1989.

Sokolovskii, Marshal Vasili. *Soviet Military Strategy.* New York: Crane, Russak, 1975.

Summers, Harry G., Jr. *On Strategy: A Critical Analysis of the Vietnam War.* Novato, CA: Presidio, 1982.

Sun-Tzu. *The Art of War.* Trans. Samuel B. Griffith. London: Oxford University Press, 1963.

Taylor, A. J. P. *The Struggle for Mastery in Europe, 1848–1918.* London: Oxford University Press, 1954.

Thomas, Hugh. *The Spanish Civil War.* New York: Harper and Row, 1986.

Thucydides. *A History of the Peloponnesian War.* New Brunswick, NJ: Rutgers

University Press, 1975.

Tuchman, Barbara. *The Guns of August: August 1914.* New York: Macmillan, 1962.

Tucker, Robert C., ed. *The Marx-Engels Reader.* 2d ed. New York: W. W. Norton, 1978.

Tucker, Robert W. *The Just War.* Baltimore: Johns Hopkins University Press, 1960.

Valtin, Jan. See Krebs, Richard.

Van Creveld, Martin. *Supplying War: Logistics from Wallenstein to Patton.* Cambridge: Cambridge University Press, 1977.

Vargas Llosa, Maria. *The War of the End of the World.* New York: Farrar, Straus, Giroux, 1984.

Waltz, Kenneth. *Man, the State, and War.* New York: Columbia University Press, 1964.

Walzer, Michael. *Just and Unjust Wars.* New York: Basic Books, 1977.

Washington, George. *Farewell Address.* Albany, NY, 1810.

Weigel, George. *Tranquilitas Ordinis: The Present Failure and Future Promise of American Catholic Thought on War and Peace.* Oxford: Oxford University Press, 1987.

Wiskemann, Elizabeth. *Europe of the Dictators.* New York: Harper and Row, 1966.

Wright, Quincy. *Study of War.* 2 vols. Chicago: University of Chicago Press, 1942.

Xenophon. *The Anabasis.* Trans. Aipheus Crosby. New York: Potter, Ainsworth, 1875.

Zabih, Sepehr. *The Iranian Military in Revolution and War.* London: Routledge, Kegan and Paul, 1988.

Zhukov, Georgi. *Memoirs.* New York: Delacorte, 1971.

Zim, Herbert. *Codes and Secret Writing.* New York: William Morrow, 1948.

INDEX

THE AUTHORS

ANGELO CODEVILLA's books cover topics ranging from comparative government to political thought to the theory and practice of conflict, especially intelligence and missile warfare. They include *Informing Statecraft Intelligence for a New Century, The Character of Nations,* and a new translation of Machiavelli's *Prince.* He is the principal author of the seven-volume series *Intelligence Requirements for the 1980s* and is at work on the intellectual history of U.S. foreign relations.

Angelo Codevilla's articles and op-eds have appeared in *Commentary, Foreign Affairs, The National Interest,* the *New York Times,* and the *Wall Street Journal,* as well as in comparable publications abroad. Most recently, he is the author of the "Victory" series in the *Claremont Review of Books.*

Since 1995, Codevilla has been a professor of international relations at Boston University. Between 1985 and 1995, he was a senior research fellow of the Hoover Institution, Stanford University. Between 1977 and 1985, Codevilla served as a senior staff member of the Senate Select Committee on Intelligence, supervising the intelligence budget. He was instrumental in the effort to develop space-based missile defense. During the same period, he served on Ronald Reagan's presidential transition teams for the State Department and the Central Intelligence Agency. He also taught ancient and modern political theory at Georgetown University. Prior to that, he served as a U.S. foreign service officer and, earlier, as a U.S. naval officer.

A U.S. citizen since 1962, Angelo Codevilla lives in Wyoming, California, and Massachusetts.

PAUL SEABURY (1923-1990) taught political science to a generation at the University of California, Berkeley. His courses stressed history–knowledge of events–over academic formulae. Known in Washington, D.C. as a critic of bureaucracy after the publication of his book *Bureaucrats and Brainpower,*

he was a member of the Consortium for the Study of Intelligence, the intellectual source of efforts to reform U.S. intelligence. Through his service on
the President's Foreign Intelligence Advisory Board, he worked at the highest
level of U.S. national security. His book *Power, Freedom and Diplomacy*
won the Bancroft prize for American history and diplomacy. A descendant
of Samuel Seabury, the first Anglican bishop of North America, professor
Seabury is also remembered for his 1978 *Harpers* cover story on the decline of American "mainline" churches, "Trendier Than Thou." Wit enliv-
ened his teaching and writings. His satirical cartoons are collectors' items.